P9-CDJ-537

# Toward the Setting Sun

ALSO BY DAVID BOYLE

*Troubadour's Song: The Capture and Ransom of Richard the Lionheart*

# TOWARD THE SETTING SUN

## Columbus, Cabot, Vespucci, and the Race for America

### DAVID BOYLE

WALKER & COMPANY

NEW YORK

Published by Walker Publishing Company, Inc., New York
Distributed to the trade by Macmillan

All papers used by Walker & Company are natural, recyclable products made from
wood grown in well-managed forests. The manufacturing processes conform to the
environmental regulations of the country of origin.

LIBRARY OF CONGRESS CATALOGING-IN-PUBLICATION DATA

Boyle, David, 1958–
Toward the setting sun : Columbus, Cabot, Vespucci, and the race for America /
David Boyle.—1st U.S. ed.
p.   cm.
Includes bibliographical references and index.
ISBN-13: 978-0-8027-1651-4 (alk. paper)
ISBN-10: 0-8027-1651-2 (alk. paper)
1. America—Discovery and exploration—European.   2. Columbus, Chirstopher.
3. Vespucci, Amerigo, 1451–1512.   4. Cabot, John, d. 1498?   5. Explorers—
America—History.   6. Explorers—America—Biography.   7. Explorers—Europe—
History.   8. Explorers—Europe—Biography.   I. Title.

E101.B794 2008
970.01'5—dc22
2008000143

Visit Walker & Company's Web site at www.walkerbooks.com

First U.S. edition 2008

1 3 5 7 9 10 8 6 4 2

Typeset by Westchester Book Group
Printed in the United States of America by Quebecor World Fairfield

*For my father*

# CONTENTS

"Heisa, heisa
vorsa, vorsa
wow, wow
one long draft
more might, more might
young blood, young blood
more mude, more mude
false flesh, false flesh
lie aback, lie aback
long swack, long swack
that, that, that, that
there, there, there, there
yellow hair, yellow hair
hips bare, hips bare
tell 'em all, tell 'em all
gallowsbirds all, gallowsbirds all
great and small, great and small
one an' all, one an' all
heist all, heist all."

English maritime hauling song sung
by sailors in the mid-sixteenth century

*"One glass is gone*
*and now the second flows.*
*More shall run down*
*if my God wills it.*
*To my God let us pray*
*to give us a good voyage,*
*and, through his blessed mother our advocate,*
*protect us from the waterspout and storm."*

The prayer told at sea by the most junior officer
of the watch, as he turned the half-hour glass,
which told the time on fifteenth- and
sixteenth-century Spanish ships

*"We sawe birds of all colors, some carnation, some crim-*
*son, orange tawny, purple, greene, watched, and all other*
*sorts, both simple and mixt."*

SIR WALTER RALEIGH, *Guiana*, 1596

# Prologue

# Setting Sail

*"Lord, what a tangle of dangers are here for the wretched mariner! Rocks and eddies and overfalls and shooting tides; currents and . . . horrible great mists, vapours, malignant humours of the deep, mirages, false ground, where the anchor will not hold, and foul ground, where the anchor holds for ever, spills of wind off the irregular coast and monstrous gales coming out of the main west sea."*

HILAIRE BELLOC, *The Cruise of the Nona,*
in the Bristol Channel

*"That Venetian of ours who went with a small ship from Bristol to find new islands has come back and says he has discovered the mainland 700 leagues away, which is the country of the Grand Khan."*

LORENZO PASQUALIGO, letter
to his brother in Venice, August 23, 1497

ON AUGUST 6, 1497, nearly five years to the day since Christopher Columbus had first set sail for the New World, his Venetian rival, John Cabot, navigated his tiny ship *Matthew* back up the Avon River to the English port of Bristol. Then he rode at speed to London to give the king the news of his extraordinary discovery on the other side of the Atlantic. Columbus had failed, he said. Despite what the intelligentsia of Europe believed, Columbus's expeditions had actually lodged in some remote islands very far from the Chinese coast he claimed to have found. But Cabot claimed that his own expedition, one ship with a crew of less than twenty, *had* found the route to China in a very different place and that Bristol was set to be the new Venice and Alexandria, all rolled into one.

We know today, of course, that Cabot was right about Columbus but wrong about himself. We know that his pioneering 1497 voyage was not really a voyage of "discovery." Other races and civilizations occupied the "New Founde Land" he had claimed. We also know, with the benefit of history, that the voyage led not to spice routes but to a staggering exploitation of the cod trade, repeated and pointless exploration for the mythical Northwest Passage for the next three centuries, and the English claim to North America.

What is less well known is that Cabot's arrival in London, and his every move afterward, was being reported to Spain by agents of Columbus, who was then working closely with the first person to correctly interpret the geography of these adventures, Amerigo Vespucci, the man whose name would eventually grace the new continent that hardly anyone had yet imagined. Cabot knew them both, certainly by reputation, but where history has been quiet—if not silent—until now is about how much his voyages were bound up with theirs.

All history involves leaps of imagination. The story of the race for America is no exception. In fact, the separate tales of Columbus, Cabot, and Vespucci have been almost unique in their susceptibility to bizarre theories, generation after generation, as critical maps or documents are alternately discredited and vindicated.

Was Columbus Jewish? Was Cabot from the Channel Islands? Was Vespucci a fraud? Were they all double agents? All these claims have been made by serious researchers within living memory, and the answer in each case is almost certainly no. But in recent decades, a broad consensus has begun to emerge about the basic facts and documents, thanks to painstaking research and vital new discoveries. Cabot's debts, Vespucci's pretences, and Columbus's religious obsessions have only recently become clear, and the three pioneers begin to emerge not so much as explorers, but first and foremost as merchants. Their primary motivation may have been glory, but most of all, the enterprise they shared was about the prospect of astonishing profits.

The last few years have yielded quite unprecedented progress in our understanding of all three men—documented evidence of Columbus's extraordinary cruelties to his followers, indications of the true achievements of Cabot's mysterious final voyage, and insights into how Vespucci had reinvented his own story. All this new evidence has added to the consensus and provided us with more fully rounded pictures of each man. Taken together, it means that it is at last possible to end the artificial divisions, which have resulted because historians and nations have told their three stories independently. Their lives have always been separated by those whose self-appointed task it has been to fight their corner and discredit the work of their opponents.

The arguments have raged across the centuries. Americans have traditionally sidelined Vespucci—"a thief . . . the pickle dealer at Seville," according to Emerson—saying that he "stole" Columbus's achievement by using his name Amerigo for their continent. Italians have pressed the claims of Vespucci, including his mythical "first voyage"—widely agreed to have been based on later forged documents—because of his apparent claim to have discovered the continent himself. The British have pressed the claims of Cabot on the grounds that the name Amerigo was part of a Roman Catholic plot to discredit a soon-to-be Protestant nation's achievement.

It is time to string the story together as one narrative, not as three rival mythologies peddled by different nationalities, but as the single tale it originally was—of three young men born within a few years and a few hundred miles of each other, who struggled against indifference, fear, and bitter rivalry to be the first to cross the western ocean. And who by doing so ushered in the end of the medieval age.

The truth is that the three men knew each other. Columbus and Vespucci worked closely together, and Cabot and Vespucci had common acquaintances interested in the possibilities of Western trade. They collaborated, knew of each other's ambitions, and followed each other's progress. Columbus and Cabot were also both born around the same time in Genoa and probably knew each other from their earliest lives. All three were admirers, and two were acquaintances, of the sage of Florence, Paolo dal Pozzo Toscanelli, who first urged explorers to sail west in order to find the East.

Writing the story of all three as one narrative has been in itself a kind of research. When you link them and put the stories in context, it becomes suddenly obvious why Cabot went to Mecca or why Vespucci abandoned his career to go to Spain. The business of profit becomes even more central to the tale than it was before, and the race for America was as much about business as it was diplomacy. Reconstructing the historical events as one story reveals aspects that were not always obvious before, and it gives an energy and thrust to that story that wasn't always apparent.

The key relationship at the heart of this tale, and the one that still remains least clear to historians, is the one between Cabot and Columbus. But the whole thrust of the story implies that the enterprise of the Indies—the plan to find a western route to China that lay behind Columbus's and Cabot's discoveries—was not originally a separate, almost identical, undertaking happening by coincidence, but rather a joint project between Cabot and the Columbus brothers, Christopher and Bartholomew, that unraveled.

The most likely interpretation seems to be an original collaboration, but it is hard for academic historians to break out of the safety of certainty—to shift from closely argued detail—and to fill in the remaining gaps in the story. It also seems that a partnership between Cabot and Columbus is the clear implication of telling the three stories together. But anyone who tries to tell it as one story, as I have, needs to be as honest as they can be about where they have to go beyond the undisputed evidence, and to explain—either in the text or in the notes—what evidence lies behind the assumptions they have made. This is the story, based on the best available evidence as it stands today. There remain gaps and uncertainties but writing a narrative sometimes depends on going a little further than a strictly academic approach would allow—and I have tried to make clear where I have done this.

The stories most of us now understand about Cabot, Columbus, and Vespucci and their race across the Atlantic are inaccurate simply because they have been told separately, as if in a vacuum, or amid such controversy and detailed argument that the main thrust of the narrative has been lost. But because those events of so long ago have had a profound impact on how we live now, it seemed right to tell the tale as it really happened.

And the tale begins not in Genoa or Florence, where the three central figures came into the world, but in the far eastern frontier of Europe in 1453, when the great city of Constantinople watched in silence as the Ottoman armies gathered outside its walls.

# I

# PARADISE LOST

*"There will come a time in the later years when ocean shall loosen the bonds by which we have been confined, when an immense land shall be revealed and Tiphys shall disclose new worlds, and Thule will no longer be the most remote of countries."*

SENECA, *Medea*

*"The world is fair to look at, white and green and red, But inside it is dark and black, and dismal as the dead."*

WALTHER VON DER VOGELWEIDE

IN THE EARLY hours of Tuesday morning, May 29, 1453, Constantine IX Palaeologus, the last Christian emperor of Constantinople, stood on the extreme corner of the city's triple defensive walls in the drizzling rain, looking down across the Golden Horn from the Caligarian Gate. Constantine was forty-nine years old and utterly exhausted. His closest advisers stood around him and peered through the gloom at the campfires of the enormous army of the twenty-one-year-old sultan Mehmet II, drawn from all over the Muslim world and stretched out along the Bosphorus. They could see, silently in the dark, Mehmet's brand new fortress that dominated the city and the straits that led to the Black Sea. The long-awaited attack, inevitable since they had been isolated by Ottoman forces a few months before, could not be far off now.

Behind them waited the great city, the magnificent capital of the Orthodox Christian world, too frightened to sleep. The lights in the distance stretched back to the opposite walls five miles away and flickered around the churches, where people had been gathering to pray since the evening. There they had been embracing each other, saying good-bye, and asking for forgiveness if they had ever given offense. There were still a few torchlight processions, hymns being sung in the far distance, blessing the vulnerable points in the city's fourteen miles of walls; walls that were in some places 350 feet high.

Constantine knew that Orthodox and Catholic alike had put aside their differences to worship together in the ancient cathedral of Santa Sophia—he and his predecessor had in fact negotiated a reunion between the two churches in the hope that it would encourage western Europe to stir itself in their defense. Constantine was patient and well respected and had taken the lead in the collection of gold and silver from the churches to melt down to pay their foreign defenders. He had overseen the desperate repairs at night, by men and women alike, of the damaged walls, and he had personally organized the latest collection of food for the most desperate in the besieged city. Now, physically drained, the emperor had fainted on his way to the city walls.

The rumblings made by the Turkish troops dragging their gun up hill, which had been heard since sunset, were still only too audible. There was no sign of the strange lights that Constantine had been warned about, but there could be no doubt that the attack must be imminent. There was no bombardment, though in the previous days they had suffered bombardment from a great twenty-six-foot cannon, which required sixty oxen just to move

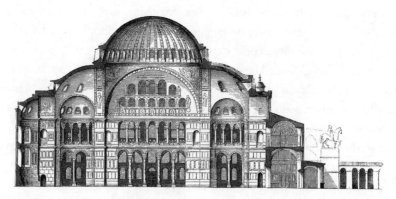

Cross section of the Santa Sophia

it into position. The cannon had been firing from ten miles up the coast and was now completely invisible in the darkness. As the remaining citizens peered through the dark toward the west, their faces wet from the rain, there was still no sign of the promised Venetian fleet. It was such a small hope, but in such terrible times anyone would clutch at straws.

The legendary city, the glory that had been Byzantium, with its vast libraries—the greatest repositories of knowledge in the known world—was locked and barred, waiting for the worst. Its great stone streets, down which the first Constantine—the Roman emperor who converted to Christianity— had once traveled, were silent and prayerful. There were only seven thousand people left to defend the city. There had been an ancient prophesy that Constantinople could not be taken during a waxing moon. But the moon had been full a week earlier and it was now waning. Worse, when the hopeless citizens had paraded around the city with the holiest of icons, the Virgin Mary, it had accidentally toppled into a gutter.

The attack finally began at half past one in the morning. As the sultan dispatched his *bashi-bazouks*, his ill-disciplined mercenary irregulars, a ball from the great cannon burst through one of the defensive stockades. At first, the forces of defenders and attackers seemed equally matched, with inspirational defense by the Genoese forces between the inner and outer walls. But when some hours later Turkish troops slipped through a small gate in the outer defenses, which accidentally had been left unlocked after a raid by the defending Genoese troops, their military strategy began to unravel.

Two contingents kept the defense alive. The Cretans in charge of three key towers, and the Genoese under Giovanni Giustiniani Longo, who had been put in command of the whole military operation. But when Longo was badly wounded and his followers insisted that he should be taken through to the inner walls, the elite Ottoman Janissaries—originally Christian children abducted by pirates—believed the Genoese were in full retreat and rushed the gate. When they succeeded in forcing their way through, Constantine realized that the battle was hopeless. He flung off his imperial insignia, led his closest advisers into the middle of the fiercest fighting, and was never seen again.*

---

*A headless body with the imperial insignia embroidered on its socks was found later and assumed to be Constantine, but its burial place is now forgotten.

Mehmet had promised his army three days of unrestricted looting, and they fanned out across the city, killing anyone they found, burning the libraries and the books inside them, and the great icons. Even the great Hodigitria, a portrait of the Virgin said to have been painted by St. Luke himself, disappeared in the conflagration. Thousands of women and children had barricaded themselves into Santa Sophia, but the doors were battered down and they were carried off to the soldiers' tents and eventually into slavery. It was widely regarded as the great retribution for the Greeks—Constantinople being the greatest Greek city on earth—for their legendary sack of the city of Troy, which had been in what is now Turkey. Only a few of the city's leaders escaped. One of them, Cardinal Isidore, a former leader of the Orthodox church in Kiev, managed to swap clothes with a beggar—who was beheaded in his place—and get himself sold at a bargain price as a slave. He was eventually able to purchase his own release. Few of his colleagues were so lucky.

But the sultan began to have qualms as the slaughter continued. Tradition suggests that he was horrified by the plunder and destruction of such a magnificent city and called a halt, protecting Santa Sophia and converting it immediately into a mosque. He even appointed one of the captured

The sack of Constantinople

Orthodox scholars, also sold into slavery, as his own Christian patriarch. But it was too late. The libraries had largely been lost; the seat of Orthodox Christianity for the past eleven centuries was in Muslim hands; and the trade routes that had taken the merchants of Venice, Florence, and Genoa up the Dardanelles through the Sea of Marmara and into the Black Sea were under the control of hostile forces. The whole axis of the Mediterranean world had shifted.

The axis had been shifted, but this was only the completion of a long-term trend. The truth was that Constantinople had long since been sidelined by the rest of Christian Europe. It was part of an old feudal world that was being elbowed aside by the new merchants and bankers. The Byzantines had forgone the massive expansion in trade over the past four centuries and found themselves without resources. As early as 1347 Emperor John VI had been disconcerted to notice at his coronation that the diadems with which he was being crowned were made of glass, rather than the gems he had expected. The population of the city had also shrunk steadily from more than 1 million three centuries earlier to only 100,000. The leaders of Italy's great cities had grown accustomed to visits from importunate Byzantine emperors begging for both military support and the means with which to pay for it.

Mid-fifteenth-century Europe was a world where money counted. Christians were not supposed to trade with "infidels," but permission to do so was usually secured by the payment of indulgences to Rome, a small tax that many merchants were prepared to pay. Mehmet's gigantic cannon, which had demolished part of Constantinople's triple walls, had been provided by a Hungarian engineer called Urban—Hungary was by then one of Europe's main exporters of iron and copper. Urban had originally offered it to Constantine, but in the end Mehmet was prepared to pay four times as much.

Even the Genoese Christian trading outpost of Pera, on the other side of the Golden Horn—and directly under the trajectory of the cannon fire from the Turkish side—was so determined to carry on the business of business that they insisted on their own neutrality. When one cannon ball accidentally sank a Genoese ship moored there, the merchants had protested to the sultan that they were nonaligned in his territorial dispute with Constantine. The pleas of Pope Nicholas V, the most energetic campaigner for a "crusade" to rescue the easternmost Christian city, had been heard with some skepticism because he still owed large sums to Venetian bankers for the last expedition in 1444. Far from joining in a new crusade, Venetian ambassadors settled down to negotiate a peace treaty and customs deal with Mehmet within months of the fall of Constantinople, to make sure the loss of the Christian city was no impediment to business.

The Ottoman advance was all very well, but far more important to the bickering and divided kingdoms of western Europe, and especially the city states of Italy, was trade. The trading system had recovered its momentum after the Black Death a century earlier, though labor was still in short supply and vast acres of agricultural land had simply reverted to forest. The big-name trading companies and bankers of Europe—Fugger of Germany, Medici of Florence—had their representatives all over the known world, in Trebizond, Cyprus, Crete, Valencia, Damascus, Beirut, and Tunis as well as London, Amsterdam, and even Novgorod. This progress was fueled by new bills of exchange in different currencies, the transmission of money by letter to foreign ports, and the underwriting of cargoes, all tracked by new systems of double entry bookkeeping to keep track of debits and credits, and by the increasing availability of loan money.

Like trading with the enemy, charging interest on loans was technically condemned by the church. In practice, as long as the lender was sharing some of the risk, this was no longer considered usury. And in any case, the popes were among the most indebted of all Europe's rulers. When Pope Paul II died in 1471, he owed so much that his successor had to appoint a team of cardinals to pay off the money by selling Paul's personal collection of precious gems and paintings. This susceptibility to borrowing was why, in a period of staggering wealth, powerful bankers like Jacob Fugger— probably the wealthiest man in Europe—could corner a monopoly of silver production in central Europe, earning a 50 percent commission on every silver florin minted there, simply by the manipulation of loans to impoverished princes.*

Money has a dramatic equalizing power when it is unleashed in force. It drives out the privileges of church and aristocracy alike. The great line-

---

*Bankers did not always win. When Edward III of England declared himself bankrupt in 1339, he brought down two of the biggest banking firms in Florence, Bardi and Peruzzi.

Jakob Fugger by Albrecht Dürer

ages of northern Europe watched in horror as the Italians gave dukedoms
to bankers and wealthy merchants, and then did exactly the same themselves. Money also levels class and spirituality to one measure alone: price.
This was, after all, a generation so obsessed with measurement that they
believed everything from love to morality could be reduced to numbers
and put on a scale. Before the invention of the thermometer, temperature
and wealth both looked to be tantalizingly possible candidates for scientific scrutiny.

Money brought other issues to the surface as well. The first concerns
about environmental destruction now began to emerge. Herring had almost
disappeared from the Mediterranean thanks to overfishing, and the first
forestry protection laws would be passed in England within three decades in
an attempt to slow deforestation and soil erosion. The monasteries—which
managed the education system and relief for Europe's poor—were the object
of deep cynicism, regarded as havens for lechers, tricksters, and loafers. The
greatest institution of the medieval world, the papacy, was creaking under
the weight of bribery, corruption, nepotism, vanity, and teenage cardinals,
while at the same time struggling to overcome the discord that remained after the schism that caused the popes to leave Rome for Avignon until 1415.

In reaction to this corruption of formal religion, there were mystics emerging all over Europe, like Margery Kempe and Julian of Norwich, and great mass preachers like Savonarola.*

So it was both the best of times and the worst of times, a period of great urban wealth and great rural poverty, and of enormous power and miserable corruption in the great institutions. It was an era of swaggering optimism in the Renaissance view of man, but of pessimistic itinerant preachers obsessed by the death and apocalypse. "When you perceive the miserable corruption of the whole of Christendom, of all praiseworthy customs, rules and laws, the wretchedness of all classes, the many pestilences, the changes in this epoch and all the strange happenings," wrote Joseph Grünpeck, official historian to the Holy Roman emperor Frederick III, "you know that the end of the world is near."

But most people did not share such apocalyptic fears. Those who worked in the fields watched the changing seasons as they always had. The urban elite comforted themselves by shopping. Consumption—not work, and certainly not spirituality—was now the most highly regarded civilized virtue. "I think I have given myself more honor, and my soul more satisfaction," wrote the magnificently wealthy Florentine Giovanni Rucellai, "by having spent money than by having earned it."

Magnificence was a virtue. It demonstrated greatness when a merchant or banker could invest in an urban palace, or surround himself with the most beautiful works of art that money could buy. The Italian Renaissance was building up to its crescendo—Donatello was sixty-seven, Giovanni Bellini was twenty-three, and Leonardo da Vinci was a one-year-old, living in a farmhouse on the slopes of Monte Albano with his mother and a man nicknamed the Brawler.

The Quentin Matsys portrait of Desiderius Erasmus, the great humanist of the age, showed him with a fur-lined purse around his neck like a merchant. Even those who were not actually merchants found that dressing

---

*The inspirational preacher Thomas Couette of Rennes used to speak in Arras cathedral in the 1420s suspended on ropes from the roof so that he could see the vast congregation who had come to hear him.

like one was a sign of confidence and sophistication. The immensely wealthy Philip the Good of Burgundy, who preferred to dress in plain black velvet, threw a party the year after the fall of Constantinople, and served a pie so big that it is said to have contained twenty-eight French musicians with their instruments, playing as enthusiastically as they could from inside it.

There was also a great deal to buy. Nearly every town with a sense of pride had its own clock. Most did not yet have traditional clock faces, but they rang the hours that let ordinary people know when to get up, go to work, or go to bed. The Florentine architect Leon Battista Alberti made a list of everything he had to do each day as soon as he got up, and then assigned times to them. No previous generation had done such a thing.

The contemporary chronicler Giovanni Tortelli wrote a list of all the inventions that were changing his world in 1450. They included clocks, compasses, pipe organs, sugar, and maritime charts. He might also have added eyeglasses. There was so much to buy for the newly rich: glass from Venice, ivory objects from Paris, carpets from India, beeswax candles from Russia and Bohemia, and silks from China. "Men sooner forget the death of their father than the loss of their possessions," said the Florentine philosopher Niccolò Machiavelli. It also appeared that they could forget the loss of Byzantium a good deal quicker than the loss of their trade routes.

Tortelli also could have included spices from the East. The nutmeg, pepper, paprika, cinnamon that kept food saleable longer—a vital element of trade—and also provided key ingredients in medicines and paints, while not new, were pouring into Europe at an unprecedented rate. With Constantinople in Muslim hands, the virtual closure of the routes eastward to the Silk Road and the Far East meant that the next generation would find themselves puzzled about these spices and how to reinvent the exotic trade that had made some of their parents extremely rich.

For the urban elite, this was a glittering new world, filled with exotic flavors, colors, and chivalry. Chivalry in the streaming banners and jewel-encrusted weaponry that were on show in the public tournaments and jousts, though—like the expensively decorated armor on sale in the cities—these were designed more for social and sartorial success than for war.* In fact, chivalry was gloriously antique, and this was an age that was fascinated by antiques. Andrea Mantegna was excavating Roman ruins and lovingly recording the inscriptions he found. Leonardo Bruni was translating Plato and Aristotle and explaining that history was divided into three ages: the classical period, the "Middle Ages," and their own wonderful new age when anything was possible.

But if chivalry looked backward to the Middle Ages, color was overwhelmingly modern. You could see it in the clothes of the wealthy in the cities. New dyes were creating ever brighter reds, indigos, and blues. You could see it in the paintings: ultramarine, made from ground lapis lazuli only available in Afghanistan, was used for the deep blues of the Virgin Mary's dress. Saffron yellow came from the autumn crocus grown in the mountains of Asia Minor. Brazilwood for brown was brought all the way from Java and Ceylon, via twelve or more intermediaries—the merchants who sold them to the artists in Florence or Siena or Venice usually had no details of the precise supply chain beyond the importer they bought from in Alexandria or Acre.

The new colors seeped down through the trade routes and into people's minds. But in 1453 one hue that really gripped people came from the parasitic kermes insect from some species of oak trees around the Mediterranean. Used to dye cloth scarlet and costing twenty or thirty times more than the madder used for ordinary reds, the color came from female lice collected in May and June before their eggs were laid, killed, and dried in the sun. Scarlet so thrilled people that there was a whole range of shades available: violet scarlets, green scarlets, white scarlets, and the very fashionable dark blue scarlets. There was even the rare black scarlet. The Querci family became so proficient at dying fabric scarlet that they were given a pension for life from the government in Florence.

But all this wealth, and the trading system that supported it, was under increasing strain. The new regime in Constantinople was threatening the existence of the western trading posts. Despite its studied neutrality, the Genoese colony of Pera was the first to go. Fewer traders were prepared to make the unpredictable journey past Constantinople to the Black Sea and, one by one, the inhabitants of Genoa's colonies there lost contact with

*Sir Thomas Malory, who would write the chivalric classic Le Morte d'Arthur, was now in prison in London charged with rape, extortion, and cattle rustling.

their trading companies or just gave up and came home. Then there was the inexorable Ottoman advance. In 1456 they were in the Aegean islands: Lesbos, Lemnos, Focea, and the others. Churches were turned into mosques and children were taken into slavery. By the 1460s, they were in Bosnia and threatening the Venetian cities on the Dalmatian coast. Soon they were in Albania, just across the Adriatic from Venice. The spice trade was stalled; even the traditional transport of sugar and olive oil was delayed by complicated permissions and heavy duties. The Islamic world watched the divisions between the rulers of Europe, and between the jealous cities of Italy, and waited for western Europe to destroy itself.

I

*"In Genoa, the word libertas can be read on the front of*
*prisons and on the fetters of galley-slaves."*

JEAN-JACQUES ROUSSEAU

On July 9, 1453, a ship from the Genoese island of Chios—near the Turkish coast—arrived in Genoa, with the devastating news of the collapse of Constantinople. People hurried down to the dockside. Not since the fall of Jerusalem in 1187 had news of such a military setback for western Europe landed there, particularly one that had such implications for the city's livelihood. The ship carried a letter from Angelo Lomellino, the chief executive of Pera, that described the full horror—not of the slaughter or the destruction, but that "the certificates of the trading companies are henceforth worthless." Though the merchants moved quickly to ingratiate themselves with the new regime—Michelangelo would even be commissioned by the sultan to build a bridge, though he never did—the long-term effects on trade soon became apparent, and did more than anything else to shift the eyes of Europe toward the Atlantic and the West.

The way through to the Silk Road for the merchants of London, Paris, Florence, and Venice was now uncertain, and nowhere was this more obvious than in Genoa, with its massive harbor, its black-and-white marble towers nestling under the mountains, and its tightly packed population of fifty thousand. Visitors to this salt-caked center of hard-headed commerce at the time described it as the "door to the world"—from the Latin *ianua*—partly because the luxurious produce of the whole earth seemed to arrive there, and partly because arriving into a city squeezed between the mountains and the sea seemed like the very entrance hall to the wealth of the whole of Italy.

The city was more vulnerable than most because of the investment it had made for centuries in an eastern empire. The Black Sea was known as "Genoa's Lake," and it was accessible only through the Dardanelles now under the control of the sultan. Genoese confederations had developed permanent trading posts at Kilia at the mouth of the Danube, at Ilice at the mouth of the Dnieper, and at Akerman (the modern city of Odessa). Genoese merchants brought shiploads of grain from around the Crimea—Genoa did not have a hinterland where they could grow their own—and they also bought slaves. Unlike the other European cities, Genoa believed that slavery was a legitimate business and invested heavily in the trade that brought young men, women, and children from the Black Sea and sold them to buyers in Muslim Spain or Egypt. Unlike Venice, who paid their galley rowers, Genoa manned their war galleys with slaves—the same way they solved labor shortage problems in their sugar plantations on the Cape Verde Islands in the Atlantic.

The center of this slave trade, Kaffa on the Black Sea coast, fell to the Ottomans in 1475. In the years that followed the demise of Constantinople, the rise in piracy—Christian piracy preying on Muslim trade and vice versa—made the whole business of business a great deal more insecure. Genoese merchants shifted their attention to Muslim Spain, and soon cities like Seville had enormous Genoese quarters. There, however, they faced growing competition from other trading cities around Europe with the same problems.

In fact, like Constantinople itself, Genoa had been suffering financially in the years before 1453. Genoa's own currency was in crisis in the late 1440s; this was solved in 1447 by the Bank of St. George, with a new gold coinage that replaced all the others. Gold was the rock that preserved the Genoese—the wealthy do better in an economy based on gold, while the poor do badly. For more than a century, Europe had also suffered from the inflation that accompanied the debasement of coinage. For those born in Genoa, the gold money provided a semimagical stability.

When the news about the fall of Constantinople arrived in Genoa, John Cabot was a four-year-old boy living in the narrow streets on the steep

Genoa as pictured in Hartmann Schedel's 1493 *Nuremberg Chronicles*

slopes above the harbor. There are problems for anyone writing about Cabot because the documentation about his life is so fragmentary, though a great deal has come to light in Venetian archives in recent years. So it is hardly surprising that there are doubts about exactly where he was born. Most contemporary documents describe him as Venetian, which was his adopted nationality by the time he was an adult. There are even some rumors that he was English, but that has never been proven. The letters from Spanish spies in England reporting on his discoveries later described him as "Genoese like Columbus," and actually there is little doubt that he was. His son Sebastian was also described as the "son of a Genoese." There is a tradition that John was actually born in the mountain village of Castiglione Chiavarese, about thirty miles down the coast toward La Spezia. Here, near the castle and Benedictine abbey—deep in wine and olive country—a ruined house is still known as the birthplace of "Giovanni Caboto."

John's father, Guilo (in Italian) or Egidius (in Latin) Cabot, and his family were seafarers—*caboto* means coastal seaman in the Genoese dialect. And although they invested heavily and apparently successfully in the spice trade, they seem to have been small-scale traders in and around Genoa when John was born. There are hints that the family may have been in-volved in the salt trade when they lived in Venice, and—since this was also a Genoese specialty—this would put them on the front line of the Genoese rivalry with Venice on the other side of the Italian peninsula.

Venice prided itself on its salt monopoly in the Adriatic, which had been the basis for the original prosperity of the city in the tenth century. Venetian barges took salt up the river Po and into Lombardy; and their raiders ventured out at night to destroy any salt pans they did not control. But at the same time, the Genoese were challenging the Venetian salt empire, refusing to buy salt from them and challenging their markets by supplying salt from the Languedoc, Spain, Sardinia, and Ibiza.* Guilo was entrepreneurial, but his efforts to climb the lower rungs of trading from Genoa were constantly upset by the unstable politics of the city and the need to back one or other faction, only to find yourself on the wrong side of the other.

Even without coming from a family of seafarers, a Genoese upbringing meant an overwhelming identification with the sea for John Cabot and his brother Piero, as well as a tough-minded approach to profit. It also meant the daily business of buying meat at the butchers and a diet of mainly fish and bread. This was before Italians ate pasta. The wheat originally came from Italy's Black Sea colonies, and the fish was from Spain and Flanders. Potatoes and tomatoes had not yet been introduced. The Cabot family garden—and most families of any standing had gardens—produced peas and broad beans to be dried in the winter, as well as onions, garlic, and herbs. They also had fruit trees. These supplemented the produce from the great grain warehouses that fed the city.

Anyone who grew up in Genoa in the 1450s would recognize the mag-nificent new palace that housed the Bank of St. George, the symbol of the stability of the city and its money, both colonial administrator and manager of the city's public debt—like the Bank of England and the East India Com-pany all rolled into one. They would know the famous Capo Faro lighthouse that provided a beacon for their harbor, a familiar landmark from land and

*Ibiza actually means "Isle of Salt."

reassurance as they sailed home. They would learn to be proud of the city's treasures: the ashes of St. John the Baptist and the emerald chalice said to have been used at the Last Supper. The phrase "Genoa the Proud" was coined in 1473 and has stuck ever since. Or as Dante had put it, "Genoa the Shameless."

Though its squares were tiny compared to those in Florence, and its artistic output puny compared to Venice, the narrow streets—it was said that a knight riding through them would have to turn in his toes to get through—were kept scrupulously clean. The mud was washed from the streets at night, and the front doors of the city's naval heroes were decorated with pictures of St. George. Like England, Genoa claimed St. George as their patron saint. Each city district was recognizable by the watchtowers at the fortified mansions of the great families who dominated there, as well as by the distinctive shops—the butchers in the district of Sosiglia, the goldsmiths in the Piazza dei Banchi, the shield makers in San Lorenzo, the dyers in Santo Stefano, and the weavers in the Borgo dei Lanaiuoli.*

Being Genoese in the mid-fifteenth century meant familiarity with the public staircases cut into the rock and the fountains in every square, fed by pipes from the mountains. It meant pride in what was the biggest and busiest harbor in the world, with its forests of masts, sails, and streaming banners, and all the fantasies and realities of the sea—the rumors of undiscovered lands and exotic spices, as well as the clang of hammers and the stench of pitch running along the beach where the tar merchants, carpenters, swordsmiths, sail makers, and pulley manufacturers did their business. The small boats from Corsica were a common sight, unloading melons and cheese to sell in the streets. So were the piles of dung and garbage that drew flies, and the merchants who put garlic to their nostrils to cover the stench as the slave vessels were unloaded.

We don't know why the Cabots left their tall, narrow, and probably crowded home; Genoese homes of the day accommodated up to six families on different floors. Maybe they felt claustrophobic among the dark, narrow streets. Maybe they dreamed of a new start in another city where they could imagine the family, or Guilo at least, having more substance than in Genoa.

---

*There were also the new phenomenon of sweet shops selling the little conical loaves of crystallized sugar known as *candi*, a word derived from Arabic.

More likely, they despaired of the continual disruption to their ambitions from the ferocity of Genoese politics.

Life in Genoa was dominated by the great families, and the network of allegiances that spread throughout the class system. The Guarco, Montaldo, Spinola, Doria, Fieschi, and Grimaldi families carved up the positions between them, and their intertwined business schemes dominated the activities at the waterfront.* But two families in particular—the Adorno and Fregoso clans—were battling for power in the middle of the fifteenth century and this increasingly spilled out onto the streets, with neighborhood brawls between advocates of the rival families. The disruption meant private prisons and miniature armies in control of some sections of the city. The violently unpredictable business of politics in Genoa meant that only four doges—the elected lifetime mayors of the city—managed to survive in office until their natural deaths.

The key issue of Genoese politics in that period was also becoming increasingly urgent. The problem was that Genoa was too weak by itself to guarantee its own independence. The question, therefore, was how to provide stable government for business to be conducted, given that Francesco Sforza, the new duke of Milan, was threatening to take control of the city and end its long history of independence. Paid agents of the king of Aragon (soon to be incorporated into Spain) were also fermenting revolt in the Genoese colony of Corsica. Florence now controlled the seaport of Pisa, but wanted another port too. The solution seemed to be some kind of alliance with a prince powerful enough to keep the city safe, and there were really only two practical alternatives—an alliance with Aragon (the nation that included Barcelona, Valencia, and Catalonia) or an alliance with France. Both alternatives carried their own heavy risks and both involved compromises that could end Genoa's independence as finally as any foreign invasion.

The Adorno party was in power in the early 1440s and supported an alliance with Aragon. But Giano Fregoso, leader of his own pro-French party, hired a galley, which slipped into Genoa harbor during the dead of night in

*The Grimaldi family remains powerful in the region. Prince Rainier of Monaco, husband of the late Grace Kelly, was a Grimaldi.

the first few days of 1447 and attacked the doge's palace. Fighting broke out all over the city and by the end of the day Giano Fregoso was in control—only to die shortly afterward. He was succeeded as doge by his son Pietro, who opened negotiations with the French king Charles VII—the man who had been crowned by Joan of Arc a generation earlier—as the price for providing some kind of guarantee to the city.

It is impossible to know for sure whose side the Cabots were on, but as members of the aspiring merchant classes it seems likely that they backed Pietro Fregoso's policy of stability under the French. It was good for business, or it was supposed to be. But the fact that they made what must have been a difficult decision to leave Genoa altogether as soon as this policy unraveled is also evidence that they were Fregoso supporters—from necessity, perhaps, rather than conviction.

Another member of the Fregoso party, this one very committed and enthusiastic, was a cloth weaver from Quinto, a man with ten different ideas a day for self-improvement and making money. His name was Domenico Columbus, and he believed that supporting the Fregoso cause would mean his triumphal acceptance as a Genoese citizen and bring success to the business ventures he dreamed of. He fought alongside Giano Fregoso in his 1447 coup and was part of his funeral procession.

Domenico's loyalty paid off. Political supporters of a reigning doge could reasonably aspire to one of the lucrative positions as warden of some part of the city's infrastructure. Domenico was appointed warden of the Olive Gate to the city, a position that carried the responsibility of maintaining it and a modest pension. His brother Antonio did even better. He was made warden of the Capo Faro lighthouse. The income from the gate made a big difference, because Domenico had recently married Susanna di Fontanarossa, who came from a similar mountain village to the one he was born in. Just after Giano Fregoso died, the young couple left their home in Quinto, with its orange and lemon trees and the blue Appenines in the distance, and moved to the outskirts of Genoa near the Olive Gate, where he was warden. Sometime between August 25 and the end of October 1451—when John Cabot was about two years old—Susanna gave birth to a son they named Christopher.

There remains controversy about exactly where Columbus was born.

Successive generations have tried to prove that he was Spanish, Portuguese, Jewish, even American. They argue that all his surviving documents are in Spanish rather than Italian, though Genoa had its own very distinctive dialect. The truth is that he was a little ashamed of his humble origins and did not emphasize his Genoese roots. But he charged his heirs "always to work for the honor, welfare and increase of the city of Genoa." "In the city of Genoa I have my roots, and there I was born," he told the Bank of St. George, writing from Castile in 1502. "Although my body be here, my heart is forever there."

A few years after Christopher was born, the family moved into a house near to St. Andrew's Gate in the Vico Diritto, now called the Casa di Columbo, where Domenico could put into practice his new scheme to sell wine. It was just inside the new walls near the waterfront and in the wool worker's quarter, surrounded by market gardens of vegetables and herbs. In the front was one large window with a door to the left of it that opened out into Domenico's workshop and wine store. Upstairs, the family could get out to the garden at the back where there was a well, right next to the city wall. There were more stories above.*

Domenico was the son of a weaver and a master weaver himself. His brother Antonio had been apprenticed for six years to another weaver, William from Brabant. They were small cogs in a giant European enterprise that bought wool from England or Flanders and exported it as finished cloth. The wool would be brought into the city from the docks or by mule, where it would be beaten, picked, washed, carded, spun into yarn, woven into cloth, measured, and cut, then stretched out to dry in sheds over a hundred feet long. It would then be combed and cut again before being handed over to the dyers, who used alum to fix the dye and remove the grease from the fabric. Finally it would end up back at the docks as yards of beautifully colored cloth.† Every one of these processes was part of a cottage industry with its own specialists, and the Columbus family was well versed in them, but even so, Domenico dreamed of a wider stage.

---

*The tiny house has consistently disappointed visitors. "I am sorry to have to say," wrote the French historian Henry Harisse in 1890, "that the house is too narrow and dark inside to be used now as a public library, school or geographic museum, as would be my intention, if I were to buy it."

†The blue cotton cloth from Genoa, exported to France, carried the sign GÊNES, which is where the word *jeans* comes from, or so it is said.

Unfortunately, the elder Columbus was one of those serial entrepreneurs who could never quite attain success. He was described later as "the sort of wine seller who was his own best customer." Later he tried selling cheese, with little more success than he achieved in the wine business. As soon as Christopher was of age, his name started appearing on his father's contracts: It was a sign that he was considered more reliable.

In 1458, when Christopher was five, Domenico suffered a serious setback that adversely affected his status in Genoa and therefore his business. The new doge, Pietro Fregoso, embarked on a series of secret negotiations to solve the problem of Genoa's vulnerability once and for all, by handing over the city to the French. The king of France's nephew was installed as governor of Genoa, and Fregoso stepped down with the promise of a fat pension. However careless the French were with the security of the city, they were quite happy to use it as a base for their own territorial ambitions. There was more than a whiff of colonialism about their rule. The Genoese were no longer the privileged elite in their own city, and Fregoso quickly irritated the new rulers so much that he was banished. In the power vacuum that followed, the rival Adornos rose to greater influence and, in the uncertainty, wool prices plummeted.

The following year, while the French governor was away on a military expedition, Pietro Fregoso returned to his city with a small force—just as his father had done a decade earlier. But this time, the battle did not go Fregoso's way. Around the corner from the Columbus home, he was caught by an angry mob and hit on the forehead with a mace. He crawled to St. Andrew's Gate for shelter, where he died a few hours later.

For three years after Pietro Fregoso's violent death, Genoa struggled to come to terms with its new masters. French rule had brought no more stability, so it was easy to blame the economic difficulties on the French rather than on more distant events like the fall of Constantinople. The desperation was such that it forced even the Fregoso and Adorno clans to join forces. Backed by aid from Francesco Sforza in Milan, the combined forces of the two rival parties sparked a better organized uprising in the city on March 9, 1461. What remained of the French garrison was taken completely by surprise and forced to take refuge in the Castelletto, Genoa's most powerful fortress. After a few more skirmishes, Prospero Adorno found himself in a powerful enough position to have himself elected doge three days later.

It was the ruin of Domenico's hopes. He had pinned his future to the fortunes of the Fregoso family, hoping for political favor, only to find his great rivals seizing the instruments of city government. But he did have a seat on a committee of the weaver's guild and heard through them that the wool trade was better in Savona, up the coast from Genoa, where the French were still in control. Keeping his house in Vico Diritto, he bought a farm in Savona, took his family there, and shifted his profession from wool weaver to wool dealer. The move was not a great success and Domenico found himself increasingly in debt. Soon he was in a debtors' court and then back in Genoa, living in the attic of the family home, having rented out all but a little space on the ground floor while Christopher tried to keep the wool business alive from Savona.

There is some evidence that the Cabot family also had links to Savona. In fact, so much about the events of four decades later, with the expeditions across the Atlantic by Columbus and Cabot, implies that they were more than just known to each other. The whole drift of the story, and the implication of the correspondence about them in the 1490s, is that they were also former collaborators. There is little direct evidence about when the collaboration began, or where they met, but the most likely scenario is that they knew each other as boys. When Columbus and Cabot were children, the number of Genoese boys under five years old was probably only two thousand or so—roughly the size of a modern-day secondary school. There is also a tradition in the town of Castiglione Chiavarese, which boasts the ruins of Cabot's house, that a neighbor from there lived next door to the Columbus family in Genoa. It is impossible to prove completely, but Cabot and Columbus probably began their friendship and rivalry either in Genoa or in Savona.

But for Guilo Cabot, Fregoso's death and the expulsion of the French from Genoa was the last straw. The family made the difficult and risky decision to leave Genoa—risky because it was the networks within a city that sustained merchants, and leaving for another city carried the risk of isolation. But Guilo had business contacts in other cities who could be persuaded to sponsor his arrival.

He chose Venice. It was a choice that said a great deal about him and his family. It meant they were prepared to turn a blind eye to the advance of the Turks into eastern Europe in return for the enormous reach of the Venetian merchant fleet. If he was indeed experienced in the salt trade, he would have valuable information about the Genoese salt business, which could be exchanged for a welcome and a helping hand in Venice. His son John was then twelve years old.

II

*"Lying on a feather mattress or quilt will not bring you renown."*

LEONARDO DA VINCI

Amerigo Vespucci was born in Florence on April 9, 1453, seven weeks before the fall of Constantinople. Another baby, Matteo, who may have been a twin who did not survive, appears to be named alongside him. His father, Nastagio, was a respected lawyer and a wealthy man, the son of the chancellor of the signoria, the secretariat of the senate that governed the city. His mother, Elisabetta, doted on her eldest son, Antonio, the only one sent to university, who later became a brilliant lawyer. Amerigo's other older brother, Bernardo, went into the wool business like Domenico Columbus. There was also a sister, Agnoletta. Unlike Cabot and Columbus, there is no dispute about where Vespucci was born. His baptism was recorded in the Church of Ognissanti the following March. Amerigo was named after his distinguished grandfather the chancellor, and he was brought up in a large home in the Ognissanti district in the northwest part of the city, along the Arno River, near the gate called the Porta Della Cana. It had an inner courtyard and a stone staircase leading to the second floor. On the door portals was the Vespucci coat of arms—a red background with a blue band with golden wasps. (*Vespa* is Italian for "wasp.")

The Vespuccis belonged to a very different stratum of society than the Columbus family, but they had at least one thing in common: Their homes were in the weaving districts of their respective cities. This wasn't a coincidence; the Vespucci's earned much of their income from the declining wool trade, and thus the wealth of Amerigo's branch of the family was dwindling. Amerigo's street, the Borgo Ognissanti, ran along the canal

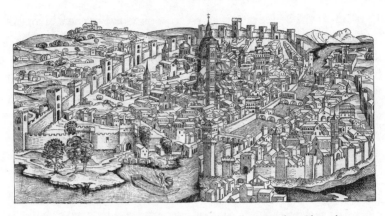

Florence as pictured in Hartmann Schedel's 1493 *Nuremberg Chronicles*

with its workshops for cloth weaving. The neighborhood was a key part of Florence's industrial sector and it smelled—not just of wine from cellars, but also of refuse dumped on the so-called island between their house and the Arno, the odors of which wafted over rich and poor alike. The next-door neighbors were a family of tanners, and the smell of hides and tanning also hung over the neighborhood. Like the Cabots, the Vespucci family had strong ties to the sea. One of Amerigo's cousins was the captain of a Florentine galley, and his uncle Piero had commanded a Florentine fleet that fought corsairs on the North African coast.

Florence may not have been as hard-headed as Genoa or as wealthy as Venice, but it was at that time the biggest and most sophisticated city in Renaissance Europe—the artistic center and the banking center that underpinned it. It was a city of expensive palaces built by Florence's merchant princes, the Pazzi with their dolphin crests, the Rucellai with their sails of fortune, or the Strozzi palace, half again as large as the White House and twice as high. And above all the Medici, then at the height of their wealth and power, with the forceful presence of Cosimo de' Medici—though he had no official position—presiding over the city from his palace behind the Duomo, rumored to have cost more to build than the Coliseum in ancient Rome.* It was the city of the famous Ponte Vecchio over the Arno, the

*It was these fifteenth-century palaces in Florence that provided the model for the Federal Reserve building in New York in the 1920s.

great red and white dome above Florence Cathedral, finally completed according to Brunelleschi's revolutionary design but not yet topped by a lantern, and the gigantic golden doors to the Baptistery, carved in relief by Lorenzo Ghiberti, the first artist in history to write his autobiography.

Florence in the 1460s was also a city of washers and carders with their wooden clogs to protect their feet from the wet floors, of colored laundry waving in the breeze, of donkey carts, tatty shops of beds, crockery, and broken casts of saints; there were the furnace makers in the Via al Fuoco, the perfumiers in the Via deli Speziali, and the hubbub of commerce in the Mercato Vecchio, with Donatello's statue of Plenty on a column at its center. It was especially a city of bankers, sitting on benches at their tables covered in green cloth at the Mercato Nuovo and the Via di Tavolini (*banco* means bench in Italian), exchanging their gold coins, and making careful notes. Florence was a city of luxury, of magnificent dinners of roasted blackbirds or capons, with wines and desserts from Corsica, Seville, and Madeira. But above all, this was a city of color—of dyes and dyers and colorful paintings, clothes, and illustrations, pushing forward the possibilities for turning flowers, insects, and ground-up precious stones into striking and permanent hues.

Amerigo knew the artists who manipulated these colors. The tanning family next door to the Vespuccis was called Filipepi, and the young Alessandro Filipepi—known to history as Botticelli—was about nine years older than Amerigo and had an older brother who was a broker in shares of the Monte, the Florentine public debt. When the Cabot family passed north of Florence on the way to their new life in 1461, the young Botticelli was an assistant to Fra Filippo Lippi, the former Carmelite monk turned artist.* Botticelli also knew the young Leonardo da Vinci, slightly older than Vespucci, but who even then was following Grandfather Amerigo in the street to fix his stately features in his mind so he could draw another interesting face when he got home.

The artists were carving out a new position for themselves in the city, thanks to the munificence of the Medicis and other wealthy patrons. Their social standing had been more akin to plumbers: You called them out and

---

*Five years earlier, Lippi had been involved in a scandal when he eloped with a nun named Lucrezia Buti. The two of them had a son called Filippino, who Botticelli in turn employed as his assistant. Lippi escaped censure because of his close relationship with the Medicis.

they would decorate your walls and furniture. They were not aristocratic in any way. Uccello was the son of a barber and Lippi the son of a butcher. Donatello—whose pert, naked statue of David in hat and boots stood in the courtyard of the Medici palace—was the son of a wool comber. A generation later, their status had so improved that Leonardo could die cradled in the arms of King Francis I of France.

Vespucci was tutored along with a few other sons of wealthy families by his uncle Giorgio, a highly respected Dominican friar. Giorgio was always immaculately dressed and knew everyone. He collected manuscripts and tended a burgeoning library of books, and he taught his pupils not just Virgil and Plato, but mathematics, astronomy, cosmology, and geography. It was Giorgio who taught him to love travel, and took him to Rome, instilling in him some of the work ethic that was to be such a feature of his career. "Arise betimes in the morning and sleep not so much, young man, who until now hath excessively played the fool, dancing and frolicking," wrote Amerigo in his ink-stained notebook. "Do not loll around or remain longer in idleness, but tire thyself out a little before old age comes upon thee and bodily vigor fails and thou moves unhappy and ill content."

Like the other Italian cities, Florence was suffering economically as Amerigo grew up. The War of the Roses in England had led to a succession of bad debts for the Medicis, and there was a string of bankruptcies in Florence in the mid-1460s. The wool trade was shrinking, as it was everywhere in Italy, and the Medicis were investing heavily in silk—ordering every farmer under their jurisdiction to plant five mulberry trees a year to feed the silkworms. But Florence also had advantages not shared by the other cities. It was the financial heart of Europe: Large sums of money from the crowned heads of Europe were deposited here—including all the papal accounts—because it was safer than in a seacoast city where it could be seized by pirates. As many as eighty Florentine banking houses controlled the credit system of the continent.

When Cosimo de' Medici died in 1464—listening to a discussion about his beloved Plato—he was succeeded by his flamboyant and astonishingly wealthy grandson Lorenzo de' Medici, known to history as "the Magnificent." Lorenzo had a better head for culture than he did for banking, and food prices continued to rise, while cloth prices fell, in the face of rising

competition from England and Flanders. Lorenzo's prescription for this economic depression was spectacle. In 1468 he held one of the most extraordinary jousts, officially dedicated to his fiancée, Claire Orsini, but unofficially
to his mistress, Lucrezia Donate, watching from a beautifully decorated balcony. Lorenzo himself entered the lists with a surcoat of purple and white
velvet, his horse clothed the same way, and with three hundred pearls trimming his cap and a golden buckle with eleven diamonds.

These were the festivals that made Florence unlike anywhere else. Afterward young people would wander outside the city in the fields, returning in
the early hours of the morning covered with dew. It was also a period of the
most extraordinary opulence, for those who could still afford it, with balls
and wedding feasts and lute music under the stars. One of these was the
wedding in 1473 of Amerigo's cousin Marco, another pupil of Uncle Giorgio, to a stunningly beautiful Genoese girl named Simonetta Cattaneo. The
heartthrob of her generation, La Belle Simonetta's arrival and her passing
became a symbol of the hope and disappointment for the age.

Shortly after her wedding, Simonetta encountered Lorenzo the Magnificent's rather over-romantic brother Giuliano at another luxurious ball.
There were fireworks, an enormous banquet, and a memorable performance
by three of the city's most beautiful women, Eleonora of Aragon, Alberia
degli Albizzi, and Simonetta herself portraying the three graces. It was the
performance that was immortalized in Botticelli's painting *Primavera*, now
in the National Gallery in London, and it was given a poignant twist when
Alberia died just ten days later. Giuliano de' Medici watched the performance and fell in love with Simonetta on the spot. For the rest of her short
life, he worshipped at her shrine. Poems, gifts, and entreaties fell at her feet,
despite the fact—or possibly because—she was married and steadfastly refused to succumb to his charms.

It was Simonetta who inspired Botticelli to paint *The Birth of Venus*. She
is also in the painting *Madonna with the Vespucci Family* in the Church of the
Ognissanti, painted by Domenico Ghirlandaio.* She remains one of

---

*The painting was whitewashed over in 1661 and only uncovered again behind the altar
in 1892. For years afterward, there was a dispute about which figure in painting was
Amerigo. The result was that medals struck in his honor by the Italian government—
Vespucci is, after all, the Italian candidate for the discovery of America—were made in
the likeness of the bald man kneeling at the feet of the Virgin.

Botticelli's *The Birth of Venus*. Simonetta Vespucci was
the model for the central figure of Venus.

history's most enticing, beautiful, and untouchable women. But reputations
like hers are enhanced by dying young, and just three years later, in April
1476, Simonetta died from tuberculosis. Her funeral cortege, with its open
coffin, was accompanied by Leonardo da Vinci, who sketched her head. She
was buried in the neighborhood Church of the Ognissanti. Peering into the
night sky afterward, Lorenzo the Magnificent glimpsed a star he had never
seen before. "That is Simonetta," he said, writing a sonnet in her memory.

> Bright shining star! Thy radiance in the sky
> Dost rob the neighboring stars of all their light.
> Why are thou with unwonted splendor bright?
> Why with great Phoebus does thou dare to vie?

Back in Genoa, Domenico Columbus had taken to describing himself as a
taverner, running a small bar from what he still retained of the family home.
He was trading small amounts of wine, cheese, and wool between Savona,
Genoa, and other local ports along the coast. Genoa had some of the most
sophisticated charities in Europe—the massive Pammatone, funded by a donation of shares in the Bank of St. George—but there was little help for political trouble-makers who like Domenico had fallen on hard times.

The years that followed the coup and the Adorno takeover saw unprecedented upheavals, as the French tried to claw their way back to a position of
control. Sforza intervened on the side of the Genoese, and doge after doge
was elected and then flung out of office. At the same time, the man who
would dominate the city for the next generation—Pietro Fregoso's brother
Paolo—began his inexorable rise to power, setting out on a long career of
piracy and populism as cardinal, admiral, and self-appointed doge. One Genoese chronicler complained that, if he had to record any more upheavals,
he would run out of paper. There was even talk of actually inviting the
French to come back. There was a new French king who might prove more
amenable than his predecessor, and the French were still in control of the
Columbus family's hometown of Savona. But it was too late for the new
king Louis XI, who declared that if "the Genoese give themselves to me, I
will give them to the Devil."

By 1464, after the first years of mismanagement by the doge-archbishop
Paolo Fregoso, the shares in the Bank of St. George had fallen to their low-
est point. Domenico asked Christopher to help him in business, and
Christopher went with him on his trips with the wine and cheese, and
helped negotiate prices. If his father was not entirely welcome in Genoa,
Christopher could represent him. But there were compensations for
Domenico's semiexile. Rubbing shoulders with Christopher on the wharves
of Savona were some of the other leading members of the Fregoso party, the
di Negros, Spinolas, and Centuriones, all formerly leading shipbuilders in
Genoa, now—like the other merchant princes of Genoa—shifting their
trading links westward. Columbus found himself on good terms with the
younger members and, sometime in 1473, he was appointed to accompany
their cargo to the eastern Mediterranean. He had a copy of Marco Polo's
*Travels* packed in his trunk.

# 2

# Maps

*"Our land is the home of elephants, dromedaries, camels, crocodiles, meta-collinarum, cametennus, tensevetes, wild asses, white and red lions, white bears, white merles, crickets, griffins, tigers, lamias, hyenas, wild horses, wild oxen and wild men, men with horns, one-eyed, men with eyes before and behind, centaurs, fauns, satyrs, pygmies, forty-ell high giants, Cyclopses, and similar women; it is the home, too, of the phoenix, and of nearly all living animals."*

Letter purporting to be from Prester John, delivered
to the emperor of Constantinople, c. 1165

*"Map me no maps, sir, my head is a map; a map of the whole world."*

HENRY FIELDING

Sometime in the middle of the twelfth century, a powerful rumor began to circulate across Europe. The story concerned a distant Christian ruler in the East, at least as wealthy and powerful as the Christian rulers of the West, who had broken the power of the Muslims near his own land, and was ready to march to the defense of Western Christendom. Jerusalem was still in Christian hands then, but the tide of affairs in Palestine was not going the way of the westerners, and the distant hope of rescue gleamed so alluringly that, on September 27, 1177, Pope Alexander III wrote an appeal to this distant legendary emperor. Then he sent his physician eastward to find the king and deliver it. It had been more than a decade since a letter from this ruler—known to legend as John the Priest, or Prester John—had been received in Constantinople. But no reply to the message ever came and the physician himself never returned.

The legend of Prester John was probably bound up with rumors of the heretical Nestorian church, which had briefly spread eastward as far as China, Sri Lanka, and Tibet. Prester John himself has been identified with Unk-Khan, a real ruler—though certainly not a Christian—in the region of what is now Kyrgyzstan. But the dream of Prester John, descended from the Three Wise Men and living somewhere along the Silk Road, or deep in Ethiopia, or perhaps ruling a great Indian empire, never quite died.

When Constantinople finally fell to the Ottomans in 1453 and the lucrative trading routes between West and East began to seize up—and Western Europe was genuinely threatened by an ascendant Islamic empire—the legend of Prester John once again became a powerful intoxicant. European adventurers dreamed not only about opening new trade routes—their closure now bearing heavily on Florentine bankers and Genoese merchants—but also of linking up with Prester John to push back the Muslim advance. The Pope sent out emissaries; the Portuguese even mounted land expeditions from the West African coast, but these efforts yielded nothing and the intelligentsia of Europe continued to puzzle over their maps of the world.

This was the age of maps. The great works of classical geography were suddenly being translated into Latin and being printed for the first time. Since Johannes Gutenberg began the first printing press in Europe in 1454, presses emerged in most of the big cities, and a new reading public was beginning to think for itself. But the intellectuals, fascinated by the dream of other lands and other opportunities for trade, wanted to see these places set out on a plan as well as read about them.

Most educated people understood that the world was round—Aristotle had worked that out seventeen centuries earlier—but there was little consensus about the shape of the land masses on earth. Maps of the world were speculative, beautifully painted works of art on rolls of vellum, with descriptions and little pictures of monsters and devils in the unknown regions. Cabot, Columbus, and Vespucci as young men were in the first generation to enjoy maps in wide circulation. It is hardly surprising that they were fascinated by them.

One of the new printed editions being read, and with enthusiasm, was *The Travels of Marco Polo*. Polo had written it two centuries before, while he was in prison in Genoa—a fact that did not encourage the academics and geographers to believe what he wrote. Learned people thought his descriptions of China and Japan were complete fiction, but they were still captivating for dreamers. Not just the descriptions of the three and a half year journey to Beijing, or the jewels sewn into the jacket of the Great Khan, but also the solid gold roofs of Cathay:

> The palace of the princes is entirely roofed with gold plates, just as our houses are roofed with lead. The halls and rooms are lined with plates of gold, and the windows have gold frames. There are pearls in great quantity and so many precious stones that you only have to bend down and pick them up.

And how could a romantic forget the women of the city Marco Polo called Qinsay, who "are so tempting and have such experience in amorous intercourse that a man who has once enjoyed one of them can never forget her"?

The difficulty was separating fact from fantasy in the maps and descriptions of foreign lands. There were authoritative descriptions of races able to survive the extreme heat and cold that geographers believed were at the equator or the poles—pygmies, giants, people who were able to live just off the smell of apples, four-eyed seagoing Ethiopians, dog-headed men. There were the Scipods, who held one foot over their heads like a big umbrella, the Blemmyae, who had their faces in their chests, and the Antipodes, who had their feet inconveniently turned backward.

Atlantis had disappeared, but what about the floating islands of the South Atlantic described by Juventius? Or the legend of St. Brendan, the Irish monk whose journey included an island of talking birds, an island of sheep, and a crystal island? At least the crystal island might have been an

A page from Marco Polo's *Travels*

iceberg. But what about the island of hy-Brasil, a version of the lost Irish island Tir na Nog, the land of eternal youth, said to be visible off the western
coast of Ireland in the right psychic conditions.*

There was Antillia, or the Island of the Seven Cities, supposed to
have been the destination of seven Portuguese bishops who escaped
ahead of the Muslim advance across the Spanish peninsula in the eighth
century. Everyone interested in such matters had heard the tale of the
ship that landed on Antillia by accident a generation before Columbus,
and when the crew went ashore and found a church, they were surprised
to discover it was Roman Catholic. The sand they brought back from
their landing place was also found to be one third fine gold, or so it was
said. That was the thrill of these debates: They were not just romantic;
even the most hard-headed skeptics were drawn toward these dreams of
untold wealth.

*As late as 1872, a professor at the Royal Irish Academy claimed to have seen it. The
last remaining memory of this mythical island was the final disappearance of the equally
mythical Brazil Rock from British Admiralty charts in 1873.

. . .

The man with the self-appointed task of separating fact from fiction was one of the most romantic characters in this or any age. Prince Henry the Navigator was the younger son of King John I of Portugal and half-English by blood (his mother was Philippa of Lancaster, the daughter of John of Gaunt). While the English and French were battling it out at Harfleur and Agincourt, Henry was dreaming up a plan to sail around Africa to reach the Indies and Cipangu, Marco Polo's name for Japan (a corruption of the Chinese phrase *Ji pen Koue*, meaning Empire of the Rising Sun). This in itself was a massive leap of faith: Apart from the legend of Hannibal sailing all the way around Africa, there was very little evidence that such a voyage was possible.

As a younger son, even of a king, Henry had few resources—certainly too few for what he wanted to achieve. He carefully conserved what he had managed to earn in his early career in piracy, preying on Muslim shipping, and what came in from his monopoly on the Portuguese soap trade. But he knew what he would need: improvements in ship building, breakthroughs in navigation using the stars, new systems of chart making using latitudes, new understandings of weather patterns and ocean currents. With promises of glory and wealth that belied Henry's actual resources, his emissaries tracked down the greatest shipwrights, mathematicians, astronomers, and geographers and lured them to his new institute at Sagres. This windswept edge of the known world, the last rocky outcrop on the edge of the Atlantic, the most southwesterly point of Portugal and Europe, gave an aura of sanctity to the whole enterprise.* Under Henry's leadership, Portuguese expeditions sailed to determine whether the sea was really boiling at the equator or if the pitch that held the boats together would melt there. One by one, each voyage pressed farther south along the coast of Africa, leaving a stone marker on the shore at the extremity of each voyage to mark their progress, until in 1445 they rounded Cape Verde and found, not boiling seas, but fertile villages and riverbanks.

But forcing the pace southward in their three-masted caravels, new ships designed to have high forecastles (the tall, multideck castlelike structure in the bow of the ship) to deal with the Atlantic swell, had some unexpected

---

*Henry devoted himself so singlemindedly to the task that he was widely believed to be a virgin. When he died in 1460, he was found to be wearing a hair shirt.

by-products. The winds in the mid-Atlantic move clockwise, so it was difficult—at least given the technology that Henry's captains used—to sail back again directly northward. His explorers found themselves sailing far-ther and farther west in order to get home, and so as a consequence of the search for the southern tip of Africa, they soon discovered the Azores and the Canary and Cape Verde islands among others.

The most westerly islands of the Azores, Flores and Corvo, were added dutifully to the maps in 1452, the result of an unsuccessful Portuguese expe-dition in search of hy-Brasil. A decade later, Portuguese mariners were be-ing offered the islands of Lovo and Capraria if they could find them, or later still the Island of the Seven Cities. None of them actually existed, but they were still on the maps. That was the problem with fifteenth-century maps: They were speculative interpretations of the world. You could not use them to mount a reliable expedition into the unknown.


Maps and geography were bound to be the subjects of intense interest among Florence's powerful intellectuals—no contemporary city had achieved a similar level of civilization. There was a breadth to Florentine thinking that matched its new broad avenues and squares—a wholly differ-ent kind of city—compared to the cramped and bustling narrow streets of Genoa and Venice. Over the past generation, thanks to the immense wealth of Cosimo de' Medici, the arts were flourishing and so was a small coterie of intellectuals dedicated to a sophisticated kind of mysticism and the rediscovery of the philosophy of Plato.

Right from the beginning, Cosimo's Platonic academy had discussed geog-raphy. There is even a sketch of Cosimo de' Medici and friends poring over a copy of Ptolemy's *Geography* by candlelight. The greatest minds in Florence were brought to bear on the problem of how to represent a spherical world on the flat surface of a book or map. Alberti and Brunelleschi, creator of the great dome, tried to see whether their insights into the laws of perspective might allow them to draw a flat map of a spherical globe. And Paolo dal Pozzo Toscanelli, a retired but celebrated doctor, was on hand to interview foreign visitors and muse aloud about the shape of the distant lands of the world.

Toscanelli was the grand old man of Florentine intellectuals. Unmarried, monkish, and astonishingly ugly, he had lived in the same house since returning to Florence as a graduate in 1424, near the public well in the Santo Spirito quarter of the city, just across the Arno from the Vespucci family. His vision, though, was truly global: He took detailed notes from all the participants at the Council of Florence—Cosimo de' Medici's attempt to broker an understanding with Constantinople and the Orthodox Christian world, with emissaries from Byzantium, Russia, and even the Great Khan—and from them developed a radical theory. He believed that the size of the earth was small enough that if you were to sail west across the Atlantic you would reach China and the spice islands of the East.

He collected the best and most expensive maps that he could find from around the world, helping the Medici family find and buy skins and spices, never eating meat or drinking wine, studiously avoiding any criticism of or gossip about the Florentine intellectual elite, and writing letters to his friends all over the world. In his spare time, he practiced as a doctor, without charging fees. If anyone in Europe yearned to know the truth, whether it was about spice islands, astronomy, or the measurement of comets—the subject of his most important book—they made their way to Florence and asked for an interview with Toscanelli.* Henry the Navigator's brother Pedro had come. So had an ambassador from Ethiopia, who arrived unexpectedly in 1441, claiming to have been sent by Prester John himself. In the 1460s his most regular visitor was the young Leonardo da Vinci, asking him about mathematical problems.

The young Amerigo Vespucci almost certainly knew Toscanelli, who was still director of the library at the monastery of St. Mark, where Vespucci's uncle Giorgio was officially a monk. Giorgio and Toscanelli traveled in the same circles within the Platonic academy, and Giorgio must have introduced him to his favorite nephew. Amerigo's growing fascination with maps may date from those meetings. With Toscanelli he saw the great planisphere— the enormous map of the world that hung on the wall of his home—and heard the strange stories of Markland and Vinland, the Viking colonies beyond the seas.

There was no more exciting time in history, with the new books and maps emerging, to be fascinated by ideas. The classical past was suddenly

*The book has a rather wonderful title: *The Immense Toils and Serious Lucubrations of Paolo dal Pozzo Toscanelli on the Measurement of Comets.*

available, and the world's intellectuals would open their doors to almost anyone who expressed interest. And of all places to be fascinated by art or ideas, Florence was the pinnacle of the civilized world, especially in the heady summer of 1476.

I

*"If you knew how you are universally hated, your hair would stand on end."*

GALEAZZO MARIA SFORZA, to the secretary of the
Venetian Republic, 1467

Venice looked to the East to trade her goods, so the frustrating closure of the Venetian links to the Silk Road and the spice routes was particularly difficult. The Ottoman advance across eastern Europe had been beaten back from the gates of Belgrade and Budapest but was, nevertheless, advancing. Yet the Cabot family, newly arrived in Venice, was managing to establish themselves successfully in the business community.

At first it was the salt trade, using Guilo Cabot's knowledge of Genoa's rival involvement in salt on the other side of Italy, that provided Guilo with the right to do business on his own account before being enrolled as a Venetian citizen. But very quickly, he also became involved in the spice market. Spices were not just an important food ingredient, they were increasingly used as food preservatives—which made the trade in agricultural products easier—and as cosmetics and pharmaceuticals. Sugar, tea, coffee, and chocolate were all drugs that later would be recognized as foods. Cinnamon was a menstrual regulator and good for sunburn, frankincense was used to unblock both arteries and bowels. The spice market was to dominate the imagination and plans of Guilo's son, John, in addition to the trade in skins that John was beginning to make his own. It was in these trades in his father's shop and his own speciality that he was beginning to learn the basics of business—the techniques that allowed you to track the profitability of a deal, even while it was still at sea, the insurance, the loans, the contracts, and the long-term partnerships that made profit possible. Night after night, by expensive candlelight, he studied their *ricordanze*, the detailed business diary that companies used before double-entry bookkeeping.

He was also learning to share the Venetian worldview. This was a city so bound to the sea that there were no roads to it at all. It had no city walls to protect it. The Cabot family could gaze out from the Moorish windows of their mansion on what is now the via Garibaldi, with the entrance to the harbor right in front of them, and watch the trading ships of the Mediterranean unloading exotic wares from every corner of the known world and beyond—gems, peacock feathers, perfume and colored dyes, carpets from the Levant, silver from Germany, wool and cloth from England and Flanders.

John seems to have thought of himself as overwhelmingly Venetian. He signed his name using Venetian spelling (*Zuan* rather than John or Giovanni). To be Venetian was to be immensely proud of the glories of St. Mark's Square and the twisting shopping street known as the Merceria, to regard the Rialto and its bridge over the Grand Canal as the center of commerce and banking in the eastern Mediterranean. He must also have frequented the new bookshops. Printing arrived in Venice in 1469, eight years after the Cabots arrived, and within five years, 130 editions of books emerged from the city.

As he approached the age of twenty, having lived in Venice for almost a decade, he came to recognize as his own the striped red and white tights of the gondoliers, the small black caps people wore in the street, the tall chimneys on the mansions along the canals, and the swirling scarlet capes of the senators depicted in the paintings of Carpaccio. In the streets, it was possible to hear the extraordinary cacophony of German, Turkish, Arabic, Persian, Italian, Greek, and every other language you could imagine. The Cabots may have been newcomers, but this was a city of immigrants.

Venice as pictured in Hartmann Schedel's 1493 *Nuremberg Chronicles*

Venice was also a civilized city compared to Genoa. There were no loud voices raised even on the Rialto. Lamps burned continuously in the dark corners of the narrow streets, with icons behind them, and the great city festivals did not degenerate into political brawls. The annual fifteen-day feast of the Sensa saw carpets hung over the balustrades of the bridges and handcarts selling wares under the golden domes of St. Mark's Square. It also marked the annual reaffirmation of the marriage between the doge of Venice and the sea: a ring dropped symbolically into the ocean once a year.

John took what opportunities he could to accompany his father's cargoes, just as Columbus was doing. It may have been due to something that happened on one of these trips—an encounter with Turkish pirates or some successful resistance to Ottoman customs demands—or simply youthful charisma that made John Cabot a popular figure in his adopted city, and at the age of twenty-one, he was elected by acclamation to one of the city's many exclusive clubs. Not just any club either, but the confraternity of St. John the Evangelist, also known as Scuole Grandi, which was highly prestigious and had long waiting lists for membership. Despite the waiting lists, Cabot was granted immediate membership at a third of the normal entrance fee. In 1470 the family had only been in the city for nine years and neither John nor his father could yet afford to pay the full amount. But Cabot's contemporaries believed in him, and not just because of whatever feat of arms or mercantile trickery had propelled him to fame.

Like so many of his contemporaries, John was also fascinated by maps and cartography, and through the Scuole Grandi, he could mix freely and intimately with some of the leading mapmakers and geographers that Venice could offer. Venice may not have been on the front line of the artistic renaissance, but it was as steeped in humanism—the learning based on a new appreciation of the classics—as anywhere else in Europe.* The great Venetian navigator Priamo Capella was a member of the Scuole Grandi. Cabot would have looked to him to learn about the shape of the world, or sat at the feet of Capella's brother Febo, the greatest Venetian humanist of the age, and later grand guardian of the confraternity. Febo Capella had recently returned from being the city's representative in Florence, and he had

---

*Though this was the city that gave us the prodigious Bellini family, now out sketching the city.

become great friends with the group of Platonists around Toscanelli and the Medici family. There is no evidence that Cabot encountered Toscanelli himself or heard his theories about the shape of the world firsthand, but Febo Capella is a clear link between them.

The news that filtered through from Genoa convinced Guilo Cabot that he had been right to leave. The turbulent politics of the city had never died down, nor had Domenico Columbus managed to inveigle himself with any of the new factions. For most of the time since the Cabots departed, Genoa had been ruled by the powerful Sforza family from Milan. But the consequences of playing off the surrounding powers was that there was never a time when the city had not been drawn into one foreign dispute or another.

Christopher Columbus found himself lodging in Savona, or sometimes in the old Columbus family home in Genoa, and accompanying his father's consignments of wine and cloth down the coast. Occasionally, he was also testing out his own abilities farther afield, sending their wool and cloth to be sold in Spain, North Africa, or the Middle East—even if he didn't accompany it himself—then using the money to buy local products like wheat, for sale back in Genoa. Sometimes the tasks required of him were brutal seagoing raids on Fregoso enemies. Christopher nursed his outrage at the indignities heaped upon the family. He seems not to have had much affection for his father and his rapid changes of mood, but Christopher was proud of his family, sometimes obsessively so. Through strength of will and a determined measure of bluff, he was keeping the family business running.

He was also determined that this was not going to be the sum of his life. Also based in Savona were some of the other mercantile clans who had backed the ruined Fregoso party, the Spinola and di Negro families and the sugar barons in the Centurione family. Soon Christopher was carrying out small tasks for them, and going to sea helping to protect their cargoes or joining in the freelance activities of a corsair, raiding the businesses of enemies of the Fregoso clan, mainly Aragonese interests along the coast. In later life, he told a boastful story of how he had joined a raiding party on behalf of the king of Naples, the Fregoso ally René of Anjou, in his bid to take the throne of Aragon.* He related how he persuaded a fearful crew that they were going home, through a little trickery with the compass, when actually they were sailing straight toward the enemy.

Whether it was true or not, the story hints at the self-image that Columbus nursed for himself in his mind: resourceful, heroic, and capably on the path to glory. He was now twenty-four and when he was offered the chance of joining the convoy for Chios in September 1475, on board Gioffredo Spinola's ship *Roxana*, he jumped at the chance.

The island of Chios, off the Aegean coast of what is today Turkey, was almost the last Genoese trading colony in the East still operating so close to the Ottomans. It was supposed to have been the birthplace of Homer, author of the *Iliad* and the *Odyssey*, and was considered critical to the struggling Genoese economy because it was one of the few places in the known world with evergreen trees that produced gum mastic. Mastic was a vital ingredient in varnishes and adhesives, and when it was mixed with sugar, it produced sweets like marshmallow and licorice. Genoese traders like Spinola would charter a convoy of large ships—three-masted caravels—and sail them to Chios in the autumn, stay there through the spring, and then travel through the Strait of Gibraltar and on to England and Flanders to sell the mastic and bring back cloth.

This convoy was to be Columbus's first long voyage, at least three weeks at sea, hugging the coasts where possible, leaving from Sicily and snaking through the Greek islands and across the Aegean. The convoy was also carrying a full complement of mercenaries, plus heavy weapons, to guard the island against an expected Ottoman attack. The weather was changing in the Mediterranean as they sailed through the Greek islands and the waves and wind were less predictable. Then, suddenly, Chios appeared. As the *Roxana* approached the mouth of the harbor, lines of windmills came into view and behind them the big houses of the traders in red and white alternating colored stone. As they unloaded the cargo, the mercenaries spread

*René was theoretically King of Jerusalem, though that city was then in Muslim hands, and was supposed to have been grand master of the secret society known as the Priory of Sion (if it actually existed). His daughter Margaret was the fearsome wife of Henry VI of England, one of the forces driving the War of the Roses, in exile at the time.

out across the harbor, much to the relief of the Genoese families they were there to defend, fearful that the sultan's galleys would appear on the horizon at any moment.


The threat to Chios was reflected all around the Aegean as, one by one, the Ottoman advance destroyed the most lucrative Venetian trading outposts and industrial facilities. It was becoming clear that Mehmet II, the conqueror of Constantinople, was maneuvering to control all the trade routes of the eastern Mediterranean. He was building up a fleet that was capable of challenging the Venetians, as well as orchestrating internal divisions in Egypt and Syria, which controlled the caravan routes from the Persian Gulf through to Aleppo, Damascus, and Beirut. The furs and slaves from the Black Sea had dwindled and almost completely disappeared. Turkish mercenaries had also been landing near Venice itself and destroying the surrounding countryside. Any Venetians who made the laborious climb to the top of the dome of St. Mark's could see the smoke from the burning villages.

In January 1475, through the unlikely intervention of Mehmet's stepmother, a peace offer from the Turks arrived at the doge's palace. The offer was bitterly controversial and was debated for two solid days and nights in the senate before it was narrowly and grudgingly accepted. But Doge Mocenigo, who had driven the vote for peace through the force of his personality, died before the final negotiations were complete. It was said that he suffered from exhaustion, not from negotiating, but from the attentions of his ten Turkish slave concubines. The uneasy standoff between the two great powers in the eastern Mediterranean continued.

While the debate over the peace offer was raging in the senate, the Cabots reached the moment they had been waiting for: They had now lived in the city for fifteen years, making them eligible for Venetian citizenship. Although Venice was a republic and nominally a democracy, 90 percent of the population were not officially citizens and had no vote. But citizenship, if you could get it, conferred added rights for independent business and trade. Still the local hero, twenty-six-year-old John Cabot applied and was unanimously elected by the senate.

John had been working as a merchant's factor, or agent, not just for his father but for other clans as well, and was now increasingly active as a trader in his own right. The glimpses we have of him, in Venice or later, imply strongly that Cabot was a talker. He was articulate, brilliantly energetic, and full of schemes and projects—more credible in some ways than his erstwhile friend Christopher Columbus, who was trying to carve out a similar role for himself in the West. Cabot was also putting his eloquence to good effect, trading in animal skins. Those who specialized in salt were figuring out ways to diversify, because the Venetian salt pans on either side of the Adriatic were vulnerable to attack from the Ottomans. Even the traditional sources of furs in the Crimea were now as good as closed to the Venetians, but there were new routes opening up that went directly to the great center of the fur trade in Bruges, bringing back mink, squirrel, or fox furs for the prestigious furriers of Venice, and this is where Cabot began to make his mark in business.

These were long voyages, through the Strait of Gibraltar and then all the way down the English Channel, bringing back sheep skins and wool in the same consignments, bought cheaply in the ports of southern Spain. It is unlikely that Cabot undertook these journeys himself at first. He had another project at hand—renovating property in Venice and selling it at a profit—while his father's cargoes were on the high seas. But so much more would be possible now that he was a full-fledged Venetian citizen.

As the winter of 1475 approached, Columbus was back in Genoa, dreaming of the East. Chios had been a frustrating trip, and while he was there, the news had arrived that Caffa—the last Genoese outpost in the Black Sea—had fallen to the Ottomans some months earlier. Yet the distress began to turn to relief as the threat to Chios lifted. It was clear that the sultan was not, after all, intending to attack them. As the relief at their escape spread, so the attitude of the Chios families toward the visiting mercenaries changed.

Within a few weeks, the authorities were so infuriated by the behavior of the soldiers that they had swept through the island rounding them up and herding them back onto the ships they had arrived on. The convoy was not going all the way to the English Channel after all, and they set sail back to Genoa as soon as the weather permitted. Still, Columbus made the most of his near adventure in Chios. His work for the di Negros and Spinolas had been noticed and soon the call came again. Christopher was asked to accompany their consignment of mastic from Genoa to England—probably originally intended for the previous year—and he accepted. So in May 1476, just eight months after his first departure for Chios, he set off to seek his fortune a second time in a convoy of five ships heading out into the Atlantic in search of English and Flemish cloth. As they weighed anchor in Noli harbor, Columbus watched the disappearing mountains, this time from the gunwales of the whaler *Bechalla*, hired by Niccolò Spinola.

As the convoy hugged the coastline of Aragon, dropping into Barcelona and Valencia through June and July, all but one of the ships was flying the Genoese flag—the red cross of St. George on a white background.* As they passed Gibraltar on their starboard side, they encountered one of the most fearsome pirates in the eastern Mediterranean, the Frenchman Guillaume Casenove, in command of a fleet of thirteen Portuguese raiders. There were few pirates in those days who simply attacked any ships they encountered. They lived under the protection of princes and were nominally Christian raiders seeking out Muslim shipping—or vice versa. France was in alliance with Genoa—a rare moment when the old Fregoso policy was in place—so, tempting as it was, Casenove could find no excuse to seize Columbus's convoy.

Or could he? The *Bechalla* was not flying the Genoese flag, although it was manned by seaman from Savona, because it was actually Flemish. It therefore flew the flag of Burgundy, which was currently at war with France. That was excuse enough. Casenove's fleet had prepared for sail and now filed out of Gibraltar harbor. They shadowed the Genoese convoy around the coast, and off Cape St. Vincent on August 13 they ordered them to stop.

There was really no decision to be made. The Genoese ships were heavily outnumbered and would have to fight. The *Bechalla* was one of the smaller vessels in the convoy but it was not ignored, and soon arrows and crossbow bolts were clattering on the deck. All around them, the engagement was turning into a prodigious confrontation. Sea battles in those days involved the terrifying screams of hand-to-hand fighting on other decks,

---

*The St. George's cross is more famous now as the flag of England. In fact, England had only just adopted St. George as their patron saint—before the fifteenth century they used St. Edward the Confessor—and borrowed George from the Genoese because of the protection the flag afforded them on the high seas, or so the Genoese say.

while arrows dipped in burning pitch would begin to fall. There was the acrid smell of burning wood and flesh wafting across the waves. Four of Casenove's ships were now burning and sinking, but two of the convoy's ships had also disappeared, and then the stench of fire became so close as to be unmistakable. Soon the *Bechalla* was on fire from one end to the other, and the crew plunged into the sea.

Columbus was about six miles from the coast—wounded and weak from loss of blood and half-blinded by the salt. Some hours later, a peasant farmer found him collapsed on the sandy beach of Porto de Mos on the Argarve, just west of a Portuguese fishing village called Lagos. He was within a few days journey of the Portuguese capital city of Lisbon, where his younger brother Bartholomew was trying to establish himself as a cartographer. Thanks to the efforts of Henry the Navigator, this was now the city of navigators.

Two ships of Columbus's convoy managed to escape and take shelter in Cadiz. The crews and the survivors made their way to Lisbon at the end of December and soon made contact with those fortunate few who had managed to land from the sinking ships. Help was also on the way. Those behind the joint venture that had sent the convoy had been considering what to do. The suppliers were still waiting in England, and there were the survivors of the battle to think of; to that end, a second convoy began preparing in Genoa to rendezvous with the survivors of the original one in Lisbon and complete the journey. By late March or early April 1477, they were in the English Channel, slipping through the Solent to dock at Southampton, and Columbus was aboard.

Like Genoa, England had been through more than its fair share of political turbulence. The dynastic battle known as the War of the Roses finally seemed settled. But the Yorkist king Edward IV, tall, handsome, and capable, was still suppressing any whiff of dissent and in the summer would execute two people for trying to kill him by witchcraft.* But although the civil war had not touched every corner of the kingdom, and the trading houses of

---

*The case for clemency was put forth by the Duke of Clarence, who, as a result, was famously drowned in the Tower of London in a barrel of fortified wine known as malmsey.

London, Southampton, and Bristol had continued their inexorable rise, there were few disputes that did not crystallize into politics.

Columbus was determined to take a ship farther north from Bristol, one of the ports that had been most affected by sudden shifts in policy. For nearly a century, Bristol merchants had been sending cloth and wheat to the isolated Danish colony in Iceland, and buying air-dried cod known as stockfish in return. Then King Edward agreed to a peremptory demand from the Danes to stop buying fish from Iceland—the monopoly for which had been given to the Bergen branch of the powerful Baltic trading group, the Hanseatic League.

The relationship between Bristol and Iceland was complicated. On the one hand, Bristol traders were almost the only sources of supply available to the Icelandic communities. On the other hand, they also bought boys and girls from Icelandic communities and took them home to England as household servants. The coastal communities in Iceland were equally furious about the fish agreement, afraid that they would simply be abandoned. The traders of Bristol, for whom the Icelandic trade had become increasingly important, were badly hit too. Columbus may not have known, but if he was going to sail north on a Bristol vessel, it would no longer be a simple matter of shipping onto the next trading voyage out of the harbor.

Southampton, on the other hand, was full of Italians; a recent mayor had even been from Florence. Columbus reported to the offices of the Spinola family in the city and joined another party of sailors through the Bargate on the road to Winchester and from there to the city and port of Bristol. He arrived there in May and the first thing he noticed was the astonishing heights of the tides. At one moment the ships along the wharfs of the Avon River were resting in the mud; a few hours later they were riding up to fifty feet higher in the water. With tides that high, they would have been on the edge of an ocean that was vast compared to the Mediterranean.

Once in Bristol, Columbus found his way to the Church of St. Nicholas, the patron saint of sailors, next to the Mariner's Institute on Marsh Street, to find out when and where ships were sailing and who needed crews. Soon he was safely on board a trading ship, carrying butter, honey, grain, and Flemish linens. The voyage was a twenty-day journey into the Bristol Channel, along the coast of Wales and Scotland, and from there directly across to Iceland. Having arrived, he made contact with the crew of an English or

Scottish dogger. These were large fishing boats that made their way along the Icelandic coast catching cod, with the intention of smuggling the catch home without paying duties—buying stockfish there was prohibited. For the next month or so, Columbus shared the tough life of the fishermen, the massive Atlantic swell, and hauling the nets in what was, even in summer, an icy sea.

But in the heaving seas west of Iceland, tantalizingly close to Greenland, Columbus was as close to the edge of the known world as he had ever been. He knew Seneca's famous prophecy that lands would emerge beyond Thule, the medieval name for Iceland. He would also have heard in Iceland, if not earlier, that there had once been Danish settlements farther west than that, on Helluland, Markland, and Vinland, strange islands inhabited by painted men or *skraelings*.* It is still not certain to where these Viking place names referred, but there is a suggestion that Helluland was Baffin Island, Markland was Labrador, and Vinland was Newfoundland. A century before Columbus sailed to Iceland, the Oxford mathematician Nicholas of Lynn traveled all the way to the Arctic on behalf of Edward III, probably to Markland, and left behind his astrolabe with the local priest.

The dogger had circumnavigated Iceland by the end of August, and as agreed, Columbus shipped a return passage on a Bristol trading ship. Bristol ships returned back along the coast of western Ireland, and Columbus knew that in the busy port of Galway he would again encounter Portuguese traders and that way get back to Lisbon. But even more important for the future was what he saw in Galway. While he was waiting for his ship in the small harbor, there was a commotion at the dockside. A small boat had been towed in, having evidently drifted for thousands of miles, with a man and a woman inside still alive, clinging to the planks. The woman was absolutely beautiful, but both were of "most unusual appearance." Today we would recognize them as Inuit, but Columbus believed they were Chinese. For him they were a tantalizing glimpse not so much of lands to the west, but of the golden roofs of Cipangu far beyond the horizon.

*The previous summer an expedition of the Danish pilot Johannes Scolvus had left from Iceland to reestablish contact with a European settlement on the east coast of Greenland—the settlement on the west had been abandoned about a century earlier. It has often been speculated that Columbus heard about this while he was in Iceland.

## II

*"Certainly I owe much to Plato, but I must confess that I owe no less to Cosimo [de' Medici], inasmuch as Plato only showed me the idea of courage, Cosimo showed it to me every day."*

MARSILIO FICINO, Plato's translator

While Columbus was at sea in the north Atlantic, a deadly conspiracy against the Medicis was beginning to take shape in Florence. Lorenzo de' Medici was increasingly unpopular, blamed for the series of disastrous harvests that had undermined the city's finances. There were irritable whispers about who this elegant young man thought he was, with his sumptuous entertainments and poets and artists in luxuriant clothes. Florence was supposed to be a republic, so why were they ruled by this staggeringly wealthy dynasty? These mutterings quickly began to take a more deadly shape, led by the rival Florentine banking family Pazzi, but with at least tacit support from Pope Sixtus IV—and very active support from Archbishop Salviati of Pisa and a hot-headed seventeen-year-old Cardinal Riario, a nephew of the pope, whose father commanded the Vatican troops. The motivations for the plot were various—dark resentments and jealousies and a frustrated attempt by the pope, using Pazzi money, to take over the main road to the Adriatic.

Lorenzo and his brother Giuliano arrived at Florence's spectacular cathedral, the Duomo, for mass on April 26, 1478, sitting in their usual places in front of the choir. But as the priest elevated the bread and wine, it was the sign for the conspirators to strike.

Francesco Pazzi stabbed Giuliano fatally, and so brutally and enthusiastically that he injured his own thigh. Lorenzo was wounded in the neck but he leaped over the choir rail and was saved by the quick thinking of his friend, the poet Angelo Poliziano, who hustled him through the door to the sacristy and slammed it shut. The archbishop meanwhile arrived at the offices of the city authorities, but the *gonfalionere*—the city's chief official— was suspicious, and locked himself in the building ordering the bells to be rung. When the other conspirators arrived, shouting "the people and liberty!" they realized the coup had almost certainly failed.

Giuliano and Lorenzo de' Medici

Some of the conspirators were killed then and there in street fighting, but the rest were caught. Within days, the leaders were hanged from upper windows of city offices—Francesco Pazzi naked, the archbishop in his full ceremonial robes. A nervous Botticelli sketched their bodies as they hung there, and his biographers dated his mental decline as stemming from the experience. Furious at such treatment of an archbishop, an incandescent Pope Sixtus put the whole of Florence under an interdict, a mass excommunication of the city. Venice and Milan backed Florence, but the rest of Italy lined up behind the pope. A general conflagration seemed to be inevitable as the pope's own troops, under Riario's father, prepared for war.

Only two of the leaders of the Pazzi conspiracy remained alive: The youthful Cardinal Riario was flung into prison; the other escaped. It soon became clear that the person responsible for his escape was Amerigo's cousin Piero Vespucci. Piero was arrested, tortured for twenty days, and sentenced to life imprisonment in the city's prison, known as the Stinche. His son Marco was exiled.

Why did Piero help? He always claimed that he was innocent, though he never denied that he had helped the conspirator escape, and he must have had some idea what was happening. One explanation is that he still harbored resentment against the Medicis for the outrageous way that Giuliano had up-staged his son Marco as the public lover of Simonetta. Whatever the reason, the city was in uproar, with crowds shouting the Medici slogan *"palle, palle!"*\* All of Florence focused their attention on the Vespucci family.

In the aftermath of the failed conspiracy, Florence was on the brink of war against a fearsome combination of Italian cities, allied to the pope, and there were desperate diplomatic attempts to avoid military catastrophe. Amerigo Vespucci, now twenty-five, had been taught that the strength of Florence lay in its intelligence and subtlety, and now he was suddenly given the chance to see this intelligence in action firsthand.

The most urgent task was to make sure that if war was inevitable Flo-rence had allies, and to delay any action until these allies could commit themselves. To lead the Florentine delegation to the Vatican—to the furi-ous Pope Sixtus—Lorenzo took the imaginative step of appointing Piero's brother Guido Antonio, who was a brilliant lawyer. Guido in turn asked his young cousin Amerigo to accompany him to Rome as his secretary.

Rome in those days was a small, dirty, lawless city. It was hardly comfort-able, being a Florentine in the city of the pope, but it was here Amerigo cut his teeth as a diplomatic secretary, listening, recording, and writing letters, in the most difficult and desperate circumstances. When it was clear that there was no alternative to war, Guido Antonio headed home. But while he and Amerigo were traveling, the news reached Florence that their ambassa-dor to France had died. The moment they arrived back under the Duomo in Florence, Guido Antonio received a request to go immediately to Paris as his replacement. It was the first time Amerigo had traveled outside Italy. He saw the galleried streets and arcades in Bologna, and brick towers hundreds of feet high, glimpsed Milan under the ruthless Sforza family, crossed the Appenines, and headed toward Lyons and deeper into France. While Columbus and Cabot were great talkers, Vespucci was becoming known as a great listener and a great correspondent, and it was this trip to Paris that

---

\**Palle* was a reference to the golden balls that were the symbol of the Medici family. The slogan was literally, "balls, balls!"

helped make him so, listening to the talk on the road and writing a stream of letters to officials back home.

Vespucci arrived in Paris in 1478, the time and place immortalized by Victor Hugo in *The Hunchback of Notre Dame*, and began to settle in at the French court. Here he met another great personality of the age. King Louis XI's closest adviser was the historian Philippe de Commines, who rapidly became a close friend of Guido Antonio, telling him how best to approach the king. Louis never quite looked royal—he wore shabby clothes and an old felt hat—but he had mastered the art of diplomacy to such an extent that he has become known to history as the Spider King. The webs of intrigue that he wove were designed to neutralize the pope, whom he disliked heartily, and increase French influence in Italy. He was therefore prepared to make friendly gestures toward Guido Antonio, including closing the Pazzi banks in Paris and seizing their assets, but it was a very ambitious project to get the French to invade Italy in support of Florence, and in this the Vespuccis failed.

Even so, the young Vespucci was discovering a city in the best way, from the privileged position of the court, being advised by one of its most civilized members. As he glimpsed the very heart of European diplomacy, Vespucci's own interest in maps began to grow more intense. In his spare moments in Paris, or anywhere else he was taken, he began to seek out and collect maps of all sorts. Not just small maps, but the big attempts to set out the geography of the whole world, with their great green watercolor seas, held down on the table by paperweights at each corner.

The maps that fascinated him the most were those based on Ptolemy's *Geography*, just becoming widely available in printed form and so popular that the word "ptolemy" was soon applied to any atlas. It was the spice routes that thrilled him most, the narrow straits between Java and Cathay, through which the spices and the silks poured into Europe, marked on these fifteenth-century maps as the Cape of Catigara. He consigned all this to memory, remembering also how Toscanelli had told him of his meeting with Niccolò di Conti, who had spent twenty-five years in the Indies and had seen these very straits.


After his voyage around Iceland, Columbus was back in Lisbon staying with his brother Bartholomew. Both had agreed to work together in a small chart-making business, satisfying the enormous demand for maps of all kinds among Lisbon's burgeoning merchant population. Christopher's most frustrating problem was that although he was ambitious and determined, he had very little education and spoke only the Genoese dialect. He therefore immersed himself in courses in Latin, Portuguese, and Castilian and began ferociously reading new books. Soon he was able to read everything he could lay his hands on about the Atlantic and what lay beyond, and became particularly acquainted with five books he carried with him for the rest of his life.

*The Travels of Marco Polo* went everywhere with him, and the young Columbus clung to Polo's dream of the golden roofs. There was also *Historia Rerum* by Pope Pius II, Pliny's *Natural History*, and *The Perpetual Almanac* by the Jewish astronomer Abraham Zacuto. Finally there was *Imago Mundi*, by the extraordinary former rector of the Sorbonne in Paris, Cardinal Pierre d'Ailly, a book full of descriptions of sea serpents, dog-faced women, and men with the bodies of lions.* In Columbus's own copy of this book, the critical phrase "India is near Spain" was heavily underlined. On these shaky foundations, mainly compendiums of classical and medieval knowledge about the earth, Columbus built his dreams.

Lisbon was certainly the place to be for an adventurer. King Alfonso V was conducting an exhausting war with Castile, which meant that the caravels of exploration were now rotting in the harbor, but this was still where everyone with seafaring ambitions came if they could. The city's forty thousand inhabitants were a varied mix of English, Genoese, Germans, and Venetians, who were mathematicians, geographers, and oceanographers, questioning everything about what lay beyond the known world. As he established himself in business with Bartholomew, Columbus could look out from their shop by the textile market in the middle of Lisbon's growing Genoese neighborhood and see the narrow lanes below the fortress of St. George snaking away toward the harbor, the tall houses painted in red and green, and the ships anchored along the broad Tagus River.

Columbus continued to carry out assignments for Paolo di Negro, who was in Lisbon in 1478, and who sent him on his behalf to buy a cargo of sugar from Madeira for Ludivico Centurione. But something went wrong

*D'Ailly also correctly predicted the French Revolution and much else besides.

with the deal, the cargo he carried could not be sold, and the merchants would not let him have the sugar on credit. Columbus found himself back in Genoa facing a court summons demanding payment for the hire of the ship. The twenty-seven-year-old Columbus explained the situation and told the court that he was leaving for Lisbon the following day. He never went back to his home city.

Within months of his return from the North Atlantic, Columbus was seeking out the kind of connections that could help him to realize his dreams. Always passionately religious, he sought out the company of Portuguese aristocrats, noticing that they frequented the chapel of the Convento dos Santos, then a fashionable boarding school for the daughters of the local aristocracy, overlooking the Tagus River near Bartholomew's map shop. He began the habit of going there for mass and vespers, and made the acquaintance of one of the teachers in the school, Felipa Perestrello. She was in her late twenties, rather too old in those days to be unmarried, but her father and grandfather were hereditary governors of the island of Porto Santo off Madeira, a thousand miles out into the Atlantic.*

Columbus was more than just singleminded. He was almost fanatical about restoring the fortunes of his family. Perhaps he always had been, but the frustrations of Chios and the shipwreck had raised the intensity with which he schemed. Columbus was now a loud and ambitious presence in the three-hundred-strong Genoese community in Lisbon, and he needed an edge. Felipa looked like the opportunity he had been searching for—a connection with the elite of Portuguese exploration—and he introduced himself.

The interpretation that Columbus deliberately seduced Felipa because of her connections goes beyond the evidence, but it fits both with what we know of his obsessions and with the fact that he barely mentions her at all in anything he wrote later. It seems, in fact, to have been his mother-in-law whose company he really enjoyed. There is also the hint in early biographies that, having slept with Felipa and made her pregnant, Columbus then had to marry her. His son Ferdinand's biography of his father says that he

---

*Felipa's father had actually shown very little aptitude for seafaring, but he was given the task of settling Porto Santo because two of his sisters were mistresses of the Archbishop of Lisbon.

"behaved honorably," which might imply something of the kind, though the context suggests that this is his explanation of why Felipa accepted him, rather than the other way around.


Columbus was a master at weaving tales about himself. It may be that the tales he wove to make possible his fortuitous marriage to Felipa began to unravel very shortly after the wedding. He was, after all, the son of a weaver and taverner, penniless, a self-educated supplicant to more successful Genoese merchant families, whose father had been—and may then have been—in prison for debt. Lisbon was a city where anybody could be almost anything but, even so, it seems to have made sense after the wedding to disappear for a while. Columbus and his bride, accompanied by his mother-in-law, left for Porto Santo soon after the wedding, as guests of Felipa's brother.

It isn't clear whether Columbus hoped to establish some business venture from the island. If he did, he was to be sorely disappointed. Porto Santo was nine miles long by three miles across. It was a stopping point for ships heading south toward the Portuguese outposts in Guinea, though there had been precious few of those since the war with Castile. Its forests had been destroyed in a massive seven-year fire shortly after it was settled by the Portuguese. Columbus's father-in-law, Bartholomew Perestrello, had taken a pregnant rabbit with him on his first voyage to the island, and—to the great delight of those who thought it a good omen—the rabbit had given birth on board. Two years after his arrival, there were so many rabbits, and so little vegetation left, that they decided to abandon the island. Even when Columbus and his family settled there, they had few companions.

The one redeeming factor for Columbus on this barren outcrop was his friendship with Felipa's mother. During the long hours staring out to sea during his two-year exile, she told him the tales of the first generation of Henry the Navigator's explorers—of the crudely carved wooden idol that had been picked up at sea, the strange trees washed ashore, and the bodies of drowned men with strange, broad, foreign-looking faces. She also brought out all the maps her husband had kept there, and his handwritten notes about sea routes, winds, and currents in the Atlantic. Nearby Madeira had been the base for Portuguese explorations, and there was enough ephemera to keep Columbus fascinated for months.* With this evidence in front of him, he also noticed other peculiarities about being six hundred miles out into the Atlantic. The wind blew from the west. The sun set later there. To a man with an inquiring mind who was curious about the size and shape of the earth, this was tantalizing evidence.

By 1480 the affair of the missing sugar seems somehow to have been settled, and Ludovico Centurione alleviated the boredom of Porto Santo by suggesting that Columbus work for him on Madeira, selling sugar to merchants from Flanders and the Netherlands. Like other nearby islands, Madeira had not been inhabited before the Portuguese arrived, but it had been transformed in one generation into a powerhouse of sugar production. Slaves from the Canary Islands were put to work on vast plantations, the model for those that would emerge centuries later in the New World.

Even so, Madeira was almost as much of an exile as Porto Santo had been, and the isolation did nothing for Columbus's melancholic obsession. Here in their new home, Felipa gave birth to their first child, Diego. Some biographers imagine that Columbus conceived the idea of crossing the Atlantic as he gazed out to sea in the summer nights on Porto Santo. It is just as likely that he had always imagined himself discovering new lands, but the possibility of where and how to profit from such a discovery began to form more clearly in the lonely evenings on Madeira. Ships from Bristol were now trading directly with the island, bringing cloth and wool to trade for sugar. Some of them even planned to trade directly with North Africa, but the Portuguese protested and the plan was allowed to lapse. In his conversations on the wharves with the Bristol merchants, or at the end of the day in his home in the rue Esmeralda in Funchal, Columbus renewed his acquaintance with the rumors that Bristol sailors held dear, of the shadowy lands to the west and the great cod fisheries.†

On one visit to the Azores, as far west as he had ever sailed, Columbus had a conversation that confirmed the Bristol view. A one-eyed sailor told him of how, on a particular voyage, he had been caught in a storm and blown far off course to the west and had seen land, which he believed was

*The islanders believe that these charts and secret documents are still there, buried somewhere on Porto Santo to protect them from Moorish raiders.
†Strangely enough, the window of his home in Madeira still exists—in the garden of a nearby property.

Tartary (Mongolia), before the weather blew them out of sight again. Columbus was a man who believed in destiny, and exactly what his destiny should be was becoming a little clearer in his mind.

The machinations of Lorenzo the Magnificent's ambassadors, and the offices of the Medici Bank all over Europe—indistinguishable from Florentine missions—had held back the tide of war for a while, helped by the tireless persuasion of Guido Antonio and Amerigo Vespucci. But the master stroke had been played by Lorenzo himself.

Lorenzo reasoned that the alliance against him included at least one weak link: Naples. But instead of the laborious business of sending ambassadors, he needed to have direct contact with the Neapolitan king, Ferdinand, as soon as possible. There really was only one way. Leaving Florence secretly, Lorenzo arrived incognito at the court in Naples and demanded to see the king. By the time the news was out and the foreign ambassadors alerted, they were sitting down at the same table laughing like old friends. Ferdinand had only one immediate request: that Lorenzo release his friend Piero Vespucci, languishing in prison for helping one of the conspirators escape. Still protesting his innocence, Amerigo's notorious cousin was released.

In fact, peace was breaking out all over Europe. After a heavy defeat at the battle of Toro, Portugal surrendered its claims to the throne of Castile and the Canary Islands in return for an exclusive right to explore southward and a free hand in Africa. The gold, ivory, sacks of pepper, and ships full of chained human beings began to arrive on the wharves of Lisbon once more, and for those whose life was exploration, the ships represented a sense of hope. Finally, a peace agreement was brokered between Venice and Sultan Mehmet, but it was a difficult one to negotiate because Venice was no longer in a position of power. Venice was forced to hand over the lemon farms they retained on the Greek mainland, and pay ten thousand ducats annually for the privilege of trading in Turkish waters—the very sectors of the Mediterranean that Venice depended on most for its wealth. Under the treaty, Venice also agreed to send the leading Renaissance artist Gentile Bellini to the sultan's court to paint him.

Still, the peace was not fully achieved. Having neutralized the Venetians, in the summer of 1480, the sultan struck at the heart of Italy itself with an assault by seven thousand Ottoman troops near the port of Otranto. There was an appalling massacre: The elderly archbishop was sawed in two in front of his own altar, after which the remaining population was carried off to be sold as slaves in Turkey, Syria, and Egypt. The pope immediately lifted his interdict on Florence, hoping that the city-states would unite around Venice to force the invaders out. But it was not to be. The Venetians agonized, but they were bound by the terms of the peace treaty, and in any case they had no money to send an armed force. Instead, Naples and Hungary gathered together what men they could afford and sent them against the Ottoman invaders.

Having established himself on the Italian mainland, Mehmet turned on the island of Rhodes, where the defending Knights Hospitaller unexpectedly held off the attack. Both sides settled down to wait. But on May 3, 1481, Mehmet, the conqueror of Constantinople, died suddenly at the age of only sixty. In the ensuing struggle for succession, his troops withdrew from Italy, never to return. The Venetian senate waited a few months, then sent a message of congratulations to his mild-mannered son Bayezid II, the new sultan, and he responded by confirming the treaty and reducing trading levies. At both ends of the Mediterranean, finally, those who dreamed of trade routes in the future could begin to make plans.

Despite the peace, and the resumption of trade, the caravels that explored Africa while Henry the Navigator was alive were still wasting away in Lisbon harbor. King Alfonso, his spirit broken by a heavy defeat by the Aragonese, was shut away in a monastery in Sintra, suffering from serious depression. When he died in August 1481, his son John II shut himself away for three days wearing white sackcloth, but then emerged to assume full control. John brought with him a new spirit of exploration. There would be new voyages down the African coast, he announced. There would be a fort built at La Mina on the Gold Coast (now Ghana) to defend their African possessions from the Spanish and a land expedition from there eastward to make contact with Prester John.

Excited by the whiff of renewed adventure, Columbus returned to Lisbon to look for work, filling any free time once again drawing maps for

Bartholomew. While he was there, he was introduced to a relative of his mother-in-law's who was a canon of the cathedral. He got on well with Fernão Martins, a future cardinal, and the subject of geography soon came up. It transpired that Martins had been in Rome in 1464 at the deathbed of another popular cardinal, and had met and made friends with the most extraordinary man he had ever met, a Florentine doctor of immense wisdom called Toscanelli.

Martins went on to explain how he had told some leading figures at the Portuguese court about their friendship and about Toscanelli's theories regarding the shape of the world. Some years later, he had been asked by the highest authority to reestablish contact with Toscanelli and ask his advice about new trade routes to the East. Toscanelli had written a reply that set out, in no uncertain terms, that the way to the East was via the West.

Columbus was thrilled. It was a small piece of information but he recognized it as vital. Would it, by any chance, be possible to see Toscanelli's letter? But Martins was not prepared to let him. Maybe he no longer had a copy. Maybe he never actually had one. Maybe the risk of showing such sensitive information to a foreigner was too high. But Martins could tell him this: Toscanelli believed Marco Polo provided evidence of the size of the earth, and that the Chinese province of what he called "Mangi" was probably only five thousand miles west of Lisbon.* It was vital confirmation for Columbus of what he had begun to suspect: that it might be possible to sail there directly across the Atlantic.

Toscanelli's theories had also reached the Scuole Grandi in Venice. Like Columbus, an idea was forming in John Cabot's mind about reaching the spice routes on the other side of the earth by sailing westward to reach the East. But Cabot had not given up on a second idea: of reaching the eastern spice routes by traveling south to Arabia and the Red Sea to cut out more of the middlemen. Perhaps, if he was clever enough, those two strategies— finding the origins of the spice trade *and* opening up a new route there via the West—might lead the way to untold wealth and glory.

But all this would require money, backers, and partners—and some way of protecting his discovery. In the meantime, he listened to Febo Capella and the other humanists and geographers at the Scuole Grandi, with their

---

*This was an enormous miscalculation. The real distance is over eleven thousand miles.

Toscanelli

tales of distant islands and roofs of gold, and practiced making his own maps and experimenting with constructing three-dimensional maps called globes.

Cabot was a dreamer and a talker. There is far less direct evidence about his life than there is about Columbus, but there is enough to get a sense of his personality as distinct from the man who became his great rival. Cabot was articulate and energetic in a different way: more believable, more confident, and calmer as well. While Columbus was determined to earn his heroism as well as his wealth, Cabot somehow seems to have enjoyed heroism from an early age and to have taken it more for granted.

After the age of steam, the idea that there were set routes across the sea became hard to understand: Steam enabled ships to cross the ocean wherever they chose. But in the age of sail, the discovery of safe routes at sea were closely guarded secrets. Go one way, and the currents and prevailing winds would frustrate your journey and risk destroying your vessels; go the other and they would speed you on your way. These routes had enormous commercial significance, and knowledge of them was valuable. So it was never sensible to ask too many geographical questions in Lisbon. For the Portuguese, maps provided their most valuable resources for the future: These were state secrets with fearsome legal protection. Maps of the routes southward down the coast of Africa, or to the newly discovered Atlantic islands, were signed out to captains when they weighed anchor and signed back in again when and if they returned. The penalty for anyone sending a chart or map abroad was death.

There was no doubt that Columbus was dabbling in dangerous areas for a foreigner, although—paradoxically—the burgeoning chart-making business in Lisbon was dominated by the Genoese. This irritated the merchants of Lisbon, who saw the expansion of the Genoese community in their city as a direct threat to their incomes. One of the first petitions the new king, John, received was a plea to have the Genoese excluded from Lisbon trade. The accusation was not just that they were muscling in on trade with Africa and the islands, but that they were stealing secrets. But Columbus had married into a family with maps and those maps were at the heart of his work and his obsessions. He knew what he was collecting could put him and his business in danger. If he hung around the right bars on the Tagus there was no end to the amount of details he could pick up. Still, others also were listening in those same bars and he had to be careful.

But the Toscanelli clue was just too valuable to ignore. He had no address, and as a foreigner it was too suspect to send such letters out of the country to a city he had no business with. Nor would a man like Toscanelli correspond about state secrets with somebody like Columbus. But persistent questioning of Martins revealed that he had used an intermediary in his relationship with Toscanelli, a Florentine merchant living in Lisbon and involved in the import of black slaves from Africa. Lorenzo Berardi had been the one who actually wrote to Toscanelli, and Columbus struck up a relationship with him. At long last, and inspired by the same idea—sailing westward to China—Berardi agreed to show him Toscanelli's reply. With great excitement, Columbus unfolded the letter and copied its contents into one of the books that was rapidly becoming his bible: *Historia Rerum* by Pope Pius II. Toscanelli explained how he had encountered an emissary from the Great Khan who had been sent to the pope in the 1440s, and who had described the broad rivers and fantastical cities of Cathay. "On one river, there are established about two hundred cities, and marble bridges of great breadth and length adorned with columns on either side," he wrote breathlessly. "I esteem your noble and grand desire to navigate from the East to the West," he told the Portuguese via Berardi. "For the said voyage is not only possible, but is sure and certain and will bring honor."

Toscanelli received the letter from Columbus apparently with irritation, judging by the tone of his reply. He was an old man who was frustrated that he had spent his whole life urging a western voyage and would probably not live to see one attempted. He enclosed a map, and with mounting enthusiasm Columbus inscribed it alongside the one Berardi had shown him. "I am not surprised that you, who have high courage, and the whole Portuguese nation, who have always been able men in every great enterprise, should be inflamed and desirous to prosecute the said voyage," he wrote.

As far as is known, they never corresponded again, but the letter was arguably the most important Columbus ever received. It convinced him that there were serious scientific foundations to the enterprise, and that this was not simply a pipedream shared by himself, his brother, and a few enthusiastic contacts. It could be done, and if it could be done, then he and his colleagues would do it.

# 3

## THE ENTERPRISE

*"Between the edge of Spain and the beginning of India, the sea is short and can be crossed in a matter of a few days."*

—CHRISTOPHER COLUMBUS, marginal note
in his own copy of *Imago Mundi*

*"Make no small plans, for they have no power to stir the soul."*

—NICCOLÒ MACHIAVELLI

EDWARD IV WAS on the throne of England, and the terrible civil war that had so bedeviled the English seemed finally to be at an end, with Edward's Yorkist faction in the ascendancy. John Cabot was thirty-one; Columbus and Vespucci were still in their twenties. In Bristol, in July 1480, the handful of English sailors aboard the 360-ton caravel *Trinity* were hauling out the bowline to tighten the foresail, as they made their way under the cliffs along the Avon River and out to sea.

The *Trinity* always attracted notice when it set sail, because it was one of the biggest ships that came to Bristol, too big to moor alongside the wharves. Its destination was Lisbon followed by Huelva, the port that served Seville in Spain, to deliver consignments of the woolen cloth that had become such a staple of the English economy, and to bring back wine. It was a voyage that *Trinity* undertook twice a year, on behalf of a consortium of the wealthiest merchants in the city, including the ship's co-owners, the mighty Canynges family.

What few on the quayside knew was that this trip had a hidden agenda. The previous year, three prominent Bristol merchants—all of them with a history of trading with Portugal—had linked up with the chief customs official of Bristol customs to search for new fishing grounds in the far West. The customs official, Thomas Croft, had finally organized the royal permission four weeks earlier, but he and the others knew that the search for fishing grounds was only part of the voyage: The departure of the *Trinity* was masking a parallel voyage by another smaller ship they had chartered to search for the legendary island of hy-Brasil.

The years of civil war in England had put every royal official at risk. It was vital, not only for their livelihoods but also sometimes their lives, that they correctly anticipate which candidate for the throne would emerge victorious, and make their choice of allegiance neither too early nor too late. As chief customs official in England's second biggest port, Thomas Croft was both powerful and vulnerable. He was an ally of the current king, but that could make him vulnerable in what was a climate of mistrust and suspicion. So it was with a familiar feeling of dread, in October 1481—more than a year after the first exploration voyage of the *Trinity*—that Croft received into his office near the dockside an armed deputation from the city's constable with a warrant for his arrest. The charge was illegal trading.

As a customs official, he was disbarred from trade. But a commission of inquiry sent to investigate claims that shipments were arriving in Bristol, which were failing to pay the required 5 percent in tax, had uncovered the fact that Croft had been sending ships abroad. It was the second legal disaster to befall the merchants who had hired the ship the previous year to search for hy-Brasil: one of the merchants, Robert Straunge, had ended up briefly in the Tower of London, accused of counterfeiting coins.

The voyage that had set out in 1480 had been arduous. With the celebrated helmsman John Lloyd in command, the crew had been forced by bad weather to take shelter in Ireland, in the port of Kinsale. Then they had pursued their regular route across the Bay of Biscay and around the coast of Portugal to Lisbon and then Huelva for a four-week refit. While they were there, some of the senior members of the expedition spent some time at the

Franciscan monastery of La Rábida, where the monks ran a kind of college for navigators, and left a donation to guarantee prayers for their venture ahead.

Next there was a stop in Gibraltar, a voyage down the African coast to Oran, then on to the Saltes estuary for a refit, after which they would normally have set sail back to Bristol loaded with wine. But this time they swung far out into the Atlantic, buffeted by storms, spending as many as nine weeks at sea, unclear as to where they were. It was a frustrating voyage, the waves lashing their faces, the compass ambiguous, and no mythical island added to the map. In September 1480 they had limped exhausted into harbor in Ireland, and by October the *Trinity* was once again at her usual mooring in Bristol, being prepared for another voyage south.

If this was the first deliberate exploration to the west, it was also the first to discover that the route westward from the latitude of Portugal was likely to be dangerously stormy and was probably impossible. But Croft and his friends remained undaunted. The following year, three months before his arrest, they had tried again. When the ships returned somebody was watching them unload, and the authorities were informed that they had been illegally landing fish. Croft's arrest was the direct result.

What Croft knew, but preferred not to discuss with the constable, the court, or its officials, was that this second voyage of exploration had in fact found land to the west. This time the route had been farther to the north, and the storms had been avoided, and now he and his colleagues believed they had at last seen not hy-Brasil but the Island of the Seven Cities. These are shadowy corners of history, and they are still controversial. But the evidence that an island believed to be Antillia was found is clear; maps showing a "Bristol influence" began portraying it not as one island, but as three.

At his trial some months later, Croft stuck to one undisputable fact: He had a license from the king himself to search for new lands. He was not trading at all; the salt and the wine had been required for the voyage. The king's involvement was critical, and Croft was acquitted. Even so, rumors of the discovery could not be entirely confined to Bristol. Croft's arrest made his colleagues wary, and when they eventually resumed the voyages westward, the islands could not immediately be found again. But something was there, and the question was how to profit from it. The immediate answer looked to be the absolute profusion of cod in the waters they had found. It made sense to Croft and his colleagues, if and when they could find Antillia again, to set up some kind of small settlement there to catch and dry the cod as stockfish. But it was vital that this information did not leak out. The islands may have been Danish territory, and English merchants were forbidden from trading there. It was best to keep silent about the whole enterprise.

Although the sedentary merchants of Bristol kept quiet, those who had been on the *Trinity* and their accompanying ships could not quite forget what they had seen rising out of the Atlantic mists. There were the amateur geographers in the bars by the Lisbon docks who overheard their conversation and the cosmographer monks of the monastery of La Rábida just over the border in Castile, who knew their objective. And among those to hear rumors of the new discovery was Columbus, on his daily wanderings down at the quayside. His own tentative maps of the world, incorporating Toscanelli's view, would from now on depict Antillia as three separate islands.

When an English double agent reported some of the details of Cabot's historic voyage to his Spanish masters later, he described the plan as "according to the fancy of this Genoese." There is the strong impression in the letter that both Cabot's and Columbus's voyages had been part of a joint endeavor, by mariners from Genoa. "Another Genoese like Columbus," said another informant about Cabot. The implication is that at some stage, Cabot and the Columbus brothers had been working together to the same end, and if they were, their plan must have begun to take shape around now.

There is other evidence too, none of it absolutely conclusive in itself, but taken together, the coincidences between the lives and plans of these two merchant adventurers are just too close to believe they were independent of each other. Both were indeed Genoese, probably with connections to the Fregoso party and to the coastal port of Savona. They were almost exactly the same age. Their plans for the enterprise of the Indies were almost identical, though Columbus in the end demanded more in return.

But that is not all. Research over the past few decades in the Venetian archives has also turned up some other connections that are hard to ignore. Both men were involved around the edges of the wool and silk trade from southern Europe to Bristol and London. Both used the same ports, Lisbon and Huelva for Seville, both ports frequented by sailors from Bristol with stories of the exploration. What is more, as it turns out, both ended up so heavily in debt in the mid-1480s that they had to leave their homes with their families and find somewhere else to live.

Most history has at its heart some uncertainties, no matter how definitively it is written, and this one is certainly no exception. But what we know about Cabot and Columbus points confidently to a common position and common plans for the Indies that was more than simply a dream of crossing the Atlantic. Those joint plans included working together to raise the money they needed—through one risky but ambitious deal that linked Venice, Lisbon, and London that went horribly wrong. Indeed, this is probably the missing element of the tale of the race for America—a race where none of the participants had any conception of where they were actually going—and without it the full story is simply not coherent.

Life at the French court was an exhausting business for Amerigo Vespucci, but even more so for his cousin and mentor, Guido Antonio. The royal court rarely spent more than a month in any one place before it packed itself up and set off for the next royal palace. On the way, in the long procession of possibly four thousand courtiers, suppliers, butchers, huntsmen, together with all the food and the whole paraphernalia of royal life, they passed through burned and abandoned villages from the aftermath of the Hundred Years War. They rested occasionally in collapsed and crumbling churches and glimpsed the wolves in the distance in the ruined landscape. Only a generation earlier, Joan of Arc and the young dauphin, later Charles VII, had yanked the nation back from the brink of complete incorporation into England. The scars were still obvious.

On the rare occasions that they were in Paris, Amerigo found that the contrast with renaissance Florence was extreme. Paris was still a medieval city. It had a narrow drawbridge by the city gate, guarded day and night, beyond which lay an enormous gibbet with the hanging corpses mummified by the weather. The wide, palatial streets of Florence bustled in their own way, but in northern cities like Paris, every street included a filthy stream of liquid manure running down the center in the winter, or a choking cloud of dust in the summer, as pedestrians had to battle past children,

beggars, ducks, geese, dogs, and every other kind of creature known to do-
mesticity.

It was a different culture. "These things carved from marble and por-
phyry are beautiful; I have nothing against them," says one of Rabelais'
characters about the Renaissance statues of Florence. "But the pastries of
Amiens, the old roast shops with mouth-watering odours, and yes, even the
girls there . . ." In short, Vespucci's education was being broadened. In Florence, they imported spoons to grace their sophisticated tables; in France
they slurped their soup using three fingers as a spoon.

But now, after nearly two years following the Spider King and the French
court, albeit in the amusing company of Philippe de Commines, Guido Antonio had been recalled. Together, the two Vespuccis made another grueling
journey to Lyons and from there through the icy mountain passes. Guido
Antonio had been appointed to be the Florentine ambassador to Rome,
partly to seal the Italian peace treaty and partly to work for Lorenzo the
Magnificent's next dream: the nomination of his young son Giovanni as a
cardinal. This task was to take up all Guido Antonio's time for the next few
years, but he pulled off the coup and Giovanni was appointed as a prince of
the church at just thirteen years old.

As part of the deal brokered with the Vatican, the Florentine artists
Ghirlandaio and Botticelli—who had both just finished painting in the
church of Ognissanti—were sent to Rome to start work painting the Sistine
Chapel (named after Sixtus himself). Both artists included a picture of
Guido Antonio in the finished picture. Amerigo must have looked forward
to a period learning papal diplomacy, in the magnificent but unpredictable
papacy of the Genoese Sixtus IV. But his career was to take a different path.
On the way home, he heard the news that his father was ill, and Guido Antonio ordered him home to Florence.

When he reached the familiar Arno River and the Vespucci family home
in Ognissanti in April 1482, it was clear that his life was going to change.
Now that old Nastagio was aging and infirm, there was nobody else who
could shoulder the burden of the family business, with its varied collection
of mills and its silk importing business. Amerigo's brother Antonio was a
trustee of the property confiscated after the attempted coup from the Pazzi
family. Girolamo was in Rhodes, and although he was supposed to be representing his father's business interests there, he had gone off to become a

knight of St. John of Jerusalem. His younger brother Bernardo was in the wool business in Buda in Hungary. This was Amerigo's destiny, by default: not to be a diplomat, after all, but a compiler of accounts, a business manager, a commissioner of cargoes.

Columbus was living mainly in Lisbon now, only occasionally with his wife, Felipa, and his baby son, Diego, earning a living as an agent for the Spinola and Centurione families when he had the chance, taking their cargoes north to England and Flanders, and filling in the gaps in his income by selling books and helping Bartholomew in the mapmaking business. Change was in the air in Lisbon. The final peace treaty between Castile and Portugal meant the wharves of Lisbon were once again receiving consignments of Ashanti gold dust, elephant tusks, pepper, and some of the first black slaves brought to Europe on a commercial basis.

The new Portuguese king, John II, was only twenty-five but exuded respect by conjuring up a profound sense of sacrifice. He had abandoned his mistress when he was crowned king, and chose an emblem for himself of a pelican piercing her own breast to feed her chicks with her blood. Not for nothing was he known as the "Perfect Prince." He looked down from his palace windows high above the harbor, with the odor of spices and the sounds of money-lending wafting up from the dockside, determined to invigorate Portuguese maritime exploration again.

Intriguing news for the amateur geographers of Lisbon was emerging already. The king of Benin had sent a messenger to Lisbon describing a great king who lived twenty moons eastward and sat screened behind curtains. It sounded tantalizingly like Prester John. The Portuguese dropped six messengers for him along the coast of Africa with instructions to go eastward. Drawn to this expectation, scholars, cartographers, and navigators from all over Europe began to arrive in Lisbon again hoping for preferment. There they were in their foreign-looking clothes and with their intellectual airs, wandering awkwardly around the docks on the Tagus River, their papers under their arms. Among them was the brilliant young cosmographer Martin Behaim from Nuremberg.

Behaim was exactly the kind of adventurer that the new king hoped to attract. He had an advanced understanding of navigation, practical theories about new kinds of rigging for ships, and was immediately appointed to the advisory council, which the king set up to take the place of his great uncle's academy at Sagres. Behaim set to work drawing up new navigation tables and building his own case for westward exploration. If he and Columbus met, and they must have, they seem not to have liked each other. Behaim, with his scholastic background and uncompromising ambition, probably did not take the wild talk of this merchant's agent from Genoa entirely seriously.

But using what influence he possessed, Columbus did manage to enter the service of the new king, and in December 1481 he was appointed to join a caravel, accompanied by Bartholomew, to sail south down Africa and secure Portugal's possessions on the Gold Coast. The fleet of eleven ships set sail from Lisbon, arrived early in 1482 at El-Mina, and began to unload the tons of stone and prefabricated timber walls required to build the fortress of St. George of the Mine near a village called Aldeia das Duas Partes that was becoming central to their trading activities there.*

Remembering the competition from Behaim, Columbus realized that if and when he reached Lisbon harbor safely again, it was time for him to start making concrete plans for the Indies.

Five thousand miles from El-Mina, in Venice, Cabot was constructing a similar life, drawing maps, and making globes in his spare time, while working as a merchant's agent for his father—and as a merchant on his own account—sometimes on the route via Lisbon to England, sometimes more ambitiously in the spice trade to Egypt. His own links to Toscanelli, via the fellow members of his confraternity, had convinced him that westward exploration was the most exciting geographical frontier. He was full of plans to exploit that route, but was also involving himself in property development in Venice and venturing farther afield. Cabot was now in his early thirties and seems to have taken advantage of the treaty between Venice and the Turks to sail past the captured city of Constantinople as far as the Black Sea, in search of skins.

*When they arrived off the Pepper Coast, Columbus recorded that he saw some sirens, the mythical sea creatures that were said to lure sailors to their deaths with their seductive songs.

Cabot's involvement in cloth and skins—linked to his father's spice trade with Egypt—implies a wider business ambition: color. The spices he sought in the East—aloewood, camphor, cinnamon, nutmeg, sandalwood, ginger—were valuable for medicine and food preservation, a critical element in a burgeoning trade. But many of them were also crucial to the dyeing industry, and there was a clear opportunity here to square the circle, and use the dyestuffs his father's business was importing to prepare the cloth and skins he was bringing in himself, using saffron for yellow, madder for red, woad from the Netherlands for blues, and of course the expensive kermes lice for Venetian scarlet.

Cabot had married in Venice. Though nothing is known about his wife, Mattea, it seems to have been a love match: He named his ship after her in 1497. Unlike Columbus, who married for political connections, he loved not wisely but too well. The time would come when he would badly need money and protection, and Mattea's family could provide little of either.

Like Columbus before him, his visits to England brought him into contact with strange stories of secret fishing grounds and shadowy expeditions to the far West. He was also passing more frequently through Lisbon, and his conversations with Columbus started to mature. What had started as enjoyable romps through cosmographical lore were now becoming concrete plans. To make the voyage westward to the Indies, they would each require a partner.

Although the two men had a great deal in common, they were also very different. While Columbus was becoming increasingly devout, Cabot was the type of man who would offer to name the lands he discovered after his barber. While Columbus appears to have been loquacious rather than eloquent—one recent biographer says that "he gives the impression of having wearied his enemies into opposition and bored friends into assent"—Cabot seems to have exercised his influence more effortlessly. Where Columbus was intense, Cabot was charming. Columbus needed Cabot's personality and contacts.

Cabot also needed partners outside Venice. This was more than just the perennial difficulty that Venice faced East and any Venetian expedition across the Atlantic would have to use some friendly port outside the Mediterranean. The problem was that, since the Venetian peace treaty with the Turks and the Ottoman assault on Otranto, it had been increasingly difficult to conduct business as a Venetian with the other Italian city-states. "If you knew how universally hated you are, your hair would stand on end," Galeazzo Sforza, Duke of Milan, told the secretary of the Venetian republic in 1467. "Know then that your enemies do not sleep. Take good counsel, for, by God, you need it." Two decades on, Italy loved the Venetians even less.

Pope Sixtus had even laid Venice under an interdict, which forbade them the basic services of the church, but it was kept secret from the Venetians themselves. Their representative in Rome refused to forward the announcement to his home city, and when the pope sent a special messenger to the patriarch of Venice, he claimed to be too ill to pass it on to the senate.

The deep unpopularity of Venice had led to a ruinous though largely uneventful war on three separate fronts, with Florence, Naples, and Milan, in the early 1480s. Surrounded by enemies, their treasury exhausted, and their trade routes threatened on every side, the Venetians took the fateful step of appealing to the king of France for help. Louis the Spider King was now dead and his place was taken by his thirteen-year-old son Charles VIII, and it was he who received the letter from the doge urging him to invade Italy and assert his ancestral claims over Naples and Milan. It was a momentous step and one they would bitterly regret in the decades to come.

This clearly was not a good time to organize a Venetian expedition across the Atlantic. Nor was it a sensible moment to expand a trade in skins and cloth across Europe, since most of those items were coming across the Alps and via Milan. That was why Cabot had begun to develop his own shipments of spices bound for England in exchange for English cloth or wool, not across the Alps, but the long way around by sea, via Lisbon and via his increasingly practical conversations with Columbus.

I

*"Lay the wood, bone, or horn in a glass jar, and pour vinegar thereon which has verdigris mixed in it so that it is quite thick and not too thin. Cover it well and let it sit seven days under warm horse manure. If it is not green enough, let it stand longer."*

Instructions for dyeing cloth green, from the *Allerley Mackel*, Mainz, 1532

If someone wanted an education in the fourteenth and early fifteenth centuries, they would have had to find a teacher, sit at that teacher's feet, and occasionally consult the great manuscripts attached by chains to lectionaries in the libraries. Thanks, however, to the invention of the printing press, even a poor man could find a Greek dictionary and learn languages, and could set about the process of imbibing knowledge by the light of spluttering, smoky candle flames. This was the process that Columbus had been putting himself through in his long nights on Madeira and Porto Santo. He could now read Latin, and was already involved in the book trade, and he scoured everything he read for evidence—not to prove that the Indies were on the other side of the Atlantic, but to have a credible argument that the journey to find them was not suicidal.

He was also showing signs of a growing obsession. His marginal notes in his books at this time were often about wholly esoteric and mildly erotic issues, like tracking down the lost land of the Amazons, the fearsome warrior women of legend. But he had returned from the Gold Coast filled with self-confidence and convinced that he was right about the route to the Indies outlined to him by Toscanelli. Even so, conviction was by no means enough, and as he watched educated men like Behaim wandering confidently in and out of the councils of state to discuss the next phase of Portuguese exploration, he knew he needed something else. He would need to be able to gather some evidence about the distance from Lisbon to Japan, or Cipangu as he knew it.

If you divided the globe into 360 degrees, the key question was how much of that was land and how much sea. Columbus managed to get hold of a book by the Greek philosopher Marinus of Tyre which estimated that 225 degrees was taken up by land. Columbus scoured the Bible for geographical references, and laid great emphasis on the obscure verse 2 Esdras 6.42 in the Apocrypha: "Six parts has thou dried up." This was the evidence he felt he needed, that actually only 15 percent of the earth's surface was sea. That meant 135 degrees around the equator was ocean, which was too far to sail with existing technology and resources.

But he rationalized that he only actually had to reach Cipangu, which he estimated as 30 degrees away from China. And the journey could be shortened at the other end by calculating the distance from the Azores instead of the mainland. By similar calculations, Columbus managed to whittle crossing the Atlantic down to a journey of just 60 degrees. Then he had to translate degrees into actual miles, and that depended on how close you were to the equator. Aristotle argued that, when you were at the broadest point of the earth, each degree represented about 60 nautical miles, but Columbus discovered a book translated from the Arabic about celestial movements that reduced that figure to 45 miles. Forgetting, or deliberately ignoring, the fact that Arabic miles were considerably shorter than Roman miles, he finally cut down the crucial distance of his voyage to something that might just be conceivable. He adopted a figure of just under 3,000 miles, and very much less than the 10,800 nautical miles that the ancient Greeks correctly believed was the distance from Europe to China, and which was far beyond the practical distance that could then be sailed.

In effect, Columbus's amateur calculations had shrunk the earth's actual circumference by a quarter. Even the wildly optimistic Toscanelli had told him that it was at least 5,000 miles.

It was at this point, in Madeira, that the story that has come to be known as "the missing pilot" is supposed to have taken place. A small ship sailed into the harbor there with only five of the crew still alive, and in the final stages of hunger. Columbus cared for the helmsman, a Castilian from Huelva called Alonso Sanchez, in his own home, and he heard that they had been heading for England when they were driven westward by an enormous storm that lasted for twenty-eight days. When the storm lifted, they had seen islands and had landed on them to find water, only to be driven away again by naked natives. The helmsman was too weak to recover, but before he died he sketched out a map of where he had been, with estimates of the winds and currents.

Biographers of Columbus have doubted the story from the beginning, though it was widely told about him in the generations that followed. It may still have happened in some form or another and been attributed to him. That is not unlikely, because the late 1470s and early 1480s were the years when Europe woke up to the possibilities of the Atlantic. There was little argument at the time among mariners that there was land on the other side of the ocean, though neither Columbus nor his contemporaries had much of a concept of a New World. The issue was whether it was possible to sail there, and for Cabot and the Columbus brothers, there was also the question of how to make the venture profitable if they did so.

Most European nations have some story about how they reached America before Columbus, and some of them may actually have done so, whether by accident or design. It could have been the Bristol expeditions. The Danish pilot John Scolvus, who led the expedition to Greenland, may have gone there, though the story that he was sent by Alfonso of Portugal is very unlikely. The Portuguese mariner John Vaz Corte Real may have run across Newfoundland as early as 1472. The Poles have a candidate, the adventurer Jan of Kolvo. And even the Basques, whose whalers regularly charged between the Bay of Biscay and the waters around Greenland, have stories about strange encounters with islands in the far West.* Columbus also would have heard about the Vikings and their settlements on Greenland as well as the legends of the Irishman St. Brendan and the Welsh prince Madoc who was supposed to have landed in Mobile Bay in 1170.†

The truth was that, although these people may not have formally discovered America, they and others seem to have happened upon it over and over again in the generation before Columbus, or happened upon something. The issue was not discovery; it was designing a method of staking a claim to the resulting trade to the Indies, if that was indeed the land on the other side.

Columbus was returning to the African fortress at El-Mina, this time as the commander of a caravel on an expedition to relieve the garrison. Cabot was buying spices and dyes in the territory of the sultan of Egypt and was selling the occasional slave in ones or twos, stopping off in Crete to sell them on the way home. They were gifts from the merchants he had been trading

---

*One story says that when he arrived in North America, Cabot was astonished to be confronted with native Americans speaking Basque. It sounds far-fetched, but in 1918, the Basque Academy of language commented on the strange similarities between Basque and the Huron language. They both, for example, used the word *orein* for deer.
†As late as 1669, the Rev. Morgan Jones was traveling through the Carolinas when he came across a tribe that understood his Welsh. A century later, the search for the heirs of Madoc took the Welsh clergyman John Evans all the way to North Dakota. "I think you can safely inform my friends," he wrote home sadly after a fruitless search, "that they have no existence."

with, and of the trio—Cabot, Columbus, and Vespucci—Cabot was probably the first to be involved in the trade in slaves that would play such a large
part in all their lives and achievements.

He was also supplementing his income by building a reputation as a
contractor that would stand him in good stead later. Those he was doing
business with in Venice were usually in the small circle of geographers
and dreamers he had met through his confraternity. There are records of
him selling a house that he had rebuilt for the sons of Taddeo da Pozzo,
who was close friends with the explorer and cartographer Alvise da
Mosto.

But with every sale and every new contact, Cabot's plans for his own
enterprise of the Indies were taking greater shape. If the Indies could be
reached by sailing westward, as his friend Columbus claimed—and everything he had learned from the Florentine humanists suggested he was
right—it came back to the same question: How was it possible to profit from
such a voyage? Here was the problem that Cabot and the Columbus brothers seem to have discussed. If they raised the money for a voyage and
brought back the news that the Indies lay on the other side of the Atlantic,
then every trader in Europe would follow them there—and cut them out. If,
on the other hand, they sailed as the agent of a monarch—as the great Portuguese explorers had done—then they would provide an enforceable claim
for their patron, but only a promise of further commissions for themselves.
They would get fame, of course, but nothing tangible.

Fame was very nice, but they were merchants. The purpose of the enterprise, the whole challenge, was primarily about profit. So, by the beginning
of 1483, their plan included three elements, each vital to this financial
success.

1. A scheme whereby they could reap a financial reward from the route
   they had discovered. They would persuade either the Portuguese or
   the English monarchs to license their discoveries—and to enforce
   their national rights to whatever territory was found—but in return
   would be granted a percentage of the profits made from their exploitation.
2. A scheme to pay for the venture. They would organize a major deal
   through their contacts in Portugal, Venice, and England, the profits

from which would pay for some or all of their enterprise. They had to share the risk of the voyage if their sponsoring prince was going to give them the concessions they needed to ask for.

3.	A scheme to find suppliers in the East. There was no point in simply arriving in Cathay without some information about the original sources of the spice trade. By the time they had tracked them down, the merchant fleets of Europe would have converged there. They needed contacts in advance if they were to cut out all those middlemen—who laboriously traded spices all the way to the Mediterranean—and before their rivals arrived.

This plan goes to the heart of the basic problem, and it is the only one that fully explains their predicament and their actions later, once the whole project began to unravel. There is no record of the plan that has survived, if indeed it was ever written down, but it can be inferred from what happened next. It also explains why Cabot and Columbus ended up so disastrously in debt at the end of that year, why they needed to approach the crowned heads of Europe, and why Cabot made such a dangerous journey to Mecca two years later to investigate the sources of the spice trade in the Far East.

It also goes some way to explaining the ambiguity at the heart of the story of exploration and discovery: If mariners had traveled regularly, if ac-cidentally, to lands on the other side of the Atlantic before, then what was special about Columbus and Cabot? The answer is that they had cracked the basic problem: how to profit from their enterprise. And that is what it was—not a voyage of discovery, but an enterprise of enormous ambition. This was a plan with the dream of fame at its heart, but it was also one that underlines their joint ambition. It was a scheme which, if it had worked, would have made them the richest men in the world.

The big deal that would finance the joint Cabot and Columbus expedition to the Indies was complete. The money was borrowed, the consignment of spices or wine was at sea and on its way to Southampton, which is where most Italian traders landed. Their backers in Venice, London, and Lisbon were committed. It was bold, but to win the kind of concession they needed, they would have to finance—or at least partly finance—the enterprise of the Indies themselves. But at that crucial moment, in the early spring of 1483, some most disturbing news arrived in Lisbon: The affable and capable king of England was dead.

Edward IV had begun to feel ill at Easter, but the disease remained a mystery to his advisers and doctors. He lingered on for some weeks, adding codicils to his will—including naming his brother Richard of Gloucester as the regent for the kingdom in the event of his death—and on April 9 he died. The cause of death remains a mystery, but recent theories have suggested he died of a burst appendix. He was just a few days short of his forty-second birthday.

By the time the rumors reached Cabot and Columbus, the news was even worse. England was paralyzed by indecision, the unexpected death of a man in his prime seemed likely to spark their disastrous dynastic struggle once again. The rightful king, the twelve-year-old Edward V, had been taken into protective custody wearing blue velvet by the regent, his uncle Richard, who had promptly seized power himself and proclaimed himself Richard III, rightly or wrongly about to go down in history as the most notorious tyrant ever to wear the English crown. Disturbing rumors about the legitimacy of Edward IV's marriage—and therefore the legitimacy of the young princes— were being circulated. Worse, they were being held in the Tower of London and had not been seen for some time. There were arrests and accusations of sorcery, and a fearful atmosphere of skullduggery and conspiracy had descended on the kingdom. Most depressing of all, the nervous merchant financiers of London and Bristol were withdrawing their promises of credit and avoiding ambitious projects, and consignments of forgotten cargoes were lying unclaimed and unsold on the wharves.

There are no records suggesting that the deal between Columbus and Cabot was undermined by the death of Edward IV, and the coup in England by his brother, but the timing suggests something along these lines. Either way, by the middle of the decade, both seem to have been forced to leave their adoptive countries, and the most likely date for the unraveling of their plans was probably 1483. Edward was unusual among English monarchs because he had mercantile interests in his own right, along with his mother, though he sold his rights to Italian managers. Through those agents, he was linked to most of the highly profitable wool and cloth trade with Italy, managed through a network of Italian merchants and using Venetian ships.

Both the partners had accepted large sums of investment money—Columbus from the Centurione family perhaps, and Cabot from the Capello, Dragan, and Mocenigo families. We know about Cabot's creditors because they were named on the letters sent after him later around Europe, and they all had strong commercial links with England. Columbus's backers are more shadowy, but before he died, Columbus asked his son to pay thirty thousand Portuguese reales to the heirs of Luigi Centurione. It is usually suggested that this was to assuage his guilt over the sugar deal that went wrong in 1479, but it could just as well have been a settlement of the debt left over from his 1483 catastrophe.

The unexpected death of one link in the chain of this deal, which connected financiers in Venice with merchants in Lisbon, Crete, and London, had torpedoed the whole enterprise. The investors were asking difficult questions. Southampton, where most Venetian shipments landed, was worryingly silent. Creditors were beginning to press. It was increasingly clear that the profits Columbus and Cabot were relying on to launch their expedition were not going to be forthcoming. Worse, they might in fact lose everything they had already amassed. Maybe the money had not been transferred to London. Maybe the goods were not going to be available. Maybe some key link lost his nerve, fearful that Edward's death had undermined the whole plan. Cabot was a master mariner used to plying the Bay of Biscay route, and it would then have been he who was forced to set sail empty-handed from England, and bring the despairing news to the Columbus brothers in Lisbon.

To make the situation doubly tragic for Columbus, he chose this moment to make one of his occasional visits back to Madeira to see his wife and son, only to find that Felipa had died from plague. Columbus was in mourning, heavily in debt, and solely responsible for his young son, Diego.

Perhaps it was at this moment that the alliance with Cabot was dissolved, but it is more likely they decided to press on with their separate aspects of the plan regardless. What else could they do? The aftermath of their disastrous business project would have delayed them, but Cabot would proceed to the East to seek out information about the sources of the spice trade. Meanwhile, the Columbus brothers would go ahead and win backing from the Portuguese court, and raise the money from the king of Portugal for the voyage if they possibly could.

## II

*"Talk of nothing but business, and dispatch that business quickly."*

ALDUS MANUTIUS, a sign on the door of his Aldine
Press, set up in Venice in 1490

The generations were changing in Florence. The city's sage, Toscanelli, breathed his last in May 1482. Vespucci's uncle Giorgio, now the librarian at the monastery of St. Mark, was distraught about the loss of his old friend and teacher. Now Amerigo's father was dying as well. Nastagio summoned Amerigo to his bedside and asked him to take over the family business completely. Four days later he was dead.

It was the beginning of a life in which Vespucci began to take responsibility for other people's affairs—a life in which he became a trusted confidante of business associates and relatives alike, and so grew to assume the role of discrete fixer, a role that he seems never to have quite shaken. Like Cabot, he had a talent for friendship. Unlike Cabot, he could be a quiet presence in the background, a civil servant as much as a business leader. When anyone connected to him had a problem—financial or otherwise—they came to Vespucci with it. Soon, his whole family seemed to be relying on him.

"I cannot but complain of all of you at home," said his brother Girolamo in Rhodes. "I wonder that you hold me in so little esteem. It has been over two years since I have had a letter from you, and I cannot understand why. I can only attribute it to the scant love that you feel for me . . . I am not in some inaccessible spot in the world. Every day, people come here on their way to Venice or Naples, and everybody gets letters except me."

Short, thick-set, with a peculiarly massive head, and known for never losing his temper, Amerigo would soothe the egos of his family, and sort out their problems. He was deeply reliable but made time—usually with Giorgio—to keep up with his intellectual interests as well. Just as his brother complained that people only passed through Rhodes on their way to someplace else, there were always intellectuals passing through Florence. One of them, who Amerigo almost certainly met in Florence when he arrived in search of academic preferment, was the controversial German humanist scholar Johann Reuchlin.

Martin Behaim's globe

Reuchlin had been sent to Florence by his close friend Lorenzo Behaim from Nuremberg, who was then living in the home of one of the most worldly ecclesiastical princes of them all, the newly appointed and stagger-ingly ambitious Spanish cardinal Rodrigo Borgia. Behaim's brother Martin, Vespucci knew, was even then working with the Portuguese king on some extraordinary new geographical ideas.

Since the violent death of her husband Giuliano de' Medici in the Pazzi plot, Simonetta Vespucci's cousin Semiramide had been living quietly out-side Florence. Her resemblance to the beautiful Simonetta, displayed now so famously as Botticelli's Venus, was disturbing. Semiramide was gathering symbolic significance in her own right for this, and for being the widow of the most romantic Medici of them all. Perhaps because of that, or because of her beauty and charm, Semiramide was receiving more frequent visits and attentions from another part of the Medici family.

Lorenzo the Magnificent's cousins, confusingly called Lorenzo and Gio-vanni di Pierfrancesco de' Medici, had been very close to their powerful relatives. But they had fallen out over money after the increasingly impor-tunate Magnificent was forced to ask them for a loan. The cousins were young and wealthy in their own right, with diverse business interests all over the Mediterranean, and were increasingly disaffected about the oligarchy that ruled Florence in their family's name. They began to call themselves the Popolano, which meant "commoners," to ally themselves with the citizens of Florence and to distinguish themselves from their powerful cousins.

The twenty-year-old Lorenzo di Pierfrancesco de' Medici, head of the Popolano branch of the family, proposed marriage to Semiramide, and she accepted. After the wedding, they set up in their own palace in the city and sought out the most trustworthy manager they could find to take charge of their business affairs. Almost immediately they approached Amerigo Vespucci to take the post and to become a member of their household.

It was not a wholly unselfish gesture. The Vespucci family felt let down by the Magnificent, feeling that he had promised them more support, and the Popolano moved to fill the vacuum, as much to irritate their cousins as anything else. "Find out what he wants," wrote Lorenzo di Pierfrancesco, sending a member of his staff to see Giorgio Vespucci, "and offer him on our behalf everything, whatever it may be." The result was that young Amerigo now had a new patron, and one he would look to for nearly the rest of his life.

Columbus and Cabot were salesmen. They were also loners and outsiders—especially now that they were in debt—making what use they could of their wits and contacts. Vespucci, on the other hand, was an insider, instinctively efficient, trustworthy, and loyal to his master, Lorenzo di Pierfrancesco. Nearly everything connected with the Popolano household went through Vespucci, but he was soon given more responsible work connected to their trading operations. When there was wheat from their Italian estates, he would arrange for its sale. When they traded wine via Seville or Lisbon, it was Vespucci who quietly and efficiently contacted their agents in Castile and Portugal. When Semiramide wanted to organize a party, it was Vespucci she consulted for advice and to make the arrangements. "My word is as good as a notarized document," he used to say, and perhaps it was, though historians have always wondered, over every aspect of Vespucci's life, whether his word really *was* that trustworthy if he had to say so.

He was also responsible for the vast number of goods in which the Popolano had trading interests: goblets, pigeons, poultry, knives, satchels, spoons, saltcellars, silver forks, napkins, tablecloths, handkerchiefs, shirts, mustard, buttermilk, cherries, wine, and fish. Sometimes he needed to travel to visit their agents around the Mediterranean, particularly in Castile, and he was usually asked by Semiramide to bring back something for her burgeoning family. Under Vespucci's discreet guidance, his aspects of the business grew, but he was also trading in a small and slightly raffish way on his own account, sending jewels to women on behalf of their lovers, debt collecting, and buying precious stones. Whatever it was, the work brought him into contact with the back streets and red-light districts of Florence. He seems to have frequented those districts on his own account as well. Meanwhile his own status and personal income began to grow, and he spent it freely.

Investing in books about geography and in maps and charts was the only way in which Vespucci could nourish his growing enthusiasm for exploration. On one trip he had the chance to buy one of the most celebrated and beautiful maps of the age, made in Mallorca in 1439, with beautiful miniatures of the monarchs and flags of the world picked out in blue, green, and gold. The map cost him 130 ducats and he brought it home to Florence and his rooms in the Popolano house. We can imagine him unrolling it for the benefit of guests, or staring at it when he was alone, dreaming of the semimythical islands in the far West where one day he would go.*

Vespucci had begun playing a leading role in the cultural affairs of the household, which was increasingly filled—as was the home of Lorenzo the Magnificent—with the stars of the Renaissance—scholars, poets, and artists. Ghirlandaio and Botticelli were now active in Florence's own increasingly influential opposition party, the Piagnoni—opposed to the Medici oligarchy over the city—which used the Popolano palace as its unofficial headquarters.

And when his masters needed a new villa decorated, Vespucci arranged for Botticelli, his childhood friend, to get the commission. When the Popolano wanted Ghirlandaio to carve a statue of John the Baptist as a

---

*Three centuries later, in 1838, the map was owned by the Count of Montenegro and was unrolled for a distinguished visitor, the French novelist George Sand (then in the middle of an affair with Chopin). The servant held one corner down with a full inkwell, but it was not quite heavy enough and the map leaped into the air and rolled up with the now-empty inkwell inside. It was restored in time for the Chicago World's Fair in 1892, when it was sent by steamboat across the Atlantic, insured for $100,000.

child, it was Vespucci who commissioned it. And perhaps, wandering through Ghirlandaio's studio on this task, Vespucci came across the young unknown who was apprenticed there and who was later known to history as Michelangelo.

While the greatest artists of any age rubbed shoulders with the poets and philosophers of Florence in the palaces of both Medici families—and Vespucci skillfully maintained his good relationship with the Magnificent's family—a strange idea was taking shape. It was in some ways a very worldly idea, in some ways enormously idealistic. It was that Christianity, Islam, and Judaism were at their roots the same, and that behind all three lay a kernel of divine truth that would allow them to be forged together in a new era of peace.

This was the dream of the coterie of friends that had grown up around Toscanelli, his old admirers and pupils—Amerigo's uncle Giorgio Vespucci, the poet Angelo Poliziano, the philosopher Marsilio Ficino, the architect Leon Battista Alberti—who gathered as often as they could for an intense debate, not just about philosophy and religion, but also about the new religion of truth that bound together Christianity and Islam.

It was an idea they had borrowed from some of the Greek Orthodox churchmen who had come to Italy before the fall of Constantinople. In fact, the papal secretary George Trapezuntius, in Naples when he heard of the downfall of his own city in 1453, had written an urgent letter to the sultan, urging him to work for the unity of the two faiths.

> If someone were to bring together the Christians and the Muslims, in one single faith and confession, he would be, I swear by heaven and earth, glorified by all mankind, on earth and in heaven, and promoted to the ranks of the angels. This work, O admirable Sovereign, none other than you can accomplish.

It was a belief that, behind the confusion and illusion of the world, there was a pure and central truth, and it derived—like so much else in Renaissance Florence—from the ancient Greek philosopher Plato. Plato may have been dead for sixteen centuries, but he was in the process of being crowned in Florence as the font of all knowledge, his birthday celebrated with great style every November 7. Poliziano, the poet and translator of pagan works, who had saved the life of Lorenzo the Magnificent during the Pazzi plot, was a central figure in this Platonic revolution. It was said that he only went to church in order to catch mistakes the clergy made in their Latin grammar. Another central figure was the new arrival twenty-year-old Conte Giovanni Pico della Mirandola, who had already mastered twenty-two different languages, as well as the ancient Jewish mystical kabbalah.*

The cult of Plato had given Florence's elite a fascination for esoteric knowledge, found in the translated pages of long-forgotten classics. It was as much about astrology and magic as it was about conventional faith, and like many of his contemporaries, Vespucci was skeptical about conventional Christianity. "In the end, I hold the things of heaven in low esteem," he wrote in his school notebook, "and even come close to denying them."

To some in Florence, like the new Dominican preacher Girolamo Savonarola, this fascination with pagan ideas seemed like a rationale for tolerating the naked dancing figures of the kind found in some of Botticelli's paintings. It looked corrupt, and so did the leadership of Florence. Not to mention Lorenzo the Magnificent's regular nocturnal rides to the villa of his mistress, returning at dawn. But there was another way of looking at it. People like Vespucci, the educated sophisticates of Florence, dreamed of a new world where the purity of this vision might be realized— and the idea began to mesh with the thrill of exploration. There might, after all, be a New World on earth. Poliziano was so thrilled at the possibility of the Antipodes that he wrote to John of Portugal and asked for help writing an epic poem about Portuguese discoveries that would make his fame immortal. John agreed and ordered his navigators to give Poliziano all the help he needed. The project was prevented only by Poliziano's untimely death.

With reverence, they repeated Plato's story of Atlantis in the middle of the great ocean to the west: "There was an island beyond the passage known as the Pillars of Hercules. This island was larger than Libya and than Asia. The travelers of those times could cross to it, and from it to others, and reach the continent lying on the opposite side of the sea." That island, de-

---

*It was said that Mirandola could recite any page of text forward or backward having read it just three times.

stroyed in a great conflagration that Plato described, may have reappeared, declared Toscanelli before he died. So while Columbus and Cabot plotted to see for themselves, the intellectuals of Florence dreamed of a similar voyage to the west where all these things would be revealed. For Vespucci, it was only a matter of time, and—if he could arrange it—he would see it for himself.

On the Atlantic coast of Europe, Lisbon was heating up, in more ways than one. There was plague in the city, and the summer's heat was making the rubbish smell in the streets. Three years into his reign John II was proving to be high-minded and, when necessary, brutal and rather puritanical. He banned silk clothing, even for members of the royal family. He made sure he ate in public and reduced royal banquets to just five dishes accompanied by nothing more potent than water. It was traditional for medieval kings to eat in public, but John took the daily ritual to extreme lengths. Any male would be allowed in to watch, once the trumpets sounded for his meals twice a day. He studiously avoided favorites at court, and was even known to go to the home of a courtier in the evening to apologize if he had shouted at him during the day.

But if he felt he had to be, John was also known to be absolutely ruthless in his determination to bring order to the Portuguese state, handing the business of government over to professional administrators rather than to the vagaries and rivalries of the great magnates. He had arrested the Duke of Braganza, the wealthiest man in Portugal, and had him beheaded in public for treason. This very year, convinced that his brother-in-law was also plotting against him, John invited him to his private quarters in the palace and dispatched him himself with a dagger.

Apart from this possibly justifiable paranoia, his main concern was to organize a diplomatic marriage for his sister Joana. Although he loved her more than almost anybody else, he was determined to refuse her permission to do the one thing she wanted to do: stay permanently in the convent where she lived. He was insisting that she should marry the prince of his choice. And in this case, John eventually decided it was time to strengthen the alliance with England by marrying her into the English royal family. When Richard III's wife died in March 1485, he seemed the prime candidate.* As Columbus was seeking out contacts that could deliver him an audience with the Portuguese king, it was these family struggles—a treasonable brother-in-law and a recalcitrant sister—that were on the king's mind more than issues of nautical exploration.

John was to be disappointed about the English alliance. In August of that year, Joana made her way into Lisbon with the entourage of nuns she had come to love, to see her brother in the Palace of Alcaçovas. John received her with alacrity, thinking she had finally changed her mind about the proposed Anglo-Portuguese marriage and her alliance with the new English king. The negotiations with Richard III were now at an advanced stage, and John was using every pressure he could bear to force his sister to agree. Her capitulation would be an enormous relief. But one look at her was enough for him to realize he was to be disappointed: There was Joana in her nun's habit and still unbowed.

"The man you want me to marry is dead," she informed him. It really was impossible that this news could have reached the convent before the court. But Joana was adamant that she had dreamed of Richard's death the night before, in battle, and that his crown had toppled off and rolled under a bush.

Nonetheless, some weeks later, the news did arrive from England that Richard III had been killed. Accompanied by only two thousand soldiers, the twenty-nine-year-old Henry Tudor, a cousin of both the rival factions in the recent English civil war, had landed at Milford Haven in Wales. He had been in exile in Brittany since the death of Edward IV and the object of a wide-ranging conspiracy to offer him the throne. As he marched out of Wales and into England, he had been greeted by crowds hailing him as king. King Richard—short but not hunchbacked, despite his description in Shakespeare's play—confronted this burgeoning force at Bosworth in Leicestershire, wearing gleaming Italian armor and riding an enormous white horse. In a rage at the height of the battle, Richard led an attack on Henry's position, and was cut down when his horse sank into the marsh. The ornamental crown he had been wearing was retrieved from under a

*Richard's wife, Anne Neville, probably died of tuberculosis, and he wept openly at her funeral. Shakespeare's allegation that he had her killed is not true. They also had rather a romantic courtship: Richard is supposed to have discovered her working as a scullery maid, having been hidden away by her guardian so that he could pocket the income from her estates.

bush, and his body was flung naked onto the back of his horse and carried into the city of Leicester.

It was the moment when English historians have dated the end of the medieval period in English history and the start of the Tudor dynasty. Two months later, during an outbreak in London of a mysterious disease, now extinct, called the sweating sickness, blamed on the arrival of Henry's Breton and French mercenaries, a glittering procession of the ambassadors of Europe gathered in Westminster Abbey in London to watch the new king crowned as Henry VII, wearing a cloak of bright violet.

Thanks to contacts at the Portuguese court, presumably through Canon Martins—a distant relative of Felipa's—Columbus finally secured his crucial interview with King John. But there he faced something of a dilemma. The maps and charts he had been shown by his mother-in-law, and those he had happened upon over the years via his various contacts around the quays, were all state secrets. If he was unable to be entirely honest about his charts and the sources by which he had obtained them, he would have to fall back on Marco Polo as an authority for the shape of the globe, and that was liable to undermine his case.

Armed with the sketchy maps he felt were safe to show the king, and accompanied by Bartholomew, Columbus made his way up the steep winding streets to the Moorish castle of St. George, towering over the two-towered cathedral. The brothers were ushered into the Palace of Alcaçovas inside the castle, where John held court. Paying court to medieval kings was a lengthy business of waiting in corridors and anterooms, patronized by courtiers, as hours—sometimes weeks—ticked by.

Finally Christopher was shown in to see the king and his advisers. His great opportunity had arrived. There was the goateed and somewhat flabby-cheeked John. If Columbus was anything like other visitors encountering John of Portugal for the first time, he must have seen a man whose eyes shone with intelligence, but who rather undermined the effect by the way he talked through his nose.

It is not quite clear what deal Columbus suggested to the Portuguese. Accounts by contemporaries simply repeat the wording of the demands that he eventually secured with the Spanish, complete with Spanish nomenclature, so it seems likely that this was used simply to fill a gap in their authors' understanding. There were no complaints about outrageous demands, as there were from the Spanish, so he may not actually have reached the stage of setting out to the court what he wanted.

He also failed to be entirely clear about the purpose of the expedition he hoped to mount. Cabot and Columbus planned to find an island off the coast of Cipangu, which they could use as a trading post with the Indies, and planned to use the royal warrant to give them rights over that trade. The demands for hereditary positions and the religious rhetoric belonged to a more obsessive and embittered Columbus, acting a few years later and alone. Whatever the deal he put to John and his court, he was careful not to reveal his secret store of maps and the knowledge they held about routes, wind patterns, and currents—too careful, in fact. He instead made the mistake of bringing up Marco Polo's description of Cipangu and Cathay. The experts brought in by John to advise him on the Columbus brothers' proposal, the so-called Junta dos Mathemáticos, exchanged glances. The committee, led by three of Lisbon's authorities on nautical matters—Diego Ortiz de Vilhegas, the Bishop of Ceuta and Tangiers, to consider the theological aspects; the Jewish scientist José Vizinho; and the court physician Rodrigo—was sent away to consider the proposal.

There was one notable absentee: Columbus's learned rival, the German globe maker Martin Behaim, was not included in the committee, even though he was known to have ideas similar to Columbus's. Having made the strongest case he could, Columbus withdrew and hoped for the best.

History does not record how Columbus received the verdict of the experts at the Portuguese court toward the end of 1484, whether he was simply handed a disappointing message or whether he made the journey with his brother again up the hill to the castle of St. George. A Portuguese play written only a century later imagines Columbus once again confronted by King John, who dismisses him with the damning suggestion to "get your head examined!"

Actually there is reason to believe that John did receive them again and was friendly. He was intrigued by the encounter and the idea, but unfortunately for Columbus, the Portuguese explorer Diego Cão had just arrived back in Lisbon convinced that he had reached the southern tip of Africa. Whatever the experts reported, John had already decided to concentrate his efforts on the route to the Indies around Africa. But he was warm enough to welcome Columbus back four years later, and warm enough now to offer Bartholomew a role in one of the most secret projects of the Portuguese state, the construction of a master atlas, using Ptolemy's basic outline but adding in every piece of intelligence acquired from the voyages south.

But though he was intrigued by Columbus, John was not impressed. "The king found this Columbus was very proud and boastful in presenting his talents, and more fanciful and full of imagination than accurate," wrote one chronicler. Nor was the proposition that Columbus be given rights over his own discoveries very popular. Vasco da Gama and Bartholomew Dias, his great Portuguese contemporaries, sailed as royal agents. They were showered with honors, but were given no personal rights. The verdict of the Portuguese advisers was also damning. Their report to John described Columbus's plans as "vain, simply founded in imagination." They were particularly contemptuous of his reliance on the authority of Marco Polo.

They were wrong about Marco Polo. But the generations to come would dismiss the Portuguese advisers, and the Castilian advisers who followed them, as backward-looking medievals. In fact, their analysis of the case Columbus put forward was largely correct. He had hopelessly underestimated the distances involved. His assumptions about the globe were manifestly inaccurate. They said he had failed completely to prove his case, and they were right. What neither side knew was that another continent, not completely unknown, but uncomprehended, lay in the way. Columbus was right that the Atlantic could be crossed using existing technology, but absolutely wrong that he could reach the Indies by that route.

While Columbus was struggling with the Portuguese committee, John Cabot's home city of Venice was experiencing an economic revival thanks to the peace treaty with their neighboring cities. The only signatory still holding out when the draft treaty was ready in August 1484 had been the elderly and ailing Pope Sixtus, but he was suffering from such a swollen tongue that he could barely speak. In a rage at the prospect of peace with Venice, he made a gesture to his closest advisers from his sickbed. They were unsure if this was an instruction for their dismissal or a papal blessing. They never found out, because the next morning he was dead.

So the peace treaty had been signed, and Venice celebrated with three days of church bells, fireworks, and jousting on St. Mark's Square. But for Cabot, it all came too late. His debts hung like a millstone around his neck, and he faced imprisonment unless he could pay back his creditors. He had done what he could to wrest back some of his position. Wandering down to the ghetto before the curfew, he had tried to raise money from financiers.* He had even tried to raise the money from his wife's family. (It is not clear why he could not do so from his father's business, but perhaps he had already borrowed as much as he could.)

Cabot also tried to dig his way out of debt by permanently disposing of some of his wife's dowry. There were powerful laws in Venice about dowries. Husbands were allowed to invest them, and enjoy the interest on the fruits of those investments, but they had to be returned to their wives upon the husband's death. So Cabot made an agreement with his wife's family to sign over the rights to all his property in Venice—the results of his precious few years in property refurbishment. The agreement stipulated that this would be returned to his heirs if and when the dowry was ever repaid. It was clearly not enough.

It was no longer safe to leave his pregnant wife and young son, Ludovicus, alone in Venice since his most lucrative contacts in the city were embarking on an attempt to have him arrested and jailed for his debts. There was no choice but to take them with him on his trading voyages, eking out a living between Southampton and the Mediterranean, forced increasingly to shift to Bristol to avoid all the Italians in Southampton. In the final month of Mattea's pregnancy, his ship crossed the Bay of Biscay once again and sailed down the Avon River and into Bristol harbor. While it was being refitted, and with the family in lodgings, Mattea gave birth to their second son, Sebastian.

The Columbus brothers had been experiencing similar problems. Bartholomew Columbus was at least employed on secret work in government service in Lisbon, but suspected the motives of the appointment and was being urged by his brother to leave and take the proposal to England.

---

*The ghetto in Venice was the first district known as such, because it had previously been a copper foundry and *il getto* is Italian for "casting metal."

Christopher was also in debt, and now outside the protection of the king, and therefore liable to be arrested himself.

Christopher was also afraid that in his enthusiasm to convince the Portuguese experts, he had given away too much. Not only had he revealed enough details of his plans that any half-informed Portuguese mariner could attempt implementing them, but he had shown how much he knew. He had said enough for an intelligent listener to realize that he had access to the most secret Portuguese maps, and was prepared to use them to better himself.

Columbus needed to leave Lisbon if he was to avoid his creditors—who were also those Genoese families who had up until then provided him with an income—but he might be refused permission to leave by the agents of the state. He knew only too well that the penalty for sending a chart abroad was death. If he was known to be planning to leave that might be enough to make him suspect. He had lived in Portugal, or Portuguese territories, since his shipwreck eight years earlier, and so much had happened since then— his marriage, his son, his plans—so leaving must have seemed an enormous wrench. But he no longer had a wife, and his plans could not be realized where he was. He needed go—but ever so quietly.

# 4

# In Debt

*"It was an intuition. The intuition became an idea, the idea a plan, the plan an obsession; after his wife's death, it became the only aim of his life."*

PAOLO EMILIO TAVIANI, *Christopher Columbus: The Grand Design*

*"It is difficult for us to realize the extent to which the men of the Middle Ages rested on venerable authorities. This is one of the things which differentiates the period almost equally from savagery and from our modern civilization."*

C. S. LEWIS, *The Discarded Image*

THERE WERE MANY legends going around in fifteenth-century Portugal about crew members of lost ships who arrived back in Lisbon claiming to have glimpsed Antillia, the Island of the Seven Cities. One of these was so extraordinary that nobody who heard it could quite forget it. It was about an adventurer called Fernando de Alma, who tried to repeat the journey and asked the king for permission to charter two caravels to go to Antillia himself.

After surviving a series of tumultuous storms, de Alma found himself becalmed at the mouth of a great river. The grand chamberlain of the city on this new land rowed out and welcomed the crew, and when he was about to leave, Fernando leaped into his boat and went ashore. There he feasted and saw wonderful buildings. While he was being rowed back to his caravels, which proved hard to find, he fell asleep . . . and awoke, centuries later, on a Portuguese ship in the mid-Atlantic bound for home. The sailors told him they had found him drifting in the ocean, clinging to wreckage. Puzzling over his fate, and that of his crew's, he landed in Lisbon and rushed to his house and then to the home of his fiancée, Seraphina. A man he did not recognize opened the door and tried to prevent him from coming inside, but he pushed past, dashed upstairs, and burst in on his fiancée in the arms of another man.

"What does this mean, Seraphina?" shouted Fernando.

"What are you talking about?" she answered, clinging to her lover. "My name is Maria."

"How can that be? There's your portrait on the wall."

"Holy Virgin!" exclaimed Maria. "He is talking of my great-grand-mother."

Columbus, and maybe Cabot as well, probably had heard this legend. They might have identified a little with Fernando de Alma, washed up a century in the future with nothing. Their debts had made it imperative that they should leave behind everything they had come to know as home. Both had lost the powerful business contacts they had relied on for their income. Cabot had his family by his side, but all Columbus had left was his five-year-old son, for whom he was solely responsible.

As the winter of 1484 turned to the spring of 1485, some months after the rejection of his plans by the Portuguese government, Columbus had also set himself adrift. Rumors had reached him that the Bishop of Ceuta, one of John of Portugal's panel of experts, had urged the king to test out Columbus's ideas for himself, and that an expedition had been organized that was planning to leave from the Azores. A furious Columbus realized this was a signal to leave. He was no longer trusted by the Portuguese court—if indeed he ever had been—which meant no prospect of either extra income or protection from his creditors.

If the authorities discovered he was planning to leave, knowing what he knew—and the access he had to maps—they might try to stop him. So very quietly, and traveling with Diego, he boarded a small vessel in Lisbon and sailed around the coast past the border and into Castile, into the great delta of lakes and bogs, the home of boars and wolves, that marked the mouth of the Odiel River.

The voyage could be risky. From their lairs on this coast, stretching up past Huelva, and the Guadalquivir River to Seville and beyond, Castilian pirates ventured out occasionally to prey on Portuguese shipping. As their ship rounded the promontory of Rio Tinto to anchor in the small port of Palos, Columbus looked up to the cliffs and saw the white shape of the Franciscan friary of La Rábida. One plan was to go to Huelva, where Felipa's sister Violante lived, and to leave Diego with her. Instead, once he had landed with Diego, with almost no money, he climbed the hill from Palos up to the friary, knowing that he had in his pocket a letter of introduction from the Berardi family.

There he knocked on the door and asked for some bread and water. The door was opened by one of the friars, the astronomer Antonio de Marchena. By chance, Columbus had stumbled into the one place on the peninsula that would believe in him and help him. La Rábida doubled as a kind of college for navigators, as well as a school, where he could enroll Diego. The monks there were knowledgeable enthusiasts about the latest developments in geography. They had strong links with explorers around the world and kept their ears to the ground. They had even played host to the Bristol pioneers on the *Trinity* when they stopped at Huelva on their way to seek out new lands to the west in 1480 and 1481. If Columbus had not yet heard of those voyages, he learned about them now.

The great contemporary Dutch humanist Desiderius Erasmus told a story, which he said was true, about four wealthy friends enjoying one another's company around the dinner table. As a drunken boast, one of them vowed to go on a pilgrimage to Santiago de Compostela. The next vowed to go all the way to Rome. All four drank to the promise and felt obliged to carry it out. One of them died in Spain, one died in Italy, and a third was left dying in Florence by the fourth, who came home prematurely gray and completely penniless.

Such were the perils of travel in the late fifteenth century, as Bartholomew Columbus was about to find out the hard way, having succumbed finally to his brother's demands. This was no time to be bound to the Portuguese state, however secret and exciting the charts he was involved with might be. They must fulfill their side of the deal with Cabot. If

Desiderius Erasmus by Matsys

Portugal had turned them down, Christopher would make a presentation to the Castilian court. But at the same time, it made sense for Bartholomew to approach the English.

There are no details in the histories about how Bartholomew made his journey. He would have had to close his mapmaking business, or put it in the hands of trusted partners, without making it too obvious that he was planning to leave. Having done that, he must have boarded a ship—perhaps not in Lisbon, where he might attract too much attention, but farther up the coast. The journey was disastrous. Somewhere along the way, and prob-ably quite early on, along the war-ravaged coast of Gascony as they hugged the shore in the Bay of Biscay, Bartholomew's ship had an encounter with pirates.

Pirates were a perennial problem for ocean-going trade. Privateers were nominally tolerated because they went after Turkish or other Muslim ship-ping, just as the Muslim corsairs on the Barbary coast sought out Christian shipping. But in practice, they could prey on anyone unlucky enough to get in their way. They would plunder the cargoes, taking into slavery anyone young and vigorous enough to fetch a high price or anyone rich enough to fetch a ransom, and hide the plundered goods on the same coast where they moored their ships, often with the tacit agreement of the local lord. The pirates that Bartholomew came upon may have been English mercenaries left behind after fighting in Gascony. The ship was attacked and boarded and he was captured along with the other travelers and crew. His baggage was seized and taken from him, but there was enough of value in his bags—sophisticated books he had brought along to sell, and sea charts—that Bartholomew fell into the ransomable category. He was taken inland and, most likely, locked in a damp cell. There with the rats and lice, his health declined rapidly. He was only too aware that because he had left secretly, only his brother Christopher knew where he was going.

In the months that followed, when he should have been set up in business in London with the help of other members of the Genoese community, Christopher received no letters. As Columbus set out on his own quest for financial support in Castile, with his letters of introduction from the monks, his brother's disappearance must have preyed horribly on his mind.

Christopher Columbus was by then in Cadiz, a port farther down the coast of Castile, near the mouth of the Guadalquivir, pulling the few strings he had been given access to since his arrival. Cadiz was the traditional stopping point for Genoese ships from Chios on their way into the Atlantic. It made sense to hang around his compatriots, but there were other reasons too.

This was a brand new country, not yet transmuted into Spain, but created out of the marriage between Isabella of Castile and Ferdinand of Aragon, the monarchs of two peninsular nations. Both partners had been forced to struggle as teenagers for their right to succeed to the throne and had flung themselves immediately into a vastly expensive war to expel the last few Muslim outposts on Spanish soil. These clustered around the continuing Moorish kingdom of Granada, whose deposed king Boabdil was now sheltering in exile with Ferdinand. No European monarchs can have been so abstemious as Isabella and Ferdinand. Always on the move, living in tents, rarely in their Alcazar in Córdoba—where they had some vestiges of comfort—Isabella is known to have made and embroidered Ferdinand's shirts. Other ways of paying for this tumultuous war included the creation of an elite new tier of aristocrats, the most recent of which was Luis de la Cerda, who had been named the Duke of Medina Celi five years earlier. They were on the front line with the Moors, these new dukes, recognizable by their gold or silver spurs in the hubbub around Ferdinand's fortified encampment outside Granada, known as Santa Fé.

Another of these new dukes, from Medina Sidonia, had links with La Rábida, and was financing semipiratical expeditions against the Portuguese all down the African coast. Columbus also had an introduction to him, not just from the friars, but again from his contact in Lisbon, the Florentine merchant Lorenzo Berardi.* The duke was a business colleague of Berardi's son Gianotto, a successful businessman himself, also dealing in slaves and now based in Seville, from where he regularly commissioned slaving raids and piracy aimed at Muslim shipping. Gianotto Berardi was six years younger than Columbus, but had already amassed a trading fortune, partly with the help of his father, whose interests he represented in Castile. Through his father's links with Toscanelli, back home in Florence, Gianotto Berardi was fascinated with Columbus's enterprise and introduced him to the Duke of Medina Celi.

Columbus had been given some unwelcome time to think since the rejection by John of Portugal. He had begun to adapt his message to Spanish politics: What was the point of expelling the Muslims from Spain if you did not also take the message westward? He had also been considering the implications of his last glimpse of the Portuguese king. Before he had left Lisbon, he was still well enough regarded in the Portuguese court to be there when the king welcomed back the land navigator José Vizinho, having returned from a trek across Africa along the equator, one of those sent to find Prester John. It had been a grueling and exhausting journey, full of dangers and bizarre encounters, and it clearly implied that the overland route to the East was just too far. But Columbus drew another conclusion. If Africa was bigger than expected, it could mean that the rest of the world was smaller and therefore Asia must be nearer in the opposite direction.

---

*Almost exactly a century later, the great grandson of this Duke of Medina Sidonia was the commander of the Spanish Armada, the disastrous expedition to invade England in 1588.

So when he managed to strike up an unexpected friendship with the Duke of Medina Celi, on the north shore of Cadiz Bay in the town of Puerto de Santa Maria, where he was developing a new shipping business, Columbus had more ammunition. The first meeting between the two men was successful, and Columbus stayed with him through the autumn of 1485 as his guest. As the visit progressed, and the two men talked more, the duke agreed he would finance the voyage with three or four caravels. But he stipulated one condition: It had to have the approval of the king and queen.

Historians have emphasized that this was the duke's idea, but actually it was just as important to Columbus. Without a royal commission, any voyage would have been little better than a sightseeing excursion. It would have meant getting a head start with direct trading links to the Indies, but that was all. With a commission, there was some chance of continuing to profit, which was at the heart of the plan drawn up with Cabot and his brother, and it was how Columbus came to approach the fateful and historic meeting with Isabella of Castile.

When in December 1485 the Duke of Medina Celi asked permission to finance this voyage of discovery, the queen sent a message saying she wanted to meet Columbus herself and wanted him to submit his proposal to her board of advisers.


While Columbus had been busily making contacts in Castile, Cabot had been in Alexandria, seeking out a disguise in which to venture farther south. We will probably never know for certain what took him on his extremely risky journey to join the annual Muslim hajj to Mecca, but it was in keeping with the plan the three of them had hammered out. We know it was a journey to find information about the spice trade—the aloewood, cinnamon, nutmeg, sandalwood, tumeric, ginger, and all the others that his father's company specialized in—which were also the final objective of the enterprise of the Indies. We also know that he was searching for the distant, mysterious sources of these spices, and doing so probably in connection with a voyage of exploration he or an ally was preparing to make. The fact that he was prepared to take this risk implies that the journey was part of a wider plan, probably part of his original alliance with the Columbus brothers.

Cabot knew that Genoese or Venetian merchants, based in Beirut or Alexandria, bought the spices from Arab merchants who had carried them from the Red Sea and the Indian Ocean. But where did they come from before that? He vaguely knew, as the merchants did, how they got there: down the Silk Road and via the Black Sea, from India and through Arabia, or from what is now Indonesia and Malaysia to the east coast of Africa and then north to the Mediterranean. But when he and the Columbus brothers had originally laid their plans, they believed they could bypass the spice trade altogether. To do that, they would need to know the sources in Cathay so they could trade with them directly when they arrived via the back door. That was the purpose of his journey, and one of his agreed contributions to the enterprise. They may have been heavily in debt, exiled from their adopted homes, and had their plans rejected by the Portuguese court, but there were other courts, and there was still time.

Leaving his poor, wandering family with the Venetian colony, amid the baths, bazaars, and coffee houses in Alexandria, Cabot set off on his own. Like the European adventurers that followed him in later centuries, he could not afford to be recognized as a Christian caught on the pilgrimage. Even in Alexandria, Christian merchants were expected to wear heavy wooden crosses around their necks and were stripped naked and searched when their goods were submitted to the customs authorities. At night the Christian enclaves in the city were sealed. Cabot needed to look like a different kind of outsider—an Ottoman or visiting Indian perhaps, or like his contemporary Ludovico di Varthema from Bologna—though describing himself as a "gentleman of Rome"—who bought a horse and dressed as a Syrian.

The first part of the journey meant three days and nights in a boat sailing down the Nile to Cairo, past the mud villages along the riverbanks and that constant succession of what Sir Richard Burton later described on the same journey as "gaunt, mange-stained camels, muddy buffaloes, scurvied donkeys, sneaking jackals and fox-like dogs." But while sailing on the Nile was cool relief from Alexandria, the streets of Cairo—with its tens of thousands of mosques—reflected the heat from the desert like a furnace. Like the rest of the city's inhabitants, Cabot would have escaped inside in the afternoons and ventured out again only after sunset.

It is one of the duties of all Muslims that at some time in their lives they should complete the hajj to Mecca. This is also a celebration of the trials of

Abraham and, in medieval times especially, it was a trading opportunity as well. Hundreds of thousands of pilgrims were converging on Mecca—Varthema joined a caravan with forty thousand pilgrims in 1503—mainly by ship down the Red Sea. With so many people, the great traders from the East would have to be there as well. It was the opportunity that Cabot had been waiting for.

The journey from Cairo began with ninety miles in the bewildering heat to the few huts that marked the town of Suez, with the caravan protected all the way by Mamluk soldiers. Mecca is a very dry place, and the pilgrims had to bring most of their provisions with them, which made them vulnerable to attacks by Arab tribesmen. Unsure who he could trust or who might understand the handful of words he had mastered in Arabic, Cabot—like Varthema—must have said little and slept nervously on the deck of the ship as it made its way out to sea, stopping at inlets along the way every night. In the daytime, his clothes were completely soaked in sweat. At night, under the gigantic moon, listening to the storytellers in languages he could barely understand, the clammy dews soaked them all over again.*

At last, the ship sailed into the port of Jedda, and on the quayside, the travelers saw before them a whole panoply of the Muslim world, with every tribe gathering in their competing caravans to make the winding, rocky journey to Mecca. Those around Cabot began changing into the white robes of a pilgrim, indicating that the next few days were going to be the most dangerous of all.

Mecca was a sweltering city, surrounded by mountains on all sides. Contemporary travelers spent much of the time sleeping on the roofs of their lodgings, which were extraordinarily expensive in the hajj season. If he had not realized it before, Cabot must have known after he arrived just how vulnerable he was. If his identity as a Christian had been revealed, he would have stood no chance of escape. But whatever disguise he had adopted, his ruse could have been revealed by real Syrians, Persians, or Ottomans, lodging

---

*Cabot was probably aware on one of these nightly stopovers that they were at the town of Yanbu, the legendary birthplace of the great geographer Ptolemy, whose atlas he may have carried with him at the time.

somewhere in the same city, rubbing shoulders with him, and liable to emerge unexpectedly to reveal him as a fraud.

The poor were everywhere, mainly Africans, described by Varthema as fighting for scraps of food as meager as cucumber rind. So were the courtesans, described by another traveler two centuries later as having hair down to their heels with little bells on the ends that jingled as they walked along. As a merchant venturer, Cabot could not resist the mosque and its parks, where Varthema claimed eighteen years later to have seen two unicorns. The great mosque at the heart of the city was also the heart of the spice trade in the region. It was shaped like an enormous vaulted amphitheater, with up to a hundred gates. Other travelers to Mecca found guides they could confide in, and Cabot—who had the kind of gregarious personality that seems to have drawn people to him—must have managed to do likewise: He needed a guide now, as he entered the holiest place in the Muslim world.

Because of the occasional contemporary descriptions by other Western travelers, we can reconstruct Cabot's arrival, wandering into the great mosque, down twelve stairs, and through an ornate porch covered in jewels that glinted in the lamplight. Once inside, he marveled at the astonishing gilded walls for a moment before realizing where he must go. At the next level down was the sight he had been looking for: as many as six thousand traders, selling nothing but ointments, spices, and powders. "It passes belief to think of the exceeding sweetness of the savors, far surmounting the shops of the apothecaries," wrote Varthema a few years later. But having breathed in the telltale smell, Cabot and his guide set to work.

Where did the spices originate from? Who did the traders buy from? Where were they actually grown, the ginger and nutmeg and sandalwood? As the visit progressed here, and elsewhere on the journey to Mecca, Cabot's mood must have plummeted. The traders actually had no idea. And the truth was that they were not being deliberately evasive. They bought their wares from other merchants who had bought them from others, and so on for thousands of miles—by ship and mule and cart, through distant straits and oceans unknown to these salesmen, just as they were unknown to Europe. The routes by which the precious medicines, dyestuffs, and preservatives made their way even to Arabia were complex beyond unraveling. His bold adventure, his appointed task as part of the agreement with Columbus and his brother, had failed.

I

*"Then take a little Allom, and seeth it with water, then*
*shall ye haue two ounces of brasill sodde in light water, and*
*put your cloth therein, fiue pater nosters long. Then if it be*
*not drie ynough, then weat it as before is sayd."*

*Recipe for dyeing cloth red*, originally in a Dutch
dyeing manual, 1513

There was a new pope in Rome, following the painful death of Sixtus IV in August 1484. Sixtus had been a Genoese through and through, and he was followed by another Genoese, Giovanni Battista Cibo, the bishop of Savona. He was a protégé of Sixtus, and he succeeded to the papacy despite bitter divisions among the cardinals, furious accusations of bribery, and riots outside in the streets of Rome. Plump and worldly, Cibo already had a reputation for corruption and nepotism that would have made him notorious if it was not for his successor, but that comes later in the story. When he died, eight years later, a Latin ditty circulated about him said: "Eight wicked boys born, and just as many girls, so this man could be entitled to be called Father of Rome."

Cibo took the name Innocent VIII, without a trace of irony, and launched his papacy with a call for action to push back the Muslims from Europe. Within five years, he had performed such a *volte face* that he had agreed to arrest the sultan's brother exiled in Rome, for an annual fee of forty thousand ducats from the Ottomans and the promise that the spear that was supposed to have pierced the side of Christ would be returned.*

The election of a pope mired in unprecedented corruption added fuel to the barely noticed speeches of Savonarola. His sermons in Florence had been so poor that he had promised himself to abandon the whole idea and do something else. Florence was still embracing the luxury they had become so used to, but Innocent's election—and Savonarola's conviction that his

---

*Innocent's problem, like so many corrupt leaders before and since, was a growing obsession with the enemy within. He goes down in history as the man who set out the principles of the *Malleus Maleficarum*, the notorious book that led to the burning of witches across Europe in the centuries that followed. Worse, he also appointed Tómas de Torquemada, the cruelest grand inquisitor of Spain.

sermons should be prophetic visions of disaster—began at last to attract some listeners.

At the same time, and in the same city, Vespucci's wealth and taste for luxury was beginning to grow along with his reputation, and he had also acquired a mistress. "Tell me how your daughter and her mother are, and that woman called Francesca," wrote one of Vespucci's Spanish correspondents. "Give them all a thousand regards." It is not quite clear who he referred to, but like Columbus, Vespucci had a romantic attachment with a woman who probably had a child, and with another regular lover called Francesca.

Meanwhile, the business success of the Popolano was only too apparent compared to the dwindling fortunes of the Medici Bank and the finances of Lorenzo the Magnificent, as well as the succession of failed harvests that was heaping pressure on Florence. Semiramide, now married to Lorenzo de' Medici of the Popolano family, was also relying on Vespucci. If he traveled out of Florence, especially to Seville, there would be a long list of items she asked him to buy for her infant children: ivory combs, beige velvet caps, silver necklaces. Also growing in status was Amerigo's older brother, the notary Antonio, who was now representing an increasingly powerful clientele, which included Columbus's old patrons in the Centurione, Spinola, and di Negro families.

As the wealth of the Popolano grew, they began to challenge their powerful cousins in more subtle ways. If Lorenzo the Magnificent could hold pagan events with poets and artists, so could the Popolano. If the Magnificent could commission portraits of Simonetta Vespucci in all her glory, so could they.

That was how Vespucci came to be involved in the commissioning of the most mysterious portrait of his cousin Simonetta. In the portrait, she is naked except for a snake around her neck, in symbolism either too deep to be understood, or just too obscure to be remembered. It remains one of the best-known paintings by Piero di Cosimo, just back from working with Botticelli on the Sistine Chapel in Rome, and it marked a subtle shift in the power relations in Florence. The Popolano had now taken control of the cult of Simonetta.

Vespucci, Cabot, and Columbus, and others of their age, had grown to maturity in a period of upheaval across Europe. The continuing political upheavals in Genoa, the tumult of civil war in England, the aftermath of the Hundred Years War in France, and the untidy dynastic wars between Spain and Portugal, had left their mark on the landscape—but also on the attitudes of the new rulers. In Florence, the future political philosopher Niccolò Machiavelli was only sixteen, but he would live to record the emergence of a new kind of ruler that was determined not to repeat the mistakes of their parents' generation. They gathered a new professional class of administrator around them and they absolved themselves of normal human morality. Secrecy, duplicity, cruelty, all were allowed—positively demanded—because on them lay the responsibility for the preservation of the state.

John II of Portugal, the so-called perfect prince, was one of these new rulers. Ferdinand of Aragon was another; so was Henry VII of England. Compared with them, Lorenzo the Magnificent of Florence was a mere dilettante. But nowhere was the business of forging a modern nation sharper than in Ferdinand and Isabella's joint kingdom.

There was little actual fighting in the south, though the Moorish archers dipped their arrows in wolfbane, which grew wild in the Sierra Nevada, and which turned even the slightest wound septic. Yet the war was still ruinously expensive, and it was part of a wider agenda for the monarchs: They wanted to forge a united, Christian nation. That meant expelling the Muslim rulers, but it also meant trouble if you happened to be a member of one of the large Jewish communities, which were expected to bear the brunt of the war with a special tax. For historical reasons, and because it was often the only profession they were allowed to adopt, the Jewish community provided most of the financial services in Europe, and were regarded as almost endlessly milkable.

The Spanish Inquisition, under the ruthless Tomás de Torquemada, had long since broken free of the pope's authority and now answered to the monarchs alone. Jews were cajoled and threatened into converting to Christianity, but having converted, they then found themselves the object of deep suspicion for those whose self-appointed role was rooting out heresy. The year 1485 marked a ratcheting up of religious tension in Spain, when an inquisitor was murdered in Saragossa Cathedral—probably by "New Christians," the term applied to Jews who had been forced to convert. But Columbus was finding that the ruthless new rulers of Castile and Aragon were hard to track down, even for someone armed with a personal request to visit them.

In the last few months of that year, it rained incessantly in Spain. To reach his audience with the queen, Columbus needed to get to Córdoba, but the city was almost cut off by floodwater.* Exhausted and damp, he finally arrived there on January 20, 1486, and went as instructed to the enormous palace of Cardinal Mendoza, who, as primate of Spain, was supposed to ride next to the queen into battle. But the floods had caused a fatal delay. The king and queen had already left. Isabella had just given birth to her fifth and last child, the future Catherine of Aragon—who would leave her mark so decisively on English history as the first wife of Henry VIII—and was exhausted herself. Columbus would have to wait for them to return.

Through the winter and early spring of 1486, Columbus found lodgings in the Genoese district of Córdoba, near the Hierro Gate on the left bank of the Guadalquivir. Meanwhile, he looked for a source of income and prepared his case. Finally, on May Day, the waiting was over. Laden down with his usual piles of books and charts and with Gianotto Berardi at his side for moral support, Columbus made his way over the Guadalquivir by the stone Moorish bridge that linked the sides of the city, passed the magnificent mosque, which was now part of the cathedral complex, and was finally shown into the great hall of the Alcazar for his famous meeting with Isabella of Castile and her royal husband.

The meeting with Isabella and Ferdinand was not as conclusive as Columbus had hoped. Ferdinand was a striking figure, tall and good-looking, with the air of the incessant seducer he was. The problem was that Ferdinand was as obsessive about Mediterranean diplomacy as any prince alive, and saw no reason why anyone should look westward. He boasted later that he had deceived the acknowledged diplomatic master—the Spider King of France, Louis XI—as many as ten times. Ferdinand had brought with him a copy of Ptolemy's *Geography*, and turned theatrically to the relevant pages as Columbus spoke, only to find they did not support what he said.

But Isabella was a different matter. Auburn-haired and blue-eyed, Isabella was the great-granddaughter of John of Gaunt and almost exactly the same

---

*When Córdoba had been in the hands of the Moors, they maintained deep flood channels, but since it fell to the Christians, these had been allowed to silt up.

hec differt· Nã corographia
toto loca abſcidens p ſe de q

Ptolemy as portrayed in a fifteenth-century
edition of his *Geography*

age as Columbus. She also shared some of his visionary sense of destiny. Ferdinand was a pragmatist, and she loved him, but Isabella was a romantic. If she had not been, history might have been different. When Columbus unveiled the map that he and Bartholomew had prepared, and spoke of carrying the gospel to the Indies, he struck a chord.

By the end of the meeting, there were some signs of progress. Isabella had prevailed upon one of her courtiers to accommodate Columbus in his house and to introduce him to key decision-makers in the court. She had also promised to ask her own confessor, Hernando de Talavera, to organize an expert commission to advise her on the enterprise. Columbus had persuaded a sovereign to take him seriously for the first time. But in the next few weeks, hanging around the court for the commission to collect itself, he caught a glimpse of what his life would be like in the next few years. Cynicism about his mission was palpable, as new projects tend to be viewed around most courts. His enterprise was at best a distraction from the far more urgent business of prosecuting the war against the Moors, and, at worst, it was a joke. "My proposition was a thing of mockery," he wrote later, a familiar figure among the assorted beggars, plaintiffs, and scholars who hung around the vicinity of the monarchs. "All who learned of my plan made merry at my expense."

It may be that Columbus's intensity and his combination of prematurely white hair and bright red features invited this kind of mockery, when more urbane meddlers of the same broad idea, like Behaim or Cabot, managed to escape it. But Columbus also saw everything in very personal terms: This was "his" proposition. His partners, coconspirators, and friends were forgotten. In the hothouse of a Spanish court focused on another enterprise altogether, he seemed to beg for ridicule. To make matters worse, the Talavera Commission had barely met in the summer before it adjourned again to follow the court to Salamanca, where it was going to spend the rest of the year.

While Columbus struggled with the Spanish court, his brother Bartholomew lay in his place of captivity, maybe a cell, maybe just a dank room, staring out at the Atlantic. He had no news of his brother or the enterprise. For all he knew, he had been given up for dead. Christopher may even have persuaded the Spanish to back his enterprise and he and Cabot might even then be on their way across the Atlantic to the Indies. He explained to his captors that he could raise no ransom, yet they seem almost to have forgotten him as well.

We can only imagine his captivity, but it was almost certainly debilitating and sapping of his strength. If he stayed there much longer, there was no doubt that he would die. Perhaps there was the very slim chance that he could tell them about the enterprise he was planning and coax them to release him in return for a lucrative share.

As Christopher Columbus waited for the decision of the commission, providing them with information as they requested it, rumors began to reach him about the aftermath of his appearance before the king in Lisbon. The Bishop of Ceuta's advice had been taken. Earlier that year, John had granted permission to a Flemish adventurer called Ferdinand van Olmen to look for the Island of the Seven Cities. Unlike the proposal of Columbus and Cabot, this was going to have to be at his own expense. If van Olmen found the island, he could have it.

Just as Columbus realized he would need a partner, van Olmen realized the same. Three months later, he found one who was able to procure and prepare two ships. They were due to set sail shortly from the Azores. Among those who had applied to join the expedition was Columbus's rival Martin Behaim.

It was agonizing news. If the Talavera Commission did not hurry up and make a decision, the route to the Indies would already be discovered and it would be too late. But before receiving the news about the move to Salamanca, Columbus had begun to enjoy Córdoba. It was one of the wonder cities of Europe, in Christian hands for two and a half centuries, but still keeping its advanced Moorish sense of luxury, with its narrow streets, high white walls, and tree-lined piazzas. The cathedral was built in what had been the biggest mosque in the world outside Mecca, and had patios of orange trees and distinctive green and purple marble columns. It was said that you could walk for ten miles through the city at night, lit by the lamps of its libraries and bathhouses.

Columbus must have felt some sense of belonging, not just because of the Genoese, but because Córdoba was overwhelmingly a wool town. People were involved in the trade at all levels of society and kept their sheep on grazing land outside the city between the market gardens. Even so, he could generate little enthusiasm for the profits in cloth anymore. In Lisbon, he had hung around on the waterfront, and now he sought out anyone with an interest in cosmography. In those days, apothecary shops had become informal meeting places for people to talk about medicine or science, and in one Genoese apothecary near his home, he met someone who was later to become a right-hand man on his first voyage, Diego de Harana. Having talked a few times, Harana took Columbus home to meet his father, and there he also met Harana's cousin Beatriz and they became lovers.

Beatriz de Harana was twenty-one and had been born in the mountains above the city, but both her parents had died when she was a child. Presumably it was his intensity and seriousness that attracted her to Columbus. Very little is known about Beatriz. Columbus never married her. He did, however, urge his sons to look after her. She was no lady of rank, as Felipa had been, and a man in his position needed his status as a widower who might possibly attract important people.

One of these was a friend of the queen, the Marquise de Moya, whom he met at court in Córdoba and with whom he also began an intense relationship. Historians have speculated that they were also lovers. But now that he was forced to follow the Talavera Commission to Salamanca, he had to leave both of them behind. This was particularly difficult because, sometime at the end of 1486, when Columbus was spending large amounts of his time in Salamanca, it became clear that Beatriz de Harana was also pregnant. Nine months later, she gave birth to a son, Ferdinand, his father's future biographer.

Salamanca in the late 1400s was a university of residential colleges, a little like Oxford and Cambridge, and there in St. Stephen's College—where its head became a close friend of Columbus—the commission finally met over Christmas 1486, and to his great relief Columbus was put briefly on the royal payroll. His appearances before the Talavera Commission have gone down in history as tremendous clashes between enlightenment and superstition. There is one story, probably mythical, that Columbus asked the commission how it was possible to make an egg stand on its end. When they were unable to answer him, he produced an egg and smashed in its end. "You see," he said. "You can do anything if you know how." But as in Lisbon, the argument was not that straightforward. Columbus was actually mistaken in his theory, as the experts correctly recognized. He was completely wrong about the size of the globe and the distance from Spain to China, and his stubbornness began to irritate the commission members.

But what infuriated Columbus—and would infuriate anyone blessed with a practical mind—was the way the commission preferred to concentrate on the theoretical aspects of his proposal rather than the practical ones. It irritated him that one of the leading members of the commission was a lawyer, not a navigator. Constantly hearing the phrase "St. Augustine doubts . . ." began to grate on his nerves.

It was true that St. Augustine, and other authorities, had doubted the existence of the Antipodes—how could the people who lived there be descended from Adam and Eve? Augustine and others had also argued that the equator was uninhabitable and so scorchingly hot that ships would simply combust. With growing irritation, Columbus retorted that the Portuguese had already ventured as far as the equator and had come back with nothing worse than a little sunburn. But the education of the commission members compared to his own unnerved him. He began to play up his own sense of divine calling, or switched suddenly to cracking inappropriate jokes. It was not a compelling mix.

Spain was the last attic of the last palace, said Peter Martyr, the historian, lecturing in Salamanca in 1488. But if it was the last attic, he said, then Italy was its main salon, the emporium of the world. Italy was the economic powerhouse that was driving the flow of goods, spices, and luxuries across Europe, and Vespucci was in charge of one of the engines. But Spain (Castile and Aragon) was more than that. The peninsula was on the very edge of the known world, and—slowly but surely—it was becoming involved in a trade at the very edges of morality. The Castilians, in particular, were also becoming drawn into a great evil, which would eventually overwhelm everything it touched.

In the Christian world it was the Genoese who started dealing in slaves, although the Muslim world had done so for centuries. Seeking out new markets after the closure of their Black Sea trading posts, the Genoese had anchored this speciality in their business colonies in Castile. None of the three merchant venturers at the heart of this story was free of the taint of slavery.

The reason slave trading was taking root in Spain was war. Slavery had always been bound up with piracy, and that was indistinguishable from the clash between East and West, between Christian and Muslim. Christian pirates lurked in the eastern Mediterranean waiting for Muslim galleys. Turkish slavers had been known to lie in wait in the Bristol Channel, ready to pounce on the regular pilgrim ships that sailed from Bristol to Santiago de Compostela in Spain, and to sell them into slavery. The Portuguese trade with Africa had begun to organize slavery into major businesses. The Genoese were controlling a huge flow of black slaves and had taken the trouble to get papal dispensation for slavery as early as 1452.

Cabot became involved before Columbus or Vespucci, during his trips to Egypt, but in Lisbon, the key organizer was a Florentine named Bartholomew Marchionni—a business associate of Lorenzo Berardi—who was rapidly emerging as the most important slave trader in the city, dominating the consignments of Africans that found themselves blinking on the quayside in the strange European light. In Castile the new slave trade city was Seville, which was close enough to the sea for the Guadalquivir to flow in both directions during the same day with the incoming and outgoing tides. Like Córdoba, it was decorated like a Moorish city, but it was fast becoming a Christian manufacturing city too. It was the center of Spanish soap production, a by-product of the olive groves all around the city, and there was a burgeoning ceramics industry using clay from the riverbanks. More dangerously, it was the headquarters of the Spanish Inquisition, its torture chambers filled with miserable Jewish tax collectors rotting in its cells, refusing to name the names of colleagues in fantastical conspiracies.

Columbus arrived in Seville while the Talavera Commission was considering its verdict, and found the city packed with foreigners, rubbing shoulders in the narrow streets and in the bars over their glasses of sweet Malaga wine. There was a German colony, which had set up a successful new printing press, and a major Jewish community, involved mainly in financial services. But the reason he went there was partly because Seville was now home to as many as one hundred Genoese merchants, filling the gaps left by the expulsion of Jews from the city in 1483, and partly because as a paid official in Queen Isabella's service he had some role in the sale of war booty for the Spanish. And war booty included slaves, which knitted him further into the business network of the slave-trader Gianotto Berardi.

The new king of England, the parsimonious Henry VII, made his first visit to the port of Bristol in the summer of 1496. He was greeted at the city gates by a colorful procession led by a man dressed as King Brennius, the mythical Trojan who had founded the city, even before Rome, or so its citizens believed. As he rode through Bristol's narrow streets, with its citizens wearing their best examples of the famous "Bristowe red," past the confluence of the rivers Avon and Frome, an enthusiastic housewife flung a sheaf of wheat down into the street in front of him, shouting, "Welcome and good luck!" After a generation of civil war, Henry had chosen a royal crest that included both the rival red and white roses of Lancaster and York. He carried about him a welcome whiff of stability, and commercial centers like Bristol were overjoyed about it.

The city fathers took him down to the docks, across the great bridge with its four huge arches and its sought-after houses and apartments built along it.

He was intended to see the dilapidated, rotting hulks at the wharves, and was told about the increasing difficulties they pose to the business of importing and exporting. Later in the day, Henry met the leading merchants on the city council, including many of the wealthy magnates behind the shadowy voyages of exploration to the west. The merchants had agreed between themselves that this was a vital opportunity to broach the tricky subject of trade with Iceland, which was still forbidden thanks to the agreement that Edward IV had made with the Hanseatic League and the Danish court. They also wanted to convey some idea of their financial difficulties, given the run of recent losses and wrecks. It was a convincing display, but Henry—who was famously suspicious of everybody's economic motives—was not won over. A little later in the visit, he pointed out that the main thing he had noticed was the fine display of jewelry around the necks of the merchants' wives. Despite what they claimed, Henry told them, they were earning money somewhere.

This was surely an unwelcome remark to the merchants, not only because of their frustration about the lost Icelandic profits, but also because they worried about how much Henry knew. It has been suggested by some historians that by then the explorations of the *Trinity* had born fruit, and that the Bristol merchants had in fact set up a small summer cod fishery somewhere on the other side of the Atlantic, maybe in Greenland. If this was so, they were realizing exactly what Columbus and Cabot had worked out for themselves—that simply discovering new lands was not enough. They needed some way of protecting their discovery so they could profit from it openly, and for that they needed a royal warrant, which is precisely what the Bristol merchants now lacked: Their 1480 license had expired, and they had not approached the new regime to renew it.

Henry took care of one other piece of business while he was in Bristol. He sacked Thomas Croft, the old friend of Edward IV, as customs officer for the port—the man who had done more than anyone to prepare the secretive voyages of exploration. He replaced him with a Welshman, like himself, a younger merchant based in the city, named Richard Amerike, a man who had built up his wealth and his collection of fine houses by pursuing other people's debts. He was not popular among those who ran the city.

When Henry returned to Bristol in 1490, the merchants changed their approach. They paved some of the main streets by the docks, where the rivers of Bristol converge, but they made sure there was no attempt to convince Henry that they were somehow suffering financially. In fact, there was a studious silence on the subject of trade with Iceland, despite the news that the Danes were now prepared once more to let Bristol traders do business there. Something was happening quietly among the divided merchants, though historians will probably never know exactly what.

Amerike was too close to the new Tudor dynasty for those behind the exploration westward to completely trust him. Whatever was really going on in Bristol, it was a closely guarded secret among the small cabal of merchants who had originally sent the *Trinity* on voyages of exploration. But there is one tantalizing clue. Some years later, when the dispatches of the Spanish ambassador in London were discovered, informing Columbus about what his former friend John Cabot was doing, Columbus was reminded of something they clearly both knew: that Bristol merchants had sent regular annual expeditions across the Atlantic for seven years—starting, in other words, in 1490—with the search for hy-Brasil and the Island of the Seven Cities. Somehow and somewhere, those who had dominated the stockfish trade from Iceland had quietly discovered a new source.

The great secret the Bristol elite was trying to protect from the king was that there was now an alternative plan to trade with Iceland. But, for now, they were only exploring. The first few voyages may have been unable to rediscover the enticing coastline of the islands that the *Trinity* had glimpsed in 1481 before Thomas Croft's arrest had undermined the whole project.

Still waiting for some answer from the Talavera Commission, Columbus was staying in Seville, but time was passing. He had now been in Castile for more than two years, most of that time spent waiting, with varying levels of impatience and irritation, for the commission to reach some conclusion. The welcome payments from the royal payroll seemed inexplicably to have stopped and he needed to find new sources of income, but the news was good from the front line. Malaga had fallen to the Spanish, and the victorious troops were marching into the city, and the queen was present, reviewing them on a prancing horse. There were flags fluttering in the breeze from every building; tapestries were hanging over the balconies, and pennants from the end of every lance. In the far distance, but visible across the plains, the spectacle was also watched by the Moors defending the city of Baza.

Columbus realized that this was a rare opportunity because every one of the inhabitants of Malaga—as many as fifteen thousand Muslims—had been taken into slavery. This was no small consignment and the Spanish needed merchants experienced in selling slaves to take responsibility for their distribution. He seems to have been involved in this with Berardi, not just because he was available—and theoretically employed in the service of the queen—but because many of the slave markets were in Lisbon. It has never been clear why he wanted to return to Portugal at this point, since he had left so furtively, but selling slaves from the war seems to have been the main reason. He may also have been thinking about Lisbon for other reasons too. Rumors had reached him about the abject failure of van Olmen's westward voyage of discovery. Having set sail from the Azores, the expedition had run into serious storms and the crew had been so terrified that they had been forced to turn back.

Columbus had talked to some of the great navigators of the age, so he may have guessed the reason for this failure—rather than chalk it up, as he tended to do, to the personal intervention of the Almighty on his behalf. He and Cabot had also sailed from the Azores with the Portuguese, and the truth was that the islands were too far north and voyages westward from there were liable to run into exactly the kind of perverse currents and adverse winds that the van Olmen expedition had encountered. Ironically, the success of Columbus's own expedition would depend on setting sail from the Castilian Canaries, far enough south to benefit from the circular currents that dominated the mid-Atlantic. Yet when the Castilian court proposed that he represent them in Lisbon—probably about selling slaves—he was prepared to consider it. The failure of van Olmen might open a new opportunity for him in Portugal now that the Talavera Commission showed no sign of a decision. He wrote to the Portuguese king and asked him for permission to return without the fear of arrest, either for debts or on any other espionage charges that might be outstanding, and in March 1488, John replied in friendly terms, welcoming him back and calling him "my dear friend":

"And if by chance you are in fear of our justice officials owing to some obligation you have incurred, we, by means of this letter can assure you that . . . you will not be arrested, detained, accused, summoned, or prosecuted, for any reason whatsoever."

Relations between Spain and Portugal were still strained. King John's scheme for an alliance with Yorkist England had come to nothing with the death of Richard III. The opportunity missed had been grasped instead by Ferdinand and the Spanish. Even now, there were two English diplomats at the Castilian court negotiating the marriage between Catherine of Aragon, his youngest child—then age four—and Arthur, Prince of Wales, the eldest son of Henry VII. But there were also plans to bring Castile and Portugal closer, with a marriage between Isabella's eldest daughter, Isabella, to Alfonso, crown prince of Portugal, and Columbus's visit may also have been connected to that.* Either way, as winter turned to spring, and the floodwaters of the Guadalquivir retreated, he made his way back along the same route by which he had originally come from Portugal.

As Christopher returned to Lisbon, his brother Bartholomew was suddenly free again, after at least eighteen months under lock and key. His health was broken, and owning nothing more than the clothes he was wearing, it is unclear how he made his escape. Perhaps he walked away; perhaps, more likely, his captors had given up ever earning back in ransom money what they were spending on keeping him alive. There must have been a real danger that they would simply kill him, for fear that he would reveal their hideaway. Perhaps, as his brother would have done, he convinced them that he was worth more to them as a grateful discoverer of the Indies than if he was left in prison to rot, or simply dumped in a shallow grave on the beach.

Whatever happened, Bartholomew managed to find enough resources to clothe himself and pay the master of a passing merchant ship to take him with them to London, where, half dead from malnutrition and all those other diseases of damp and despair, he was entirely at the mercy of the Genoese colony on the Thames.

Toward the end of 1488, Christopher Columbus watched as a small fleet of battered caravels sailed up the Tagus to dock in Lisbon. Both he and the crowd at the dockside were aware of the significance of their return, but

---

*The wedding never actually took place, because Alfonso was trampled to death by a horse in July 1491.

Columbus must have felt alone in his despondency. After a year and a half at sea, the exhausted crews acknowledged the cheers that signaled that the days of Henry the Navigator had returned. Older inhabitants said that it reminded them of the return of Gil Eanes or Antonio Nóli.

An interview was hastily arranged between the king and the triumphant expedition commander, the former pirate and slave trader Bartholomew Dias. It is hard to imagine that Columbus was deliberately invited to such a potentially secret meeting, knowing that he was now an agent of the Spanish sovereigns, but using his friends at court, he made sure he was there. It was an explosive historic event. Dias had sailed with two caravels and a stores ship in August 1487 to find a way around Africa to India. After surviving the most appalling weather, which drove him far to the south, he sailed eastward along the African coast until it was clear that Africa did not, after all, reach all the way to the Antarctic, and a sea route to India was possible. He came across the very tip of Africa on the voyage home, in May 1488, and named it the Cape of Storms.

The implications of what Dias had found sunk slowly into those around the room in John's palace, at least those who had not immediately understood when they heard the news of his return. The problem of the Indies was solved. The Indian Ocean was not landlocked as the geographers had feared. There was therefore a sea route to the spice trade that bypassed the Muslim stranglehold over both the Black Sea and Arabia. That was reason enough for John, there and then, to rename the Cape of Storms the Cape of Good Hope. Even so, the interview with Dias did not go as well as he had clearly hoped. John of Portugal was furious that he had turned back so soon, instead of pressing on up the east coast of Africa, and it would be Vasco da Gama not Dias who would be chosen later to lead the expedition to push through to the Indies.

But Columbus was congenitally optimistic, and the news was not all bad. Africa clearly extended much farther south than the Portuguese had hoped. The new route to the Indies was hardly a shortcut. Even so, Portugal was now a hopeless case as far as his own enterprise was concerned, because all their resources would now be concentrated on opening up the new trade route around Africa. There was no point in spending any more time in Lisbon. By the end of the year, Columbus had returned to Castile and changed

his name permanently to the Spanish Colón, with its deliberate hint of the
Roman consul Colonus, and was waiting for the endless Talavera Commission to reach some conclusion.*

"English girls are divinely pretty and they have one custom which cannot be
too much admired," wrote Erasmus on a visit to London a few years after
Bartholomew Columbus was there. "When you go anywhere on a visit, the
girls kiss you. They kiss you when you arrive. They kiss you when you go
away. They kiss you when you return. Once you have tasted how soft and
fragrant those lips are, you could spend your life there." This is not a view of
London that has passed down through history, nor do we have any idea
if this was the side of London that Bartholomew experienced on his visit
to the city. But in this delightful, confused, and dirty playground for rich
and poor, with its market gardens along the river outside the city walls,
Bartholomew began to recover some of his strength and to make contacts
outside the Genoese community.

It was now two months into 1489. Bartholomew had been in touch with
his brother—had probably even heard about Bartholomew Dias—and was
being urged to find some way of seeing the English king and discussing the
enterprise of the Indies with him. Physically fearless and impressively tall,
Bartholomew was later an effective deputy to his brother in the New World,
but he was younger, less experienced, and more careful than Christopher.
Even the most articulate son of a wool salesman would find it difficult to see
a foreign monarch.

By March 10, 1489, Bartholomew had been hanging around for months
in the court in Westminster, the royal palace to the west of the city. His
health had been improving steadily. The Genoese colony had been supporting him with advice and contacts, and he had been earning some money by
drawing maps and making globes. He was a particularly skillful globe maker. In
fact, his was the first generation, thanks to the spread of Ptolemy's *Geography*,

---

*There is one theory that Bartholomew joined his brother in Lisbon at this time and
used his access to official cartographers to secretly copy some of the most protected
maps. He is supposed to have smuggled these out on pieces of paper and tried to re-
assemble them back in Spain. This is possible but unlikely.

to have undertaken such a thing. He knew how to make spheres, and he knew how to paint them to demonstrate his brother's ideas.

In the three years since his first visit to Bristol, Henry VII had been establishing his authority on the creaking national administration, another modern prince in the mold of John of Portugal. He had also suppressed the most dangerous challenge to his rule, a Yorkist uprising led by a young man claiming to be the missing Richard of York—the younger son of Edward IV—one of the "Princes in the Tower" under the care of his uncle Richard III. The rebellion had been defeated in Stoke in June 1487, and the leader had turned out to be a young adventurer named Lambert Simnel. Henry pardoned him and set him to work in his kitchens for the rest of his life.

Henry was now thirty-one. He had been king for nearly four years, and although he used pageantry and color to great effect to bolster his own position, he was seriously short of money and by temperament parsimonious to the point of obsession.* He had no experience in administration, and the sophisticated financial control systems that Edward IV pioneered had collapsed after his death. Henry was a faithful husband and loving father with a passion for learning and music—the first English monarch to build a palace with a purpose-built library—but he was also reclusive, miserly, and suspicious of almost everyone around him.

Presumably through his Genoese trading contacts, Bartholomew was granted the interview with the king that he had been seeking. He weighed himself down with charts, like his brother had done at the Spanish court, practiced his arguments, and prepared himself with angles that might be favorable to the English. To clinch the deal, Bartholomew had lavished attention on a beautiful world map to present to the king, bearing an inscription that was designed to tantalize, but probably simply irritated.

> Thou which desirest easily the coast of land to know,
> This comely and right learnedly the same to thee will shew:
> Which Strabo, Plinie, Ptolemey and Isodore maintaine:
> Yet, for all that, they do not all in one accord remaine.
> Here also is set downe the late discovered burning zone
> By Portingals, unto the world which whilom was unknown,

---

*He dressed his bodyguard of old soldiers in red with flat black caps. Their successors still wear something similar, and are known as the Yeomen of the Guard or Beefeaters.

*Whereof the knowledge now at lengthe thorow all the world is blown.*

This piece of fifteenth-century marketing reveals Bartholomew's lack of experience. But it was also an approach that showed the brothers had learned from their hearings in Lisbon and Salamanca, where they had been confronted with church fathers, like St. Augustine, and other authorities, and how their evidence conflicted with the proposal. In London, they tried an alternative tack: They began by quoting authorities—only these were the challenging classical authorities of ancient Rome and Greece so beloved during the Renaissance. They were intended to seem modern and, if not exactly free-thinking, then at least intellectually challenging.

It was, as ever, a bad moment. Parliament was locked into a marathon forty-one-day argument about a £100,000 request for new archers for a possible war against France. Henry VII was also not known for his sense of humor, though his treatment of Simnel, slaving away in his kitchens, suggests that he had one. And like all the crowned heads consulted by the Columbus brothers, he seemed both intrigued and uncertain how to proceed. He kept the map and had it examined by his own panel of experts, who quickly advised Henry to reject the idea. But Henry was not sure he wanted to reject it, and it certainly made sense not to drive this young man into the arms of a rival court. He therefore delayed a final decision and left Bartholomew once again wandering aimlessly around London, earning what he could and waiting for a final decision that seemed unlikely ever to arrive.

Christopher was back in Spain and close to despair. He had turned his back on his lucrative slave-trading contacts in Seville to go back to Lisbon to represent the queen for a year, but found he had simply been forgotten there and his allowance from Isabella had dried up completely. Columbus was now too obsessed with the enterprise of the Indies to put his mind to anything else, yet time after time his ambitions were thwarted.

He was also becoming increasingly religious, saying his prayers with an almost trancelike devotion. He had forsaken swearing—now he never said anything worse than "May God take you!"—and constantly reminded himself that, although he believed he had enemies everywhere, he must not hate them. "He wished nothing more than that those who offended against him should recognize their errors," said his son later, a peculiarly irritating stance to take for any of his sparring partners. Only the monks seemed to remain the least bit supportive. "He alone never treated my ideas with ridicule," said Columbus later about Antonio Marchena from La Rábida.

Inevitably, it was not a very good time to return to Castile. There was disease among the ranks of the army outside Granada at Santa Fé. Ferdinand was directing the siege of the Moorish city of Baza, and it was obvious that there would be no clear decision until the Granada campaign was completely over. Even that would have been comforting if the Talavera Commission had come to any conclusion at all, but it seemed in no hurry to do so, aware that the queen would like them to approve the enterprise yet unable intellectually to do so. But what could Christopher do? He had no money so couldn't hang around the court forever. One story suggests that he joined the army outside Baza. But when Baza finally fell, on December 4, 1489, his true situation had come home to him. He was completely ignored.

Cabot was in Milan, together with his family. This was the city that was electrified at the time by the wedding of Isabella of Aragon to the duke, the slightly feebleminded Gian Galeazzo Sforza. It was a sumptuous affair, with fireworks, music, and pageantry, but the heart of it was an extraordinary masquerade representing paradise, together with a riot of music, movement, and color, organized by Leonardo da Vinci.

Milan was known as the orchard of Italy. It combined the urban modernity of one of the most important financial centers of Europe with all the exotic charm of pomegranates, lilacs, roses, and pineapples, and more than a whiff of Persian-style sophistication. Gian Galeazzo Sforza was nominally the ruler, but in practice, the decisions were made by his powerful uncle Ludovico, known as "the Moor" because of his dark complexion. Ludovico in turn passed on many of the day-to-day decisions to his astrologer—he was wildly superstitious—while he spent most of his time with a succession of mistresses. Ludovico's ambition was to turn Milan into a new Athens. His agents were scouring Europe to bring back treasures for the Castello, attracting people like Cabot to build the new wonders and the future architect of St. Peter's in Rome, Donato Bramante, to design them.

Leonardo was another footloose genius attracted by the glamour of Milan in the 1480s. He had become frustrated with his life in Florence—the prosecution for homosexuality he had faced ten years earlier, his father's crowded house—and embittered by his failure to be included among the artists invited to decorate the Sistine Chapel. When Botticelli and the others packed their bags for Rome, Leonardo had written to Sforza offering his services as an engineer of war machines. His letter of application claimed that he could make bridges that were "indestructible by fire and battle" and "chariots, safe and unassailable." He barely mentioned painting and never mentioned music at all. Yet it was as a musician that he eventually made the journey north to Milan, carrying with him a lute he had made himself. And, in keeping with this ambiguity about his future role, he was soon employed on a variety of projects, including the wedding celebrations for the poor sidelined duke and his bride, later building her a luxurious silver bath.

When Leonardo arrived in 1481, Milan was still at war with Venice, and the Castello was the epicenter of Sforza power. His war machines were never built, as far as historians know, but Leonardo was given enormous freedom to conduct experiments, dissect animal and human cadavers, fill his sketchbooks, and make plans. One of these was a scheme to build an enormous statue of Ludovico's father on a horse, and Leonardo's failure to make progress with it infuriated the duke. A cast was completed, but—since it required eighty tons of bronze, which not even a Sforza could afford—the life-sized equestrian statue, probably the biggest to date, waited for its chance to be transmuted into metal.

Another of the freelance exiles around the Sforza court who Cabot must have encountered was Piero Vespucci, Amerigo's disgraced cousin, still banished from Florence for his small part in the Pazzi plot. He was now a gentleman-in-waiting to the Sforza family and increasingly trusted with difficult assignments. One of these, while Cabot was also living in Milan, involved leading a punitive expedition to the small town of Alessandria. There, Piero was captured by local outlaws and hanged from a balcony like the Pazzi plotters. When the rope snapped accidentally, he was finished off with daggers.

When Cabot heard that instructions were arriving at the Milanese court to arrest him for debt, he must have despaired. In Milan, he had some kind of future, working on construction projects for Ludovico. He may not have bargained that his creditors in Venice—the former associates behind the English cloth deal that went so wrong—would be so determined. Milan was just too close to Venice. What could he do?

Cabot chose the small but sophisticated kingdom of Savoy, partly cut off by the Alps, between Italy and France, and ruled at the time by King Charles I—known as "the Warrior"—and then, nominally at least, the hereditary exiled Christian king of Jerusalem.* We have no records of what Cabot did there, or how long he stayed, except that it was probably less than a year. But if he believed the Alps offered some protection, he was mistaken. Soon the news of where he was reached Venice and the letters demanding his arrest began to arrive in Savoy. There was little support he could expect as a newcomer, and once again, it was time for him to leave.

We do not know when or why his arrangement with the Columbus brothers came to an end. Was it when they failed to engage the Portuguese court in 1484, or when Cabot failed to find the sources of the spice trade in 1485? Whichever, Cabot's sojourn in Milan and Savoy—so far from the sea—implied that it was indeed over. If it was not, he would have been in Castile or somewhere else where he could have helped the cause. It is possible that he was trying to raise money in both those cities, but he could have made a greater impact in London where Bartholomew Columbus, who knew almost nobody, was still eking out a living among the Genoese. Cabot had connections in London—albeit through his creditors—and he should have been there to help. Instead, he was moving from city to city, dragging his wife and three children along with him.

Even so, the decision about where to go next seems to have been influenced by his determination to get back into the race. And if it hadn't been a race before—when he was working with the Columbus family—it was one now that he was working alone. There really was no alternative but to base himself somewhere on the Iberian peninsula, with access to navigators, merchants, and ocean-going investors. So, packing up his family once more and making his way to the coast—probably to Marseilles—he took a small ship down the coast to Valencia, the thriving seaport in Aragon with its plethora of printing presses.

---

*The Royal House of Savoy are also the ancestors of what became the royal house of Italy, until 1946, when King Victor Emmanuel III abdicated and went into exile.

He chose Valencia because it was the center for the cloth and fur trade in the Mediterranean, which was his primary area of expertise, but also because there were possibilities for other kinds of development. The records of Cabot's negotiations over a major harbor-building program there implies that he knew a development project was possible, and this kind of contracting seemed a suitable way of making money. It required no investment, used skills that he possessed, and paid a simple salary. Valencia may have been suffering from an outbreak of plague—as he discovered when he arrived sometime in the summer of 1490—but it was reassuringly distant from his creditors, and it was a potential base from which he could plan and equip an enterprise of the Indies all his own.

## II

*"Know then that this opinion is untrue,*
*For it is possible to sail on,*
*Since the sea everywhere is flat,*
*Even though the earth be round of form."*

LUIGI PULCI, a poet and friend
of the Vespucci family, 1481

Going over the accounts for the Popolano from their agent in Seville, Tommaso Caponi, Vespucci realized that there was something missing. There were irregularities everywhere and it was not clear where Caponi's trade in velvets, satins, damasks, and taffetas for the Popolano ended and his business for other merchants began. Over a period of months, Vespucci asked for documents, but even those did not address his central questions.

The Popolano were tough about money. They really trusted nobody but him with their business, and they were keen to rid themselves of Caponi altogether. Vespucci struggled with the vague answers he was receiving from Caponi and then suggested Lorenzo di Pierfrancesco consider replacing Caponi with a trader he'd heard of named Gianotto Berardi. "Find out what sort of person he is, and whether, in your opinion, he is trustworthy," wrote Lorenzo as Vespucci prepared to leave. "If you decide he is, he could replace Tommaso."

Vespucci did not go to Seville himself. He was involved in a court action in October 1489 and could not get away, but he was finally able to immerse himself in Caponi's documents. Double-entry bookkeeping was in its infancy, and most merchants kept what they called a *ricordanze*, a sort of business diary in which political developments, currency values, and investments were all recorded.* Caponi's books, such as they were, only confirmed Vespucci's concerns. Through intermediaries, he made contact with and approved of Berardi, who was just launching into a new business venture in the Canary Islands that dealt in indigo and also in the indigenous population, which had now been reduced to slavery. From then on, Berardi would also be the Popolano's agent in Seville.

All his life, Vespucci had dreamed of western exploration, and although he was not actually in Seville, the shadow of Columbus, who often was at that time, selling his remaining books and charts to raise a little money, was beginning to loom over his life. Now at last he was in contact with people who could almost smell the Atlantic, communicating to or about men who were taking practical steps to make the journey. He was now nearly thirty-seven years old. The distant whiff of Seville had got under his skin, and it seemed like the right moment to change his future and go to Seville himself.

The homes of the two branches of the Medici family have gone down in history for their enlightenment, for the skeptical questioning philosophy they developed, and for the poetry and the extraordinary art they commissioned. They have been praised for their intellectual and prototypical liberalism, the way they fostered a taste for beauty, their satire, and their wisdom. But there was also a Medici dark side, and Vespucci—well acquainted with both Medici households—knew it as well as anybody. Florence was nominally a republic, but in the name of that ideal, the city was actually ruled by an oligarch, who though enlightened was an oligarch nonetheless. He was also one whose hold on the economic future of the city was faltering: Both the Medici bank, and the coffers of the Florentine state, were diminished

---

*The definitive manual for bookkeeping was being written at that very moment by a friar called Luca Pacioli, later a friend of Leonardo in Milan. It was to stay widely in print for the next four centuries.

and in decline. Repeated bad harvests and rumors of wars had taken their toll. Lorenzo may have been magnificent, but he never had the sure instincts his ancestors had for making money.

Meanwhile, both the bright magnificence and dark underside of Medici Florence were producing personalities who would dazzle their contemporaries, and Vespucci must have known them. One was a young man named Michelangelo Buonarotti. His master Ghirlandaio never recognized his talents, but his friends did, and it was they who arranged for him to work in the gardens of the convent of St. Mark—where Vespucci's uncle Giorgio kept the library—to help look after the sculptures made by Donatello that had been collected there.

Under the benevolent eye of Lorenzo the Magnificent, the gardens had become a sculpture school, and it was here that Lorenzo and young Michelangelo came face-to-face for the first time. Discussing the head of a fawn, Lorenzo suggested that it should perhaps lack a few teeth. When the Magnificent found that a skillful cavity had been carved the next time he passed that way, he sensed the genius of whoever had done it and invited Michelangelo to live with him in the Medici palace so he could oversee his progress personally. The fifteen-year-old Michelangelo was given his own room, a black velvet mantle, and some pocket money, and there he wandered through the library, befriending the other members of the wider Medici circle like Ficino and Poliziano.

The other extraordinary personality was Girolamo Savonarola, the Dominican friar whose sermons on the corruption of the church had begun to attract attention in northern Italy—so much attention that Lorenzo the Magnificent had invited him back to Florence. He made the journey on foot, collapsing with exhaustion on the road south.* Savonarola began a new dramatic series of sermons in Florence in August 1490, describing a Roman Catholic Church corrupt to its very core and Italy as a spiritual wilderness. And, like an Old Testament prophet, he predicted a coming disaster. The sermons immediately began to either inspire or enrage his audiences in almost equal amounts.

*He is supposed to have been rescued by a stranger who took him all the way to the city gate at Florence, and left him, saying, "remember to do that for which God hath sent you."

Savonarola

By the following spring, he was one of the most famous people in Florence. At Easter, the Duomo, the striped cathedral at the heart of the city, was packed to hear him tearing into the morality of the Church—using lines that would a generation later be developed by Martin Luther—and terrifying his congregations with the moral force of his rhetoric. It was said that women in the congregation regularly began to scream and weep. Even the most cynical men began to shiver.

Steeped in tolerance, and sympathizing with those Platonists around him working for the unity of Christianity and Islam, we can guess Vespucci's distrust of the religious revival that began to grip his city. His old neighbor Botticelli even began to destroy his pagan paintings. Michelangelo's elder brother was inspired to become a monk. Even the worldly, but now sick, poet Poliziano was a convert to the cause of purity. Women dressed in white, carrying red crucifixes, and parading through the city weeping for forgiveness became a familiar sight in Florence. This was the summer where the very public effort to build the gigantic Strozzi Palace in the center of the city left heaps of dust and rubble in the surrounding streets, a potent symbol of luxury and waste. But something extraordinary was happening as well, and one look at the papacy was enough to see why. The extremes of corruption suddenly became unbearable to a section of the population, many of whom had benefited the most. They sent their children out on demonstrations to purify the city. They lit bonfires and burned the accoutrements of luxury, Botticelli's pagan pictures, Leonardo's musical instruments, and anything else considered sinful.

But not only was Savonarola predicting the destruction of the current papacy, he was also predicting an imminent end to the Medici rule over supposedly republican Florence. And when the monks of St. Mark's, which was also home to Vespucci's uncle Giorgio, elected Savonarola to lead them as prior that summer, he refused to carry out a diplomatic call on Lorenzo the Magnificent. He rose further in people's estimation, and in the estimation of the Popolano family: Savonarola's extraordinary rhetoric was also an opportunity to undermine the dictatorship of their Medici cousins. Even Giorgio began to support the friar.

But Amerigo's other mentor was fearful about where this religious hysteria would lead. Ever the diplomat, Guido Antonio Vespucci called on Savonarola with four other city leaders and urged him to meet Lorenzo the Magnificent. The new prior was not sympathetic. "You have come to tell me that you have come here on your own initiative," he said from inside his cell. "You lie. You are here because Lorenzo has sent you here. Go back to him, tell him to comply with the will of God. Tell him he will go and I will remain here in Florence to purify it."


Back again in close contact with his brother, Bartholomew Columbus had decided that it was pointless to prolong his stay in London. King Henry VII had not absolutely closed the door on a commission to sail westward, but there was clearly little chance that he would help finance the voyage. Since Africa was recently found to have a southern tip, the Portuguese were unlikely to support an Atlantic voyage, and Columbus had almost given up hope in Castile. That meant going to the only other place with an Atlantic coast: France and the peripatetic court of the young French king Charles VIII.

Charles was the son of the Spider King. He had inherited the throne six years earlier at the tender age of twelve. He was never strong physically, and he never looked like a king either, any more than his father had. He had bizarrely thick lips; a long, pointed nose, and long, spindly legs. He spoke very slowly and was extremely nearsighted. He was not the first choice of royal sponsor for the enterprise of the Indies, but who else was there?

So Bartholomew crossed the English Channel, armed with whatever contacts he had managed to broker from the Genoese community in London with the French court. His finesse with the English did not single him out as especially skillful in selling himself. But he made an absolutely vital friend at the French court: the king's sister. She was in contact with members of the Spinola family, who had an office in London's Lombard Street where Bartholomew had wandered in search of support, and this was precisely the stroke of luck he needed.

Anne of Beaujeu was twenty-eight and at the height of her considerable powers. Her husband was officially the regent while her brother was a child, but her father had known that by appointing him, he was actually handing over power to his formidable daughter. She had dark eyes, high intelligence, and the same long Valois nose that dominated her younger brother's face. She also had enormous experience of the court under her father, and from an early age knew and learned from those who could remember riding into battle with Joan of Arc. She was brilliant at manipulating those who could have become more powerful than she. It was her decision to move the court so often, originally as a way of preempting any attempt by one of the rival factions in the French aristocracy to kidnap Charles while he was young.

Traveling with the French court was an exhausting business. Every fortnight, when the long procession began to snake its way through the countryside, as many as four thousand members, with their merchants, servants, and horses, went by for a period of hours, watched by cattle, wild boar, and open-mouthed peasants staring from the fields. Also with them was Bartholomew, but in a place of greater honor and safety, with her vast array of dogs and parrots, was Marguerite of Austria, only a child, but betrothed to the young king.

Bartholomew Columbus was an urban animal: He knew his way around the great ports of Europe—Genoa, Lisbon, and London—but France was his first real brush with rural life, and often it was an impoverished sight. The abandoned farms and churches, the result of the war, that Vespucci had seen ten years earlier were all still in evidence. But a new generation of chateaux was appearing too, built not by the nobles who were usually heavily in debt but by the new merchant classes. Thanks to his years in captivity and his winters in London, Bartholomew was beginning to get used to the perils of the cold in northern Europe. Vast quantities of wood were loaded up and fed into the fires. Too far away from a fire after nightfall in the long winter evenings, huddled in coats and hats, and you were liable to freeze. Too close to the fire and you were liable to fry.

But despite this discomfort, Bartholomew had managed to entrance the clever Anne of Beaujeu, and so through the summer of 1490 and until the court finally moved to Moulins in the Auvergne for Christmas, Bartholomew was with them and encouraged by her. Anne was immensely strategic, but her grip on power was coming to an end. Charles was almost of age. Eight-year-old Marguerite of Austria was about to be sent home in tears when he decided to marry Anne of Brittany. Not only were Charles's obsessive sexual conquests becoming more evident, but left to his own devices, that letter to him from the desperate doge of Venice suggesting an invasion of Italy still on his mind, he would choose not a voyage of westward discovery but a perilous military expedition across the Alps.

As Bartholomew arrived in Moulins, his brother was facing yet another disappointment in Castile. Rousing themselves from their stupor, the Talavera Commision finally gave its verdict. They were aware that Isabella would have liked a more favorable report, but they were too nervous about the consequences of making a mistake. Both Columbus and the court were in Seville for Christmas in 1490, and as Christopher desperately awaited news from Bartholomew he must have begun to fear the worst about his own plans. According to Talavera and his advisers, the enterprise of the Indies was a concoction of "colossal errors." The commission "judged his promises and offers were impossible and vain and worthy of rejection" and "not a proper object for their royal authority to favor an affair that rested on such weak foundations, and which appeared uncertain and impossible to any educated person, however little learning he might have."

That barb about "educated persons" was calculated to go straight to the heart of Columbus's insecurities, but the actual decision was worse. The western ocean was infinite and probably unnavigable, they said. If you reached the Antipodes, it would be impossible to get back again. Most of the globe was covered by water, and if there were any unknown lands left undiscovered in the world, they were unlikely to have any value. It was a complete trashing of his plan.*

But Columbus was left with a glimmer of hope. Isabella refused to reject the idea outright and said it would be reconsidered once Granada was safely in Christian hands. But there was a limit to the length of time Columbus was prepared to wait for Isabella, and the early months of 1491 were spent trying to decide whether he should stay and beg the queen again for an audience or join Bartholomew to close the deal in France. Bartholomew was still moving pointlessly from chateau to chateau with the French court, snatching the very occasional audience with his patron, and made aware by the court gossip of the growing independence of the young king now that the main threat to his power, the pretender to the throne, Louis of Orleans, had been outmaneuvered. It was becoming urgent to make some kind of decision before Anne's power and influence slipped away. By the summer of 1491, Christopher had decided to concentrate on France and made the grueling journey, mainly on foot—he could no longer afford any other mode of transport—to La Rábida to fetch Diego from the care of the friars, ready to leave Castile for good.

Once more, Columbus arrived at Huelva and made the exhausting trip up the cliff by foot. For a second time he rang the bell on the door of the friary, penniless and exhausted.

*Talavera was appointed archbishop of Granada after the city fell, and aroused the fury of the Inquisition for his tolerance toward Muslims. When his protector, the queen, died, they imprisoned him.

# 5

# TRIUMPH AND DISASTER

*"This night of October 11–12 was one big with destiny for the human race, the most momentous ever experienced aboard any ship in any sea."*

SAMUEL ELIOT MORISON, *Admiral of the Ocean Sea*

*"If you can meet with Triumph and Disaster*
*And treat those two impostors just the same . . ."*

RUDYARD KIPLING, *If*

IT WAS THE second day of 1492, and the royal standard of the sovereigns of Castile and Aragon was flying from the walls of Granada, and from the topmost towers of the Alhambra palace inside. The city had fallen to the Christians and the era of Moorish Spain was at an end. In the final months of the previous year, King Boabdil of Granada had decided the situation was hopeless. He had spent the past fifteen years desperately patching up bitter divisions between his father and the Muslim court. Part of that time was spent in exile in Christian Castile. He knew that if Ferdinand was allowed to storm the city, then everything would be lost. The garrison would be massacred and the Muslim population sold into slavery. But there was still one chance: a negotiated settlement that handed over the city to the Christians, but which protected the rights of the Muslims. With the agreement of his nearest advisers, but the bitter opposition of his mother, Boabdil sent messages out to Santa Fé that he was prepared to surrender.

Through October 1491, secret negotiations set out an agreement that would allow the population of Granada to keep their mosques and to dress as Muslims. They would be allowed to keep their language and customs and be judged by Muslim law. The agreement even stipulated that disputes between a Christian and Muslim would have to be heard in court presided over by judges of both religions. It was an agreement unprecedented in its liberalism, and the date for handing over the city was set for Epiphany. But under the same terms, Muslim prisoners began returning to Granada, bringing rumors of the impending surrender and, at Christmas, riots began breaking out around the Alhambra. There was no choice, Boabdil decided, but to move the date up, and he urgently sent messengers the six miles across the military lines to Santa Fé.

And so it was that on January 2, Columbus watched the triumphant and colorful procession as Isabella and Ferdinand rode side by side, followed by thousands of soldiers and knights with banners, and riding behind them the whole Castilian aristocracy, with their golden spurs and their lances and armor glinting in the fitful sunshine. They were met by Boabdil carrying the keys to the city. Ferdinand took them and handed them to Isabella and the procession continued toward the last Muslim city in Spain.

Boabdil and his companions stopped at a spot known as the Hill of Tears, where the king glanced back at his lost kingdom and the palace that is still one of the wonders of Europe, tears streaming down his face. "You do well to grieve like a woman," said his mother, without pity, "for what you could not defend like a man."*

The news reached Florence a few days later and celebratory bonfires for a great Christian victory were lit all over the city. It was missed by Vespucci, who had already sailed for Barcelona and his new life. But in Rome the Aragonese cardinal Rodrigo Borgia, then dean of the College of Cardinals, held a bullfight in the city—a Spanish custom never seen in Italy before. There was already a sense around Europe that 1492 was going to be an extraordinary year.

---

*Boabdil was given a title in Castile but moved soon afterward to Morocco where he lived until 1527. His former subjects rose against their Castilian masters in 1499 and the liberal surrender terms were abandoned. This was not yet the era for tolerance.

. . .

In the weeks after Columbus made his last despairing journey to La Rábida to pick up Diego and leave Castile, events had unraveled at frightening speed. Arriving at the familiar front door of the monastery, ready to ask for financial support to join his brother in France, he was taken instead to see one of the most influential monks, Juan Pérez, to whom he poured out his frustrations.

The monks at La Rábida had been his most consistent supporters, and Pérez urged him to reconsider going to France. To add weight to his arguments, he sent a message to nearby Palos and asked one of the local shipowners, Martin Alonso Pinzón, to come and offer some advice. It was the first fateful meeting between the two men, and Pinzón agreed with Pérez that Columbus should not give up on the Castilians yet. They no doubt pointed to France's lack of a tradition in exploration and their shortage of expertise. And then Pérez made an offer. He was another former confessor to the queen, and he promised to arrange another audience for Columbus if he would stay in Castile for one more throw of the dice.

Isabella was then at Sante Fé, preparing for the siege of Granada. Pérez found a mule and set off by himself on a grueling journey to the front line. He told Isabella how poor Columbus was and that he was on the verge of giving up. She agreed to see Columbus and sent money for him to buy some clothes and another mule on which to make the journey. She even agreed to pay him for two years of service in Portugal working on her behalf.

Columbus set off as soon as Pérez returned with the exciting news. His new suit of clothes was delivered to Sante Fé in the searing heat of August 1491. This time he presented the monarchs with a new map, with details that Bartholomew had gleaned from his stay in England, and which Columbus had been working on in the long, depressing weeks since returning from Lisbon. The map included the Island of the Seven Cities, following the rumors of its discovery by the Bristol merchants and shown looking remarkably like Newfoundland—more evidence that the secretive Bristol voyages had found something.

Isabella was friendly. But to Columbus's horror, she referred the project to yet another committee of astronomers and mariners. He must have felt he was fated to live his life in continuous circles, and he settled down with great frustration, ignoring the looks of the other hangers-on at court. But this time, there was to be no repeat of the Talavera Commission. These experts realized the political nature of the decision they were being asked to make, and referred it immediately to the Royal Council of Castile.

So as summer turned to fall, with every eye fixed on the beleaguered garrison in Granada, Columbus waited for the Royal Council to decide his fate. As he watched the celebrations as the city fell in January 1492, and the unprecedented procession across the plain to take possession, he knew a decision could not be far off. But when it finally came a few days later, he was told by officials that Castile was facing absolute bankruptcy because of the war. For that reason, they said, they rejected the plan. There was just no money to finance it. A dejected Pérez and Columbus retrieved their mules and slipped through the west gate of Santa Fé on the long journey back to La Rábida. The enterprise of the Indies would now be offered, rather hopelessly, to France.

It is not difficult to reconstruct something of the conversation between Columbus and Pérez as they made their way through the wintry Spanish landscape, their bitterness and frustration, and the divisions between them: Had he, Columbus, hinted too much at the unprecedented honors he would demand as the discoverer of the Indies? How could merchants profit from the discovery? Was it inevitable that the new king of France would accept the proposal, when all the other crowned heads of western Europe had refused? After four miles along the road to Córdoba, they reached the small village of Pinos-Puente. There was a clatter of hooves behind them, then a call. It was clear that something had taken place after they left Santa Fé.

Having watched the pathetic figures ride out on their mules, the keeper of the privy purse, the banker Luis de Santangel, had sought out Isabella. The proposal that Columbus put forward, and the rewards he looked likely to stipulate, would be extremely expensive, but they could also have enormously beneficial consequences. If any other country successfully found a different way to the Indies, it could be deeply damaging to Castile, so the cost was well worth the risk. Columbus would get none of the rewards he was hinting at if he failed. If he succeeded, they would be cheap at the price. Santangel explained that he had become convinced that it was in the national interest to let Columbus try. He believed this so strongly, he said, that he would finance the expedition himself.

Isabella protested that that would not be necessary. "I will pledge the crown jewels if I have to," she said. In fact, she had already done this to pay for the siege of Baza. They were in Santangel's own bank, as both of them must have known. But the mood had changed, and a messenger was sent after Columbus to bring him back.

Bolstered by the capture of the last Muslim outpost in Spain, Ferdinand and Isabella had decided to take the risk of tackling the Jews. Their mass expulsion from Spain in 1492 is one of the great crimes of Europe, but it was linked both to the fall of Granada and the decision to send Columbus westward. While Columbus was negotiating his settlement with the Castilian court, the finishing touches were being put on the edict of expulsion, published on March 31. All were a direct result of the same triumphal mood, and of the messianic romanticism that Isabella and Columbus shared.

Under the terms of the edict, Castile's and Aragon's Jewish communities were ordered to convert to Christianity or leave the country within three months and were told they could take no gold or silver with them. Within weeks, in every city in Spain, there would be the pathetic sights of Jewish

A later engraving showing Columbus being seen off by Ferdinand and Isabella

families desperately exchanging their homes for a donkey, or their land for a few scraps of cloth, gathering together for the long journey south to the ports. Oblivious to the emerging human tragedy—a serious miscalculation on behalf of Ferdinand and Isabella, who thought most would simply agree to be baptized—Columbus was setting out his demands, strengthened by his firm belief that negotiations were also coming to a head in France between Bartholomew and Charles VIII.

Pérez acted as his negotiator, but he must have blanched when he heard Columbus's proposal in detail. He wanted to be appointed admiral—a Moorish term giving jurisdiction over dockyards and fleets—over the Atlantic, and for this title to be inherited by his heirs. He wanted to be viceroy and governor over anywhere he found, and he demanded a tenth of all the gold, silver, pearls, gems, and spices he brought home, tax free, on the grounds that if he really found a route to the Indies, all this would be a small price to pay. The so-called capitulations were finally agreed to on April 17.

There was also the problem of how to afford the original investment in the expedition by the crown. There was a peace dividend, but Isabella was also in the process of expelling from the country most of those involved in financial services. If the wealthy Jews were gone, who could they borrow money from? The cost of fitting out the expedition was estimated at 2 million maravedis, of which the crown managed to find 1.4 million, which had been set aside by the federation of Castilian cities to pay for the war. The royal officials also began to trawl through other accounts and found a court decision that instructed the port of Palos to provide two caravels for royal service for one year. Despite the protests from Palos, transfering these to the enterprise was a simple matter. They were the sixty-ton *Niña* and the similar *Pinta*.*

Santangel invested considerable sums, and Columbus himself contributed 250,000 maravedis. Here Columbus was very lucky to be in the right place at the right time. His friend Gianotto Berardi happened to be in Santa Fé with his new partner, Amerigo Vespucci—just arrived from Florence—trying to get approval from the crown to invade the island of Palma in the Canaries on behalf of a business consortium that also included Santangel. Berardi was

---

*A ton originally meant the number of "tuns," or pipes, of wine a ship was capable of carrying. It is impossible to say precisely what the equivalent of a maravedis was in modern money, but in terms of its ability to buy unskilled labor, a maravedi seemed to have power similar to a U.S. dollar today.

therefore on the spot to provide the financing for Columbus to invest in his own voyage, and to form a company with him to manage the undertaking. Vespucci was able to confirm that this investment showed foresight. He immediately recognized the idea of a westward route to the Indies as stemming from Toscanelli, his old teacher. It might be a risk, but the idea was not insane. Berardi, Columbus, and Vespucci formed a company to manage the investment, and raised the necessary finance from the Medici Bank.

A crew would cost another 250,000 maravedis every month they were away. In Castille anyone could be a sailor, and the poor often found that they'd be better fed working aboard a ship than begging in some alleyway. Portuguese regulations insisted that anyone going to sea needed to first develop some relevant skills. But in Spain, where every ship had rats, simply procuring a cat to control the problem was considered skill enough. And anyone who agreed to sail out on this dangerous voyage had any prosecutions against them suspended. But it was the intervention of the other captains—Juan de la Cosa who owned the *Santa Maria*, leased as flagship, and two brothers, Martin Alonso Pinzón and Vicente Yáñez Pinzón, both respected seafarers from Palos—who made the difference in persuading men to join crews.

Rather peculiarly, the actual owner of the *Pinta*, a merchant from Palos named Cristobál Quintero, was so determined to come on the expedition— or so determined to keep an eye on his ship—that he signed up for the voyage as an ordinary seaman. It was an unconventional voyage, and in strictest secrecy, Columbus and his captains struggled to equip the fleet as soon as possible before the summer was too far gone.


Vespucci had made the decision to leave Florence at the end of 1491, and the divisions that were emerging in the city were making him more certain with every day that it was the right thing to do. There were also divisions within his own family: Of his two beloved mentors, Giorgio had taken vows to enter the monastery with Savonarola, while Guido Antonio stayed loyal to the Medici. Amerigo himself would stay employed by the Popolano family, but he would not work exclusively for them, and he now knew for certain what he had agonized over for a decade: His heart lay elsewhere. If he was going to play a role in the discovery of Cathay and Cipangu, he needed to be in Seville, with the Florentine community on the Atlantic coast. So over Christmas in 1491, still ignorant of the dramatic project that was about to come to fruition, he was saying farewell to his mistress and his daughter, making promises to them and his family of continued love and support, and packing his most treasured possessions and charts. By the end of January 1492 he was in Barcelona with his young nephew Giovanni, sorting out a problem with one of the Popolano's consignments of salt that was stuck at the quayside in need of a ship.

He then sailed down the coast to Cadiz before finally making his way to Seville to find a home and an office and to track down Berardi and discuss possibilities for the future. The two men immediately took to each other and before long Vespucci was being included in Berardi's schemes—one of which, as we have seen, involved working closely with Columbus and his preparations for the voyage.

In fact, there was another reason why Vespucci was glad to have left Florence. At some point he would have had to choose between the different branches of the Medici family, and in the first few weeks of 1492, that choice was made more urgent: It was becoming clear that Lorenzo the Magnificent was dangerously ill. Through the spring, he became weaker as a mysterious disease took hold. A succession of doctors arrived to treat him, bringing in the most exotic medicines. There were doses of ground-up pearls and precious stones, all—perhaps not surprisingly—having no effect.* In early April, he went to bed in his villa at Careggi outside Florence and could not get up. When it was clear that he was dying, he asked Savonarola to visit him, to come face-to-face for the first time with the man who fulminated in his pulpit against him, Sunday after Sunday.

Savonarola asked him two questions. Would he hold to the faith? Lorenzo said he would. Would he amend his life if he recovered? Again, Lorenzo said he would. Then he urged him to meet death with resignation. "Nothing should please me better should it be God's will," he said, and his great rival blessed him and said the prayers for the dying. In a letter a few weeks later, Poliziano claimed that Savonarola told him to give Florence back its liberties and Lorenzo de' Medici had turned his face to the wall.

---

*This was a habit shared by the extremely wealthy. Pope Julius II was fed molten gold in a vain attempt to stave off his inevitable end.

This has now been disproved by other contemporary accounts, but it does show that the faithful Poliziano was beginning to lean toward those who preferred to oust the Medicis altogether.

Lorenzo died in the early hours of April 9 at the relatively young age of forty-three.*

In his more prophetic and terrifying sermons, Savonarola had predicted the demise of three of the key figures in Renaissance Italy. The first of these, Lorenzo the Magnificent, was dead and the second was showing signs of serious decline: Pope Innocent lay in a coma for weeks, despite attempted blood transfusions from three boys, all of whom died as a result, while the two great rival cardinals Guliano della Rovere and Rodrigo Borgia screamed insults at each other from his bedside.

Pope Innocent finally died on July 25, 1492, and from all over the Christian world the cardinals hurried to Rome to choose his successor. It was a bitterly divided conclave. On the one side was della Rovere, the ambitious and militaristic nephew of Sixtus IV and the influential power behind the throne for Innocent as well. Charles VIII of France and the Genoese were paying vast sums in bribes to support his candidacy. On the other side was Borgia, the effective but wholly corrupt friend of Ferdinand, allied to the Sforzas in Milan.

During the third day of the conclave, it became clear to Cardinal Ascania Sforza that *he* could not win, so he threw his considerable weight behind Borgia. That night, four mules loaded down with silver were seen moving quietly between the Borgia and Sforza palaces in Rome. But the next morning, the conclave was still deadlocked. Everyone who possibly could be bribed had been. The only cardinal left undecided was the senile ninety-six-year-old patriarch of Venice, and at this critical moment, supporters of the Borgias took him aside and persuaded him to cast the crucial vote with them. So at dawn the next day, the dark-eyed, wide-mouthed Borgia emerged from the most exhausting week of his life, bursting with energy and self-satisfaction, and announced that he would call himself Alexander VI, the most notorious of medieval popes. Alexander charmed the Roman

*As he did so, one of the most prominent church spires was hit repeatedly by lightning and the city zoo's two lions fought and mauled each other to death. All three incidents were thought to be auguries of disaster for Florence.

rabble with his joking bonhomie, but his cardinals feared for the future. "We're in the wolf's jaws and he's going to gobble us up," whispered Cardinal Medici during his coronation.

Borgia was then sixty-one, born near Valencia, and had narrowly missed being elected Pope at the conclave that chose Innocent. He had extraordinary energy as an administrator and was a brilliant orator, but his excesses were flagrant. He quickly installed his mistress, Giulia Farnese, the seventeen-year-old wife of his one-eyed cousin, in apartments through a private door inside his cathedral. His son Cesare had been bishop of Pamplona since he was a teenage student in Pisa, but now the wheels to make him a cardinal were set in motion.

Alexander's priorities were to rescue Rome from itself and the disorder and gang warfare that left new corpses in the streets with every morning light. Ferdinand and Isabella welcomed the election of a pope from Aragon as recognition of their achievement in Granada, but Savonarola fulminated from his pulpit in the Duomo in Florence: "In the primitive church, the chalices were made of wood, the prelates of gold. In these days, the Church has chalices of gold and prelates of wood."

Throughout the winter of 1491 and into 1492, John Cabot had been in Valencia, looking for a way to earn money. His experience as a construction engineer, helping to rebuild homes on the waterlogged streets of Venice, had given him an expertise in dock building. There had been little chance to exercise this in Milan or Savoy, but in Valencia during the months while Columbus was shaping his expedition, Cabot had been drawing up plans for a new stone jetty on the city's beach to replace the existing wooden wharf.

Valencia was the biggest financial center in Ferdinand's kingdom of Aragon; it was a major port on the Mediterranean and a center for silk, oranges, wine, almonds, and cloth. It was the cloth that had originally attracted Cabot there, but his reputation as a debtor did not make him popular with merchants. Even so, there were clearly other opportunities for a man of vision. The city was also the center of massive irrigation systems that distributed water from the nearby rivers and brought it into the city. These had been built some centuries earlier, under the Muslims, and had been allowed to decay, but Valencia was now overflowing with ambitious plans for the future. There was the scheme to bring water in from the Júcar

River by canal, among others. The difficulty was that all these projects were awaiting approval from the divided city rulers and for financing in a period where every bit of extra money for municipal investment had been siphoned off by Ferdinand for the war against Granada.

The city's palm and fig trees gave an impression of coolness and relaxation, but its network of streets and alleyways—culminating in the great mercado where business was carried out—seethed with tensions between the local Aragonese craftspeople and the incoming foreigners who were flocking there because it was such a successful mercantile center. There were silk and paper manufacturers from Italy and seven printers from Germany—Valencia was now one of the key printing centers of Europe. There was also a large Muslim population under royal protection. The burgeoning economic success of Valencia was symbolized by the huge Lonja de la Seda, the silk exchange, now being built above the market.

But by the summer of 1492, Cabot had managed to build a close alliance with the governor-general of the city, Diego de Torres. He had identified where the stone for the jetty could be found, in Cap de Cullera, procured ships that could carry the cut stone at the best time, and worked out how to build the jetty the following summer. It was a coherent and serious plan, and the city authorities brought it to the attention of the king. Finally, at the end of September, Cabot and his local partner, Gaspar Rull, were shown in to see Ferdinand.

In Palos, the process of preparing for the voyage had been exhausting and frustrating. When Columbus arrived there on May 12, he had planned to leave in ten days. In fact, the preparations took ten weeks. Part of the problem was the security that surrounded the expedition. Instructions to the ship fitters and suppliers provided only vague details about the destination, described as "certain parts of the ocean sea." All mention of the Indies was excised from the agreement between Columbus and the monarchs. Nor was the secrecy effective. Seville was packed with Portuguese spies, and the news of a mysterious expedition led by Columbus soon reached Lisbon, where King John was sufficiently alarmed to prepare warships to intercept the expedition if they could.

Palos harbor is today silted up and the scene of a patchwork of small, run-down agricultural holdings, but in July 1492 it was the scene of feverish activity as the three ships were loaded. The final supplies were delayed by the surrounding roads now crowded with Jewish families, stripped of almost everything they possessed. Almost eight thousand families had sailed from nearby Cadiz, their designated port of departure, before the last weeks of the deadline on August 1. Others were camped in the hills above Palos, singing lamentations, their remaining possessions on carts, waiting for someone who could ship them elsewhere. In a few weeks time, many would be seized by pirates off the African coast and taken to Tangiers, and sometimes even back to Cadiz, to be sold into slavery.*

On August 1 the fleet was finally ready. In the early hours of the following morning, all three crews made their confession and received mass. Columbus was the last aboard, and the small fleet made its way slowly into the Saltes estuary, the white shape of La Rábida above them. Their special expedition banners, which bore green crosses on a white background, each with crowns over the initials F and Y (for Ferdinand and Ysabel), fluttered in the breeze. The ships carried provisions for a year, an Arabic translator, and diplomatic letters addressed to Magnus Canus, the Great Khan, along with some duplicates where the names had been left blank.

Vespucci was settling down to his new life in Seville, no longer at the beck and call of his relations and employers, though still working partly on behalf of the Popolano. He had dreamed of exploration and discovery all his life, and now he was engaged in helping Berardi plan for what might be the greatest voyage of exploration in history.

Vespucci was growing into a man whose appearance belied his personality. He was bald, thick-set, and brawny, with a low forehead and an enormous head—like an aggressive wrestler—but one who never lost his temper. He had a talent for friendship with those more powerful than he, like Berardi. Vespucci and his young nephew Giovanni now moved in with the Berardi family in the wealthiest part of Seville, united in their commitment to Columbus and his voyage.

---

*A few of the families were so certain they would return that they simply locked their homes and took the keys with them into exile, passing them down from generation to generation. When Franco died in 1975, nearly five centuries later, and these descendants returned to Madrid, some of the keys were found to still fit the locks.

They had heard from the island of Gomera in the Canary Islands about the final stopover for the *Santa Maria* and the other ships, including the rumor about Columbus and his passion for the fearsome Beatriz de Bobadilla who ruled the island after the murder of her husband. They had heard about the fleet's departure and how Columbus had dodged the Portuguese squadron sent to intercept him. And then nothing, as Columbus and his ships headed directly west out into the Atlantic.

Across the Guadalquivir, in the bars of Triana, the rough nautical suburb of Seville where the sailors lodged—a second home for Vespucci because he worked there so often, supervising cargoes and engaging ships and crew—it was a common belief that Columbus would never be seen again.

I

*"For a time, its sun-gilt peaks and long shadowy promontories would remain distinctly visible, but in proportion as the voyagers approached, peak and promontory would gradually fade away until nothing would remain but blue sky above and deep blue water below."*

Washington Irving describing the expedition leaving
the Canary Islands in 1492

Some thousand or so miles westward in the middle of the ocean, it was apparent that the *Santa Maria* was not a good choice of vessel. It was no caravel, and at nearly a hundred tons, was bigger, slower, and less seaworthy than the *Niña* or the *Pinta*. Columbus's flagship was constantly falling behind, to the irritation of Martin Alonso Pinzón in the *Pinta*.

The decision to leave from the Canary Islands was forced on Columbus: They were Castilian; the Azores, his preference, were Portuguese. But Toscanelli urged him to take the Canaries route because that was where the prevailing winds were likely to be. The first few weeks of the voyage were so successful that it began to raise a slight doubt in the minds of the nervous crew. If the winds always blew from the east, as they seemed to do, how would the fleet ever return home?

Day after day Columbus worked out the voyage's course by dead reckoning, judging position by speed and direction, estimating their direction using a compass and their speed by the bubbles on the surface of the sea. He also measured latitude using the tried and tested method of the Portuguese, who would watch the height of the North Star at night. Congenitally optimistic, he endlessly overestimated their progress, but kept a second set of charts to reassure the crew that they had not traveled too far, "so that if the voyage were long the people would not be frightened and dismayed." This public chart turned out to be rather more accurate than his personal one.

Through the first few weeks of September, the three ships raced before the wind, in perfect weather, close to the top speed for caravels of around eleven knots. Daybreak was the best time of day, with the cool breeze filling the sails and driving them westward. "The savor of the mornings was a great delight," wrote Columbus in his journal. "The weather was like April in Andalusia. The only thing wanting was to hear the nightingales."

Below, through the hatchway, the helmsman steered the course he had been ordered to follow—blind to the sea and the weather, peering at the small compass point in front of him. Seafaring was a business of rituals, from daybreak until dusk. There was a succession of prayers, with a hot meal at eleven A.M. cooked on the ship's stove, near the quarterdeck, set on a large box of sand. Other meals consisted of olive oil, wine, salt-dried fish, elderly bacon, and maggoty ship's biscuit, eaten by the crew with their utility knives on the deck. There were no shaving facilities, so every sailor was soon sporting a beard.

September 21, surrounded by an expanse of green and yellow seaweed in the Sargasso Sea, marked the expedition's first nervous moment, but the journey went on, deeper into what seemed to be the unknown. By October 9, still no land had been sighted—despite endless false alarms—and this was becoming a serious concern. There were mutterings that the way home was now impossible and that they should quietly throw Columbus overboard and turn around. Martin Pinzón had his own theories about the route they were taking. On a visit to Rome the year before, he had been to the Vatican Library and was shown an ancient document about a legendary voyage made by the Queen of Sheba to Japan. It was this that had convinced him to take Columbus seriously, but he was beginning to resent the man he saw as a Genoese upstart and believed he had brought at least as much to the expedition as Columbus had. By his own calculations he came to the conclusion that they had missed Japan altogether.

At a conference with the worried captains in his cabin on the *Santa*

*Maria*, Columbus persuaded them to continue westward for three more days, after which he agreed they would have missed Cipangu, and he would turn back. But once the captains had rowed to their ships, the crew of the *Santa Maria* erupted in open revolt. They were only slightly reassured by a speech from Columbus making the same promise: three more days, and if no land was found, they would go home.

Luckily for him, the following day revealed possible evidence of land: plants and sticks floating in the water. Columbus gathered his own crew and told them the monarchs had promised ten thousand maravedis to whoever first sighted land. He would also donate a silk doublet. At ten P.M. on October 11 Columbus thought he saw something on the horizon, "like a little wax candle rising and falling." But he stared out to sea and could make out nothing more. Then at 2 A.M., with the moon high, Rodrigo de Triana on the forecastle of the *Pinta* made out a white sand cliff in the moonlight and shouted "land, land!" Pinzón fired the agreed signal and waited for the *Santa Maria* to come alongside. They had been at sea for thirty-seven days.

"Señor Martin Alonso, did you find land?" shouted Columbus.

At dawn the small fleet edged into a shallow bay and saw naked people on the beach who appeared staggered by the monstrous shapes that had slipped into their world. Columbus took the royal standard ashore and fell to his knees on the beach, bringing the other captains and the notaries together for a ceremony to take possession of the small island, which he named San Salvador. Then he turned his attention to the people watching him and gave them red caps and glass beads "and many things of slight value, in which they took much pleasure."

The delighted Tainos—the subset of the Arawak race that Columbus had stumbled upon—spent the rest of the day swimming out to the ships, carrying presents of colored parrots and darts. But his remark about "things of slight value" foreshadowed a fatal mistake—the confusion about what these people took to be worth something—which was to damn this collision of Old World and New. Columbus believed the native populations understood little about the value of the goods they accepted and would easily be cajoled into handing over the gold he believed they possessed. This was the fundamental flaw at the heart of the European idea of money. Columbus believed there was no equal exchange that could be made, and that apart from gold there was nothing of value in this culture. In fact, he very much needed information from the locals about how to support a colony in this unfamiliar environment, about what crops were grown and how his own might be adapted.

He did dimly sense that there were other less substantial things he might learn from the Tainos: "No-one would have believed it, who has not seen it," he wrote. "Of anything that they possess, if it be asked of them, they never say no; on the contrary, they invite you to share it and show as much love as if their hearts went with it, and they are content with whatever trifle be given them." They enchanted him, but with the arrogance of the European merchant class—backed by the supreme arrogance of the aristocracy—he believed he could not be taught anything valuable by them.

There were immediate disappointments too. There was no sign of the expected lions, elephants, and camels. The only creatures of note were the extraordinary parrots, which were to become the unofficial symbol of America for the next few centuries. There were some iguanas and the mysterious dogs without a bark, which the Tainos ate as a delicacy ("none too good," according to Columbus's party).*

It was also clear that the Arabic translator would be of no use at all.

In the West Indies—the very name conjures up the enterprise of Columbus—Pinzón was becoming increasingly infuriated with his expedition commander. He heard a rumor of gold to the south and decided he would benefit by getting there first. So on November 22 the *Pinta* left. Columbus continued to explore the island, which the Tainos called "Haiti" and he renamed Hispaniola, with what remained of the fleet, aware that the natives they had aboard were getting increasingly nervous. They said they were now in the territory of the Caribs—fierce people they described as being one-eyed with the faces of dogs—who captured them and ate them.† Going onshore, Columbus's men

---

*The first iguana they found was seven feet long and on the island of Isabella. They killed it and kept its skin for the sovereigns. They were not impressed back home. Historian Andrés Bernáldez said it was "the most disgusting and nauseating thing which man ever saw." Iguana later became a delicacy for the conquistadors.

†This word was incorporated into the languages of Europe to imply something alien—as in Caribbean, cannibal, and even Shakespeare's character Caliban in *The Tempest*.

were horrified when they went into a hut and found a man's head in a basket. Whether this was actually what they saw—the reality of cannibalism remains controversial—that is certainly what they believed.

As Christmas approached, Columbus and the rest of the crew of the *Santa Maria* were exhausted because the Tainos had been climbing all over the ship for the previous two nights. In the early hours of Christmas morning with little moon, and the sea dead calm, the ship's captain Juan de la Cosa went to bed, leaving the ship's boy at the tiller. A little later, the ship slipped so gently onto a coral reef that at first nobody noticed. When it did become apparent, part of the crew panicked and set off in a boat for the *Niña*. By the time they had been sent back, the coral had cut into the hull and water was pouring in.

Columbus sent an urgent message for help to the local chief, Guancanagarí, and through the day the weeping admiral, his crews, and the local Tainos struggled to rescue the stores and as much from the ship as they could before it broke up completely. Shocked, bedraggled, and frightened, the crew of the *Santa Maria* lay on the beach and wondered if they would ever get home.

There was still no sign of the *Pinta*, so what was to be done with the *Santa Maria*'s crew? Columbus's solution was to use the wood from the ship to build a fort and have the crew man it until his return. That day, the first European settlement in the Americas was founded and called La Navidad, after Christmas Day. By early January, a tower was built, together with the first of the thatched huts that would form the basis of the new town. Columbus set off with emotional farewells to the *Santa Maria*'s crew, leaving Diego de Arana, the cousin of his mistress and now Marshal of the Fleet, in charge. Later that day they saw the *Pinta* sailing toward them, having heard about the wreck through the native grapevine. There was a furious exchange between the two commanders in the *Niña*'s cabin.

Now that Columbus was considering what to tell the sovereigns, the fatal whiff of empire was clouding his mind. "All the islands are so utterly at your highnesses' command that it only remains to establish a Spanish presence and order them to perform your will," he wrote to Isabella and Ferdinand. "They are yours to command and make them work, sow seed and do whatever else is necessary and build a town and teach them to wear clothes and adopt our customs."

. . .

"I am still determined to proceed to the mainland and the city of Quinsay to present the letters of your highnesses to the Great Khan," Columbus had written in his running letter to Ferdinand and Isabella on October 24, 1492. Back in Spain the following day, the governor-general of Valencia, also the chamberlain of Aragon, was writing to Ferdinand to say that he had examined all of John Cabot's plans for a new jetty and thought they would work. But he warned that if the various factions in the city had to come up with the money, they would never agree, so some other way to finance the project would have to be found.

It was time for Cabot's second meeting with Ferdinand about the jetty proposal. It is hard to imagine that during the meeting, as Cabot stared into the eyes of the great strategist of the Mediterranean, Ferdinand did not ask him about Milan. He knew this Venetian in front of him had lived there for some time, knew about the tension between Ludovico Sforza and his own relatives in Naples, and would want to know every detail. At the same time, it is hard to imagine that Cabot could have resisted the temptation to mention that he had his own plans for an expedition to the Indies. History does not record the conversation, but we can imagine that Ferdinand looked amused—he had his own doubts about Columbus—but kept his own counsel.

It was a deeply frustrating time for Cabot. By then, he knew that Columbus had left on his voyage—the expedition in which he should have been an equal partner—claiming the most extraordinary titles and financial concessions. He deduced the close relationship between Columbus and the queen. If Columbus should fail, it made sense to put down a marker with the king. That done, all he could do was hope for the best—and first of all, hope for the jetty.

But that hope barely survived the winter. Letters from his creditors in Venice urging his arrest were soon arriving in the city, and thanks to irreconcilable differences among those who ran Valencia, there now seemed no hope of agreement about his jetty plan. In February 1493, Ferdinand wrote to the city canceling the project, given that extra money was not available. Cabot must ruefully have thought to himself that the money he required had been invested in his former friend's enterprise to the Indies.

Once again he had to pack up his home and his growing family and move. As he made the painful, expensive, and exhausting preparations, he heard the almost unbelievable news that Columbus had returned.

· · ·

Finally back on European soil, after being battered by storms across the Atlantic, Columbus stood before the last person he wanted to see: John of Portugal.

The winter was cold and tempestuous. Genoa harbor froze over, and as the *Pinta* and *Niña* (with Columbus on board) made their uncertain way back across the Atlantic, they ran into a succession of disastrous storms. The terrified, exhausted sailors drew lots with peas, one of which had a cross marked on it, to see who would go on a pilgrimage of gratitude if they survived. Columbus drew first and got the marked pea, but the storm carried on.* At the end of February, separated again from Pinzón, the crew of the *Niña* took shelter in the Azores. When half of them went ashore to give thanks, they were immediately arrested by the Portuguese authorities under suspicion of illegally trading in west Africa.

Having talked their way out of the charges and back aboard, the crew set off again, only to have the storm hit them with renewed force. By March 3 it was at its height, and by the light of the full moon they sighted land— only to find to their horror and discomfort that what they saw was Lisbon. Sailing reluctantly up the river, Columbus moored four miles outside the city next to an enormous man-of-war, and sent a preemptive message to the king, asking to see him. He persuaded the master of the warship, who happened to be the explorer Bartholomew Dias, that he was speaking the truth about the Indies. Having done that, Columbus made the thirty-mile journey, with three of the ten "Indians" he had brought back with him, to the monastery of Santa Maria das Virtudes, where John was staying. After a month in a raging ocean beyond anything they had conceived, the hapless near-naked Tainos found themselves struggling on mules in the mud in a completely unfamiliar world.

John received Columbus honorably, asked him to sit down, and immediately remembered how irritating he found the man's exaggerations. John explained gently that as far as he could see, Columbus had strayed into areas of the ocean that were Portuguese under the 1481 treaty that divided the Atlantic between their two countries, north and south. Realizing that his survival probably depended on his answer, Columbus said that he had not

*He never went on the pilgrimage.

seen the treaty, but he had been ordered to go nowhere near the African coast and he had obeyed.

Intrigued by Columbus's claim that the Tainos were intelligent, John suggested a test. He asked one of them to arrange a pile of beans in the shape of the islands he came from. Then he upset the shape and asked another Taino to do the same thing. Staring down at this whole new world they set out, John banged his hand on the table. "O man of little comprehension," he said, of himself. "Why did I let slip an enterprise of so great importance?"

Back on board the *Niña*, and making ready to sail again, Columbus realized how lucky he was to have escaped imprisonment or assassination, and spent his time busily writing letters—long accounts to the royal treasurer Luis Santangel and others to Berardi, Medina Celi, and the sovereigns themselves, including a request that they ask the pope to make his son Diego a cardinal. He knew his forced visit to Lisbon was bound to raise suspicions in the Castilian court, so it was urgent that he should get his own account to Isabella.

Before he sailed out of Lisbon harbor, breathing an enormous sigh of relief, he passed a Bristol ship called *Nicholas of the Tower*, importing wine and oil and owned by a shadowy English merchant called John Day, one of Berardi's partners back home, who he seems to have met on the dockside. Columbus knew Day from Seville, but this may have been when he first involved him as a kind of personal espionage service.


In the *Pinta*, Pinzón was having similar thoughts. He had landed in Castile, just north of the Portuguese border at Bayona in the last week of February, desperate to beat Columbus home with the news. He dashed off an immediate message to the sovereigns in Barcelona, asking permission to come there and tell them what had been found. The reply, when it arrived a week later, was a snub: They preferred to hear the news from the admiral himself.

Mortified, Pinzón set sail southward, rounding Cape St. Vincent at the same time as the *Niña*, but out of sight. As he sailed up the Saltes estuary and into Palos, there ahead of him was Columbus, the sails of his ship being stowed away. His last hopes dashed, furious and jealous of Columbus and his exaggerations, and sick and exhausted from his stormy crossing, Pinzón asked to be rowed ashore. From there he went straight home and to bed.

He never got up again, and in the few days left to him, local doctors treated him for a strange disease involving ulcers all over the skin, which they had never seen before and which would reappear catastrophically the following year in Barcelona and Naples. Those early European victims of syphilis died quickly, sometimes within months. It is quite possible that Pinzón was the first European to die from the disease.

After arriving at Palos, Columbus recovered for two weeks at La Rábida and then set out with his ten Taino captives for Seville, arriving on Palm Sunday. There he received his first reply from the sovereigns that they had heard the news, addressing him by all the titles he had demanded: "Admiral of the Ocean Sea" and "Viceroy" and "Governor of the islands that have been discovered in the Indies."

"We have seen your letters and we have taken much pleasure in learning whereof you write, and that God gave so good a result to your labors," they wrote, encouragingly. They urged him to make the eight-hundred-mile journey to them in Barcelona, but also to start preparations for going back to Hispaniola as soon as possible. Setting out via Córdoba, Columbus was welcomed by Beatriz and his sons, and then in Murcia and along the coast of western Spain, he organized a series of public displays. But it was in Valencia, where a frustrated Cabot was preparing to leave again, that he gave a glimpse of himself to his former partner in the enterprise of the Indies.

There was Columbus, standing like a Roman senator, proud and unsmiling, wearing as much gold and finery as he could find, six of his almost naked Taino captives around him, each of them carrying a brightly colored parrot in a cage. Everything brought back in triumph from the expedition was on display: hammocks, pineapples, iguana skins, gold masks. It was one of those great events that nobody in the surging crowds who saw it can ever have quite forgotten.

But nobody paid such close attention as did Cabot, with mixed feelings of exhilaration and fury that his former colleague should have carried out this bold plan—their plan—and come home alive to tell the world. And the more he stared at his sumptuously dressed rival, the more his doubts began to gnaw at him.

The triumphal northward march of Columbus with the Tainos and the parrots culminated finally in a massive public reception at the Alcazar in

Barcelona before Ferdinand and Isabella. Ferdinand was still recovering from a knife wound in a near fatal assassination attempt in December, but Isabella was radiant. When the admiral kissed their hands, they gave him the extraordinary privilege of sitting beside them and Prince Juan on the raised dais in the throne room of the Plaza del Rey, with its gothic murals and high vaulted ceiling. Then on to the royal chapel for a celebratory mass, tears running down the faces of Columbus and his royal mentors.

Before he hurried back to Seville to prepare for his second expedition to the Indies, there was a ceremony baptizing the six Indians. Of these, just one stayed behind as a servant in the royal household—he was baptized Don Juan, after the heir to the throne.

The celebrations in Barcelona led directly to the ambitious plans for a fleet of seventeen ships. Columbus was now at the height of his prestige and favor at the court. Those who had ridiculed and frustrated him during his years of waiting were silent. He rode down the streets next to the queen, and she had appointed a powerful representative to assist him, Juan Rodriguez de Fonseca.

Fonseca was a protégé of Talavera's, a distant cousin of the Hungarian royal family, and a collector of Flemish painting. He had only just been ordained, but had already proved himself as an administrator and diplomat. He was sent to Seville to take charge of the Indies operation, a position which he filled with growing power and influence, shaping policy in the new world, until his death in 1523. That is how Seville became what it was to be for two centuries or more—the "Great Babylon of Spain," the gate through which all trade with the Indies passed.

Already in the weeks since Fonseca's appointment on May 20, 1493, Seville—later the backdrop for Don Quixote, Don Juan, and Carmen—was showing the first signs of what it was to become. The narrow winding street through the heart of the city—the Calle Sierpes running from the palace of the Duke of Medina Sidonia, past the royal prison to the Plaza de San Francisco and the cathedral—was already filling with assorted adventurers, beggars, and laggards hoping for a chance in the Indies. The prison was soon to be receiving eighteen thousand prisoners a year, and even now the city was bursting with a new underclass. The traditional place where merchants like

Berardi and Vespucci sealed their deals was on the steps of the still-unfinished cathedral and this was increasingly crowded and uncomfortable.* Already, the seafaring and gypsy suburb of Triana, across the river, was packed with sailors from all over Europe dreaming of gold.

For the first and only time in this story, the three key figures in the race for America were in the same city at the same time. Columbus was basking in glory, writing secret messages to the queen, aware of the danger posed by spies, but also enjoying the intrigue. They were rather taken with each other, and with each other's dreams. "By this post I am sending you a copy of the book you left me," Isabella wrote to him. "The delay has been caused by the fact that it had to be written secretly, so none of those who are here from Portugal, or anyone else, should know anything about it."

He was also finding that he did not really see eye to eye with the formidable Fonseca, who was coming to very much the same conclusion about him. While Isabella saw in Columbus an enlightened visionary, Fonseca could see only an accomplished dissimulator and liar.

Across the city, Vespucci was beginning to work less as an inspector for the Popolano and moving more permanently into a new role as Berardi's partner, helping him with a schedule and set of business responsibilities that was rapidly burgeoning out of control. Seventeen ships needed to be bought or leased for the new voyage. Their crews had to be persuaded to enlist. The equipment and food had to be procured: cannons, ammunition, swords, biscuits, wine, oil, flour, vinegar, bread, cheese. It was clear from the outset that Fonseca was an inspired administrator. He put an official from the Inquisition in charge of ordering supplies of bread for the voyage, a magnificent idea to discourage cheating. But it was Berardi and Vespucci who were organizing most of the contracts.

Vespucci had been desperate to volunteer for the fleet himself, but he was held in Seville by duties for the Popolano family and his work with Berardi. As a lodger in Berardi's house, Vespucci was rubbing shoulders with four of the Tainos brought over by Columbus. These refugees were now in a desperate state—cold and ill, exhausted by all the new tastes, smells, and sights—and

---

*The vast cathedral in Seville was the brainchild of one of the clergy there: "Let us build a church which is so big," he suggested, "that we shall be held insane."

subject to the enthusiastic experiments by the gentlemen of the house, who were trying to teach them Castilian Spanish.

Even after the fleet had been equipped, a still bigger task remained and that involved equipping and manning a whole new colony. Masons, carpenters, and smiths needed to be recruited. Farmers needed to be lured away from the land, together with tools, seeds, and equipment. It was exhausting but had the potential to be enormously lucrative—though Berardi had already invested a great deal of money in the voyages.

Cabot was also in town, attempting to persuade the city to use his skills to rebuild the pontoon bridge that linked the main city with Triana across the river. Perhaps he was attempting to organize an audience with his former friend, but in any case he was knocking on Fonseca's office door urging a different approach, farther to the north, and begging to be allowed to lead an expedition there himself. Time and time again he was rebuffed. If he were allowed to launch an expedition it seemed likely to be a disruptive influence on Columbus's second voyage. But to everyone he talked to about the Indies—and that was about the only conversation taking place in Seville—he urged them to look again at Columbus's "Indians," who bore no resemblance to the traders from the East he had encountered in Mecca.

Here Vespucci shared some of Cabot's doubts. Columbus had spent some days staying at Berardi's house as well, and had discussed details of the voyage with Vespucci there. He had seen the calculations Columbus had made about the length of a degree around the equator, and knew how much it had been underestimated. He knew there were grounds to doubt Columbus's interpretation of what he had found.

The news of the discovery of a western route to the Indies was spreading across southern Europe. Columbus's letter to Santangel was published in Latin twelve times within months of his return, in six European cities and five different countries. Such was the power of the new printing presses. What those hearing the news for the first time tended to remember were the descriptions of the naked women, the new animals and birds—mainly in terms of how they tasted—and Columbus's portrayal of the Tainos. "They love their neighbors as themselves," he wrote, planting in European minds the seed of the concept of the noble savage.

Ever protective of his own image as a competent pioneer, his letters glossed over the disappointments. The loss of the *Santa Maria* was not mentioned. His original letters explained simply that he had "left" the colonists at La Navidad one caravel, omitting the detail that he had left most of it at the bottom of the sea.

The first surviving evidence of the spreading news is a letter dated April 9, 1493—when Columbus was still in Seville—from a Barcelona merchant named Hannibal Zenaru to his brother in Milan, explaining that a new province had been discovered where men were born with tails. Zenaru gave a copy of the letter to Jacome Trotti, ambassador for the Italian city of Ferrara in Milan, who sent it on to the duke. The Duke of Ferrara understood the diplomatic significance immediately and wrote an urgent message to his ambassador in Florence, passing on a rumor that Toscanelli—apparently the originator of the whole idea—had left all his books and papers to his nephew Ludovico, and urging him to contact Ludovico and find out if Toscanelli had written any more about these islands.

Letters were also arriving in Florence via the Medici network, thrilled with the stories of the naked Tainos with "only their private parts covered." Peter Martyr in Spain also wrote to his Italian humanist friends explaining that the Antipodes had been found. Suddenly it seemed to those who followed such matters that Toscanelli had been right after all. But even Peter Martyr had his doubts. "I do not deny it entirely, though the magnitude of the globe suggests something else," he was writing later in the year. But then in November, in a letter to Cardinal Sforza, he was the first to coin a critical phrase, describing "the famous Columbus, the discoverer of the New World."

What had been an obscure theory among geographers and obsessives was suddenly now high politics. Ambassadors were primed. Spies were commissioned to report back on anything related to the discoveries, and, especially in Lisbon and Seville, a heavy diplomatic and intelligence traffic crisscrossed the continent.

One of the courtiers in Lisbon, when Columbus and his Indians had stood before the king of Portugal, was Francisco de Almeida, the future governorgeneral of Portuguese India. He had watched John's experiment with the beans and the maps with consternation, aware that the Tainos exactly fit the description of Indians that he had in his own mind. In the urgent consultations in Lisbon that took place after Columbus had gone, Almeida had urged the king to act. If the Spanish had landed near Asia, they were in the Portuguese sphere of influence, and these islands must be seized back by force.

Almeida's argument prevailed, and as Columbus's new fleet took shape in Cadiz, a similar expedition—but with specifically warlike intentions—was being prepared in Lisbon harbor, with Almeida in command. The preparations had been noticed by spies who now were working in every European port, and were reported back to Castile. Ferdinand and Isabella responded by fitting out six warships in the north, ready to sweep through Portuguese waters and intercept the fleet—and, at the same time, carry King Boabdil of Granada into exile in Morocco. But when the small fleet was ready and sailed south along the Atlantic coast of Portugal, there was no sign of the Portuguese. Almeida's war fleet remained in the harbor.

What had happened was that Ferdinand realized he needed to exert an urgent diplomatic effort. He sent emissaries to the new Aragonese pope, in order to provide a legal protection for their new discoveries, and Alexander responded immediately. On May 3, 1493, he issued the bull *Inter caetera Divinae*—mentioning "our dear son Columbus"—which divided the world down a line one hundred leagues west of the Azores, giving the eastern half to Portugal and the western part to Spain.

The full text described the people who lived in Hispaniola and the other islands as "living peaceably and going naked" and that they "seem apt to be brought to embracing the Catholic faith and to be imbued with good manners." It was a vital moment in diplomatic history, and it also implied something else: The justification for the whole enterprise, both for the pope and the Spanish sovereigns, had shifted. It was no longer just about business, it was about converting souls.

The Portuguese had held back from military action to wait for the pope's decision, and they were horrified at this new division of the world. Previous treaties had divided the Atlantic along the line of latitude; now there was an entirely new division along the longitude line, which would not be measurable for centuries, and certainly was not verifiable then. What could they do? Defying the pope was a dangerous path, but something had to happen. In July, John sent an ultimatum to Ferdinand and Isabella, ordering them to suspend preparations for the second expedition, or Almeida's fleet would be dispatched immediately across the Atlantic. The Castilians made no response, but Isabella sent a secret message to Columbus urging him to leave as soon as possible. She also told him—as a matter of absolute priority—to find out precisely the position of the new islands.

It was not until September 25 that the fleet finally got under way from Cadiz. One of the last things Columbus did before walking aboard his new flagship, *Maria Galante*, was to give power of attorney to his trusted friend Berardi. In practice, this meant that both Berardi and Vespucci could act on his behalf while he was away.

Compared to the first voyage, the second was an enormous undertaking, with at least thirteen hundred men, including the former captain of the *Santa Maria*, Juan de la Cosa, rapidly emerging as the preeminent cartographer of his generation; Columbus's slightly ineffectual brother Diego; and his boyhood friend Michele de Cuneo, the son of the man who had sold old Domenico Columbus a house in Savona. The captains of each ship carried sealed instructions about what to do if they became separated from the fleet. As well as the future colonists bound for Hispaniola, leaning over the rails of the ships as the coast of Spain drew out of sight, there was a contingent of *hidalgos*, gentlemen cavaliers—forbidden by law and by their position from pursuing "base and vile offices" like tailoring, carpentry, or shopkeeping—swaying with their horses below, present on the voyage because the court believed a contingent of the gentry would help the new settlement. There was also a physician from Seville, Dr. Diego Álvarez Chanca.

And since the other purpose of this expedition as set out by the sovereigns, with the encouragement of Columbus himself, was to convert the people who lived in the newly discovered islands, there were specific instructions from the queen to treat the natives kindly. This meant there was a party of friars included on the voyage, led by a reformed Francisan, a Minim friar named Bernardo Boyle, and enough equipment to set up the first church.*

---

*Boyle is variously described by historians as Irish and Catalan; his name is spelled a variety of different ways. I have used the Irish spelling, for obvious reasons. As someone who had taken a vow of chastity, Boyle is unlikely to have been an ancestor of mine but, then again, who knows.

As the first swell hit the seventeen ships, the thousand or so passengers sharing the space with their animals realized what an ordeal the month ahead was likely to be. These tiny spaces would be their homes. They would eat salt-cured meat and rancid lard and drink a quart of stale water a day, crowded on deck in all weather to throw up over the side. Spread out ahead of them, a powerful naval squadron scanned the horizon for any signs of the Portuguese.

Some days later, the fleet drew into the harbor in Gomera, and soon afterward those on board watched the distant volcano on Tenerife—the last sight for westward voyages—dip below the horizon, and they were alone, seventeen small dots on the Atlantic Ocean.

The day after the fleet sailed from Cadiz, the pope issued another bull. Papal bulls are known by their first two words in Latin. This one, *Dudum siquidem*, favored Alexander's native Spain to an outrageous degree: "Since it may happen that your envoys and captains or subjects, while voyaging to the West or South, might land in eastern regions and there discover islands and mainland that belong to India . . . we amplify and extend our aforesaid gift . . . to all islands and mainlands, whatsoever to be found . . . sailing or traveling towards the West or South."

When the news arrived in Lisbon, there was serious consternation. What was the point of them having the exclusive right to explore for trade routes to the east—if, indeed, that was where Columbus had gone—if the Castilians were simply being given the right to encircle the world and take possession of everything they found there as well? John made the decision to abandon diplomacy at the Vatican: there was obviously no point in trying to persuade a pope who was quite immune to any cause other than that of the Spanish. They would have to take matters into their own hands and open negotiations directly with Ferdinand and Isabella, while holding open the possibility of their own expeditions.

It was at this point that Columbus's rival Martin Behaim arrived back in Lisbon. He had spent the previous year at home in Nuremberg, irritating his family—"Martin does nothing in particular, but goes daily into the garden," complained his brother Wolf. But now, sensing some opportunity, he roused himself to send a letter to Lisbon in July proposing exactly the voyage that Columbus had suggested—and enclosing a globe that demonstrated the route—clearly not knowing that Columbus had already achieved this.* But John bided his time, as Castile and Portugal seesawed between peace and war.

There were still overwhelming reasons for peace. Both sides knew that sending Almeida and his fleet across the unknown ocean, without definitive charts or positions, would be enormously risky. And if, as Cabot said, Columbus had really made a mistake, then it would be a serious waste of time to seize a handful of irrelevant islands. Yet the Castilians also knew that if they wanted to, the Portuguese navy could play havoc with their supply lines to the Indies. Backing a rival voyage under Behaim was just too risky in this delicate situation. It would also flout the decision of the pope. Lisbon decided that the best option was to negotiate instead, and that another voyage around Africa in the path of Bartholomew Dias might be a better use of resources. So Almeida's fleet was stood down.

The news of the discoveries took longer to reach northern Europe and London—where Henry VII was still considering Bartholomew Columbus's proposal for a voyage of his own to the Indies—and the French royal court, where, as the finishing touches were being put on Columbus's new fleet, the young Charles VIII finally asked to see the patient Bartholomew Columbus, who was now employed, rather miserably, making maps for Anne of Beaujeu at Fontainebleu.

The king gave him the news that his brother had come back safely, having found a route to the Indies, and sent Bartholomew to see him in Spain. Before he left, the French king handed him a small purse for traveling expenses containing one hundred crowns, then Bartholomew set out on the long journey south across the Pyrenees and along the dusty road to Seville. There he found the second fleet had already sailed, but his brother had left behind a letter asking him to conduct his son Diego and the baby Ferdinand to the Spanish court. Isabella took to Bartholomew immediately and asked him to take

---

*Behaim's famous globe can be seen to this day in the background of Holbein's eerie picture *The Ambassadors,* in the National Gallery in London, with the strange foreshortened skull in the foreground in the shape of a dagger. He left Lisbon again at the end of 1493, claiming to be on a secret mission for the Portuguese king, but was actually debt collecting for his father-in-law, and was captured by the English and had to bribe his way to freedom.

charge of the convoy of provisions that was about to leave Seville for the Indies. To do so he would have to negotiate with Fonseca, Berardi, and Vespucci and persuade Berardi, in particular, to advance him more money.

It seemed that the moment Columbus set foot again on the other side of the Atlantic, his dreams began to unravel. The fleet sighted the island of Dominica at dawn on November 3, 1493, and he summoned all hands on deck for prayer.* From there, they made their way toward Hispaniola again via Guadaloupe, and made horrifying—though still controversial—discoveries there about the habits of the Caribs, rescuing a number of Taino captives and boys who were being fattened up for eating and "had the genital organ cut to the belly." It was clear that these were not quite the peaceable, docile people he had portrayed to the sovereigns.

On the nearby island of St. Croix, there was the first recorded fight with the natives, and the landing parties returned to the ship with rescued Tainos and captive Caribs. The admiral's friend Michele de Cuneo personally captured a beautiful Carib girl, and Columbus let him keep her as a slave in his quarters. "Having taken her into my cabin," he related later, "she being naked according to their custom, I conceived a desire to take pleasure. I wanted to put my desire into execution but she did not want it and treated me with her finger nails in such a manner that I wished I had never begun." De Cuneo then beat her with rope and reached some kind of economic agreement. It is hard to see what other choice she had. There are precious few descriptions by the early discoverers of the sexual side of their achievements, but—reading between the lines—it was considerably more time-consuming an activity than their memoirs would have us believe. Rape was not just a metaphor for imperialism; sometimes it was half the point of the journey.

The fleet arrived off the southeast coast of Hispaniola on November 22 and worked its way around to La Navidad. But when, a week later, the nearby Tainos came out on canoes to welcome them, there was disturbing news. There had been war on the island. Guancangarí had been wounded by a rival chief and the new colony attacked. At dawn on November 28

---

*Columbus did not stay at Dominica, but the Caribs there were said later to have eaten a friar and been so sick afterward that they never ate anyone else dressed as an ecclesiastic.

they fired a salute toward La Navidad to herald their arrival. There was no answer, but another canoe came out carrying a man who turned out to be Guancanagarí's cousin, shouting "Almirante, almirante!" After three hours of difficult conversation through a translator, he confirmed that the fort had been destroyed. Columbus refused to believe it. But when they arrived at the site the next morning, it was all too true. The fort had been burned almost to the ground, and there was no sign of the thirty-nine-member crew of the *Santa Maria* they had left behind. The local Tainos were hiding in case they were blamed for the disaster, and when Columbus paid a visit to the wounded Guancanagarí, together with Dr. Chanca, it was clear that there was actually no wound underneath the bandages of leaves on his leg.

A powerful faction, led by Bernardo Boyle, within the leadership of the expedition urged Columbus to have the chief punished immediately. But the admiral remembered the invaluable support he had received from Guancanagarí in those crucial hours as the *Santa Maria* sank, and he was afraid to spark a native alliance against him. In any case, the truth soon became clear: A faction inside La Navidad had left the fort and roamed across the island, stealing gold and women from villages, and eventually another chief, Caonabo, had taken a terrible revenge on the whole enclave. He captured the gang and put them to death and then descended on the fort. Only ten colonists were left under Diego de Harana, plus five native women in each hut. Three were killed in the attack and the rest of the new colony were driven into the sea, where they drowned.*

Since the lightning in Florence that marked the death of Lorenzo de' Medici, the omens in Italy had all been bad. Three suns were reported to have been seen in the sky over Puglia. People in Arezzo claimed to have seen hundreds of ghostly horsemen in the skies. And in January 1494, the news emerged that the third of Savonarola's doomed tyrants, king Ferrante of Naples, had died. He was worn out by his frenetic efforts to prevent war, threatened by an alliance between the Sforza in Milan and the young Charles VIII of France.

---

*The site of La Navidad remained a mystery until 1977 when it was discovered at a remote site near Libe—now two miles inland—by the local Baptist missionary and doctor, William Hodges.

Since Cabot had left Milan, Ludovico Sforza's nephew Gian Galeazzo had come of age and his new wife was pressing for Ludovico to hand over the reins of power. Ludovico responded by seizing power in his own right. She appealed to her family in Naples for help. King Ferrante—linked to the Aragonese royal family—threatened to march north, and once again Ludovico made the fatal error of asking the French for help. In the months that followed, it was clear that this—and the sudden vacancy on the throne of Naples—was all the excuse Charles needed for his dream of an invasion.

Since coming of age and abandoning the guiding hand of his sister, Charles had developed the habit of obsessive womanizing and of muttering to himself when in company. Rumors were going around the court that he had six toes, and looking at his great bulbous lips and long protruding nose, people believed it. Throughout the spring and summer of 1494, an enormous army of thirty thousand gathered in the south of France, the biggest to cross the Alps since the days of Hannibal.

Vespucci had been right to leave Florence when he did. Lorenzo the Magnificent's son Piero was finding himself increasingly at odds with the other side of the Medici family, and the dispute reached a head over a row with his cousin Giovanni di Pierfrancesco, brother of Vespucci's old Popolano employer Lorenzo, when Piero publicly slapped him in the face. After agonizing about it for a while, Piero went further. He had all his Popolano cousins arrested on trumped-up charges of sending sympathetic messages to the king of France, and imprisoned them in the Medici villa at Cafaggiolo.

## II

*"The fish here are so different from ours that it is a wonder. There are some that look like John Dory, of the finest colors in the world—blue, yellow, red and every sort of color—and some are streaked with a thousand tints, and the colors are so fine that there can be no man who would not marvel at it and feel refreshed by the sight."*

Christopher Columbus's diary, October 1492

On Hispaniola, there was no choice but to abandon La Navidad and head out again. The passengers and animals were still cooped up in the fetid air belowdecks and were now desperate to disembark, and Columbus made the hasty and imprudent choice of a site fifty miles eastward, which he called Isabella. The first three months of 1494 were feverishly active, laying the foundations for the new town. The first crops were planted and expeditions mounted into the interior of the island, but it was soon clear that Isabella was a bad site to have chosen: There was little freshwater and the fishing was poor. But Columbus had to offset the dreadful news about La Navidad with good news about something. So Dr. Chanca was sent home with a letter to the sovereigns, together with thirty thousand ducats of desperately collected gold, sixty parrots, twenty-six Indians, three cannibals, and large quantities of cinnamon.*

Columbus's objective was increasingly becoming the elusive gold. Quite apart from the need for a financial return to investors in the voyages, like Santangel and Berardi, the discovery of gold would prove that Columbus had indeed discovered the outlying islands of Cipangu and the East. Time after time, though, the Tainos or Caribs, hoping to please the new arrivals, indicated the source of gold to be elsewhere, pointing at their own rings and then far over the mountains or to another island. But very little gold was actually being found, so Columbus decided to leave his brother Diego in charge of Isabella, and sent Pedro Margarit, a Catalan noble, to set up a new fortress inland to recruit Tainos to help find gold in the riverbed. His third lieutenant, Alonso de Ojeda, was dispatched to roam the island looking for gold—and for Chief Caonabo, held responsible for the massacre at La Navidad.

Ojeda was from an obscure family in Cuenca and had been a page in the service of Columbus's friend the Duke of Medina Celi. He had been noticed by Isabella on a visit to Seville when he danced on a beam 250 feet above the street, and so when Medina Celi had been allowed to send a ship as part of the fleet, Ojeda had been appointed to take command. He was a small man with breathtaking good looks and a quarrelsome streak that could become extremely violent.

---

*Something else that was picked up on this voyage seems to have been syphilis, which appeared for the first time in Europe as a recognizable disease in Barcelona later that year. Within months, it had spread to the Aragonese forces in Naples, who would shortly encounter the French troops of Charles VIII and from there it would spread throughout the continent.

On Ojeda's second expedition inland, three Spaniards had their clothes taken by locals while they were swimming. Ojeda exploded, cutting off the ears of one of the chief's men and sending his brother and nephew to Columbus for execution. They were reprieved, but the damage had been done. "This was the first incident," wrote Bartholomé de Las Casas, the tireless campaigner for the dignity of the Indians in the next generation. "The first injustice, with vain and erroneous pretension of doing justice, that was committed in these Indies against the Indians, and the beginning of the shedding of the blood, which has since flowed so copiously in this island."

Columbus meanwhile was pushing on to find the mainland, once more sailing with three caravels, himself aboard the *Niña*. Approaching Cuba some weeks later, he made an impromptu speech to the crew: "Gentlemen, I wish to bring us to a place whence departed one of the three Magi who came to adore Christ, which place is called Saba." The crew exchanged glances. Asking about one gold object from the local natives, Columbus believed he heard the words *El Gran Can*. On this flimsy evidence, he ordered his interpreter to prepare an embassy for the emperor of China, and sent him deep into the interior. Six days later, he was back. There was no gold, but a local chieftain had entertained him royally and he had been offered "certain herbs the smoke of which they inhale." Within a century, tobacco smoking would spread across Europe.

Navigating the reefs was exhausting work, and the truth was that Columbus was showing the strain of both leadership and his failure to live up to his hopes or his hype. He became convinced that he had seen griffins, and when one crewman thought he saw a man dressed in white on the shore, Columbus decided that this must have been Prester John himself. Once more, he exhorted his crew, urging them to go all the way around the world, and back via the Holy Sepulchre in Jerusalem.

The admiral's intense mental balance was approaching a crisis as the expedition followed the seemingly endless southern coast of Cuba. The reefs were particularly dangerous and at some point they would have to return to Isabella. There was no alternative: with no end in sight, this simply had to be a promontory of the mainland of China that he had been searching for. Desperate to bolster this opinion, he gathered the ship's scribes and drew up a fearsome oath—with punishments of fines and loss of tongue—and insisted that every member of all three crews with him should swear to it. This was China, there could be no doubt.

Only his old friend de Cuneo was allowed to dodge the oath. Crossing their fingers as they did so, the crews made the required confession of faith and Columbus set course for Hispaniola, barely acknowledged doubt gnawing away at his mind.

Columbus returned to Hispaniola suffering from the debilitating disease that marred the rest of his life, probably Reiter's syndrome following dysentery, a condition that inflamed his lower legs, lower spine, and feet, causing painful and disconcerting bleeding from the eyes. He was completely exhausted and so weak that he had to be carried ashore from the *Niña*.

Worse, it was clear that Isabella was utterly unsustainable. Without red wine or red meat, most of the colony was now seriously anemic and many were too sick to work. Water was scarce and the European crops were already failing. The provisions they had brought with them had almost run out and relations with the local Tainos had broken down completely. Most of the colonists were desperate to go home and furious that there had been no sign of the gold they had been promised. The criminal element, whose crimes back home had been pardoned in exchange for taking part in the voyage, were now roaming the island creating havoc. The former mercenaries from the war in Granada, who were hoping to use similar slash-and-burn techniques in India, were enraged to find themselves among what they saw as savages. The *hidalgos* were not only refusing to take part in the business of cultivation or construction, on the grounds that it was beneath them, they were also refusing to let anyone else use their horses.

The only silver lining in this sky full of dark clouds was that Bartholomew Columbus had arrived from Spain and now greeted his brother for the first time in nearly a decade. He quickly proved a much more effective administrator than his younger brother Diego. Christopher was sick for another five months and Bartholomew was forced to take his place as head of the new colony. He had a streak of ruthlessness that Christopher lacked, and this made him all the more unpopular with the colonists. To be ruled by one foreigner was a peculiarity; to be ruled by two of them—and brothers at that—began to smack of indignity and impropriety.

But for the brothers, there was an even more urgent problem. If there was no gold, then some other means of financing the continued expedition must be found. Despite Queen Isabella's final instructions to Columbus to treat the natives kindly, the answer was becoming obvious to him: He would send consignments of Tainos back to Europe and sell them as slaves.

The decision flew in the face of his remarks about their peaceable nature—loving their neighbors as themselves—and it concerned many of his colleagues, particularly among Boyle's team of clergy who had been sent to convert the Tainos, though none had actually yet been baptized. It quickly became a focus for discontent. Margarit had been responsible for his own share of brutality, and his own men were now involved in extortion all over Hispaniola, but when Diego Columbus ordered him to stop this behavior it was the last straw. He marched to Isabella in a rage, furious, he claimed, about the whole idea of enslaving the Tainos. But having failed to persuade Columbus's council of his point of view, he linked up with Boyle and some others, seized the three ships that had brought Bartholomew and the supplies, and set sail for home. Boyle had been bombarding the sovereigns with letters begging to be allowed to return home and had been told he could do so only if he was ill. By November 1494 the requisite illness had been produced and Boyle and his colleagues were back, talking to sovereigns, filling their minds with doubts about Columbus, his conduct, the lack of food, and the absence of the mythical gold.

Joining them in their audience before Ferdinand and Isabella was the admiral's friend Juan Aguardo, another disappointed former supporter of Columbus, who had returned ahead of them. Aguardo had witnessed Alonso de Ojeda, left almost alone among Columbus's lieutenants still in Hispaniola, coming into his own. It was Ojeda who had captured the elusive chief Caonabo by trickery, presenting him with manacles and persuading him that they were the same bracelets the king of Spain wore. Once Caonabo had put them on, he was shackled to Ojeda's horse and was whisked at top speed toward the Spanish fort. Hispaniola had reached the boiling point.

Back in Europe, largely oblivious to the unfolding crisis in the Indies, most diplomatic attention was focused on avoiding war. Spain and Portugal had both become convinced that conflict would be disastrous and that negotiation was the best way to proceed. The stage was therefore set for an unprecedented international summit at the convent of Santa Clara in Tordesillas in Castile.

The Portuguese delegation arrived in early May 1494. They were experienced mariners up against experienced diplomats on the Castilian side, who were rather less knowledgeable about geography. The Portuguese opened negotiations by explaining how their ships returned from Africa, forced by the circular wind patterns to swing far out into the Atlantic before turning eastward for home. If one of their ships accidentally slipped across the hundred-league line, it would risk unnecessary war.

The line dividing East from West had originally been suggested by Columbus, who felt he had detected a change in climate about a hundred degrees west of the Azores. Over the month that followed, the Portuguese negotiators persuaded the Spanish to push this line that would divide the world another 270 leagues farther west. As they signed the treaty document, both sides secretly congratulated themselves for having managed to deceive the other. In fact, both had unwittingly handed over the still undiscovered immensity of Brazil to the Portuguese.

The treaty has been at the center of a whole series of conspiracy theories: that long before the discovery of Brazil, the Portuguese already had an inkling of land to the south which lay farther east; that the Castilians were thinking of the future, and extending the line to the other side of the globe gave them more of the Indies there. Either way, both sides went away happy.

But if peace seemed more secure on the Atlantic coast of Europe, thanks to the initial intervention of the pope, dividing the world between the two exploring nations, war was becoming inevitable in Italy. Nearly four months after the Treaty of Tordesillas, in the first few days of September 1494, Charles VIII and his enormous French army crossed the Alps, dragging their artillery behind them. The Italians welcomed them at first with open arms, but their urban centers were unprepared for the onslaught to come. The French moved fast and brutally—this was no gentlemanly game of warfare as practiced by the Italian aristocracy, it was a matter of iron cannonballs that could devastate the defenses of any town in minutes, and then hideous medieval retaliation, of the kind the gentle Italian humanist intellectuals believed had disappeared with the Renaissance they heralded.

Only two of Charles's advisers approached the perilous invasion with any degree of optimism. One was his tutor and the other was his cousin Louis of

Orleans, though he had a hidden agenda: Louis had his own claim to the troubled duchy of Milan. Also hanging around the court was an assortment of Italian exiles, all of them, for conflicting reasons, urging Charles on and promising him a liberator's welcome. His other diplomatic advisers urged caution, but despite their predictions of disaster, the French army met little resistance as it stormed southward. Traveling with the king, Vespucci's old friend from Paris, Philippe de Commines, described how ordinary Italians were greeting the French invaders like saints, hoping they would cleanse the Italian peninsula of the in-fighting among the city-states. Soon only Pisa stood between the French and Rome, and it was in Florentine hands. At this moment, the Popolano family finally escaped from captivity and fled to Charles's camp, and Florence's young ruler, Piero de' Medici—remembering his father's dramatic mission to Naples—tried to follow suit and make a similarly dramatic peace. It was a disastrous mission. Charles confronted Piero with a fait accompli: The Florentine garrison defending Pisa was overrun and everyone there was killed. Piero had no option but to agree to everything the French demanded. In fact, French diplomats laughed later that Piero had pressed Florentine castles on them that they had not dared request.

Arriving back in Florence on November 8, the doors of the Palazzo della Signoria were slammed in his face by a furious city council. Crowds outside began jeering and throwing stones and, in the early hours of the next morning, Piero and his family escaped from the city in disguise and went into exile. That night, Michelangelo dreamed of Lorenzo the Magnificent dressed in black, and also fled the city the following day to Rome, ahead of the advancing French.

The Medicis had finally gone, and the Florentine council sent Savonarola to negotiate instead. He insisted on walking the whole way, a gaunt, spindly, Gandhiesque figure in simple clothes. Standing before Charles, he launched into a furious tirade, first welcoming him as the instrument of God and then warning him that God would turn against him if he harmed Florence. Then he turned on his heel and walked out. Unnerved, Charles marched into Florence wearing golden armor, accompanied by Scottish mercenaries playing bagpipes, and gave strict orders to his twenty thousand troops that there should be no looting. When he continued southward some days later, he left Savonarola, armed only with his hypnotic oratory, as ruler of the city. To make it more democratic, Savonarola immediately began reforming the voting system and shifting the burden of tax from the poor to the rich.

In Rome, as November turned to December, Pope Alexander was surprised by the speed of the French approach. His daughter Lucrezia and lover Giulia fell into the hands of the invaders as they swept southward, and he was forced to personally pay their ransom. They were escorted to the gates of Rome by a large force of French troops, and were met by the pope himself in a black doublet and Spanish boots, armed with a sword and dagger.

Then the news filtered through to the city that Charles was ill. He had contracted smallpox and though it was soon clear he would recover—with his bizarre features even more scarred than they were already—the march south was delayed. It was a critical moment of decision for the pope. He had already sunk to begging the sultan in Constantinople for help, and there was no one else he could turn to. The obvious response was to escape, but then his great enemy Cardinal della Rovere—now in exile in France as bishop of Avignon—would call a council of the church and have him deposed for nepotism and corruption, and all those divisions of the globe in favor of the Spanish would be reversed as well. If he could stay and brave it out, there was still a chance, at least to save himself. In a few weeks, the army would be on the move again, and he would have to decide.

Rome's independence was hanging in the balance in the last weeks of December 1494. Charles was recovering, and there were French ships at the mouth of the Tiber River. Pope Alexander and the city leaders met and agreed to surrender. On the last day of the year, the French marched through the gates and into Rome. Courageously, the Spanish pope decided to face down the situation. He stayed put in the Vatican and sent his diplomats over to see Charles, explaining that if he wanted to be crowned King of Naples it made sense not to split the church. Then at least there would be an undisputed pope to legitimize his claim.

The unpredictable and violent Roman crowds also had their first sight of the French king and decided he was ugly and boorish. They knew he had all his food tasted—and had publicly condemned all Romans as poisoners; they objected to the way the French were seizing the empty homes of bishops, and to the rumors of murdered Jews in the ghetto. It made sense for

Charles to agree to terms and get out of Rome on the march south as soon as possible.

Within two weeks he had been invited to stay at the Vatican. Soon he had succumbed to the combination of Alexander's charm, skill, and innuendo and had sworn allegiance to the Borgia pope. Charles and the French army then marched on to defenseless Naples, arriving on February 22, 1495, to a rousing welcome. The Neopolitans had seen off three Aragonese rulers in the space of just over a year, and welcomed Charles rather as the Genoese had welcomed the French a generation earlier—as a guarantor of independence. Charles had achieved his goal and barely been forced to fight a battle to do so. For a while, after his coronation as King of Naples on May 12, he relaxed, confident that his victory was permanent.

By the time Charles had resumed his advance, Columbus had become absolutely desperate. With so little of the gold he had promised, there was no money to buy the supplies he needed, and no prospect of further financing. There was no sign of Cipangu, let alone Cathay. His backers like Vespucci and Berardi were expecting their money back. The struggle to keep up a front for his original claims was exhausting his health. He simply had to produce some economic return. There was no alternative but to implement the slavery plan, and, as seems to be the way of the world, when one small cruelty is permitted, it opens the way to the most horrific kinds of tyranny.

So it was that Columbus committed the great original sin of the New World. He sent out his *hidalgos* with their horses and dogs—which were known to terrify the native population—who rounded up 1,660 Tainos from all over the island. Of those, 550 of the healthiest men and women were loaded aboard the ships that would take his friend de Cuneo and his brother Diego home to put his case to the sovereigns against Boyle and Margarit. He told his men they could choose any that were left, and 400 remained even after that division, who were told to go. But they were by now in such blind fear and panic that many of them ran off into the bush, leaving their own babies behind on the beach.

The small fleet sailed on February 24, 1495. It was the first consignment of slaves to make the Atlantic crossing that would be made by so many hundreds of thousands more in the centuries to come. They were packed belowdecks, alternately freezing and lying in their own vomit and excrement, tossed into unconsciousness by the storms that hit during the crossing. By the final leg of the voyage, half of the 500 had died and been thrown overboard.

In Seville, Berardi and Vespucci watched their arrival with considerable misgivings. They were no strangers to slave trading, but there were complications here. The admiral's reputation at the Castilian court was in decline. Already the sovereigns had been persuaded to lift the monopoly of expeditions to the Indies that Columbus enjoyed. From now on he would keep his sole rights over Hispaniola, but anyone could go to the other islands. It was also clear that the sovereigns had serious doubts about the legality of taking their new subjects captive and selling them. Influenced by Boyle and Margarit, they were coming to the conclusion that the Tainos were heathens, not pagans, and were therefore potential Christians. They instructed Fonseca to slow down the sale of the slaves and make sure that any that *were* sold could be taken back if the sales turned out to be illegal.

In April they suspended sales altogether. A few of the Tainos were given to Berardi as a way of deferring his burgeoning expenses, nine more went to him to be trained as interpreters, and a few more were sent to the royal galleys. The rest moldered away at the docks, waiting for their fate to be decided, and in those conditions, they did not live long.

Berardi and Vespucci had risked considerable sums to equip and supply the ships and realized it was time to intervene, not so much on behalf of the beleaguered admiral, but on their own. They claimed the exclusive right to equip all the ships to the Indies, by promising to cut their price and to undercut any lower offers. Having won this concession, it became obvious that with Berardi's health failing, Vespucci would have to shoulder considerably more responsibility for the business.

Vespucci, who up until then had been supporting Berardi in business, had begun organizing his own rudimentary intelligence service, collecting every scrap of information he could and collating it on charts of islands and routes. Increasingly he was going to have to run what was now a massive undertaking by himself, and find some way of paying for the supplies

Columbus was demanding out of the—still theoretical—8 percent of the proceeds that was in Columbus's original agreement. It was a tough problem—8 percent of almost nothing was still almost nothing—and he would need to use all the persuasive business skills he possessed.

Also in Seville, in the endless round of meetings between city officials and financiers, John Cabot was equally frustrated. He could attract no attention for his inconvenient innuendos about Columbus's discoveries, but his scheme for the new bridge to Triana was also frustratingly becalmed. Toward the end of 1494, as the controversies grew about the Indies, he decided to try his luck in Lisbon, realizing that there, at least, there would be a sympathetic hearing for his opinions about exactly what had been discovered. So in this atmosphere of mutual distrust in the Iberian peninsula, and deep frustration at the Vatican's bias, Cabot arrived in the Portuguese capital and asked for an audience with the king.

As the disaffected former partner of Columbus, Cabot himself was of great interest to Lisbon and John listened closely to his arguments. Columbus had not in fact found the Indies, he said. The so-called Indians he had brought with him looked like nothing more than offshore islanders. The real prize of a westward route to the Indies was still within grasp, by going farther north, where the latitudes and therefore the distances were shorter. And he, Cabot, was prepared to lead such an expedition for the Portuguese. But there was another reason why John wanted to meet Cabot. Both of them were emerging as skeptics about the whole business of the Indies; not that such a route was impossible, just that it had so far eluded Columbus. The king was an intelligent man with a strong sense of the possibilities of geography, and of the real size of the globe. He had personal reasons, as well, to be very skeptical about the enterprise he had turned down.

But the geopolitics remained the same as it had with Almeida and Behaim. There were better reasons for peace than for provoking the Castilians into war. So Cabot was thanked and sent on his way. Christmas was approaching, and with not much of a future back in Seville, a penniless Cabot was desperately puzzling over how to feed his family. After New Year's Day, 1495, the news arrived that Seville had turned down his proposal for a new bridge. So, homeless again and desperately searching for employment—chased halfway across southern Europe by his creditors—Cabot set sail once more, perhaps back to Seville, perhaps back on the familiar voyage across the Bay of Biscay to Bristol.

The truth was that even the Columbus brothers were having their doubts about what they had found, though they dared not admit them to anyone but their closest allies like de Cuneo—and he was gone. Where *was* China? Like Cabot, they began to suspect that it was probably farther north—that they had misjudged the latitude of Cathay and had overshot it and were now lost in the islands south of Indonesia.

The answer, they believed, was to plan a new voyage, with what supplies they could spare, using two ships, plus a small vessel they had constructed from spare parts at Isabella; Bartholomew would take it northward. The expedition was planned quietly, alongside the slave fleet, and was designed to find Cathay. For de Cuneo, explaining their thinking once he was back in Europe, this was the very last chance for the admiral: "If in that direction no more will be found than we had found in the above related [voyage to Cuba], I am very much afraid that he will have to abandon everything."

But it was not to be. The business of rounding up slaves had roused the Tainos across Hispaniola into action. The chief of all the chiefs, Guaniguana, united as many of the tribes as he could on the island in the early months of 1495 and advanced on Isabella to drive the Europeans into the sea. Putting aside Bartholomew's expedition, the Columbus brothers and Ojeda hurriedly knit together an army of defense. They led two hundred soldiers out to meet Guaniguana, and a combined charge of lancers with dogs terrified the Tainos and put them to flight. Effective resistance was at an end, but Bartholomew's voyage to the north had now been fatally delayed.

When the ships had been prepared again, later in the summer, a hurricane swept across the Caribbean and smashed them to pieces.

# 6

# HEADING NORTH

*"Of Yseland to wryte is lytill need*
*save of Stockfische; yet for sooth in dede*
*out of Bristow and costis many one*
*men have praticised by needle and stone*
*Thiderwardes wythine a lytel whylle*
*Wythene xij yeres, and wythoute perille . . ."*

"The Libelle of Englysche Polycye," 1436

*"I see that the world is not so large as the vulgar opinion*
*thinks it is."*

CHRISTOPHER COLUMBUS

IN NEWS, POLITICS, and diplomacy, stories that people desperately want to be true can take on a life of their own, however unlikely they might be. The canny and parsimonious Henry VII of England had, it seemed, united the nation and ended the civil war, but he was never quite loved. There was also continuing speculation and nostalgia in England and beyond about the so-called Princes in the Tower—the young heirs to the Yorkist dynasty who had not been seen since they were sent under protective custody to the Tower of London in 1483. So when rumors spread across Europe in the early 1490s that one of the princes had been seen alive, people wanted to believe it.

Henry was fated to be haunted by young men claiming to be one or the other of the missing princes, and it was frustrating to him that whether or not he knew of their fate, he couldn't produce them as evidence that the pretenders were frauds. No sooner was Lambert Simnel safely imprisoned in his palace kitchens, than another, far more convincing, imposter emerged on the continent, claiming once again to be the missing Richard, Duke of York. Some time in 1489, just as Bartholomew Columbus was proposing the enterprise of the Indies to the English court, a fifteen-year-old apprentice to a Breton merchant, known to history as Perkin Warbeck, was asked by his master to model some of the silks they were selling in Cork harbor in Ireland. A passerby immediately recognized him as Edward, Earl of Warwick, a Yorkist claimant to the throne.

Embarrassed and a little scared, Warbeck swore he was wrong. He was almost certainly from a converted Jewish family, actually the son of John Osbeck of Tournai. But later in the day, more visitors swore oaths that he looked like the bastard son of Richard III, John of Pontefract. But he couldn't have been, they reasoned, because Pontefract was in prison in England. Yet what else could explain his extraordinary likeness to the family of

Perkin Warbeck

York? He must be none other than the missing prince. It has never been quite clear how this misunderstanding, or practical joke, came to be taken so seriously—except that those who claimed to believe it, and Perkin Warbeck himself, seemed to want it to be true. So much so that Warbeck, a most extraordinary fantasist and confidence man, began to see the possibilities, and to act out the part until the role trapped him and there was no turning back.

Two years later in France, when rumors of the reappearance of one of the missing princes reached the ears of the king of France, Charles received Warbeck. It made diplomatic sense to him—because it was so inconvenient to the English—for him to officially recognize Warbeck as the Duke of York. He involved Margaret of Burgundy, Edward IV's sister, who hailed him as a "white"—a member of the family of the white rose of York. She in turn funded and opened to him the doors to the royal rulers of Europe.

Again, it has never been clear whether she did so out of malice toward the Tudors or the conviction that this was, indeed, her long-lost nephew. Whatever it was, in the autumn of 1493, as Columbus was setting out on his second voyage, Margaret of Burgundy introduced Warbeck to Maximilian, the Holy Roman emperor, who was equally taken with the youth. Between them, they encouraged his attempted landing in England in July 1495, and watched fascinated as he fled first to Ireland and then Scotland, and into the welcoming arms of the thoroughly convinced James IV, the romantic young king of Scots.

Unknown to Columbus and Vespucci, and probably Cabot—and probably also unknown to Henry VII of England—a small clique of Bristol merchants were continuing their voyages of exploration westward, building on the voyages of the *Trinity* fourteen years earlier, in flagrant defiance of the new treaty that had carved up the world. Despite glimpsing an island in 1481 they believed was hy-Brasil, they seem to have been unable, after repeated attempts, to find the right winds and currents to take them back there, with only very basic navigation equipment at their disposal. In the summer of 1494, their efforts seemed to have been rewarded with another sighting of what they believed to be the lost isle. They followed its coastline southward, but heavy seas and a disaffected and frightened crew forced them to turn back. It was the perennial problem for explorers.

But unlike Columbus, with his triumphal return only two years before, these scouts had to sneak up the Avon and swear their crew to secrecy. Since the original license for exploration had been allowed to lapse thirteen years earlier, after Thomas Croft was put on trial, these voyages had been clandestine. What is more, the small group of Bristol merchants who knew about them—now that Thomas Croft's partners were mostly dead—kept the closely guarded secret to themselves for fear that any trading advantages they could gain would simply be lost to others. Yet without admitting the discoveries and making them legal, they were forced to explore in secret. It was precisely this dilemma that Columbus and Cabot had set out to resolve. The result was deep factions among the merchants of Bristol. The new chief customs official, Richard Amerike, appointed to replace Thomas Croft, suspected the voyages but could not prove them.

One man who also watched carefully was their fellow merchant and English spy, John Day. He saw the return of the voyage and bided his time.

We may only have the sketchiest details of the personalities of some of the key figures in the race for America, but it is possible to discern a great deal from the way people behaved toward them. Columbus clearly inspired a strange mixture of awe and exasperation—it is the contradictions here, not the lack of evidence, that make him hard to read. Vespucci seems to have consistently inspired both trust and affection among those more powerful than he, and irritation with his pomposity among people of lesser importance. Cabot's confident bonhomie seems to have impressed those he came across with his abilities as a cartographer and globe maker, as a leader, navigator, and negotiator, but he seems to have turned others into immediate opponents. He impressed Ferdinand in Valencia, but inspired such suspicion among local officials that his jetty plans were scrapped. Reading between the lines, this seems to have also been the pattern after his arrival in Bristol, sometime early in 1495.

Whatever the merchants told the king, this was a good time to set up business in Bristol. After the loss of Gascony and Bordeaux to the French in 1453, the cloth and wine trade to Bristol had been cut in half. Many Bristol merchants had been forced to shift part or all of their business to London. But now the wine, cloth, and sugar trade between Bristol and Lisbon and

Madeira—which Columbus and Cabot had both taken part in—was replacing it and then some. This was now a successful port, home to ten thousand
people, perched at the confluence of the Avon and Frome rivers, which met
in a great basin at the heart of the city, and where ships from France, Ireland, and the Spanish peninsula could be seen loading and unloading.

Cabot had been drawn back to the city once again, because of the cloth
trade, which had dominated his life before his debts banished him from
Venice. His proposal for the Indies had been rejected in Lisbon, and the
Bristol ships at the quays brought to mind not just the sight of Columbus
and his so-called Indians, but also the notion that the English might be candidates for an alternative approach.

Cabot had probably always known sketchy details of the western voyages
by the Bristol merchants. When the *Trinity* had returned in 1481, there
were Venetian galleys docked in Southampton and London, and they
included crew members from his Scuole Grandi confraternity. He had also
spent enough time around Seville and Lisbon, since catching the glimpse of
Columbus in Valencia, to work out precisely what mistakes he believed
Columbus had made. If there was land to the west of Ireland—and there
seemed to be evidence that there was—and if it wasn't an island, then the
way to the Indies was to follow the coast southwest all the way to China.

Cabot now believed Columbus had marooned himself on some midocean
archipelago. That meant the enterprise of the Indies was still alive, and the
great advantage for anyone sailing from Bristol was that the latitude was
that much shorter than it would be sailing from the Canary Islands or the
Azores. Cabot was a globe maker. He understood all too well the implications of shorter latitudes farther north. The key for Cabot was what kind of
land had been found by the Bristol merchants. If it was an island, as they
clearly believed, then he was no better off. But if it was the mainland, or
near the mainland, then he would claim it under the authority of whatever
ruler backed him, and follow the coast down to the spice trade. This was not
welcome news for the close-knit coterie of Bristol merchants protecting
their secret. Since the *Trinity* voyages, they had been thinking in terms of
an island; Cabot was saying that it was actually an eastern continent.

Because of the furtive westward voyages since 1480, Bristol was also a
somewhat secretive city. The old alliance that had first sent the *Trinity* on
expeditions to the west had ended. Croft died in 1488, Spencer that very

year (1495), and de la Founte would die within months. Those who protected their secret, the island of hy-Brasil, were naturally suspicious of this Venetian seeking support for a westerly voyage. Cabot kept quiet about his Genoese origins: Genoa had been deeply unpopular in Bristol since the local merchant Robert Sturmy and 128 Bristol crewmen had been killed in a naval engagement with pirates employed by the Genoese in 1458. But Bristol was already divided in its loyalties. Croft had been chief customs official, loyal to the Yorkist dynasty, and had been sacked by the new king. His successor, Richard Amerike, was a successful merchant and ferocious moneylender in his own right, but a distant relative of Henry VII, and therefore the object of suspicion among those privy to the secret of hy-Brasil.

Enter Cabot, almost penniless and armed only with contacts in the Thorne family of merchants, one of whom he had met in Castile. As a foreign merchant, he would normally have lodged in another merchant's home. As a penniless adventurer, he may have been forced to live with his family outside the city walls, in the crowded foreign community known ironically as Cathay, but within hailing distance of the wealthiest merchants' homes around St. Mary Redcliffe, the great church on the outskirts of Bristol. From there, at least before the nine P.M. curfew when the city gates were closed, those lodged outside the walls could watch the ships arriving from Venice, Lisbon, or Seville, next to the great bay windows of the customs house in front of the docks, with the bearded crews staggering ashore, the women selling bread and ale in the streets, the prostitutes in their striped hoods, and the colorful cargoes of Gascon woad for dying cloth blue and the Spanish lice used for dying the famous Bristol Broadmead cloth scarlet.

But his lack of money made Cabot's enterprise urgent. He was given an introduction to Richard Amerike, and convinced him that the enterprise was worth the risk. For Amerike, it was the same calculation as it was for Isabella of Castile. If Cabot failed, then he lost little. But if he did what he said he would do, then, at the very least, the near monopoly of the Mediterranean spice trade enjoyed by Southampton would shift to Bristol, and that would make Bristol very rich.

As Cabot was making his home in Bristol, the eyes of Europe remained focused on the momentous events in Italy, where the continuing French invasion had lost momentum behind long supply chains stretching back along the Italian coast.

For the first time in living memory, the fractious Italian city-states were beginning to work together to face this unprecedented threat. Even Venice and Milan, which had both initially welcomed the French, had been persuaded by the pope that—if Charles were allowed to wander unchallenged around Italy—they would all soon become French possessions in a burgeoning French empire. It was time to act, and a Holy League—holy because Pope Alexander proclaimed it as such—was created in April 1495 to resist the French army. It included the emperor Maximilian and Castile and Aragon. In fact, Ferdinand was one of the main architects of the alliance. Together, they persuaded the veteran mercenary, the Duke of Mantua, to lead an army against Charles.

The treaty was signed beside the Grand Canal in Venice, and the sultan's ambassador was allowed to watch from behind a hanging carpet, having been reassured that, despite the rhetoric, the league had no designs on Constantinople. When Charles heard about it, he flew into a rage and threatened the Venetian ambassador with a rival alliance, realizing as he did so the danger he was now in. By the following month, the league was threatening his communication routes and Charles realized it was time to withdraw—if he could. He set out with half his army, plus twenty thousand mules carrying the spoils of victory, each cannon lashed to a hundred men to get them through the Apennine passes. For a second time, the cardinals cleared out of Rome to make way and, this time, Pope Alexander went with them.

On July 4 the main French army reached a village south of Parma called Fornovo and found their way blocked by the combined forces of the Holy League. Charles faced the coming battle on an enormous black horse called Savoy, his long nose poking out of a full suit of armor. In the ensuing battle, he lost his valuable wagons and most of his artillery when the league's ill-disciplined cavalry left the battlefield to chase them. But, as a result, he was able to fight the league to a standstill and negotiate a truce, allowing the remains of the French army to pass unmolested back across the Alps.

Naples was retaken by an Aragonese army later in the month. The gains from the greatest French army ever to cross the Alps were precisely nil, though the knowledge of the Renaissance was taken back home by the retreating soldiers when they dispersed at Lyons. They also left behind the so-called French disease, the syphilis brought to Europe by Columbus's crew-men, and caught in Naples from the Aragonese defenders. Within seven years, it had reached Canton in China.

The league now knew how vulnerable Italy was to a renewed French at-tack and were desperate to widen the alliance. Would England join? Diplo-matic messages crisscrossed the continent in the weeks before Christmas, 1495, and in London King Henry realized he was in a strong negotiating position. He told Ferdinand's emissary that his price would be the marriage of his son Arthur to a Spanish princess. It was also made clear that Maxi-milian would have to drop his support for Perkin Warbeck, and this he re-fused to do.

It is one of those peculiar ironies of history that, as preparations were be-ing made for the most extraordinary year of navigation and exploration in history, the minds of the rulers were very much on other things.

In Portugal, minds were not concentrating on the fate of the Holy League in Italy. The wily King John, the perfect prince, had not been well since the accidental death of his son and heir, Alfonso, in 1491, thrown from his horse within sight of his father, who always suspected he was the victim of one of Ferdinand's spies. In the years since, John had consistently made the case that he should be succeeded by his illegitimate son, George, but this was against the bitter opposition of the queen. So bitter, in fact, that when John's health spiraled into sudden decline in October 1495, just as Cabot was arriving in Bristol, it was rumored that the queen had poisoned him. After all, had not John personally assassinated her brother for his plot to overthrow the throne?

Whether this was so or not, a few hours before he died on October 25, at the age of only thirty-nine, John had apparently changed his mind. He named his wife's younger brother, Manuel, as his heir. Manuel was vain, fair, and slight, with a love of luxury and music, and slightly indolent. Negotia-tions were accelerated for him to marry the widow of Alfonso, Ferdinand and Isabella's daughter Isabella.

This alliance proved to be a disaster for Lisbon's Jewish community, 120,000 of whom had taken shelter there when they were expelled from

Aragon and Castile in 1492. Now, to win the favor of the Spanish court, the new king Manuel I decided he must toughen up his policy. So in the new year, Portugal copied Isabella's policy in Castile and Aragon, setting a deadline of December 1496 for all Jews to either convert or leave the country.

At least Ferdinand and Isabella had believed they would convert, but Manuel had no such excuse. So when Portugal's Jewish community—many of them facing this kind of deadline for the second time—arrived at the dockside to leave, they were met by mobs backed by soldiers and priests who had them forcibly baptized. But even then they were not left alone. From a haven of safety for Europe's Jews, Lisbon became the scene of one of the most horrific series of brutal riots, leaving thousands of converted Jews dead.


All was not well with Columbus's company in Seville. Vespucci was dealing with the complexity of his and Berardi's effective monopoly on equipping supply ships for the Indies. His former employers in Florence were now fighting for their very survival and he could hardly rely on them. Berardi was increasingly infirm—exacerbated by the stress of the heavy debts he incurred as a result of financing Columbus's original voyage. There was also little prospect that the meager returns from the voyages to the Indies—a little gold and an embarrassing and unsaleable profusion of slaves—was ever going to pay them off. At this difficult time, the most dangerous threat yet to their business venture emerged. Fonseca, now appointed bishop of Badajoz, though he hardly ever went there, was determined to wrest the monopoly on equipping the ships from Vespucci and Berardi. As a consecrated bishop, Fonseca was growing into the personality that would dominate business to and from the Indies for the coming decades. Proud, impatient, bullying, and scrupulously honest, he was also implacably opposed to everything Columbus stood for.

Berardi had a consummate business mind. His first proposal was to slash the guaranteed cost of fitting and supplying ships from the usual rate of three thousand maravedis per ton to two thousand, plus undercutting the lowest bid by one thousand maravedis, whatever it was. On this basis, he and Vespucci signed a contract to supply twelve ships, four large supply ships in Cadiz to be ready that summer, and two more groups of four ships,

also in Cadiz, to be ready within six months. A stream of complaints now issued from Fonseca's office, claiming that cutting costs on that scale would
make the ships unseaworthy. When Vespucci discovered that Fonseca was
chartering other ships, Berardi appealed to the sovereigns. Some agonizing
weeks later, they were vindicated. Ferdinand and Isabella wrote back: "The
bishop will use your ships and not others, and we have so instructed him,
even though he has them loaded."

At the same time, Berardi was receiving letters from Columbus by way of
the returning ships, urging him to resupply the colony. The problem was
that most colonists actually wanted to come back and Hispaniola was already in debt to the sum of between 10 and 12 million maravedis, with no
prospect of repayment. Columbus's miscalculations may have been a source
of personal embarrassment, but for Berardi it was a very serious threat, especially as he was not well and was relying increasingly on Vespucci to do the
work. Something had to give and it was at this point that Berardi put forward a plan of his own.

The idea was to populate the new islands in such a way that they could
increasingly provide for one another's needs, and to earn money by trading
with one another and with Spain. To reach that position required a considerable investment—probably the same amount as had been invested so
far—but this time it would be properly managed. The sovereigns retained
the right to a fifth of all precious metals and pearls found in the Indies, and
if enough colonists went there and brought them back, then this fifth could
pay back the investment. What was required was other ways in which new
colonists could make fortunes in the Indies. The twelve ships would therefore carry tools, seeds, cattle, and more colonists. These would then stay
based in Columbus's islands and be available to travel and trade between
new colonies there or to discover more islands. Notaries, lawyers, and accountants would have to go on the same ships to begin tallying up exactly
what was owed to the crown.

Of the 12 million maravedis required, two would be amortized and 10
million more would be provided by the crown. But at the end of six months,
those fifths owed to the sovereigns would begin to pay off the mortgage in
such a way that no further investment would be required, and, it might be
added, a means would have been created to pay Berardi's debts as well. The
amortization plan would have to be underpinned by new rules that governed

investors. Anyone who wanted to try their luck in the Indies would be as-signed to a commander and would have to buy a license to conquer and set-tle some land. They would have to finance their basic costs, and a fifth of the profits they made over and above that investment would go to the crown.

It was a bold proposal and, as much as anything else, the foundation of the economic underpinnings of Europe's transatlantic empires. It also subtly recognized what Vespucci had begun to suspect, that Columbus might not have discovered islands near the Indies after all, so gold and spices might never be forthcoming. The difficulty was that combined with the cost-cutting they had agreed to with the ship supply contracts, the exhausting workload could only get heavier. But Vespucci, ever efficient, managed to prepare the first four of these supply ships by August 1495, and Columbus's former friend, the royal butler Juan Aguardo, was appointed to command them. He was charged also by the sovereigns to investigate the complaints made by Boyle and Margarit and report back.

With the slave shipments from Hispaniola finally suspended, the Columbus brothers were back where they had been before with no way of paying their debts. Most of the inhabitants of Isabella were seriously weakened by mal-nutrition, syphilis, dysentery, and malaria. The ability of the new colonists to feed themselves depended on supplies from Castile, and they had to be paid for. There had to be a way of extracting gold from the island.

The system devised by the Columbus brothers was brilliantly simple. It was also, according to Las Casas, "a moral pestilence . . . invented by Sa-tan." But it was not unprecedented, and related systems were to emerge in many other empires over the centuries, from Mexico and Peru to British In-dia. The gold was to be extracted by taxation. Every adult native of the is-land over the age of fourteen had to provide a tiny brass bell, called a hawk's bell, of gold, about a thimbleful, exhaustingly panned from the rivers. If they lived in an area that was known to have little gold, or too far from the rivers, they could pay the tax with twenty-five pounds of spun cotton in-stead. It was a tragic irony that the hawk's bells, brought over by Columbus to delight the Indians, were now to become a symbol of their oppression.

For a race that was unused to heavy work, this was disastrous. Their agrarian economy provided the Tainos with sufficient food for their needs without hard labor. Like later imperial administrations, it may even have been that Columbus's council, which had once hailed the natives as noble innocents, was offended by the Tainos' slow pace of life and their easy access to necessities. Either way, what small amounts of gold the Tainos possessed was the fruit of generations of work, and extracting it from the soil or riverbeds was extremely difficult and impossibly exhausting and humiliating, especially when the lowest Castilian convict demanded to be treated by any passing Taino as if he were royalty. Those that managed to pay the tax were rewarded with a copper token. Those without copper tokens were hunted down with hounds and hanged in groups of thirteen—in memory of Christ and the apostles. By the end of the decade, there were 340 gallows across Hispaniola. Some Tainos escaped to the mountains; others fought back, incurring the most horrific reprisals against their families.

Regimes that institutionalize even the mildest tyranny seem to in effect remove any qualms rulers might have about further brutality, and so it was on Hispaniola. The new taxation regime was enforced with a series of campaigns all over the island led by Ojeda and Bartholomew Columbus, who was gaining a reputation for severity almost as fearsome as Ojeda's. These campaigns were partly to install a chain of forts across the island, partly to seek out sources of gold, and partly to reinforce the message that rebellion would be a serious mistake. When rumors emerged about gold in any location, brutal roving bands would descend on the locals and terrify them into providing more information about the source, even when it never existed. "Infinite was the number of people I saw burned alive," wrote Las Casas a few years later, describing how they forced this information out of the miserable Tainos.

It was said that what horrified the Tainos most about the new arrivals wasn't their violence or their greed, it was their coldness—their lack of human emotion. Often there was no purpose in the brutality at all. Las Casas describes how groups of colonists "made bets as to who would slit a man in two, or cut off his head with one blow; or they opened up his bowels. They tore the babes from their mother's breast by their feet, and dashed their heads on the rocks." There were horrific descriptions of villagers watching while colonists honed the blades of their swords, only to have them test the sharpness by putting the observers to death.

The combination of all this cruelty was disastrous for the miserable Tainos, who had so enchanted Columbus less than four short years before. As well as the brutal killings—organized or spontaneous—the diversion of farmers away from the land was even more fatal as the effects of famine were beginning to appear. Columbus had also brought cattle with him on the second voyage and began using the Castilian methods of cattle ranching, which tended to devastate everything that grew in the area, leading very quickly to soil erosion—just what had happened on the Cape Verde Islands and Madeira. Those natives who worked with the colonists found themselves shunned by their own people. Even Chief Guancanagarí, who had helped Columbus save the stores from the stricken *Santa Maria*, died ruined and wandering alone in the mountains.

By 1495, according to Peter Martyr, up to 50,000 Tainos had died. The population of Hispaniola at the time has been variously estimated at between 300,000 and 8 million. The speed of the destruction of the Tainos population depends on which figure you believe. But two years later, after the imposition of the taxation system, perhaps a third of the population of the islands had been killed or died from the famine or the diseases brought over by their conquerors, mainly influenza. By 1507 only 60,000 were left; by 1542, only 200.*

What has become apparent only recently was that the agents of this oppression, the settlers who had joined Columbus so greedily and hopefully on his second voyage, were themselves suffering under a form of tyranny. It was milder than that suffered by the Tainos, but it was just as bitterly resented. To be fair to Columbus, he clearly decided that fear was the only option open to him to control his disparate and recalcitrant followers, but his judgment was nonetheless disastrous and his policies erratic.

It soon became clear that he was ignoring instructions from Queen Isabella, not just about slavery, but about the prices he should charge for food, the rations he should allow, and the punishments he should inflict. His strict policy on baptism—only for children—was designed to maximize his choice of slaves, because Christians could not be enslaved. It was bitterly resented by the colonists, especially when their native mistresses were refused baptism because it meant they could not marry them. Columbus's insistence

---

*Today they are extinct or entirely subsumed into the colonial population.

that colonists should attend mass was equally unpopular, as was his refusal to allow rations to be given to anyone who was ill. Those caught swapping gold for food were whipped through the streets. Those selling it were hanged.

Queen Isabella had also insisted that all malefactors should be sent home, with records of the evidence against them, for punishment in Castile. But the Columbus brothers preferred unexpected and often brutal punishments instead, often on the basis of rumor alone. "His guilt is written on his forehead," Columbus said, condemning one colonist. Others were tortured to death.

In October 1495 the beleaguered colonists in the new city of Isabella were relieved at last by the sight of four sets of sails on the horizon, cautiously making their way around the reefs of Hispaniola. But the relief Bartholomew Columbus felt about the badly needed supplies was tempered by the discovery of who was on board.

Landing by the makeshift dock at Isabella, Juan Aguardo had the trumpets sounded to herald his arrival, followed by a contingent of soldiers. Marching up to the government building, he immediately began countermanding Bartholomew's orders. There was a scene outside as Bartholomew tried to delay him by questioning the authenticity of his papers. Aguardo responded by taunting him about how displeased the sovereigns had become. Bartholomew sent an urgent message to his brother to return as soon as possible to tackle the most serious threat to their authority so far.

Aguardo began immediately investigating the situation on Hispaniola. He discovered that almost everyone on the island was ill and desperate to go home, and this was the main reason the new colony was still so dependent on supplies—few had either the health or the will to start cultivating crops. Almost nobody was interested in putting down roots. They just wanted to leave. It had not been Aguardo's intention to stay on Isabella any longer than he absolutely had to. But shortly after his arrival, a hurricane swept through the Caribbean, tearing off the roofs of houses and swamping part of the shore. This was the storm that ended Columbus's ambitions to explore northward but it also flung Aguardo's ships onto the beach, smashing them beyond repair. Of all the ships anchored off the coast, only Columbus's favorite, the *Niña*, escaped. Until the next fleet arrived from Castile, or they could rig up some interim solution, Aguardo was trapped with Columbus.*

If the Italian Renaissance was, at its heart, about money, banking, and investment as much as it was about art, as historians say today, then Berardi epitomized it. In his house in Seville, where he lived with Vespucci—a small piece of Florence transported to Castile—they had debated the emerging shape of the world, tried to teach groups of Tainos to speak Castilian Spanish, and soothed Columbus's tortured brain on his visits. But now the period of Vespucci's life dominated by his great friendship with Berardi was coming to an end. Berardi was on his sickbed, exhausted by months of political battles with Fonseca and the overwhelming tasks of supplying the vessels for the Indies, carrying the weight of Columbus's debt, and lobbying at court on Columbus's behalf about money he believed was owed to him.

There was some respite in October when 40,000 maravedis from the sale of slaves from the Indies appeared in the accounts, just before the ban, allowing the company to cobble together more supplies for Columbus. Berardi continued to work on his fleets, but his health was failing fast. On December 14, 1495, he wrote his will, setting out in some detail how to handle his personal debts. The will undertook to pay all his creditors, but it was also realistic: Paying his creditors depended on Columbus repaying the 180,000 maravedis, which were to be paid to his executors, one of whom was Vespucci, who he described as "my agent and special friend."

The following morning the lawyers gathered around his bed to witness the signing of the will, only too aware that the prospect of Columbus ever being able to repay his debt was increasingly remote. By now Berardi was too weak to hold a pen. But he made his mark and slipped into a coma and died in the evening. He was only thirty-eight. Businesses then tended to be inherited by the partners, so Vespucci was now alone as agent for an undertaking that was both exhausting and possibly unviable.

*The Tainos may have died out as a result of the arrival of Columbus, but they have left some traces of culture behind and the word "hurricane" is one of them. It is their word meaning "sudden storm."

I

*"One crew member on the topsail called Navarro shouted
'Land ahoy! Land ahoy!' Everyone was so excited that he
who expressed it least came across as the craziest, as anyone would feel in such a state."*

Spanish transatlantic sailor, 1521

Cabot was in London. He had been employed by some of the Bristol merchants a few months earlier to put their case to the Danish ambassador
about Bristol's trade with Iceland. It was more evidence of his peculiar
charisma that he should have been employed in this way by Amerike's faction among the Bristol merchants and so soon after his arrival. But this
time, armed with introductions arranged by Amerike, he was there—
probably around November 1495—to put forward the case that he lead an
English voyage of exploration and trade to the Indies. And these would be
the real Indies, he emphasized, not those islands discovered by Columbus.

Cabot was not a man to operate in a city quietly, and he soon became
known to one of the few others in London with genuine knowledge and interest in the Indies. This was a rare thing in Cabot's recent life—a genuine
stroke of luck. Giovanni Antonio de Carbonariis was an Augustinian or
Austin friar. He may have been sworn to poverty, but he was also an emerging prince of the church, the deputy papal tax collector in England, and a
recognized theologian, originally from Pavia in Italy but now living in London. He was in close contact with the Minim friars, who had led the expedition under Bernardo Boyle, and through their stories—and scandalous
descriptions of Columbus's attempt at colonization—had become fascinated
with the whole idea of exploration. But he had also been Henry VII's emissary to Milan, in which role he must have met Cabot when he was living
there. Carbonariis had the contacts and the interest to drive Cabot's plans
to fruition, and with his protection and friendship, and leaving his family in
Bristol, Cabot moved into the palatial London abbey of the Austin Friars.

Austin Friars, with its dominating spire, included an abbey, a famous library, and extensive grounds, with Throgmorton Street on its south side
and the city walls on the north. From the accommodation there, visitors
could gaze over the walls across the Moorfields, with its skaters on the

frozen ponds in winter, to the fields of Finsbury and the village of Islington in the distance. That was where, amid the black habits, Cabot spent his evenings. But during the day he was following up on any contacts in the city who might provide him with the investment he needed.

The original scheme with the Columbus brothers had involved generating investment from the Spinola family—who had recently been helping Bartholomew Columbus—and there Cabot proceeded, past the other offices of the Italian banking houses on Lombard Street, to the Genoese bankers Agostino and Benedetto Spinola, with whom Carbonariis had close links. It was they who agreed to back Cabot's voyage, conditional of course on getting royal backing. Then the area of activity shifted westward, down Ludgate Hill, across the Fleet River, and past the great palaces of the Strand to Westminster, and the lawyers and court officials Cabot and his backers now needed.

In the weeks that followed, he became a familiar figure around Westminster and in the streets of London farther up the Thames. London was then a city of riotous apprentices, of hot pies sold in the street, heavy bar-room drinking, and the ghoulish sight of traitors' heads on poles at the southern end of the extraordinary—and crumbling—London Bridge, with its houses, chapel, and drawbridge.* London Bridge was also one of only two ways over the river. The pavements were often unpaved and the footpaths muddy, and it made sense to climb down the river steps and shout "oars" if you wanted to get around.

This was also a city in the grip of one of its periodic crazes. Playing cards, with the famous representation of Elizabeth of York—Henry VII's wife—as the queen, had just arrived in London and could be found in nearly every inn and tavern. So popular had they become that the king himself had banned servants and apprentices from using them that very Christmas, though he regularly gambled with cards himself. Cabot undoubtedly came across them on this visit.

Cabot was keeping to the original plan that he and Columbus had outlined. His voyage was to be explicitly about trade, and he would enforce his

---

*The man in charge of the upkeep of London Bridge at this time was John More, whose son—Sir Thomas More, the writer, chancellor, and future martyr for his refusal to abandon Catherine of Aragon—was then seventeen years old.

own claim to any lands that were discovered with a royal warrant. There would be no simple fee and dismissal with honor as there was for the Portuguese commanders, and there would be no secrecy forced on them as there had been for the Bristol explorers.

An official voyage to the Indies was a tricky affair diplomatically. For one thing, it would fly in the face of the pope's decision to divide the world between Castile and Portugal. But it also required careful thought, and most English diplomats were engaged at the time in intricate negotiations with the Holy League, which were taking place in Nordlingen near Augsburg. It was there that Italian diplomats were hammering away at the emperor Maximilian to persuade him to drop his support for Perkin Warbeck so that England would join. The main player in the league was by then Ferdinand of Aragon. At the beginning of 1496, just as Cabot was becoming entrenched in his own negotiations in London, Ferdinand sent his emissary Rodrigo Gonzales de Puebla to negotiate a marriage between the young Prince of Wales, Henry's nine-year-old son Arthur, and his own daughter Catherine of Aragon—as long as Henry sealed the deal by joining the league.

Only one thing seemed likely to defer the plan: Warbeck was now in Scotland as a guest of James IV of Scots, and they were planning a joint attack over the border into England. James had taken an instant liking to Warbeck, installed him in a magnificent suite in Stirling Castle, and married him rapidly to one of his cousins. Ferdinand was kept fully informed about this by his spies in Edinburgh, and he was determined that the attack should not happen. He therefore launched a sophisticated intelligence scam to persuade the Scottish king—a bachelor—that he had another available, unmarried daughter. If James dropped Warbeck and his invasion plans he could marry her. As part of the same intelligence plot, Warbeck would be lured to Castile and quietly disappear.

As Cabot and his advisers sat in the corridors and antechambers of Westminster, they heard rumors of the negotiations with the Holy League and they realized one aspect was playing firmly into their hands: As long as Ferdinand and Isabella were desperate for Henry to join their league against France, they would not quibble about minor infractions of their monopoly on what Columbus called the Indies. What is more, a rumor had reached Henry's ears that Warbeck was in fact in Castile and being sheltered by Ferdinand himself, in which case he would hardly care what

Ferdinand thought. But of course Cabot also emphasized the economic benefits to England of having a handle on the spice trade, and having met Bartholomew Columbus, Henry was familiar with the basic idea of sailing west to go east.

Even so, waiting on the will of kings was a difficult and expensive business. Even if Cabot managed to get to see Henry at this tense moment in diplomatic intrigue, there were still detailed negotiations with the royal lawyers, and almost everyone involved—even the man who warmed the sealing wax for the final document—had to be paid. Cabot and his investors sat for days, even weeks, in the drafty corridors of Westminster, unsure which lawyers they could trust and which superior courtiers could really give them access, paying out money and talking. Like Columbus in a similar situation a decade earlier, Cabot's main weapon was his powers of persuasion.

Cabot's exertions in Westminster had not gone unnoticed by Ferdinand's network of spies, who were particularly vigilant about any threat to their unexpected foothold on the Indies. On January 21, 1496, de Puebla—now Ferdinand's ambassador in London—wrote home to warn that "one like Columbus" had arrived there and was trying to persuade King Henry to mount his own enterprise of the Indies. He reassured Ferdinand that, in fact, Henry was not listening to this proposal, which was in any case (he said) a plot by the French to undermine Anglo-Spanish relations at this crucial diplomatic moment.

De Puebla was a shabby figure around Westminster, who had become so close to the English king, on this and previous visits, that he attracted some suspicion from his compatriots. He was short in stature and came from humble origins, and his father was rumored to be a tailor and a converted Jew. He supplemented his income by representing the pope and the emperor in London as well, but he was paid so badly by Ferdinand, and so irregularly, that he was forced to spend much more time hanging around the court than he wanted.

"Why does he come to court?" Henry asked one of his courtiers, according to the Tudor chroniclers, wondering why this somewhat poorly dressed visitor was always at Westminster Palace.

"To eat," they said. Henry roared with laughter.

To make matters worse, once Ferdinand's other ambassador Pedro de Ayala had finished his work in Edinburgh—and James had discovered with disgust that there was no other unmarried Spanish princess—de Ayala was sent to London to reinforce de Puebla. But the two diplomats loathed each other, and the English court thoroughly enjoyed watching them fight it out in public.

In fact, de Puebla was wrong: Cabot had managed to wangle at least one meeting with the king himself, spreading out his maps and, like Columbus, faced the prospect of the whole project being referred to a committee. But he had won over both king and committee as well as the royal lawyers. When de Puebla was writing to Ferdinand, the patent that would give Cabot the right to explore with the king's authority was already being negotiated. It was finalized on March 5, 1496, addressed to "John Cabotto, Citizen of Venice, Lewes, Sebastyan and Soncio, his sonnys," and finally signed by the king.

The documents gave the Cabots the right—and their heirs and those merchants to whom they had assigned some of those rights—to send five ships to "the eastern, western and northern seas" to discover "whatever islands, countries, regions or provinces of heathens and infidels, in whatsoever part of the world placed, which before this time were unknown to all Christians." The document was carefully written to give some grounds for defense if Ferdinand and Isabella complained. The southern seas were not included, and Cabot's patent extended only to undiscovered lands "unknown to all Christians." If Columbus knew about a place, they must not go there.

The patent also set out that these lands would be occupied in the king's name, and that all goods that came from there would come through Bristol, and, as in Castile and Aragon, the king would take 20 percent of the profit. Other merchants could go there and trade, under the same conditions, but they needed to have the permission of Cabot and his deputies. It was very similar to the deal done with Columbus, and further evidence that he and Cabot had hammered out the original plan between them.

As soon as the deal was done, and Cabot and his advisers were on their way back to Bristol, the English diplomat Sir John Egrement arrived in London with the news that Maximilian had agreed to drop all reference to

Perkin Warbeck, and there was now no barrier to England joining the Holy League—as long as the Scots stayed within their borders.

By late May or June 1496, Cabot's small expedition was already at sea. Historians do not know exactly when or where, but he was in stormy weather in a tiny caravel, somewhere southwest of Iceland, and in serious trouble. Bad weather, poor charts, and disease were the continuing threats to all voyages of discovery. But the real challenge in those days, when sailing anywhere except along a coast meant sailing into the unknown, was in managing the fears of the crews. Bartholomew Dias had been forced to turn back as soon as he had navigated the Cape of Good Hope. Columbus was nearly thrown overboard by terrified crewmen. And now, somewhere in the mid-Atlantic, with gales laying the tiny ship *Matthew* almost on its side in the turbulent ocean, its crow's nest touching the waves, Cabot's crew decided they had gone too far.

Cabot's dash to sea after signing the royal documents was precipitous, perhaps because he wanted to guarantee better weather by sailing in the spring or because he feared the diplomatic window that allowed the English to ignore the pope's division of the world might close. Bristol's merchant community seems to have closed ranks against him, except for Amerike and two of his business associates—Robert Thorne and Hugh Elyot. The king was famously frugal and was not investing in the voyage, and there was clearly little chance of raising enough money for the fleet of five ships that had been agreed to in the documents. In fact, Cabot would have been forced to assign a large proportion of the rights in his royal patent to Amerike and his associates. The patent had specified that all trade from his discoveries would have to go through Bristol, which meant that, initially at least, only Bristol financiers would have been prepared to invest, and they were fatally divided between those who were party to the secret of the earlier discoveries and those who were not.

It seems likely that the lease agreement on the fifty-ton *Matthew* had been arranged while Cabot was still in London. Matthew is an unusual name for a ship and probably was a nickname used after Cabot renamed the ship after his wife, Mattea. But then Matthew was also the name of a tax collector in the Bible, and the apostolic equivalent of a chief customs official, so it may also have been a tribute to Amerike, the expedition's main investor.

In the stormy North Atlantic, the whole enterprise was now threatened. It has been suggested that the crew was particularly worried about ice building up in the rigging. This was not a problem Cabot had ever faced before, and it was hard to pretend that he knew what to do. Columbus seemed to have been a master of navigating by dead reckoning, but we know nothing about Cabot's preferred methods of navigation, though he would have had a quadrant for measuring latitude by the stars. Both methods were all but impossible in bad weather. Previous experience, as Cabot must have known, suggested that three thousand miles was probably the limit before most crews would mutiny. The *Matthew* had actually sailed only two-thirds of that, but in such bad weather under such exhausting conditions, buffeted from one anonymous area of unknown ocean to the next, it might well have seemed like the full three thousand miles. Added to that, they were by then short of food. If there was to be no landfall to stock up, and no freshwater, they would have to return. They had tried—God knows they had nearly given their lives—but there was no sign of land, let alone of the Indies. It was time to turn around.

It is impossible not to wonder whether Cabot was also a victim of the coterie of Bristol merchants who knew what was on the other side of the Atlantic. There were crewmen aboard, perhaps, who had been paid to make sure the *Matthew* never stumbled upon their islands, of hy-Brasil or their newly discovered fishing grounds. Cabot also had no choice. The ship's marshal would normally punish sailors who threatened extreme actions of this kind, which might include ducking or even keelhauling, dragging the man underneath the ship, his skin torn off by barnacles. But if the ship's marshal and the crew were united, there really was no alternative but to consent to their demands. Historians have no idea how long they were battered at sea—there is no record of the date Cabot left England —but if the crew of twenty decided unanimously that they must turn around, they would have. The crew, even in medieval times, had maritime law on their side—the so-called Laws of Oléron—which gave crews in these circumstances the right to vote on whether to go home.

Bitterly disappointed, Cabot stood on the quarterdeck of the *Matthew* as they sailed back down the familiar parallel coastlines of the Bristol Channel, and waited for the tide to sweep them back up the Avon to the ignominious encounter with his critics and an embarrassing confrontation with Amerike.

He returned to Bristol, sometime in August 1496. Henry himself was in the city on August 12, and it is tempting to suppose that he took the opportunity to meet the king and retain his support for another attempt. This time Cabot was determined that there would be no mistakes. Advised by Amerike and his other backers, he handpicked his crew of eighteen for the *Matthew* and made sure that there would be allies aboard to support him. He would take his two merchant backers, Elyot and Thorne, plus two friends of his: an unnamed Burgundian and a Genoese barber from Castiglione who Cabot had persuaded to accompany them as the ship's surgeon. It may be that his fifteen-year-old son Sebastian joined them as well.

Autumn and winter 1496 to 1497 was a peculiar and sometimes alarming period in Britain. Ferdinand's plot to neutralize Perkin Warbeck unraveled and, in September, he and his new ally James IV of Scotland, led a disastrous raid over the border into England. James was nearly captured in Berwick and returned home chastened and fed up with Warbeck, who slipped away to Ireland on the *Cuckoo*, the only ship James could spare. It was then that Ferdinand's emissary Pedro de Ayala came to London and clinched the long-awaited deal to have England join the Holy League. When the news was announced in November 1496, every street in London from London Bridge to St. Paul's Cathedral was decorated with the banners of the great livery companies that presided over London's traders. The church bells rang through the morning and bonfires were lit across the city. Similar celebrations were held in Bristol, where Cabot was working.

In the new year, news arrived that the Anglo-Spanish alliance was agreed to. The treaty to marry Prince Arthur to the baby Catherine of Aragon had been signed. Henry VII had sent Catherine a wedding ring in gold and silver. This had implications for Cabot's voyage, though, as suddenly it was important that the English not upset Ferdinand and Isabella by trespassing on their islands. Cabot crossed his fingers in the hope that his patent would hold until his departure date in May.

Juan Aguardo's aggressive arrival at Isabella in October 1495, when Cabot was first in London, and his brandishing of what amounted to a royal warrant, was evidence of a shift of loyalty at Isabella and Ferdinand's court. It was imperative that Columbus should return to Spain before Aguardo had the chance to make his report. The last thing he wanted to do was to leave Hispaniola at this crucial moment in the unpopular, though capable, hands of Bartholomew, but it had to be done. To that end, Columbus and his remaining loyal followers—and the crews of Aguardo's ruined fleet—struggled through the winter to assemble something from the wreckage of the hurricane. From the larger pieces of the wrecked caravels, they managed to construct one seaworthy vessel, which they christened *India*. From the end of January 1496, Columbus shut himself away, fully aware that he had not obeyed the queen on the question of sending evidence home against his settler malefactors. For six hard weeks, he constructed evidence against everyone who had been hanged or mutilated. He may not have sent them home for punishment, but at least he would have some evidence that they had been dealt with properly.

On March 10, five days after Cabot's negotiations were concluded in London, Columbus and Aguardo squeezed into the *India* and the *Niña* with 30 slaves and 225 disillusioned Spanish colonists. The *Niña*'s original crew numbered only 25, so this meant desperate overcrowding on the decks and below. Among those on board was "rebel" leader Chief Caonabo, who, like many of the other Tainos on board, died on the voyage back. Food ran so low over the next six weeks that the crew even suggested eating the slaves or at least throwing them overboard.

Apart from the desperate crowding and shortage of food and water, Columbus was able to recover some of his physical health during the weeks at sea. But his mental health was still under severe strain. He could not accept, let alone admit, that his judgment had been wrong. All the evidence, and it mounted week by week, was that his islands were not the outlying borders of China and Japan. But why then had God guided him there? It had to make sense. Instead of cerebral rest, Columbus sat in his cabin at the stern of the small ship, writing feverish letters of self-justification to the queen, trying to counter the influence of Boyle, Margarit, and Aguardo. "The more I said," he complained, "the more these calumnies they uttered were redoubled and abhorrence shown."

When his inspiration for letter writing had temporarily been expiated, he sat hunched over his Bible, searching for clues. He became particularly obsessed with Isaiah 60:9:

*Why, the coasts and islands put their hopes in me,*
*And the vessels if Tarshish take the lead*
*In bringing your children from far away,*
*And their silver and gold with them,*
*For the sake of the name of the Lord your God.*

Sometime during his long second journey to Hispaniola, Columbus began signing his name with a mysterious cryptic set of symbols, which no historian has quite been able to decipher. The signature referred to him as Christo Ferens, like his namesake St. Christopher, the Christ bearer, carrying Christ on his back across the Atlantic. Since Tarshish was usually identified with Spain, the verse from Isaiah seemed to be self-referential. He was God's chosen instrument. But if so, then surely the suffering he had undoubtedly caused could not have been what God intended. Making steady progress in the mid-Atlantic, the spring sunshine and the occasional sea spray on his face, he remembered the delight with which he had first encountered the innocent Tainos. When he landed in Spain, he would arrive not as a conquering hero this time, but wearing the garb of a penitent. And if God was not appeased by this show of humility, it might at least help his cause with Isabella.*

On June 10, 1496, while Cabot and his recalcitrant crew were being buffeted in the North Atlantic, Bristol had been torn apart by a brutal riot between the forces of city government and the church. Bristol was the center of anticlerical feeling in England, and the heart of an underground trade in heretical books. So when the mayor became involved in a fracas while he was checking the weight of bread sold on the abbot's precincts on College Green, the townspeople hurried up the hill from the docks to join in. At the height of the fighting, which involved fists more than swords, the mayor was seen swinging his ceremonial sword around his head.† That very same day,

---

*Those disillusioned Franciscans who came back on this voyage found their order in chaos in Castile, where a new leadership was insisting on stricter lifestyles. Some friars were said to have gone to North Africa and converted to Islam so that they could keep their mistresses.

†He claimed later that he was in fact shouting, "Keep the peace, keep the peace!"

two thousand miles away in Cadiz, Columbus sailed quietly into the harbor, to find no crowds and no welcoming committee.

Berardi's elegant amortization plan was now under way. New money had been raised, and those who had put their faith in the Indies venture were waiting with confidence for repayments to begin. Unfortunately, all the colonists returning from Hispaniola brought with them were the most terrible tales of brutality and crop failure. Their disappointment was now widely understood. There was a little gold, but it was hardly lying around waiting to be picked up and, in any case, the foreign Columbus brothers took it all for themselves. Why sign on for a voyage with the next generation of investors when you were promised nothing at all and ran a 50 percent chance of not returning alive?

Those few who did volunteer for the crews tended to have nefarious, ulterior motives: They were escaping serious debts, prison sentences, or heresy charges, or they were criminals with nothing to lose. Those who had risked sailing with Columbus's first voyage had still not been paid and information like that got around the wharves of Seville and Cadiz, where Columbus became known as "Admiral of the Mosquitoes."

Despite these obstacles, Vespucci had succeeded in equipping four more of the twelve supply ships in January 1496, shortly after Berardi's death. Then disaster struck. The convoy ran into storms in the middle of the Atlantic and were badly damaged, forcing them back to Cadiz for repairs. Three more set out in June, and Vespucci's enormous head was still to be seen among the merchants of Seville or along the docks in Cadiz. His gray hair was nearly gone and he was prematurely bald, but he was well respected; not only for his supreme efficiency but also because, despite the most trying circumstances, he never lost his temper. Unfortunately, the destruction of the fleet at the beginning of the year was to be the last straw for the company. Berardi was dead and his company was bankrupt, and Vespucci was having to consider his position in the community. He had continuing responsibilities as Berardi's executor, but it made no sense to continue to struggle with the business of finding ships and crews when there was no longer an obvious role for him.

It was at this point that Columbus arrived back in Seville, marching in his gray Franciscan habit down onto the dockside. As soon as he arrived, it became apparent that just along the quay four ships—which he knew nothing

of—were being prepared to set out for the Indies. Clearly the control Columbus believed he could exercise over his discoveries was beginning to ebb. He
forwarded his letters of self-justification to the queen and asked for an urgent
meeting, but she and Ferdinand were a hundred miles northeast of Madrid,
at Almazán, and replied disconcertingly that he must be tired after his journey and really ought to rest.

In fact, they were busy with both the details of a new military expedition
to Naples and a whole string of diplomatic marriages to buttress the Holy
League against the French. There was the forthcoming marriage of their
daughter Juana to Philip of Burgundy, the union that, as it turned out,
would carry on their line. There was the parallel marriage of their son and
heir, the wild Juan, to Philip's sister Marguerite of Austria,* and the marriage of the new king of Portugal, Manuel, to their daughter Isabella.

Rumors had also reached the sovereigns about Columbus's peculiar arrival. Not just that he looked ill, or that despite being given the title of a
hereditary admiral he was dressed in the habit of a Franciscan, he had also
failed to bring back consignments of the anticipated gold, pearls, and spices,
as one might have expected from the discoverer of the Indies, but instead
carried peculiar native masks, necklaces, and carvings of what looked like
the devil. This was the very picture of a man on the verge of a nervous
breakdown.

While the various wedding preparations continued, the sovereigns kept
Columbus at bay, to see if his mental state would improve while he was staying at the home of the historian Andrés Bernáldez and then through the
summer at a Jeronymite monastery in Medina del Campo. Rumor had it
that Columbus had not returned to his long-suffering mistress in Córdoba,
who he was now banned from marrying because he was a member of the
Spanish aristocracy. He was seen wandering around the city with his hair
unkempt and his beard uncut.

Ferdinand and Isabella left him to wait for nearly four months and when
they finally agreed to see him, at the luxurious palace of Casa del Cordón at

---

*We last met Marguerite as an eight-year-old, betrothed briefly to Charles VIII of France.
"Here lies Margot, a proper little girl,/Who, despite two husbands, is still a virgin," she
wrote, as her own epitaph, at the height of a vicious storm at sea on her way to her own
wedding.

Burgos at the beginning of October, he found that his long letters had done their job. The sovereigns were still friendly and solicitous. They confirmed both his original patent and Bartholomew's position as *adelantado*, or military governor. He wanted to support Bartholomew, but most of all, he wanted to be there to choose a new capital city for Hispaniola now that it was clear that Isabella would not do as a site. But there were still disagreements about his legal position. Early in the new year, he was writing to the sovereigns, claiming a full quarter of the whole yield of everything that came back from the Indies. This was impossible, they replied. It would render Berardi's amortization plan completely unworkable. All he could have was the agreed upon tenth share of their 20 percent. Then there was the question of who was allowed to go to the Indies, and here Columbus began to realize—perhaps under Vespucci's influence—that the more people who went, the more lucrative it might be for him.

While these discussions continued, it became obvious to Columbus why money was so tight in the royal coffers. A gigantic fleet of 130 ships accompanied Princess Juana to Flanders for her wedding, and then brought back Marguerite. Her wedding to Juan took place in Burgos on April 3, 1497, and Columbus was there. As soon as it was over and the royal couple safely dispatched, Ferdinand and Isabella finally turned to the question of Columbus's return to the Indies.


The Success of the Holy League had led to an uneasy peace in Italy. The French had gone, at least for the time being—though Charles was known to be preparing to return, delayed only by his grief at the death of his infant son—and the city-states were unusually and suspiciously united. The one exception was Vespucci's hometown of Florence, where the French had been hailed by Savonarola as God's chosen instrument.

Vespucci was in constant touch with his friends there, despite his heavy schedule in Seville. He knew that the rapid departure of the Medicis had left Florence once more a republic, which, despite his loyalties, pleased him. He also knew that under Savonarola's influence, the city had clamped down on the usurious moneylenders, declaring all their debts void and setting up a city bank—the Monte della Pietà—that lent money at no more than 7.5 percent interest. It meant that people could once more risk opening small businesses and that farmers could once again borrow to buy seeds. He knew Savonarola was urging the churches to go further still and to give their accumulated gold and silver to the poor, and to encourage them, the city was busy selling off the treasures of the Medici palace. Vespucci's elderly uncle Giorgio managed to siphon enough of the proceeds of the sale to buy the Medici library and bring it to San Marco for protection.

The other cities looked askance at this dangerous religious radicalism, and to an extent Vespucci shared their fears. As a quintessential Renaissance man, he regarded Savonarola as dangerously medieval. Pope Alexander, deeply fearful of Savonarola's prophetic influence and furious that Florence had refused to join the Holy League, invited him to Rome and offered to make him a cardinal if he came. A suspicious Savonarola stayed put, and intensified his rhetoric against the pope. "Be prepared, I tell you, Rome, to suffer dreadful punishments," he thundered from the pulpit of the Duomo. "You are going to be bound in iron chains, you're going to be put to the sword, fire and flame are going to eat you up. If you want to be healed, give up feasting, give up pride, ambition, lust and greed, since it is food like this that's made you ill."

But God seemed to be looking in the other direction. There were disastrous floods that were destroying Florence's harvests, bringing unaccustomed political pressure to bear on Savonarola. Opposition parties were emerging in Florence, and the Popolano family were encouraging them. There was the Arrabbiati (the Angry Ones), a group of wealthy families who derided Savonarola's supporters as "the Nodders" and the Compagnacci, led by the homosexual banker Doffo Spini, who spread intense hatred against Savonarola and his purity campaigns. This combination of intense religious fervor and reform, and the growing opposition, led to a series of extraordinary spectacles that have gone down in history as the Bonfires of the Vanities.

On Shrove Tuesday, 1497, while Cabot was busy preparing his second voyage, and just as Columbus's permission to prepare a third voyage finally arrived, as many as ten thousand boys carried olive branches and banners of the cross through the center of Florence, singing hymns written by Savonarola himself. They then converged outside the cathedral in the Piazza dell Signoria, where they piled in a sixty-foot pyramid all the wigs, perfumes, pagan books, musical instruments, and sculptures and paintings of naked women and pagan gods they could find. On top was an effigy of Satan himself. As the procession arrived, the crowd sang the *Te Deum*, the giant bonfire was lit, and some of the greatest works of the Florentine Renaissance were consumed by the flames.

Columbus had been forced to wait ten months, but finally, on April 23, 1497, Ferdinand and Isabella issued instructions for a fleet of eight ships to make a third voyage to the Indies. The news was greeted with great relief by Columbus, but there were immediately complications about where the money would come from.

In the end, it was borrowed from the dowry of their daughter Isabella, the new queen of Portugal. Berardi was dead and his company was no more, so the old Florentine financiers in Seville were no longer adequate middlemen. Columbus fell back on those he could really trust: the Centurione family and another Genoese acquaintance, Bernardo Grimaldi. Fanatically vigilant about whispering against him at court, or the merest whiff of a threat to his privileges, Columbus—still dressed as a Franciscan penitent—wrote to Bartholomew that he had never experienced such anxiety, exhaustion, and difficulties.

Bartholomew was already in the process of choosing a new capital city for Hispaniola. While his brother was still clamoring for an audience with the sovereigns, a party under Miguel Días had found a site on the south coast of the island with a good harbor and good rivers, which looked likely to produce gold. Later in the year, while Columbus was in Burgos, the first bricks were laid on the site of what would be the city of Santo Domingo. Isabella itself was abandoned. Even Columbus's own house, with its sentry posts to guard him against a murderous assault by his followers, was left to rot. Within a decade, its ruins were said to be haunted by the spirits of slaves or executed Castilians screaming in the night.*

Vespucci was still involved in the business of financing Columbus's voyages, both as a friend and as a trusted supplier. As 1497 dawned, he had managed to get two more ships ready for Férnandez Coronel in Sanlúcar, as

---

*It was said that Días had chosen the spot because he fell in love with the woman chief of the territory, the formidable Cathalina, but las Casas, writing only a few years later, said this was not true.

well as the twelve that had already been arranged, and because of his friendship with Columbus, he was busy preparing his ships as well. In the intervals, the two friends spent some time in discussion. Columbus had become obsessed with the political implications of living on a round planet, fears he had been agonizing over on his voyage home. Should there also be a dividing line between Castile and Portugal in the Far East? Should not the line set by the Treaty of Tordesillas go all the way around the planet?

Vespucci found this interesting, but he had his own priorities: He wanted to influence Columbus's choice of route. In Hispaniola, the Columbus brothers had been obsessed with sailing north or northwest, to where they believed they would find Cipangu or Cathay, but having been back in Castile for nearly a year, Columbus had changed his mind. Vespucci's research had led him to the same conclusion, and he was now determined to persuade Columbus, when he returned, to head southwest. There he believed he would find the Cape of Catigara, through which Marco Polo had left China and sailed to India, and urged this approach on him.

And it was not just Vespucci's influence. Both men had heard rumors, reinforced by Ferdinand's spy network, that the Portuguese believed there was land to the south of Columbus's islands. Historians have since wondered whether the Portuguese success with the Treaty of Tordesillas, where they successfully pushed the line dividing the Atlantic a hundred leagues farther west, was because they knew more than they let on. Maybe they had sent secret voyages themselves to the area and knew there really was land to the south of Hispaniola and Cuba. Maybe it was just intelligent guesswork. Either way, Columbus now needed to see for himself.

What worried Vespucci was that Columbus's other priorities seemed to be becoming increasingly bizarre. It wasn't just the religious mania, it was his growing obsession with the island of the Amazons—an island of semi-naked warrior women or, as he put it, the island "where all women were communal"—which Columbus was now determined to find. It was becoming clear to Vespucci, with his growing experience of voyages of exploration and his great knowledge of experimental geography—learned at the feet of Toscanelli himself—that waiting around for other people to make the required journeys might just be folly. He would have to do it for himself.

Berardi was gone, and apart from their friendship, Vespucci's five years in Seville seemed exhausting and somewhat thankless. He had some reason to hope that his association with Berardi would catapult him to higher things, to exploration and recognition. In fact, it had given him the tedium of association with a bankrupt business and the whiff of failure. But Savonarola's revolution ruled out going home to Florence, where he would be forced to take sides among his bitterly divided family and friends. Vespucci knew all the wealthiest merchants and Medici agents in Spain and he was still respected enough. There really was no reason why he should not accompany an expedition himself, if he was determined to do so.

In the early months of 1497, while Cabot was making preparations for his second attempt to reach the Indies, another fleet was being prepared in Lisbon which was to go in the opposite direction. The new Portuguese king, Manuel, was proving to be unexpectedly decisive on the throne. He had consulted his astrologer, Abraham ben Zacuto—a privileged member of the Jewish community who had escaped the expulsion and pogroms—who told him that the stars favored an attempt to reach India via the East.

In fact, John of Portugal had been planning such a trip for years, and had put the experienced royal servant Estêva da Gama in command. Da Gama had died unexpectedly at the same time as John, and Manuel decided, after further astrological advice, that his son Vasco should take his place. Manuel hailed him as he was passing through the palace in Lisbon and made the announcement, which was as unexpected to the inexperienced Vasco as it was to everyone else. Bartholomew Dias, the discoverer of the Cape of Good Hope, was overlooked because Manuel knew he needed a diplomat.

Vasco da Gama was then twenty-six, a discreet, diplomatic loner from a fishing village in the north of Portugal and in service to the Almeida family. His mother was partly English. But there would be no scrambling for investment or leases for ships: Manuel's expedition would include four specially built, specially designed galleons—much bigger than caravels, after Dias's advice about the weather around the cape. As winter turned to spring, da Gama, Vespucci, and Cabot were all putting the finishing touches on what would be historic expeditions.

.   .   .

It was dawn on May 2, 1497, and high tide in Bristol, where the fifty-foot tides rose and fell with such tremendous force that they propelled ships over the mudflats of the Avon River and out to sea. For the second time, Cabot received mass at the mariner's church of St. Nicholas by Bristol Bridge, walked down to Redcliffe Wharf, and boarded the *Matthew*. It again seemed extraordinary, to Mattea and those families who watched from the dockside, that such a small ship could travel to the sources of spices on the other side of the world.

On a good day, Cabot could have expected to reach north Devon and anchor there for the night. This was not a good day: History suggests that Cabot's first day at sea was frustratingly slow once the tides had stopped changing, and he put into port before even reaching the mouth of the Avon, perhaps to take on kegs of salt. This journey was so underinvested that some of the bills would have to be paid with a consignment of cod caught in the North Atlantic.

In the days that followed at the quay, there were disturbing stories: talk of a rebellion in the far west of England over the taxes levied to pay for defense against the Scots, and rumors that Warbeck was considering another landing in their support. Within days, the stories were confirmed and the uprising had spread to Somerset. Up to forty thousand rebels were said to be on their way toward Bristol, sending demands ahead that the mayor should surrender the city. The last thing Cabot wanted was for the *Matthew* to be caught up in any kind of civil disturbance, especially since it looked as though Bristol was going to be the focus of the fighting. But something— whether it was lack of wind or basic repairs—held up the *Matthew* for more than a fortnight, as the news filtered down the river. The mayor of Bristol had sent back an insulting refusal to the rebels and called out the city's militia. Guns were being hauled onto the city walls.

On May 20 the *Matthew* left from the quay and made its way out into the Bristol Channel, avoiding the Turkish pirates that lurked just beyond and pressing on between the two coasts and out to sea. He docked in Bantry Bay in Ireland a few days later to take on extra crew, rather as Columbus had on the Canary Islands, before passing the last glimpse of Cape Clear on the southern tip of Ireland. When it was out of sight, Cabot turned north for some days on the familiar route to Iceland known to the Bristol merchants, then once again turned west and into the unknown.

. . .

Cabot's course kept the North Star firmly on the right of the ship and at a constant height to stay on the same latitude. Columbus had found the compass could be erratic in the Atlantic, as it shifted from true north to magnetic north. This time, whatever tactics Cabot used with the crew—perhaps faking the charts as Columbus had done—the crew and the ocean remained calm. On June 21 the *Matthew* ran into its first serious gale and the tiny ship once more found itself flattened against the enormous waves. But by dawn the next day the sea was calm again.

The day after that some birds were sighted, an unambiguous sign that they were near land. Elyot and Thorne gazed over the side in astonishment at the number of cod, which were thick in the sea wherever they looked. That night, there was the unmistakable odor of fir trees. At five A.M. on June 24, St. John the Baptist's day, there was land ahead and in great excitement the crew watched as they approached it. But this was unmistakably an island, and only the mainland would mean success for this voyage. Cabot named it St. John and moved on. Only a few hours afterward, more land was on the horizon. As they moved closer, everyone on board was craning to make it out. There were clearly enormous forests there and a beach where a landing could be made.

Rival historians have battled for centuries about whether the land that Cabot named Prima Terra Vista (first land seen) was Cape Bonavista or Cape Breton, whether it was in Newfoundland, somewhere in modern Canada, or in Maine, or even farther south. The Canadian consensus is that he landed somewhere in what is now Newfoundland, though the name itself was previously applied to almost anywhere along that coast. Critics point to the fact that there was no mention of fog, which he must have encountered if he landed on Newfoundland in June. Any glance at an atlas implies that Newfoundland—with its ambiguity about whether it is an island or promontory—is the more likely landmass Cabot first encountered, probably near Cape Bonavista. But for most of the past century, a slim majority of historians have leaned toward a landing on Cape Breton Island on the northern tip of Nova Scotia, partly because the scenery seems more like it was described by contemporaries and partly because the other circumstances make better sense that way.

They edged the *Matthew* closer to the shore and launched the small landing boat they carried with them for this purpose. It is hard to imagine anyone but Cabot leaping first over the side and into the shallows. Those with him carried three banners and a telescope. Once the *Matthew*'s passengers and most of the crew had gathered on the beach, they walked nervously a little way inland, to a high point and clearing from where they could see their battered ship, bobbing in the bay. Cabot supervised raising a large cross and the banners of England, Venice, and the pope. This was the mainland, he said, and not just any old mainland, but the country of the Grand Khan, the foothills of the Far East, with its gold and spices. The decision to call it Prima Terra Vista was Cabot's.

The banners fluttered and Cabot stood with his closest friends, one from Genoa and the other from Burgundy, and the two Bristol merchants who accompanied him, and surveyed the scene. The soil seemed suitable for brazilwood and silkworms, but there was no doubt that the path from the beach was a track that had been made by humans. One sailor shouted: he had found a snare and an old campfire; another had found what looked very much like an arrow and a needle. They looked up at the enormous trees, tall enough for the masts of ships, and peered into the dense undergrowth. They had to assume they were being watched. After a quick discussion, they agreed to make their way back to the boat, fill their water bottles in the stream, and explore the coastline. It would be tragic to have found the Indies and not live to report it. So it was that the first "discovery" of mainland America was cut short because it was in fact already inhabited.

## II

*"Mammon, the least erected Spirit that fell*
*From heav'n, for ev'n in heav'n his looks and thoughts*
*Were always downward bent, admiring more*
*The riches of heaven's pavement, trodden gold."*

JOHN MILTON, *Paradise Lost*

Having stowed the oars and the boat back aboard the *Matthew*, and bid a reluctant farewell to Prima Terra Vista, Cabot's team debated how to proceed: If Cabot's enterprise was going to be achievable, and they had not just found any mainland, but a mainland that could be followed south all the way to China, then their first priority was to sail south to make sure such a voyage was possible, before they returned with greater resources to finish the journey. There is still debate about which way Cabot went next, because the only written evidence is ambiguous, but since he badly needed to confirm his basic proposition, it is likely that he actually turned southwest, along the North American coast, in the direction of where he believed China to be.

Over the next two weeks, the *Matthew* sailed quietly down the coast of Nova Scotia. The merchants and Cabot's friends watched carefully, along with the rest of the crew, for any signs that this was a continent: large animals, for example, or the mouths of enormous rivers. They saw clear signs of cultivated fields, an extraordinary forest like nothing those on board had ever seen before, and, on one occasion, saw two forms running on the beach, but were too far away to make out if these were men or animals.

Deciding whether they had found *the* mainland was precisely the problem Columbus had faced sailing along the south coast of Cuba. How far would you have to sail to be sure? Cabot, though, was luckier than his rival. He had, in fact, found the mainland—he was just mistaken as to which one it was. The proof that he needed was probably going to be, as it eventually was in Latin America, the mouth of a river so vast that only a continent could have produced it. The documents suggest that the *Matthew* sailed three hundred leagues—about a thousand nautical miles—in those weeks. In the days that followed, Cabot hugged the shore southward, around Cape Sable, into the Bay of Fundy, satisfying himself that this was not a passage into another sea, and to the mouth of either the St. John River or St. Croix River, near the present border between Canada and the United States. Realizing that such large outflows of freshwater implied this was indeed the mainland, he was able to turn north again and retrace the journey. He then struck out across what is now the Cabot Strait to Newfoundland, going counterclockwise around the coast, perhaps as far as Cape Bonavista, maybe even Cape Bauld, staggered by the profusion of cod, which would one day make these waters famous.

The mood on board was exuberant, but not so much that the crew was prepared to take any unnecessary risks. The priority for Cabot, Thorne, and Elyot was above all to get back with the news, and stake their claim. There would be no more landings with all their attendant difficulties to ship and men. Staring obsessively at the charts as they drew them, they agreed what must have happened. The *Trinity* and those other adventurers over the previous seventeen years may indeed have found hy-Brasil, but they may, in fact, and in all fairness to them, have also found a promontory, and mistaken it for an island. On the return journey northward, they passed two islands they had missed before. On an impulse, Cabot gave one to each of his friends, the Burgundian and the Genoese barber. It is worth pointing out the contrast with Columbus, who named every place he found after saints or members of the royal family; Cabot named them after his friends. This was a trading voyage: It had no religious purpose.

There remained one task before them: They needed a cargo of cod to raise the outstanding two hundred pounds. Off the coast of Newfoundland, they set about this task and hooked something else without altogether intending to. It was a small whale. They hauled it aboard and stripped it and salted it along with the codfish. Cabot was as sure as he could be that he had reached mainland Asia, and his readings of the North Star implied that they were now on the same latitude as southern Ireland, so they set sail for home.

As Cabot was sailing back up the coast of Nova Scotia, five large ships were riding at anchor outside Lisbon harbor. On board the flagship, *São Gabriel*, Vasco da Gama was checking the details of this fleet, which constituted the renewed Portuguese assault on the Indies from the east. Three of the ships had been built to specifications set out by Bartholomew Dias, and one was to carry stores for the others. Dias himself was commanding the fifth ship, which would accompany them as far as El-Mina.

On July 7, 1497, King Manuel received da Gama and his captains at a solemn ceremony onshore, presenting them with a silk banner of the Order of Christ, and marching with them down to the quayside. Then, to the beat of drums, they climbed into the waiting boats that would row them through the sparkling waves out to the Tower of Belem in the middle of the harbor, and to their ships. The following day, the fleet sailed slowly down the Tagus and out to sea. It was an impressive sight, far removed from the *Matthew*'s quiet departure from Bristol two months before. Ferdinand's spies reported back to Spain that the Portuguese fleet had sailed to the Indies. A sharply worded protest followed to the court in Lisbon. If Vasco da Gama was heading for the Indies, then he must be trespassing on the Castilian side of the line drawn by the Treaty of Tordesillas, which allowed Castile to claim everything west of the line, even if that included the Far East and Asia. Manuel chose to ignore it.

Out of reach of any diplomatic fallout, it took four months for da Gama's ships to reach the southern tip of Africa, where they ran into repeated storms that divided the fleet and battered the ships back to the positions they had been in days before. It wasn't until November 22 that the commanders persuaded their frightened crews to keep at the sails long enough to round the Cape of Good Hope. On Christmas Day, 1497, the fleet reached a coast they named after Christmas, Natal, and headed north toward what is now Mozambique, where they would collect supplies and repair the ships. They had then been cut off from news of Europe for more than six months.

If Columbus was right, da Gama might expect to encounter the Castilian colonists in the East. He had been chosen to lead this expedition because he was believed to be up to the required subtlety of such an encounter.


Cabot's return journey had been extremely fast, with the Gulf Stream wafting the ship back toward Europe. There were disputes between Cabot and his advisers, who were certain they had drifted too far north, and Cabot agreed to change course farther south. As a result, after fifteen days sailing, they made landfall and it was obviously Brittany—the lighthouse at La Rochelle must have given it away. They turned back north and sailed around Land's End and into the Bristol Channel.

On August 6, 1497, the *Matthew* was carried by the tide back up the Avon River and, having notified the quays on their way, to a tumultuous welcome. The tax rebels at the gates had bypassed Bristol and the city was untouched: They had spent the summer moving slowly toward London, only to be surprised by Henry's troops near Kingston and an ignominious series of humiliations.

London was three days from Bristol along the Great West Road, and Cabot was only too aware of the potential fate that so nearly defeated Columbus on his return—being beaten to the court with the news by a recalcitrant underling. He had to get to the king as fast as possible. So he just had time to greet his family before setting off, making sure as he did so that he had reliable information about where the king was.

Henry had, in fact, shifted his crisis headquarters to Woodstock Palace in

Oxfordshire to be more centrally located. But he was now briefly back in London, so Cabot rode out—probably with at least some of his investors—down the Great West Road to Chippenham, past the strange unnatural shape of Silbury Hill, through Marlborough, Hungerford, Newbury, and Reading, across the Thames at Maidenhead, through the small villages of Hounslow and Hammersmith, with the Thames snaking away in the distance toward London. Three days later, an exhausted Cabot made his way down the main road from the west, known since Roman times as Akeman Street, through the village of Kensington, and turned right into Whitehall, to the great gates that led to the Palace of Westminster. His first priority was to make his arrival known, leaving his horse in the stables then taking the narrow road that led past Westminster Abbey to the gates of Westminster Hall, past the house of the first English printer, William Caxton, and the abbey chapter house where the House of Commons met.*

On August 10, history records his interview with Henry and his advisers. Despite the nervousness of some of his diplomats about a possible source of conflict with Ferdinand and Isabella, and a threat to the royal marriage, Henry was pleased with the achievement and gave him an immediate reward of ten pounds. This was not quite the welcome that Cabot had planned. Perhaps the king had not fully understood the significance of what had been achieved, so Cabot went straight from Westminster to find Carbonariis at Austin Friars to hammer out a strategy to explain it to him better. Some weeks later, they made their way together back to the palace, and Carbonariis managed to bring Cabot before the king for a second time. This time Henry was made to understand the significance and made two immediate decisions: He renamed Prima Terra Vista New Founde Land, and he awarded Cabot with an "annuitie or annuel rent of twenty poundes sterling, to be had and yerely perceyved from the fest of th'anunciation of our lady last passed." At long last Cabot's money worries were over.

The decisions about how to capitalize on the discovery were made over the next few months. For the moment, London was at Cabot's feet and keen

---

*Westminster was then still all but separate from London and had a fearsome reputation for disorder: One in four buildings there were alehouses or brothels. Caxton had actually died in 1492, but his business continued under his colleague Wynkyn de Worde.

to invest, eager to hear more about the continent and how it would make London and Bristol the wealthiest cities in Europe.

Henry was heading back within days to Woodstock to deal with the looming threat of a second rebellion in one year, once more emanating from the far west of England, but also a threatened invasion from Scotland. In the following week, it was clear that Perkin Warbeck himself had landed in Cornwall, smuggled aboard a Castilian ship in Cork, and hidden in an empty wine cask when the ship was intercepted and boarded, and was now on Bodmin Moor having declared himself King Richard IV.

There was no point in hanging around an empty Westminster, so Cabot was soon back in Bristol with his family, with an enormous sense of relief of having at long last escaped the degradation of debt. Not that his had been paid, of course, but he was now too important to have his debts enforced against him, and he finally had money of his own. He immediately rented a house in the prestigious St. Nicholas Street, next to the mariner's church and the Welsh Back, where the coasters unloaded. He took the lease from Amerike's assistant John Kemys at a hefty two pounds a year.

It was an excellent street to set up a headquarters. One end led to the city's pillory and stocks and the main wharves at the docks. At the other end were steps down to the Avon where the local women did their washing. There was a view of Bristol Bridge, a smaller version of London Bridge with houses all along it and a chapel in the middle, and one large mansion, which had once belonged to the ill-fated Robert Sturmy. This was now the Cloth Hall, which also acted as a trade exchange and an office for the local fellowship of merchants, where those who operated out of Bristol kept their closely guarded maps. The jaw bone of the whale he had so laboriously returned, was placed over the door inside St. Mary Redcliffe Church.*

Cabot was in high spirits. The first thing he did in London, having been

---

*Where you can still see it today. Legend also has it that this was a rib from a monstrous dun cow that terrorized Bristol in the Middle Ages. The story that Cabot brought it back is far more likely, especially as there is evidence in an old accounts book of a 1497 bill to have it erected in the church ("Pd for settynge upp ye bone of ye bigge fyshe . . . brote over seas").

granted his pension, was to wander down Cheapside where the goldsmiths and silk merchants operated, to shop for clothes and buy himself a silk out-fit. Cabot was at his most gregarious, but there were hints that his bitterness about Columbus still ate at him. What Columbus had achieved, but he had patently not, was a title, which is perhaps why Cabot allowed himself to become known around London society as the admiral—an Arabic word without a formal use in English at the time. Having constructed a map and globe to demonstrate where the New Founde Land was, and how it connected to the Indies, Cabot returned to London to put them on display and to give a series of public lectures in the city. Both the map and the lectures were also ammunition in the threatened war of words with Castile. They demonstrated where he had gone and set out the official English view: that Cabot had not been to, and was going nowhere near, Columbus's discoveries.

But what his map implied about the dead end Columbus had reached was bound to irritate in Castile and Aragon. One of the rival Spanish ambassadors, Pedro de Ayala, informed Henry that his sovereigns regarded Cabot's voyage as trespassing on their territory. They had discovered islands around the Indies, and that was where Cabot was going—how could it not be trespassing? Henry deftly dismissed the charge: If that was what the Spanish believed, they were simply wrong.

It was said in Italy that by inviting the French to come, Ludovico Sforza of Milan had turned a lion loose in his house—with the inevitable consequences still to come. Even so, as the official beneficiary of the French invasion, Milan had escaped lightly from the recent war, though it had now joined the Holy League. The eminent artists and engineers that clustered around the Sforza court were still there. Leonardo da Vinci had just finished painting his magnificent *Last Supper* on the wall of the refectory of the Dominican friars at Santa Maria delle Grazia, one of only six paintings he managed to finish during his stay as a Sforza employee.

Cabot was well known in Milan—he had lived there for nearly five years—and some of the first letters to reach Italy about his achievement arrived there. The very first was a letter dated August 23 from a Venetian merchant named Lorenzo Pasqualigo sent home to his family. "That Venetian of ours who went with a small ship from Bristol to find new islands has come back and says he has discovered the main land," he wrote, explaining that this was "the territory of the Grand Khan." But the news arrived in Milan the following day, and there Leonardo at least would have understood the significance. He had not been a pupil of Toscanelli's for nothing. The new Milanese ambassador to London, the elegant and witty Raimondi de Soncino, was soon writing home about the impact the victorious Cabot was now having there. He described Cabot as a well-known figure around the court with his public lectures and his vociferous advocacy of a scheme to "make London a more important mart for spices than Alexandria."

It is from Soncino that we know about Cabot's taste in silk clothing, though there may have been an element of projection here. Soncino himself had taken Henry's court aback by arriving in September dressed in a robe of crimson damask with four rows of pearls and jewels around the collar. Soncino also made merry at the expense of Cabot's two friends, who had islands named after them, and therefore "consider themselves counts."

"As I have made friends with the admiral," he went on, "I might have an archbishopric if I chose to go there, but I have reflected that the offices which your excellency reserves for me are safer . . . Meanwhile I stay on in this country, eating ten or twelve courses at each meal, and spending three hours at table twice a day, for the love of your excellency, to whom I humbly commend myself." There is an exuberance implied here that goes beyond the mere collecting of supporters, though we have to discount Soncino's ironic deprecating tone. Cabot had, according to Soncino—and this is easier to believe—a "kindly wit." It is what drew people to him.

Cabot also still needed support. Henry's offer shortly after their meeting to equip ten ships rapidly seems to have dissolved. Cabot needed to raise more money in London as well as Bristol, but the stakes were high. The fleet would be equipped—rather as Columbus's second voyage had been—to facilitate the formation of a colony that would be the basis of a trading outpost near the Indies. They would need colonists—probably mainly pardoned prisoners—as well as food, agricultural equipment and seeds, animals, and construction materials. They would need Franciscans to come on the voyage as well to minister to them. Compared to Columbus, Cabot had played down religion, but it was politic to include it as part of the agenda. All these necessities required money, loans, fixers, and middlemen in both cities, and just as Henry was financially straining the nation to defend his throne.

The Scottish threat was disposed of without too much difficulty. We don't know whether Cabot was in Bristol or London at the time, but he might have watched on November 28, 1497, as the captured Perkin Warbeck was paraded through London in chains, and then put in the stocks outside Westminster Hall. If he missed the spectacle, he must have heard about Warbeck's capture and confession with relief. It was one less distraction for the officials and financiers he was dealing with.*

Reassured by de Puebla in London that Cabot had been refused support by the English, Ferdinand and Isabella had stopped worrying about English journeys to the Indies. They had been much more alarmed by the news from Lisbon about the departure of Vasco da Gama, so Cabot's success took them by surprise. They urgently needed more information. Historians have not seen fit to chart the growth of espionage in this period, before the great Elizabethan spy-masters, but it was becoming increasingly sophisticated. This was partly the new role of diplomats, among which Vespucci had cut his teeth in Paris in the 1470s, and was now providing a wealth of sometimes daily information about thinking in foreign courts.

Diplomats had various methods. Some spent all their time writing dispatches. One used the technique of interrupting with irrelevant comments when anyone was being indiscrete, on the grounds that the less people wanted to listen to you, the more they seemed to be prepared to say. But the rulers needed more. We hear about Ferdinand's spies at the Scottish court in Edinburgh or at the Portuguese court in Lisbon. We know the great lengths the Portuguese went to to protect their new sea charts, and some Portuguese historians believe Columbus's voyage was based on deliberate misinformation planted by their spies. The English had their own shadowy networks. The accounts of the merchant king Edward IV record various sums paid out to people he describes as secret "explorators," which seems to mean spy. Often these spies were merchants, who had reasons to come and go. Ferdinand's formidable network of spies sent a constant stream of information

---

*Warbeck's new wife refused to accept that he was not who he claimed to be. "Most noble lady," Henry VII said to her, "I grieve too, and it pains me very much, second only to the slaughter of so many of my subjects, that you have been deceived by such a sorry fellow."

into the court. But it was weakened by having no proper way of cross-referencing or even indexing the information. A generation later—faced with a threatened divorce—Ferdinand's successors hunted for months to find the crucial papers about Catherine of Aragon's marriage to Henry's son.

As soon as it became clear that de Puebla was wrong, and that the English were indeed taking up the offer of the "one like Columbus," Ferdinand's network was once more watching the wharves in Bristol. Ferdinand and Isabella also seem to have asked Columbus's advice on whether Cabot's voyage was likely to be any kind of threat. History does not relate what Columbus—locked in combat with Fonseca—told the sovereigns about this or about his own previous relationship with Cabot.

But Columbus felt the need for his own information and remembered the English merchant John Day, who he had met on the docks in Lisbon on his first triumphant return, before he had even reached Castile with the news. The man had put himself unreservedly at the admiral's service, and he was also likely to be discreet—Columbus knew he was an associate of Berardi and Vespucci's. Whether or not they had corresponded in the interim, Columbus thought of Day now, and wrote asking for his help. What he needed was information, as long as it was not prejudicial to his loyalties to his own king.

Day was a shadowy cosmopolitan figure, working under a pseudonym—his real name was Hugh Say, an indebted member of the Mercer's company in London, which had been operating between Portugal, Castile, and Bristol, and was therefore in a position to observe Cabot's arrivals and departures. He had been a business partner of Berardi's in the days when Berardi's business was prospering. Day's reply addressed Columbus as "Lord High Admiral" and was clearly a letter written after an interview between the two men, presumably in Seville. Day promised to send a copy of Marco Polo's *Travels* and another of a fourteenth-century book called *Inventio Fortunata* about an Oxford friar who went to Greenland, and probably also Labrador, which has since been lost. He also agreed to supply a version of Cabot's map in London as soon as he had been able to copy it.

Day has been described variously as a spy and a double agent. In fact he was a merchant and was not keeping Columbus informed in return for money, but for continued contact with the great man, whom he addressed as "magnificent Lord." "In payment for some services which I hope to render you," he wrote, "I beg your lordship to kindly write me about such matters, because the favor you will thus do me will greatly stimulate my memory to serve you in all things that may come to my knowledge."

The letter is fascinating because Day reminds Columbus that "it is considered certain that the cape of the said land was found and discovered in the past by men from Bristol who found 'Brasil' as your Lordship well knows. It was called the Island of Brasil, and it is assumed and believed to be the mainland that the men from Bristol found."* If this question about what Cabot's Bristol rivals had discovered before was being discussed openly in letters to Columbus in Castile, it must have been deeply divisive in the Bristol merchant community, especially when Cabot was honored for finding land which some of the locals believed they discovered nearly two decades earlier.

Cabot and Columbus, so long rivals, were now facing similar difficulties getting their new fleets equipped. Vespucci was assisting the management of getting Columbus's six ships ready for the Indies, but he was mainly engaged with the tedious business of being Berardi's executor and untangling the catastrophic debts they had incurred on the Indies expeditions. Fonseca was now actively obstructing his old enemy at every stage, determined not to let the voyage go ahead, and only 6 million maravedis had been forthcoming to pay for the ships from the crown. Time after time, Columbus was forced to appeal to the sovereigns. They replied, when they chose to respond, either with support—they wrested control of this voyage from Fonseca and appointed de Torres in charge instead for this voyage—or, more disconcertingly, with more detailed stipulations: There could be no murderers on the voyage, they said, or counterfeiters, traitors, heretics, or homosexuals. They were also now absolutely determined that there was to be a policy of conversion to Christianity not slavery. They wanted the islands colonized, and if there was no gold, they wanted Columbus to supervise this by providing plots to enable colonists to produce sugar. Then, suddenly, the intricate diplomacy of Ferdinand and Isabella unraveled in a series of tragic episodes.

*Day's letter came to light only in 1955, when it was found filed under "Brazil" by a professor of romance languages, who happened to be friendly with the Columbus scholar Louis Vigneras. Vigneras immediately recognized that the Brazil referred to was actually the mythical island of hy-Brasil.

The first blow was the death of their only son, the nineteen-year-old Juan, who developed a dangerous fever after a feast in his honor in the university town of Salamanca. On October 6, 1497, he died in his father's arms. It was never quite clear what had made him so suddenly ill. There were rumors about eating a bad salad the night before, or even about too much sex with his new bride, Margaret. Columbus realized immediately that his sons Diego and Ferdinand, who were pages to Juan, were now out of a job, though, in fact, Isabella took them on herself. Still reeling from this disaster, the news came through in August of the following year that their eldest daughter, Isabella, now queen of Portugal—an alliance that would have united all the nations of the Iberian peninsula—had died in childbirth. "It seemed as if God had been offended with both those illustrious families," wrote the French diplomat Philippe de Commines, "and would not suffer the one to triumph over the other."

Neither Ferdinand nor Isabella ever fully recovered from these bitter blows, which destroyed their family and blew apart their carefully constructed alliances. The twin thrones of Castile and Aragon would now be inherited by the Hapsburgs, the dynasty into which they had married their next eldest living daughter, Juana. After Juan's death, they withdrew from the world to the Episcopal Palace at Guadalajara and saw almost no one until the following April. Columbus had to do without either their instructions or support.

This was a moment in history where a series of deaths unexpectedly shifted the direction of politics. It was Lent, and in Florence for the second year running Savonarola's supporters were building a giant bonfire on which to throw accumulated art, music, and anything considered to be a luxury. But this time the atmosphere was different. Florence was suffering economically after a succession of failed harvests, and from outbreaks of famine and the plague. The city was almost isolated in Italy and regarded as standing almost heretically against the pope and the Holy League. The news that a Florentine grain fleet bound for Livorno had been driven back by ships belonging to the league was a bitter blow on the streets.

Savonarola himself was defying an excommunication from Pope Alexander. The Popolanos' campaign against the new regime was reaching a crescendo, and forged letters were circulating around Italy purporting to be from Savonarola urging Charles VIII to bring his armies back to Italy. When he refused to take part in an ordeal by fire against a Franciscan opponent, Florence finally rose up against him, attacked the monastery of San Marco—while Vespucci's uncle hid in his library—and took Savonarola prisoner. Two papal emissaries arrived to conduct his trial with "the verdict in their bosoms." On May 23, 1498, he and his closest allies were simultaneously hanged and burned at the stake on the same spot where Savonarola conducted his Bonfires of the Vanities. Vespucci's old friends the Popolano were prime instigators of his destruction.

Savonarola had been transformed into ashes, collected in secret by his admirers when they were still floating in the Arno, but fate had also overtaken the man Savonarola had believed was God's chosen instrument for punishing Italy. The day before Palm Sunday, on April 8, 1498, Charles VIII of France was making his way around the back of the castle at Amboise to watch a tennis match. He banged his head on a low door lintel, suffering no ill-effects at the time. But walking back again after the game, he collapsed in the same area.

It was the spot where the castle's drains discharged, "a place where every man pissed that would," according to de Commines, but it was felt it might be best not to move him. Charles lay there for nine hours and died just before midnight. His young son had died two years earlier, so his only heir was his cousin Louis of Orleans, a man determined to return to Italy and to wrest Milan from the control of Ludovico Sforza.

If Vespucci had toyed with the idea of going home, he must have put it aside now. He was fed up with his predicament and his constant disappointments in Seville. He had burned his bridges with the Popolano family, and was no longer handling their business. He would go instead to the Indies, or wherever it was that Columbus had discovered, and prove to the world that he had unrecognized wisdom and cosmographical skills.

# 7

# STRANGE MEETINGS

*"The land which God has newly given your Highnesses on this voyage must be reckoned continental in extent."*

CHRISTOPHER COLUMBUS, letter to Ferdinand and
Isabella, October 1498

*"God made me the messenger of the new heaven and the new earth of which he spoke in the Apocalypse of St. John, after having spoken of it through the mouth of Isaiah, and he showed me the spot where to find it."*

CHRISTOPHER COLUMBUS,
letter to Juana de la Torre, 1500

THE WHARVES OF the port of London were noisy places. Walking along Thames Street, close to the river, as Cabot did day after day, past the huge warehouses and massive cranes of the various trading leagues and companies, it was possible to hear almost every European language being spoken. The many distinct dialects from around London made communication hard for locals and foreigners alike. When William Caxton set up his first printing press down the river in Westminster, the profusion of them made it nearly impossible for him to print his books in words that could be widely read.

It was, as always, a city of violent contrasts. On the one hand, the future scholar and martyr Thomas More was a successful law student at Lincoln's Inn in 1498, just across the fields from the Fleet River that emptied slops into the Thames. His friend Erasmus was about to visit the city for the first time, steeped in the new literacy that was sweeping across Europe. On the other hand, the city remained a playground for its traditionally wild and brutal apprentices and maintained its schizophrenic attitude to foreigners and its seedy dockside taverns, and the Bow Bell still tolled the curfew each evening.

On these streets in the early months of 1498, seeking out investors to whom he could sell a share of his rights to the New Founde Land, was John Cabot. The accounts we have describe him as being dressed in the finest clothes and joining enthusiastically into the life of the city—the games of cards over stingo, London's distinctive spiced ale, until the early morning and then buying pies filled with beef or mackerel or sheep's trotters in the streets on his way to the next meeting with investors.

After fifteen exhausting years moving from city to city, one step ahead of his creditors, Cabot was hailed as a hero and widely recognized. London's amateur cosmographers and geographers beat a path to his door, to hear his lectures and to see his globe showing the sloping coastline across the Atlantic, all the way to Cathay and Cipangu and the wealth they represented.

"The English run after him like mad," said Pasqualigo, reporting home to Milan. "So do our own rogues." What the merchants of London recognized, though they were no more credulous about the risks than other investors, was that Cabot was planning to make Bristol and London the economic equivalent of Alexandria, the lynchpin of the world's spice trade, and as wealthy as the Levant. Even so, the original rumors that the king was going to give him ten ships, paid for by the English crown, had unraveled quickly as the treasury was faced with paying for armies to counter an invasion from Scotland, a taxpayers' uprising in the West Country, and the reappearance of Perkin Warbeck.

Warbeck was under house arrest at the Palace of Westminster, but the English treasury was seriously depleted as a result of mobilizing armies against the uprising he had led. Henry had finally agreed to Cabot's pension payments—they would be paid at Easter and Michaelmas by the Bristol customs—and he had reinforced the original grant to Cabot in February 1498 to go to "the land and isles of late found by the said John in our name and by our commandment," but the royal ships had not been forthcoming. Nor had the promised criminals to man the ships on a journey into the unknown and—like Columbus's early settlers in Hispaniola—to provide the human foundation for an English trading station in the Indies.

The new letters of patent allowed Cabot to hire six ships of not more than two hundred tons each. To hire them he needed to offer shares in the rights given him by the royal patent to investors in Bristol. Since the Bristol merchants were still suspicious of this Genoese Venetian announcing discoveries in seas they had believed were their own, and which they had hoped to keep secret, he had no choice but to go to London for the money instead.

Armed with introductions from Amerike, Cabot made the 120-mile journey from Bristol to London and back several times in autumn and winter 1497 to 1498, and was soon able to interest a powerful syndicate of London merchants led by two partners, Lawrence Thirkill and Thomas Bradley. They were able to raise the money for the king's ship as coinvestors with the crown and were given the contract to fit it out—the exhausting work that Berardi and Vespucci had been doing for Columbus. They then traveled back to Bristol to supervise the provisioning of a fleet that looked to number five ships. It was only half the promised number, but it was a respectable expedition nonetheless.

In early May 1498, exactly a year since the lonely and quiet departure of the *Matthew*, Cabot's five ships were ready to sail, and this time all of Bristol had turned out for his departure. There were processions and pageantry, as the mayor and abbot vied to outshine each other, and Cabot attended mass at dawn in St. Nicholas Church.

Cabot and his sons were in the biggest of the ships, the one provided partly by money from the king. The royal banners streamed from the mainmast at the head of this impressive fleet. On deck with him were Thirkill and Bradley, and below were stored "slight and gross merchandises, as coarse cloth caps, laces, points, and other trifles, to trade with the Indians." Also packed belowdeck in all five ships were water and provisions for a year. Even if they found no land, and reached no trading ports in China or Japan until then, Cabot could sail on—provided that he could persuade his crews to sail with him.

Elsewhere in the fleet were a number of Italian friars who had been given the task of looking after the spiritual needs of the new trading colony. They were led by Giovanni de Carbonariis, referred to as another Friar Boyle, a reference to Bernardo Boyle who had sailed so unsatisfactorily on Columbus's second voyage. Carbonariis was finally achieving his ambition to get involved personally in exploration, and he sailed with Cabot on the king's ship.

Amid the grief at the Castilian court, Columbus had finally received royal permission to prepare his fleet and leave for the Indies for a third time. He drew up a new will that left the vast wealth he still believed would be his to his son Diego, with a percentage of revenues for his brothers and uncles, and more to go into a fund at the Bank of St. George in Genoa. This would be used to help relieve the taxes on his fellow citizens back home. He left nothing for his mistress Beatriz. His new concern for Genoa was something of a change, and it followed a reconciliation with his former employers and creditors. For this third voyage, his investors would not be Florentines like Berardi or Castilians like Santangel, but his old Genoese colleagues, the Centurione and Grimaldi families.

Later in the same month that Cabot had put out to sea from Bristol, Columbus's fleet of six ships lay ready at the dockside in Seville, and sailed down the river to anchor outside the castle of Sanlúcar de Barrameda, where the admiral followed the fleet himself, having written to his son Diego that "Your father loves you as he does himself." On May 30, 1498, they hauled up the anchor chains, and floated slowly on the tide, past the white houses and fig and olive trees, out of the mouth of the Guadalquivir and into the Atlantic.

Enormously relieved at last to be underway, Columbus had come aboard his flagship shortly before departure, only to find the man he disliked most in the whole of Castile, the royal paymaster and Fonseca's right-hand man, Jimeno de Bribiesca, waiting for him on deck to question more of his purchases. Columbus was still tired and ill, and had only recently dispensed with his Franciscan garb and his studied air of humility. This was the last straw. He hit Jimeno squarely on the jaw and knocked him down on the deck.

Columbus planned to divide his fleet in two. He had appointed Beatriz's brother Pedro de Harana to lead the three supply ships that were sailing directly to Hispaniola. For his own exploration, Columbus had chosen the seventy-ton *La Vaqueños* (the cow) and the similar-sized *El Correo* (the mail). Unfortunately he had made the same mistake as he had with *Santa Maria*, and had chosen a larger ship that had not been designed for exploration and that would prove not nearly as seaworthy as the others. His favorite, the *Niña*, had sailed back to Hispaniola in January, along with the *India*.*

Among those shipping out on the voyage were crossbowmen, priests, agricultural laborers, gold panners, and about thirty women, among the first to go to the Indies from Europe. Also by his side on the flagship was the short but energetic figure of his old lieutenant, the queen's favorite, Alonso de Ojeda. Ojeda had also become a favorite of Columbus's great enemy Fonseca and, although Columbus may not have realized it, was deliberately placed as Fonseca's eyes and ears on the expedition.

Packed in his trunk were his instructions for the voyage from the queen: "God willing, you will try with all diligence to inspire and draw the natives of the said Indies to ways entirely of peace and tranquility and impress on them that they have to see and be beneath our lordship and benign subjection, and above all that they be converted to our Holy Catholic Faith . . ." It was impossible to interpret any part of this letter as somehow giving the green light to slavery in the Indies. Also packed away was the copy of Cabot's map, which he had been sent by John Day. One of Columbus's self-appointed tasks on this third voyage was to try to square this map with his own.

Columbus had ended his second voyage determined to press forward his exploration to the north, toward the region where he believed Cipangu lay, but the influence of Vespucci and the sovereigns had convinced him that the real challenge lay to the south. Maybe the story that the Portuguese king had somehow identified a continent south of the Indies was

---

*The *Niña* had experienced the most bizarre adventure in the meantime. Chartered for a voyage to Rome, it had been captured by corsairs outside the port of Cagliari and taken to Sardinia, where the crew was removed and taken to a pirate ship. Four of these crewmen managed to escape, steal a boat, row back to the *Niña*, cut her cables, and sail back out to sea and to Spain, just in time for the *Niña* to return to the Indies.

nonsense, but it made sense to find out. But most of all, there was Vespucci's intriguing theory that the Cape of Catigara—the way that Marco Polo had originally returned from China—lay southwest of Hispaniola instead.

But there was another idea behind the third voyage, which related directly to his absolute failure to find the promised gold. There was a popular view, based on Aristotle's geographical theories, that precious metals were found in increasing quantities the farther south one sailed, as well as at similar latitudes around the world. If the Portuguese had sailed south and found gold in Africa, then there was a reasonable chance that the pattern would be repeated on the other side of the Atlantic. He was also more aware than anyone how much the future of his islands depended on the discovery of gold. Without paying for their upkeep, he feared that they would simply be abandoned.

In the meantime, Columbus had to deal with a more pressing and familiar problem. When he left on his second voyage, he had been forced to take evasive action to dodge a Portuguese naval squadron that had been sent to intercept him. This time, Castile was in open conflict with France along the border region, and French agents had relayed the message that the admiral was about to leave for the third time. A French fleet therefore stood off Cape St. Vincent waiting for him, so Columbus was forced to take his six ships directly southward along the African coast.

From there, he sailed to his old home on the island of Porto Santo, where the inhabitants believed he was a pirate raider and fled into the hills, so they were not available to sell him the food and water he needed. So at San Sebastian instead, where his old romance with Beatriz seems to have died, he divided his fleet and set off southwest. "May our Lord guide me and lead me to something that may be of service to Him and to the King and Queen, our sovereigns and to the honor of Christendom," he told his captains. "For I believe that this way has never been traveled before by anyone and that this sea is utterly unknown."

It was indeed. Columbus and his small squadron became among the first Europeans to record a terrifying journey through that part of the mid-Atlantic known to later generations as the Doldrums, a windless area of intense and deadly heat. For nine terrifying days, the three ships lay becalmed in searing temperatures, while the exhausted crew lay on the decks and the food went rotten below. The wine turned sour, the water supplies evaporated, and their meat supplies putrefied. Without wind to set them free again, Columbus feared they would undoubtedly die.

Cabot and Columbus had set sail within three weeks of each other. Columbus knew about Cabot's forthcoming voyage. Cabot assumed that Columbus would return to his islands before long. Both knew about the dispatch of the Portuguese fleet around the Cape of Good Hope the previous year. What neither of them knew was that on May 20, 1498, just ten days before Columbus sailed, Vasco da Gama had finally anchored outside Calicut in India, and opened trade negotiations with the local rajah.

Da Gama had battled his way around the cape and faced down a rebellion by his own navigators by throwing their instruments into the sea. Disguising his crew as Muslims, they made their way up the ports of east Africa, leaving Mombasa to cross the Indian Ocean on April 7. The scale of possibilities before the Portuguese were only too clear: Anchored outside Calicut with da Gama's small fleet were as many as seven hundred other ships from all over the East as far as China.

It was a defining moment in business and maritime history. Nothing would be the same again.

The sailing of Cabot and Columbus, together with Vasco da Gama's arrival in India, coincided with the untimely and slightly sordid last hours of Charles VIII of France. Charles was the most powerful monarch in Europe, and had flexed his muscle terrifyingly in Italy only two years earlier. His death at the age of only twenty-seven, and without an heir, was an enormous shock for Europe's diplomatic elite, and they dashed off dispatches home with the news. The messenger galloping home to Venice with the news from Paris rode thirteen horses to death in his haste.

The crisis in France meant real uncertainty for Italy, because Charles's nearest relative and obvious successor was his cousin Louis of Orleans, who had been one of the most powerful advocates of the invasion of Italy in 1494. Louis had a claim to the dukedom of Milan, Cabot's former home, which was now ruled by Ludivico Sforza, the uncle of the rightful duke.

When Louis XII was crowned in Rheims Cathedral, the worst fears of the Sforza clan were realized. He assumed the title Duke of Milan during the ceremony, to the joy of the Milanese exiles who surrounded Louis at his new court. Louis was thirty-five, at the height of his powers, immensely ambitious and a brilliant diplomat, rivaling even Ferdinand of Aragon. His first act was to have his marriage to the disabled Jeanne, daughter of Louis XI the Spider King, annulled so that he could marry his predecessor's widow, Anne of Brittany, the key to keeping Brittany in the kingdom of France. His second act was to choose his most able negotiators and send them out to the great cities of Italy to unravel the Holy League.

In fact, the league was rapidly unraveling on its own, largely because of a change of heart by Ferdinand of Aragon. Naples had just crowned its fifth king in three years, and the only route open to secure his family's hold over the kingdom in southern Italy seemed to be taking Naples for himself. That meant conflict with the rest of Italy.

Pope Alexander, the architect of the league, was relatively easy to bribe. He agreed to marry off his son Cesare Borgia—who was bored with his life as a cardinal and yearned for military adventure—to the sister of the king of Navarre. It was already clear that the Borgias no longer had any interest in Milan or the Sforzas. The pope's daughter Lucrezia Borgia was desperately tired of her husband, Giovanni Sforza, and managed to persuade him to escape from Rome in fear of his life, forcing him before his departure to sign a letter claiming that he had never consummated the marriage because he was impotent.

To the Venetians, Louis offered part of the duchy of Milan. After long debates in the council, they accepted the offer, and the Holy League was no more.

Cabot's and Columbus's parallel expeditions had been gone less than a month before London's uneasy peace was briefly at risk again. Perkin Warbeck escaped from Westminster Palace on Trinity Sunday. He was captured a few hours later in the village of Sheen in Middlesex, put in the stocks at Cheapside, and then sent to the Tower of London. For a moment, it looked as though England's dynastic struggles were about to break out again. Warbeck was executed eighteen months later, alongside the only living Yorkist claimant to the throne, for whom he had originally been mistaken less than a decade before.

Perhaps it was because of this excitement that Ferdinand's agents in London missed Cabot's departure. Maybe they had been persuaded that there would be a delay before sailing. Maybe there was nobody listening on the wharves at Bristol to hear that Cabot, Thirkill, and the others had actually left. But then a chastened Thirkill reappeared in London early in the summer, explaining that his ship had been damaged in a storm in the Irish Sea and the crew had been forced to put into an Irish port for repairs and he had been left behind.

The two rival Spanish ambassadors were determined to be first with the news. Pedro de Ayala was beginning to outwit Rodrigo Gonzales de Puebla in their daily skirmishes at court in Westminster. De Puebla was now distrusted by both sides: The Spanish wondered about him because of his obvious friendship with Henry VII; the English worried about him because he was always there, looking for something to eat, and was now actually being subsidized by Henry. De Ayala was solving the problem of the nonpayment of his salary in another way, by persuading the king that he deserved preferment. He was in the process of being made archdeacon of London and canon of St. Paul's Cathedral, an unprecedented honor for a foreign ambassador.

Both ambassadors dashed to send rival messengers with the news home to Castile. "The king of England sent five armed ships with another Genoese like Columbus to search for the island of Brasil and others near it. They were victualed for a year," wrote de Puebla on July 25. "They say that they will be back in September. By the direction they take, the land they seek must be in the possession of your highnesses."

The same day, Pedro de Ayala was dashing off a rival dispatch saying the same thing, and even using a similar phrase: "I have seen the map which the discoverer has made, who is another Genoese like Columbus . . . The people of Bristol have, for the last seven years, sent out every year two, three or four caravels, in search of the island of Brasil and the seven cities, according to the fancy of this Genoese." This was dramatic evidence to historians that there were Bristol expeditions across the Atlantic in the 1480s.

De Puebla had copied Cabot's maps, showing the Atlantic journey to the Indies and where he had gone, and sent them out to Ferdinand, just as John Day had sent copies to Columbus. The Spanish sovereigns had already been able to digest the implications and were convinced that under the Treaty of Tordesillas, Cabot had landed in territory that had been ceded to Castile and Aragon by the pope. Ferdinand and Isabella told de Ayala to make a formal protest to the English king.

It may be that what had delayed their dispatches was the news of the storm that had hit Cabot's fleet and seriously damaged the king's ship, which carried Cabot as well as his chief investors. If the expedition had carried on decapitated, then little could be expected of it. The king's ship was back in Bristol and Thirkill was back in London, but there was no sign of Cabot. He seems to have switched to another ship, probably with his son Sancio and Carbonariis, taken command of his diminished fleet, and headed off across the Atlantic from there.

Columbus and his three crews sweltering in the heat of the Doldrums for those nine terrifying days were actually lucky. Throughout their period of captivity in midocean, the sky was overcast and it drizzled. If they had been exposed to the full force of the sun, they would probably have died. On the ninth day a faint ruffling of the sails indicated a breath of wind, and soon there was enough to power them out of the area. By the end of July the weather was perfect, and Columbus's flagship plowed through the waves at a rate of nearly two hundred miles a day. But the crew was becoming increasingly nervous, having been disorientated by their ordeal, and one of them was even convinced they had drifted so far that they were now lying somewhere off Scotland. The water supplies on all three ships were dangerously low, and Columbus agreed reluctantly to turn northward to get supplies in the Lesser Antilles, unaware that the American continent—which still eluded him—had been just ahead of them.

On July 31, a seaman from Huelva named Alonso Pérez sighted land from the crow's nest. The crew sank down to their knees and sang "Salve Regina" on the deck. The three regular peaks they saw on the island ahead of them reminded Columbus, in his heightened state of religious intensity, of the trinity, and he named the island Trinidad. By nine P.M., the ships stood off Galley Cape and he sent expeditions ashore to look for water. The distress of preparing for this voyage, and the ordeal in the Doldrums, had brought back Columbus's sickness, his bleeding eyes and swelling limbs and bladder. He lay below when he could, trying to conserve his dwindling sight.

A welcoming committee of canoes paddled out to greet them, but when Columbus peered over the rail to look at them, he was bitterly disappointed. These were clearly not Asians. They were Caribs. Trying to get them to come closer, Columbus ordered the crew to play the tambourine and dance. The locals took this for a war dance and a hail of poisoned darts rained onto the deck. But he took comfort, as ever, from one detail: The men wore a kind of bandana around their heads, like the women did in the Moorish regions of Spain, which was at least a whiff of the East.

Within days, they had sailed through the Serpent's Mouth and into the rough water of the Gulf of Paria, where on August 4, the trio of ships escaped disaster from the effects of some kind of tsunami. There was, according to records, a great roar from the south followed by an enormous wave that lifted the ships high in the air and snapped their cables, before dropping them down again. Once more, Columbus's attempt to land on mainland America was shelved. When they anchored the following day, on the southern tip of the Paria Peninsula, on the coast of what is now Venezuela, Columbus decided not to go ashore. He sent Pedro de Terreros instead with a small party to raise a large cross on this new coast claimed for the monarchs of Castile and Aragon. Out of sight of the admiral, Pedro was soon surrounded by canoes, including some large ones with cabins in the middle for carrying goods, and was offered the usual selection of colorful parrots and necklaces and, in this instance, a powerful local brew called *chica*, made from fermented maize. But when representatives of the locals came back with him on board, he saw they had something else: The women all wore necklaces of the finest pearls, which they said came from pearl fisheries farther westward along the coast.

As they sailed on, they realized they were in freshwater, which was flowing into the sea from tributaries of the River Orinoco. The more experienced seamen on board insisted that huge amounts of freshwater like this must be from a vast river, and if that was the case, this could not be another island. But as they sailed carefully along the peninsula, and back out into the Caribbean, heading for the island of Margarita, Columbus refused to draw any conclusions, though he accepted that they had stumbled upon a "large mainland which, up until now, no-one knew existed."

By Columbus's reckoning, they were slightly southeast of the Chinese province of Mangi, which is what he believed Cuba to be. There was no continent to the south of Mangi on any atlas that had ever been drawn. So either every cosmographer in the world was wrong, or his identification of the Indies was mistaken. There was no contest here for Columbus, who had stuck to his theory through greater contradictions than a new continent. But the effort of holding his original views in the face of mounting evidence to the contrary was increasingly exhausting, even without the strain on his eyes and limbs.

There were other peculiarities too. He took detailed readings with the astrolabe and realized that the North Star was deviating in its position, a phenomenon that he and Cabot had become familiar with farther west, but this time the readings were more extreme. It required a truly magnificent theory to explain it, and in his heightened emotional state, Columbus provided one:

> Now I observed the very great variation which I have described and because of it began to ponder this matter of the shape of the world. And I concluded that it was not round in the way that they say, but is of the same shape as a pear, which may be very round all over but not in the part where the stalk is, which sticks up; or it is as if someone had a very round ball, and at one point on its surface it was as if a woman's nipple had been put there; and this teat-like part would be the most prominent and nearest the sky; and it would be on the equator, in this Ocean Sea, at the end of the Orient.

He added that the Garden of Eden was at the top of the pear, and it was impossible to go there without God's approval. He believed he was now sailing uphill through the Gulf of Paria. Ahead of them lay not just pearls, but paradise as well.

There wasn't much to be done. The holds were full of rotting supplies, their freshwater was severely rationed, and he desperately needed to get back to Hispaniola and link up with Bartholomew. The bond between the two brothers was ever stronger the more isolated they became. So regretfully, Columbus asked the locals to collect pearls for him to trade on his return and abandoned what was until then his most valuable find. His failure to quite comprehend its significance laid him open to the whisperings of

Ojeda, who suggested later that Columbus had failed to reach the pearl fisheries because he was planning to seize them for himself.

Feverish from dehydration and bleeding from the eyes, Columbus spent the journey to Hispaniola drifting in and out of sanity. He unwisely began a stream of consciousness letter to the sovereigns setting out his growing conviction that he was the "Christ-bearer," like his namesake St. Christopher, who would usher in the end of the world. Meanwhile, his lieutenant Alonso de Ojeda had also been busy. In one of his admiral's moments of inattention or pain, Ojeda had slipped into Columbus's cabin and made his own copy of the map of the Gulf of Paria, the coast of what is now Venezuela, and the location of the pearl fisheries. When Columbus's peculiar letters were making their way back across the Atlantic on board *El Correo*, Ojeda and the stolen map went with them.

Bartholomew Columbus had been facing one of the most dangerous challenges to his authority from one of the leading members of the new community in Hispaniola. Francisco Roldán's initial complaint was that, having been named as chief magistrate for Isabella, Bartholomew then chose Santo Domingo as the capital and abandoned Isabella altogether. But Roldán quickly became the focus for all the frustration against the Columbus brothers and their small group of acolytes, with their arrogance, cruelty, and inability to communicate properly with those they now administered. Bartholomew seems to have been behaving with increasing pomposity and was a major focus of discontent.

But Roldán was also a romantic. Like Columbus, he had been moved by the beauty of the landscape on this island they had annexed. He was also fascinated by the gentleness of the Indians and appalled by the moves to sell them into slavery. And he was a bitter opponent of the tax and the various brutal alternatives used to force the natives to offer up their gold. But he was also romantic in more self-interested ways, and when he seduced a wife of the Taino leader Guarionex, Bartholomew was furious. Roldán bided his time, but when he was sent by Diego Columbus with forty men to pacify Indians near Concepción, he made this the centerpiece of a plan to take over the outpost and use it as a headquarters from which to challenge the Columbus brothers across Hispaniola. But the fort's commander stayed loyal, and the plan was frustrated from the outset. Roldán marched back with his men to Isabella, tried and failed to launch the only ship in the harbor there, and instead escaped to the southwest part of the island—the most beautiful part—taking tributes and gifts from the Taino leaders on his way. The news that Bartholomew had been appointed *adelantado* by the monarchs was a blow to the legitimacy of his rebellion, and he settled down in his private fiefdom on the Jaragua Peninsula.

For some time, Roldán had been busy rebuilding his friendship with Guarionex after the seduction incident. Guarionex was one of the five most powerful Taino leaders on the island and also one of the most interesting. He had been the only leader to embrace Christianity, but had rejected it later because of the behavior of Christians on Hispaniola, and that made Roldán interesting to him. The two men had agreed to support each other, and when Roldán's revolt fizzled out in minor exchanges of brutality, Guarionex retreated with his Taino supporters into the mountains, where Bartholomew, infuriated at the murder of two of his messengers, followed him, burning villages as he went. When it was clear that he had taken refuge with a neighboring chief named Maiobanex, Bartholomew threatened to burn their villages as well unless he was handed over.

Despite pleadings from the local Tainos, Maiobanex held firm, telling them that Guarionex was a good man, but that the Christians were violent and he refused to have anything to do with them. As Bartholomew's soldiers approached, Guarionex felt that the honorable thing was to leave and give himself up. He did so, but Maiobanex and his family were taken captive anyway, and they were all taken back to the fort at Concepción, and chained up there.

When Columbus finally arrived at Hispaniola with his three ships, he landed by coincidence in territory controlled by Roldán and his men. With no knowledge of the revolt, Columbus invited him on board and Roldán took the opportunity of speaking to the crew, persuading a number of them to follow him instead. Leaving quickly for an emotional reunion with Bartholomew on Beata Island, it became clear that Columbus's plans for the pearls—he was hoping to set up a trading colony in the Gulf of Paria—were going to have to be shelved for the time being while he tried to bring some semblance of government to Hispaniola.

Columbus had arrived on his own island exhausted, nearly blind, filled with conviction that God had a leading role for him to play, and astonished that his own chief magistrate should have been the leader of a revolt against him. The short-term answer was obvious: no more magistrates drawn from the colonists. He needed a man who understood the law and held some authority in order to uphold it. He immediately sent a missive asking Ferdinand and Isabella to send a trained lawyer, or as he put it, a "lettered" official. This letter also went aboard the *El Correo*.

The problem underlying everything was the utter failure of his island to pay for itself. The gold was coming in tiny quantities and although there was brazilwood, it was hardly likely to pay for the vast investment that had made Columbus lord of Hispaniola and beyond. In this mood, he set aside what he knew to be Queen Isabella's views about turning her new subjects into slaves. There was no suitable alternative, as he explained, and he assured her that Hispaniola could export four thousand slaves a year, bringing in 20 million maravedis.

"Even if they die now," he wrote reassuringly, explaining that about half the Taino slaves had died on the voyage home so far, "it will not always be this way, for this is what the blacks and Canary Islanders did at first."

Back in Castile, Ferdinand and Isabella were unnerved by Columbus's letters. They were not reassured that he was in charge, as he had intended that they should be. Nor did they find his theorizing that the earth was perhaps pear-shaped at all convincing. They were painfully aware, as he kept telling them, that the privileges they had given him meant that they were denied a clear, objective view of the situation in the Indies. Isabella also received with disgust the letter with this extraordinary flouting of her instructions about slavery. "What power of mine does the admiral hold to give my vassals to anyone?" she asked later.

The effects of the letter's arrival were immediate. The sovereigns decided they could no longer rely on Columbus alone for exploration. From the following May, they commissioned a whole range of voyages under other commanders, most of them people who had sailed previously with the admiral. In the meantime, they were actively on the lookout for intelligent, trustworthy, calm, and sensible merchants or cosmographers who could be their eyes and ears.

The second decision was in response to Columbus's request for a lawyer. They decided to take him at his word, and send an official who could genuinely sum up what was going on around Hispaniola and act in their name. They chose Francisco de Bobadilla, a careful, well-respected, and aristocratic administrator, chamberlain to the monarchs, and the brother of Queen Isabella's closest friend. They initially gave him powers to act as governor of Hispaniola and to limit Columbus's responsibilities if necessary, but then they delayed sending him, unsure whether these powers would be enough or exactly what they wanted him to do.

The decision to send Bobadilla was not just a result of Columbus's intemperate and bizarre letter. A period of peculiar suspicion of foreigners had infected the court in Castile, in part due to the conflict with France and the demise of the Holy League. And of all the foreigners who excited the most suspicion, the wealthy, stateless Genoese merchants in every Spanish port, cornering the market in slaves and sugar, had a special place on everyone's list of those most distrusted. Rumors were flying around the court that the Genoese Columbus brothers were plotting to hand over Hispaniola to the city-state of his birth.

Ojeda had returned to court along with the letter, having briefed Fonseca on his way and handed over his stolen copy of the invaluable map of the pearl fisheries. He was a special favorite of Isabella, who admired his combination of courage and good looks, and she listened carefully as he described the pearls. Why had the admiral not investigated more closely? Ojeda could not imagine. It was enough to raise the question and encourage the idea that Columbus was somehow holding back. There was a reason so little gold had been forthcoming from Hispaniola, after all. Because, it was said, the admiral was concealing it, leaving his poor investors and the depleted Castilian treasury to pick up the pieces.

In Bristol, Cabot's wife, Mattea, reunited with her son Sebastian, who was either not included on the expedition or was on the king's ship, scoured the horizon for the return of her husband and other sons, due back in September 1498. She knew, of course, that if they had the opportunity to press on into the unknown, they would do so.

In London, the investors waited less patiently. The Great Chronicle of

London made an entry as the old mayor of the city retired on September 29, and it was about Cabot, "of whom," it said, "in this mayor's time returned no tidings."

I

*"The land and all its joys,*
*The beach, the harbor, all we know,*
*The trees fade out of sight,*
*And the shore becomes enwrapped by mist;*
*Already we begin to want it back*
*When hardly any time has passed—*
*And the more time we are away,*
*The thicker the clouds that we encounter."*

LOPE DE VEGA, *La Dragontea*, 1598

For Vespucci, unable to go home and unable to fully extricate himself from the tentacles of Berardi's old debts, Columbus's third voyage was a thrilling chance to test the hypothesis of the Indies, to find Marco Polo's Cape of Catigara and sail into the Bay of Bengal. He had urged Columbus to take the southwesterly route, and Columbus had done so. The news that returned with Ojeda was a bitter disappointment. Vespucci simply could not understand why Columbus had failed to grasp the opportunity. Why had he not continued along the coast to find out whether it would take him to the Indian Ocean, and prove the enterprise of the Indies once and for all? Why this frustrating drawing back to Hispaniola, to have his energy dissipated in pointless tussles with his fellow colonists? As for this bizarre plan to find the island "where all women were communal"—another possibility floated in letters home—it was the kind of project dreamed up by a man who had been too long on board ship.

In fact, Columbus now reasoned that it was impossible to go farther toward paradise without God's permission. Whether Ojeda passed this on to Vespucci or not, he undoubtedly heard rumors to that effect. The idea of asking divine permission to explore anywhere flew in the face of Vespucci's whole humanist education. Columbus had been Vespucci's business partner and was now his trusted friend. But there came a time when if you wanted to find out something badly enough, you had to carry out the exploration yourself. Vespucci knew all the wealthiest merchants in Spain, and all the Medici agents who handled the investment. All he needed to do was let it be known that he would like to accompany an expedition across the Atlantic. If Elyot and Thorne, Cabot's backers, could accompany him on an expedition to the New Founde Land, then Vespucci could go to the Cape of Catigara.

He was in a position to know the latest plans for Indies sailings, and it soon became clear that Alonso de Ojeda was to command an expedition, partly to map the coastline Columbus had discovered and partly to seek out the pearl fisheries. That was Fonseca's plan, but it was the sovereigns who insisted that trustworthy experts should go too. It was objective information they needed, so Ojeda was told to take with him two people who could record the geography of what they saw. Juan de la Cosa, once the captain of the *Santa Maria* and now one of the most respected mapmakers in Castile, was to be one of them. But to provide an objective view of the geographical evidence, Vespucci was invited as the second, partly as astronomer, partly as director of policy on behalf of the investors, and partly as the eyes and ears of the sovereigns. For Ferdinand and Isabella, it was a dream combination, and hopefully also a solution to one of their nagging questions about Hispaniola: On which side of the line drawn by the Treaty of Tordesillas did it actually lie?

"It was my intention to see whether I could turn a headland that Ptolemy calls the Cape of Catigara, which connects with the Sinus Magnus," Vespucci wrote later. It was clear from the beginning that, although he had barely ever ventured to sea before, if he wanted to exercise command, he might also be given some measure of independence. Whether or not he would actually be in command of part of the expedition, he would at least have some influence over where they went.


Ojeda had come a long way since he entertained Queen Isabella by balancing on a wooden plank above the street in Seville. He was now in full command of his own expedition, with the trust of Fonseca and the queen, a powerful combination. Ojeda had in his pocket a copy of the stolen map of the pearl fisheries that Columbus had sailed past, and may have had secret instructions from Fonseca about what to do if he encountered Cabot, from whom there was still no news. Vespucci had with him his full collection of navigation equipment, atlases, charts, and astronomical tables, and left behind his nephew Giovanni, who had lived with him since his arrival in Seville, and his new fiancée. Over the recent months, Vespucci had become engaged to Maria, the sister of Fernando Cerezo, with whom he had worked trying to disentangle the difficulties of Berardi's will.

Ojeda's fleet of four ships moved out of Cadiz harbor early on May 18, 1499, almost a year to the day since the departure of Columbus. In the flagship, Ojeda had on board not just Juan de la Cosa, but three pilots, a surgeon, and an apothecary. In Palos, a little to the east, and almost ready to sail, was another ship commanded by Peralonso Niño, a former pilot of the *Santa Maria*, also bound for the pearl fisheries and furnished with the same maps. (Niño would be arrested on his return for failing to pay the regulation fifth of the value of his pearls to the crown.)

The mild-mannered Vespucci and Ojeda had little in common. Both were reinventing themselves, but as rather different characters. Deeply suspicious of everyone, and particularly the ship's chandlers who equipped his ships, Ojeda took part of the fleet immediately into Puerto de Santa Maria at the mouth of the river. There he hijacked another ship that lay at anchor, transferred his stores to it, and left the suspiciously unseaworthy ship he had been given in its place. If he had any doubt about the adequacy of his supplies, he indulged in a little light piracy to make up the difference. At Lanzarote in the Canary Islands he even plundered a house belonging to the daughter of Columbus's old mistress from San Sebastian. In the Portuguese Cape Verde Islands, Ojeda divided his fleet into two and he and Vespucci set different courses across the Atlantic, agreeing to meet somewhere between the pearl fisheries and Hispaniola.*

On June 27, 1499, the moment of truth arrived for Vespucci. For some weeks, Ojeda had left him responsible for two ships, supported by captains

---

*The Cape Verde Islands were a peculiar place. Already shorn of the greenness that gave them their name but known also for their turtles, they had attracted a large population of lepers, who bathed in the turtles' blood in the belief that it cured leprosy.

and pilots, but, as the representative of the investors, effectively in control. Vespucci had now seen enough of how his commander operated to be absolutely determined he would not, in fact, link up again with Ojeda.

Vespucci had dreamed of exploration his whole life, and facilitated it for seven exhausting years in Seville, and now ahead of his two ships was a looming shadow on the horizon. As the two ships drew closer to the land, probably near Cayenne in what became French Guyana, the shadow became a green mass and with just a few miles to go, it was clear that up ahead was a vast tropical forest. The smell of rotting vegetation and stagnant water was obvious even several miles out to sea. It was a rich aroma and beautiful in its own way: It smelled of life. Vespucci called it the Land of St. Ambrose, a Christian way of dedicating it to a Renaissance idea, the ambrosia of the gods. While Columbus named his new lands after saints and Christian festivals, and Cabot after his friends, only a Florentine like Vespucci—steeped in the artistic revolution of Botticelli—would name them after a pagan idea.

The crews said prayers on deck for their safe arrival and anchored offshore, and Vespucci's large balding head descended over the side of the ship and into one of the exploring boats. According to his calculations, they were about five degrees south of Columbus's landfall the previous year.

"We launched the boats and with sixteen men went ashore, to a land we found so full of trees and verdure too, for they never shed their foliage, and the sweet scent emanating from them (for all are aromatic) was so soothing to our nostrils that it had quite restorative effect on us," he wrote later. But when they reached the shore, the vegetation was so thick, with the roots of the mangrove trees so deep in the mud flats and sand below the waterline, that there was nowhere to beach the boats. For the rest of the day, until it grew too dark to continue, Vespucci and the two boats searched for a way inland through the trees. They went back to the ships bitterly disappointed.

The following day, they turned east along the coast. It was a matter of basic precaution to follow the coast some way off but just in sight, in case of shoals and unexpected rocks. Noticing the peculiar behavior of the waters around them as they proceeded some distance offshore, they hauled a bucket of water onto the deck, tasted it, and to their astonishment found— just like Columbus had farther west—that it was freshwater, and they filled their casks with it.

The forest wall continued for days, but on July 2 they turned into a great gulf, about 150 miles across as it later turned out. Vespucci called it the Gulf of Santa Maria, the feast of whose visitation it happened to be that day, returning to conventional methods of naming new places: in practice, all three of the explorers named their discoveries after dates in the church's calendar, with the name of the saint celebrated that day. To celebrate their arrival, as they moved nearer to the mouth of what looked like a gigantic river, there was a spectacular electrical storm, with lightning flashing in the rigging and masthead with St. Elmo's Fire, the bright electrical glow from the masts when there is high voltage in the atmosphere. It was beautiful and terrifying.

This could not be Catigara because that was a sea-lane and therefore salt-water. The obvious explanation, as Columbus's sailors had insisted in the mouth of the Orinoco, was that this was the mouth of some vast river. Vespucci turned the ships in toward the shore and soon found himself in an archipelago of islands at the river's mouth, far bigger even than the one Columbus had stumbled across. Neither Vespucci nor his captains could have known that pouring out onto the coast, there were two rivers, which we know as the Tocantins and the Amazon, carrying one fifth of the world's freshwater out to sea.

There was still no letup in the wall of mangrove roots that prevented them getting ashore. Vespucci chose the most northerly channel and the ships battled against the current and sailed into a river so broad that you could not see across it. The two tiny caravels, dwarfed by this vast freshwater torrent, made their way slowly upstream. Vespucci and his pilots feared reefs, so he anchored the ships and took nineteen men in two boats farther along the river, keeping away from the dangerous banks.

For two days, and by the light of the moon at night, they rowed continuously in teams. There was still no space to land, but Vespucci and his men marveled at the extraordinary colors of the parrots, only too aware—like Cabot in Nova Scotia—that they were being observed. Although there was no sign of people or buildings of any kind, there were lines of smoke rising from the trees which made it obvious that this vast forest was populated.*

It took less than two days to sail with the current back to the ships that

*For the next century, the Amazon was known as the River of Smoke.

were anchored near the mouth of the river. Vespucci hauled up the anchors and carried on along the coast to the south, where it became clear at night that the North Star had disappeared below the horizon. They had crossed the equator. It was a relief for those new to exploration, having heard all the stories about ships combusting at the equator or the air disappearing completely, to have survived with no more ill-effects than a bit of sunburn. "Rationally, let it be said in a whisper," wrote Vespucci later, "experience is certainly worth more than theory."

The next morning, the crew gathered on deck and Vespucci explained to them the significance of where they were. They were on the line that marked the hottest part of the world, where the sun was directly overhead at midday, and the stars—well, what were the stars in the southern hemisphere? Nobody, as far as he knew, had ever mapped them. He asked for volunteers among his crew to stay up through the night and help him draw the southern heavens for the first time. Nobody volunteered, so night after night he watched alone, searching with fascination for some heavenly body the equivalent of the polestar in the north.

They were still too close to the equator to work out which star this was but, after some nights, four stars that moved against one another in the same part of the sky were visible. In an intuitive leap, Vespucci realized this might be what he was looking for, pinpointing the constellation that mariners in future generations would know as the Southern Cross. Vespucci was not the first European to glimpse the Southern Cross, but it was an experience that changed him forever. Before reaching the equator, he retained at least one foot in the world of merchants, accountants, and profits. Afterward, it was knowledge he craved: He would give his allegiance and his labor to whichever employer allowed him to pursue knowledge for its own sake.

Alone at night, listening to the faint lap of waves against the ship's hull and with the night breeze on his face, Vespucci stared at the new stars and lines from Dante's *Purgatory* leaped into his mind. He recited them quietly to himself on the quarterdeck, and set them down again in his description of that moment in his letter to his Popolano mentor Lorenzo di Pierfrancesco:

> *I turned to the right hand, and gave heed*
> *to the other pole, and saw four stars*

*never seen save by our first parents.*
*The heavens appeared to rejoice in their rays.*
*O widowed northern region,*
*Since thou art deprived of beholding these.*

While Vespucci was sailing southward along the coast, the most extraordinary news was finally reaching Lisbon. The fleet under Vasco da Gama, to which they had waved farewell two years before, had rounded the Cape of Good Hope successfully, made their way up the east coast of Africa, and linked up with traders in India itself.* Europe had finally achieved the trading dream of a direct link with the East, and it had been done by the Portuguese sailing eastward, not the Italians sailing west.

Vasco da Gama had run into immediate difficulties in Calicut, aware that there were divisions within the local population, some of whom were determined that this first European mission should not be encouraged to return. By August 1498, only three months after Cabot and Columbus had set sail, da Gama had decided he would leave and return with a much larger fleet.

It had taken da Gama's ships another three months to sail back across the Indian Ocean, and by early in the new year 1499, they were so short of men that the *São Gabriel* was beached and set on fire to concentrate the crews in the remaining ships. On March 20, they had rounded the cape going the other way, and da Gama had sent his fastest ship on ahead, reaching Lisbon with the news on July 10, personally taking his sick brother Paolo from the Cape Verde Islands to the Azores, where Paolo died. When da Gama finally arrived in Lisbon on September 8, he was welcomed as a hero and given a triumphal homecoming into the city.

The Portuguese were keenly aware of the significance of Vasco da Gama's achievement. But there were also those in Bristol and London who had been listening quietly to news of Cabot's preparation for his small fleet of discovery to the Indies. Like Ferdinand and Columbus, the Portuguese king Manuel and his advisers had been struggling with the implications of the Treaty of Tordesillas for a round globe. It was all very well to divide the

---

*Da Gama met his first Hindus, among the first ever encountered by Europeans, at Malindi on the African coast, and immediately assumed they were Christians.

world between Portugal and Spain down the Atlantic, but what about the other side of the world? It was hardly surprising that the first reaction from Castile about Vasco da Gama's return was to lodge a formal protest that he had been on their side of the line laid down by the treaty.

Vespucci was sailing as fast as he could down the coast of what is now Brazil, the first European to do so. His ship (we don't know its name) had managed about eight hundred miles since the equator, but Vespucci was certain this was not far enough to be anywhere near the Cape of Catigara, and the currents were getting stronger in the opposite direction.

"We encountered an ocean current which ran from south east to north west, and was so great and ran so furiously that we were terribly frightened and hastened away out of this great danger," he wrote. "The current was such that the waters of the Strait of Gibraltar and around the lighthouse of Messina were those of a pool by comparison. It was such that when it struck our bows, we could not make any headway, even though we had a brisk fair wind."

It is hard to work out exactly where they were, because there is no obvious current that Vespucci could have encountered in this part of the south Atlantic, unless it was the one that eventually becomes the Gulf Stream. Whatever it was, Vespucci's captains sailed the two ships in a great arc out into the Atlantic, and turned south again. Still the going was no easier. On the first day away from the coast, they managed to make only twenty miles. The following day it was even less. Time and supplies were also running out and, even if there had been gaps in the thick forests, there was really no time to land. Marco Polo had not recorded this difficulty when he passed through the Cape of Catigara.

Clearly they could not continue. Bitterly disappointed that he had failed to identify the sea-lanes to India, there was no option for Vespucci but to turn around and sail back north.

The first people Vespucci had seen since sighting the coast of Guyana in July were back in Trinidad, where his ships had arrived about a month behind Ojeda and the rest of the expedition.

While Vespucci had been sailing down the coast of South America, Ojeda and Juan de la Cosa and the other two ships had been taking a more leisurely journey in the opposite direction, along the coast that later became known as the Spanish Main. Ojeda's expeditions were never short on bloodthirstiness. He had no sense of negotiation and was inherently suspicious of almost any situation. Landing at bay after bay, his sailors left dead locals and burned villages behind them. When they reached Capo de la Vela in Venezuela, they turned north—as Columbus had done almost exactly a year before—toward the Lesser Antilles, and headed for Hispaniola, for rest and repairs.

By then, Vespucci was following along behind and was much more impressed with the locals than Ojeda. They had, he said, "the skin of tawny lions." The people of Trinidad welcomed him and his crews, treated him and his men to breakfast, and gave him eleven large pearls and some colored parrots. "They all go naked as they were born, without having any shame," he wrote later, in some amazement. "If all were related of how little modesty they have, it would be entering upon obscenity. It is better to keep silence."

His two ships had made their way back up the coast, more than twenty miles apart, but still in sight of each other, until on August 4 they reached a point just north of their original landfall. Vespucci persuaded himself that it was still possible that Catigara was farther to the west along the coast, but after six hundred miles it was quite clear that this could not be the extreme tip of Asia in the west. The rivers were undeniable evidence that this was a vast continent.

They met more locals in the Gulf of Paria, following the map sketched out by Columbus the previous year, where they were entertained again with fruits, wine, and juice and presented with exotic birds and the most enormous pearls, and—if the implication is correct—they enjoyed the local women, with or without their consent. Vespucci was particularly fascinated by the local languages, and claimed largely as a result of this voyage that there were at least a thousand languages on the planet, at a time when most scholars believed there were only twenty-six.

Around the Paria Peninsula, and along the coast of what is now Venezuela, mapping as closely as he could, and going without sleep to map the sky at night, he found that the locals were less welcoming. Often their trips ashore encountered armed parties waiting to ambush them. It is hard to escape the impression that since they were now sailing about three weeks

behind Ojeda and company, the "welcoming" committees were largely a reaction to Ojeda's bloody raids. Normally the crew was able to anticipate
these attacks and escape back to the boats before there was any confrontation. But on one occasion around August 16, Vespucci's men were taken by
surprise while they were still on the beach and had to fight for their lives.

The weapons at their disposal were considerably more powerful than
those of their attackers. They had guns and swords, but they had little defense against poison arrows or a well-aimed machete. Vespucci's men fled
back to the boats, when the boatswain, the oldest member of the crew,
urged them to stand their ground so that God could give them a victory.
Vespucci described later how the boatswain emphasized the point by falling
to his knees on the beach, praying aloud, then running ahead of the rest
into the melée. The attackers were soon overwhelmed, and the crew turned
into a raiding party, moving quickly inland to the nearest village and burning 180 huts to the ground, before following the wounded back to the ships.

There were so many wounded after this run ashore that Vespucci set sail
immediately to find a quiet bay where they could recover. They did so for
a week, near what is known today as Puerto Cabello. One of the crewmen
died there from his wounds, and Vespucci dubbed the place the Bay of Arrows. A week's recuperation meant that Vespucci could look more inten-
sively at his new maps and consider the evidence that this was indeed an
enormous continent. From the ship they had seen lions, pumas, deer, and
boars, and it was believed at the time that you did not find large animals on
islands. On one expedition into the bush, they also came across an ana-
conda nearly twenty-five-feet long and as thick as a man's waist. Terrified,
the crew dashed back to the ship.

Hanging back for fear of too close an association with Ojeda, or perhaps
because he did not yet want to relinquish his temporary command, Vespucci
turned north somewhere near the island of Curaçao, which he called Brazilwood Island. There occurred one of the most bizarre encounters between
civilizations. Vespucci took eleven men ashore in a boat and followed an
obvious human path for seven miles or so inland, where he found a village
of large huts. Around the huts, to their surprise and delight, were a number
of huge women, none of them less than ten inches taller than he was. The
women entertained these outlandish visitors in their huts, where the sailors
caught sight of two beautiful teenage girls, both also enormously tall. Dur-

Vespucci and the natives, from a later engraving

ing this meal, one of the sailors suggested quietly to Vespucci and his col-leagues, in an outrageous flouting of the laws of hospitality, that these girls might make a wonderful gift for the king of Spain.

They were just discussing how they could steal them away when there was a rattle of voices outside the huts, and a large number of well-armed men arrived back from hunting. They were even bigger than the women. The men questioned their visitors closely using sign language. Where were they from? What did they want? Outnumbered by giants, Vespucci's sign language—and the few words he had picked up from the Taino slaves in Seville—conveyed that they were journeying around the world and had no hostile intentions. The idea of kidnapping the two girls was quietly dropped, and the men escorted Vespucci and the crewmen politely and firmly back to their boats.

Back at the coast of the mainland, on Cape de la Vela, Vespucci was de-lighted to see a conjunction of the moon with Jupiter, which would help in his calculations later. The following day, on September 16, they finally turned northward toward Hispaniola. They were now only two and a half weeks be-hind Ojeda's ships in their tumultuous journey in the same direction.

But the Curaçao story is revealing, partly because of what it says about Vespucci himself. Of the three explorers, he is by far the most modern: even-tempered, civilized, learned, and tolerant, even if he wasn't wholly trustworthy. Yet he still takes us by surprise, although we do know him as a man steeped in the slave trade in Seville, and reveals himself as a potential kidnapper and looter after all. But it is revealing also because this is one of the very few stories of discovery in the new world where the locals emerge with power and dignity. Perhaps this was the pattern of an alternative relationship between the new arrivals and those they had discovered. Perhaps, if things had been only a little different, this could have been a vision of a more equal relationship between the Old World and the New.

Once Columbus had arrived back on Hispaniola, the most obvious problem that required attention was Roldán's revolt. A quick review of the resources at his disposal made him think twice about a direct confrontation. He had only about seventy soldiers available, and he was unsure of the loyalty of at least half of them. The rest—about a third of the forces theoretically available to him—were now too ill with syphilis to be able to fight. Roldán was a former friend and he seemed contented with his fiefdom in the west, so it made sense to come to terms. Columbus initially sent him a placatory message, addressing him as "my dear friend." The negotiations that followed kept them both busy for nearly a year. Roldán set out his terms: He wanted to be appointed magistrate of the island as a whole. He also wanted his supporters to be given what they longed for: the chance to go home, and take with them what gold they had managed to extract, their concubines, and their slaves.

Columbus had signed a document to this effect in November 1498. In Columbus's view, the decision to make Roldán chief magistrate of the island for life was unimportant, if this senior official requested from Castile would outrank him, but it made Columbus a laughingstock on his own island. The agreement also said that anyone who wanted to go back to Castile could do so on the ships that had brought them, and these would sail within fifty days. "Our people here are such that there is neither good man nor bad who hasn't two or three Indians to serve him and dogs to hunt for him and, though it perhaps were better not to mention it, women so pretty that one must wonder at it," he complained to the queen. "With the last of these practices I am extremely discontented, for it seems to me a disservice to God, but I can do nothing about it . . ." He also told her that because he had not negotiated the agreement himself and had signed it at sea, it might not be legal and she could cancel it if she wished. Isabella was unimpressed.

Columbus had hoped to use the small fleet to set up his station in the pearl fisheries, but two months later it was ready to take Roldán's supporters instead. Under the terms of the agreement, three hundred colonists were able to go home and to take one slave each with them. As for Roldán and his remaining backers, they also wanted some kind of settlement that did not involve imposing the hated tax system on the Tainos. The formula they worked out through the first half of 1499, which involved assigning land to settlers with rights over the Indians who lived there, was the beginning of the *encomiendas* system that introduced a similar pattern all over the Spanish empire. Those who saw the system in action a few years later believed it was a worse tyranny even than the tax, but at the time, it seemed like a relief.

In any case, the gold tax was unraveling, and Columbus's officials were already beginning to organize the remaining Tainos into work parties led by Castilian landholders. The *encomiendas* system treated them less like free men who must be taxed and bludgeoned into submission, and more like Russian serfs who could be bought or sold along with the land. It wasn't Columbus's design, yet in practice it allowed a much more systematic exploitation.

At this point, on September 5, Ojeda and de la Cosa landed in southwest Hispaniola at a place called Yaquimo, on the long peninsula that was controlled by Roldán and his rebels. Their journey there had included a brief visit to the island of Aruba in what is now the Dutch Antilles, where they found people living in strange stilt houses above the water. Ojeda sent a party of men to force their way into the homes and found that they were full of cotton and brazilwood. These products normally came from the East, and were a small piece of evidence that Columbus would have welcomed. Juan de la Cosa said the watery place reminded him of Venice, and the term "Little Venice," or Venezuela, was used later as the name for the region on the mainland opposite.

Ojeda knew about Roldán's revolt—he had been in Hispaniola the previous year—and so he had an advantage once he arrived there again. He therefore claimed to be Fonseca's representative and began ordering about any colonists he could find. When Columbus heard of his arrival, he sent a message to Roldán—now the chief magistrate of the whole island—to send an expedition to arrest him. The last thing either wanted was a rival rebel leader, and Roldán and Ojeda approached each other gingerly and took the precaution of taking a handful of each other's men hostage. Yet they had known each other in Isabella in the early days of that abandoned city and were old colleagues, and Ojeda persuaded him without much difficulty to take no action.

On September 23, 1499, a little over a fortnight later, Vespucci landed on Hispaniola as well. There were worms eating his hulls and maggots in his remaining stores, and his crews were still recovering from wounds and exhausted. He was well aware that this was a potentially awkward visit. He knew how Ojeda would behave on the island. He knew a little about Roldán's rebellion and did not want his own arrival to become confused with it. He also wanted to protect his friendship with Columbus, and concluded that the best way to do so was to have as little contact with either him or Ojeda on Hispaniola as he possibly could. He therefore steered along the north side of the island, and landed somewhere near the original city of Isabella, now all but abandoned.

There are no records of meeting Columbus during his time there, but Juan de la Cosa seems to have sought Vespucci out, in order to gather the information for his definitive map of the world. The two men, the preeminent geographers in Spain, pored over each other's charts, comparing notes about the coast that would become the Spanish Main, while Vespucci explained his pioneering voyage south along the coast of Brazil and the vast rivers he had seen there. Which raised the question: Exactly where were these places? The accuracy of their measurements of latitude were pretty reliable, at least as far as the equator when the North Star disappeared below the horizon. But longitude was a tougher proposition, and longitude mattered very much under the Treaty of Tordesillas. Having time on his hands on Hispaniola, while his ships were being repaired, meant that Vespucci had the leisure to do some serious calculations based on his observations of the sky at night on his long voyage.

He had been puzzling over the problem of measuring longitude. Columbus had done it by dead reckoning, estimating course and speed each day to work out how far west he had sailed. Vespucci had come up with something more precise, which used the position of the moon compared with other planets at a set time on a given day. If he was stuck in harbor, as he had been for a week in the Bay of Arrows, and now in Hispaniola, he realized he could compute when midnight was by using half-hour glasses to measure the length of time between sunset and sunrise.

If there were any planetary conjunctions with the moon on those days in Ferrara in Italy—and he had charts setting out, rather inaccurately as it turned out, the precise times of these in Ferrara—he could look for the same conjunctions in his own sky and pinpoint when they happened. The difference between the time in Ferrara and the time where he was on the other side of the Atlantic meant he could then work out how many degrees of the earth's 360 they were away. Though he claimed to have invented this "lunar distances" method himself, it was in fact known in the Middle Ages, but only in theory. Vespucci's contribution was to put it into practice. He reckoned he could measure the longitude of his position to within two degrees—though this was another exaggeration. He was using inaccurate tables and took most of his measurements at sea, and was forced to borrow Columbus's reading of a lunar eclipse in 1494.

Taking readings was extremely difficult in those days anyway. Accurate astrolabes needed to be big, but if they were made of metal they were then too heavy, and if they were made of wood, they warped at sea. It is hardly surprising, under those circumstances, that Vespucci's calculations remained inaccurate, nonetheless he had made the first steps of reinventing himself as a mysterious man of science, who would later pour scorn on mere mariners.

## II

*"In the endeavor to ascertain longitude, I have lost much sleep, and have shortened my life by ten years, but I hold it well worth the cost, because if I return in safety from this voyage, I have hopes of winning fame throughout the ages."*

AMERIGO VESPUCCI, letter to Lorenzo
di Pierfrancesco, July 1500

In the first few months of 1498, as Cabot and Columbus were preparing to sail, Milan had seen a flowering of intellectual life in Ludovico Sforza's court. The duke launched a series of great debates in his castle, bringing together Leonardo da Vinci, still basking in the success of his painting of the Last Supper at the convent of Santa Maria delle Grazie, and some of the other thinkers attached to the court.* One of these was a Venetian friar, Luca Pacioli, whose mathematical masterwork would go down in history as the first clear instructions for double-entry bookkeeping, a work still in print four centuries later. Along with these contemporaries, Leonardo knew about his former colleague Cabot's discoveries in the Atlantic. As a pupil of Toscanelli's, he had also followed the achievements of Columbus, apparently proving Toscanelli's old theories about sailing west to get to the East. As a friend of Vespucci's since childhood, he may also have known about his prospective voyage.

But since that intellectual flowering, the life of Milan's court had been torn apart by wars and rumors of wars. The intentions of the new French king were very well known in Milan, but there seemed to be nowhere Ludovico Sforza could go for help. Naples was in ruins and the Holy League in tatters. Florence was barely holding itself together. Venice was in alliance with the other side. His only comfort was the miserable defeat of the Venetian fleet in a series of four battles in April 1499 at the hands of the Turks, after which the Venetian admiral was sent home in chains and the Turks sailed to Lepanto and took the city.

Even so, it was soon clear that the travails of Venice would not delay Louis and the French. In the middle of August 1499, as Ojeda and Vespucci separately prepared to leave the coast of Venezuela, the French army once again crossed the Alps under the command of a Milanese exile named Gian Giacomo Trivulzio. The first Milanese garrison was massacred, and as the army approached the city, there was an uprising against Sforza rule in the streets. On August 30 Ludovico's own treasurer was killed by rioters, and three days later Ludovico fled with his family to Innsbruck in Austria. On October 6 Louis marched into Milan at the head of his army and confirmed himself as duke.

---

*Leonardo is said to have scoured the streets of Milan to find the right models for each disciple, and to have threatened to use the convent's prior as the model for Judas unless he was given more time to finish the painting.

For Leonardo the invasion was a personal disaster. He needed a new patron, and in the weeks before the arrival of the French, Sforza had requisitioned the sixty tons of bronze earmarked for his gigantic equestrian statue of the duke's father to make cannon instead. Worse, when a detachment of Gascon archers came across the full-size clay model for Leonardo's statue, they used it for target practice and destroyed it. Still living near the convent, Leonardo sadly gathered his belongings and headed for Mantua. Six months later, in the spring of 1500, Sforza was briefly back to reoccupy the city, but he was unable to pay his own army, which then abandoned him. He tried to escape in disguise, but was arrested and taken to France. He was a imprisoned at the castle of Loches, where he died in 1508. Only two years before the invasion, ironically, his ambassador in London had joked about preferring to hang onto his steady job with the Sforzas rather than accept any of Cabot's flimsy promises about being made ruler of some new island.

For Venice, also at war with Milan, the worst was yet to come. On September 9, 1499, the disastrous news about Vasco da Gama arrived in the city. The city's days as the international clearinghouse for the European end of the spice trade were not quite over—the old spice routes would be reestablished in the middle of the next century—but for a while, Lisbon would be the new Venice. The Venetians feared they would become instead a small outpost on the edge of the Turkish empire. There was already a financial crisis because of the advancing Turks, and now two Venetian banks failed. The Doge briefly discussed cutting a canal to the Red Sea at Suez, but it was considered impractical. It was a turning point in Italian history.


Ojeda and Juan de la Cosa set sail again for home sometime in the new year of 1500. It was exactly half a millennium since Christ's birth and a new age seemed to be dawning. The map they had drawn—though it did not include the discoveries of Vasco da Gama in East Africa and India—was beginning to take shape, and it would set out a world that no geographer would have recognized before. It was going to be a momentous six months in all their lives. By the end of the summer that year, the news about the eastern route to the Indies would have spread, the Portuguese would have stumbled on the coast of Brazil, Columbus would be facing his second revolt, and his nemesis would be on his way from Castile to Hispaniola.

Vespucci stayed determinedly apart, careful not to let his own efforts be compromised by Ojeda's ambition. He set sail in spring 1500 for the Bahamas, but ran into serious storms and unpredictable oceans full of rocks and shoals. Food and water began to run short—rationed to six ounces of bread a day—and, after some weeks, the crew approached Vespucci formally and requested that the voyage be brought to an end. The natives of the Bahamas had failed to capture Vespucci's imagination. He dismissed them as "timid people of small intellect," adding ominously, "we did what we liked with them." It was another example of how even the most cultured of people can fall for the doctrine that the weakest somehow deserve to be mistreated.

Columbus breathed a sigh of relief that Ojeda, at least, had gone. He had been the latest in a long line of former friends and colleagues who he now believed had betrayed him: He never forgave Ojeda for going to the pearl fisheries, and was aware that of all the people who might appear unexpectedly on his island, Ojeda had more potential than any so far for making trouble.

But only a few months after he had sailed, and after Vespucci followed him home a little later, there was another unfamiliar Castilian sail on the horizon, and once more Columbus was forced to ask himself whether this was a welcome supply fleet or another unwelcome adventurer trespassing on his island and his monopoly. It was, in fact, the latter. Juan Díaz de Solís had teamed up with his old colleague from the the *Niña*, Vicente Yánez Pinzón, and his nephew, Aruas.

Solís was a member of an impoverished aristocratic family from Asturias, who had been in Portuguese service but had been forced to escape to Castile because he had murdered his wife. They had set sail from Palos back in November, run into freak weather, and ended up in the mouth of the Amazon, believing it was the Ganges. They had even rounded Cape San Roque, the eastern extremity of Brazil. Eight of their crewmen had been killed in clashes with the locals on the way north again, presumably those who had first encountered Europeans at the hands of Ojeda. When they reached Santo Domingo on June 23, 1500, they were utterly exhausted and down to their last rations.

Columbus realized that the sovereigns were not keeping what he believed to be their side of the bargain, and it seemed that worse was to come.

. . .

Enthralled by the possibilities of redirecting the Indian spice trade via Portugal, King Manuel was determined to capitalize on Vasco da Gama's achievements as soon as possible. But two other things bothered him: One was Columbus and the other was Cabot.

The rumors from Columbus's third voyage, confirmed by spies at the Castilian court, were that a continent-size landmass had been found south and east of Hispaniola. It seemed quite possible that some of this land did, in fact, lie on their side of the Tordesillas line. The rumor from Cabot's voyage on the *Matthew* was also that he had found land around the same longitude far to the north, and had set off to follow where it went. There had been no news since he left, now nearly two years before. But was it not possible that this New Founde Land was also on their side of the line? What if his English fleet encountered the Portuguese in the Indies? There was an opportunity first to warn the English off their territory and, second, perhaps to reach some agreement that could provide them with an ally against Castile. So one of Manuel's first new acts of policy after Vasco da Gama returned was to send a diplomatic mission to London to discuss Cabot's voyage.

But he took more aggressive steps as well. First, he gave permission to sail north to a trader from Terceira in the Azores called John Fernandez, known also by his nickname as yeoman farmer or "labrador." Fernandez and his associates had long experience in the North Atlantic, because they had been sailing to and from Bristol since at least 1492. He was an obvious choice to push forward Portugal's knowledge of the ocean in the far northwest. Fernandez the Labrador and his colleagues huried to prepare an expedition. Sometime in the summer of 1500, while Vespucci was sailing home from the Bahamas, they found part of Greenland, believing it to be much farther west. They were prevented from landing by ice, but named the new land Labrador, more as a joke than anything else. The name was later applied to the coast north of Newfoundland.

Second, Manuel gave secret orders to Pedro Alvares Cabral, commanding the fleet of thirteen ships that was going to consolidate Vasco da Gama's route to India, to swing far out into the Atlantic on their way south to see what they might find. Cabral sailed from Lisbon on March 9, 1500. The bishop of Ceuta, Diego Ortiz, who had been on the committee of scientists that first turned down Columbus's enterprise of the Indies, presided at mass on the beach in front of the king and the court to send them off.

On April 22 Cabral reached Brazil, convinced that the land he had found was the same as that found by Columbus in 1498. He named it *Terra Sanctae Crucis*. He stayed ten days then headed back on his voyage to India, certain that this was a large island and absolutely not Asia. He sent one ship, the *Anunciada*—chosen presumably because of her name—back to Lisbon via the Cape Verde Islands, with the news and a consignment of parrots.*

The owner of the *Anunciada* was a Florentine merchant living in Lisbon named Bartholomew Marchionni, a business partner of Vespucci's, who, though Vespucci may not have known it—was spying for the Portuguese. He was also a fellow agent for the Popolano family back in Florence, and deeply involved in the slave trade. Marchionni had paid for one of the ships in Vasco da Gama's original fleet, and had underwritten some of the costs of Cabral's as well. The discovery of Portuguese land on the Portuguese side of the treaty line was precisely what he had hoped for.

Faced with a potential revolt by his crews, Vespucci held a conference with them to decide what to do. Apart from a number of massive pearls, his part of the voyage had not in fact filled the hold with spices and precious stones. Like Columbus before him, Vespucci fell back on a tried and tested solution. He continued to sail around the Bahamas, sending expeditions ashore to seize slaves. Having filled his two ships to capacity with a miserable human cargo, Vespucci set off into the Atlantic and sixty-seven days later he arrived in the Azores, where he heard the extraordinary news of Vasco da Gama's return. After six days at sea, his two ships sailed into Cadiz harbor in June from Madeira, having thrown thirty-two dead slaves overboard. Two hundred were left, and these he sold immediately, repaying his investors the other money he had borrowed to equip the ships. There were just five

---

*Only three weeks later, Cabral's fleet nearly met disaster rounding the Cape of Good Hope in an unprecedented storm. Four of his ships capsized and their entire crews were lost. The commander of one of them was the man who had first rounded the Cape for Portugal, Bartholomew Dias.

hundred ducats left to pay the crew. He divided this equally among them at the rate of about ten ducats each—and just in time. Only a few days later, Ferdinand and Isabella declared a general amnesty for all slaves brought from the Indies. Those that were still just alive on the dockside in Seville, after Columbus's other voyages, would be sent home to Hispaniola and resettled.

Vespucci lost no time making the journey to Granada where the sovereigns were based, dealing with an uprising by Moorish insurgents. Along with the enormous pearls they had been given on Trinidad, he presented them with two large precious stones, one the color of amethysts and the other the color of emeralds. Ferdinand and Isabella were delighted and were fascinated by Vespucci's cosmographical calculations. They were right to be. Vespucci had outlined to them more new coastline than anybody since 1492, although he still was unsure where it was in relation to his mental atlas. His method of measuring longitude was used for three centuries until the invention of reliable chronometers in the eighteenth century. He also promised to make a globe explaining his discoveries for the king and, in return, Ferdinand made him an unprecedented offer. There were three ships being fitted out for a new expedition and they would leave in September. Would Vespucci go with them? Not even Columbus had managed a response so immediate.

Basking in royal favor a few weeks later, Vespucci began to reach out to his various contacts. He had been suffering from malaria since his return and was not well, so he had time to write a full account. He decided to write to his old Popolano employer Lorenzo di Pierfrancesco de' Medici, now thirty-seven and steeped in the turbulent politics of Florence's uneasy new republic, having played a leading role in the brutal overthrow of Savonarola. He promised that a map and globe were following, to be brought by a friend of his from Seville called Francesco Lotti, and described the journey in colorful detail, obviously intending it for a wider audience. He added that he hoped to go back soon and find Ceylon, and rather exaggerated his own importance on a voyage where he was simply representing the investors to one of the subcommanders but not a commander himself. Lorenzo had also had Giorgio Vespucci as a tutor, and as a result, understood something about geography.

The letter made it clear that Vespucci regarded the land he found as a "continent." Columbus had written something similar in his letter to the sovereigns. They could not escape the evidence. But which continent? Both men in their conversations in Hispaniola leaned in the same direction. It had to be the Antipodes, the legendary continent in the far south, but stretching much farther north than anyone had realized. What else could it be?

The second, more sensitive, question was exactly how far west it was. As he repeated his calculations now, back in Spain, Vespucci realized there were inaccuracies in the Ferrara almanac he had used. He also realized he had miscalculated the length in miles of one degree of the size of the earth—most likely a consequence of spending too much time in the company of Columbus. He reworked the figures, based on his new calculation of the circumference of the earth—27,000 Roman miles, just 50 miles out—and there was one inevitable and rather shocking conclusion. When he had sailed down the coast of the new continent, he had clearly crossed to the Portuguese side of the line drawn under the Treaty of Tordesillas, and the treaty was clear: if anyone found land in the area of the other, they must report it immediately.

He did not know then that just three months before, Cabral, the leader of the Portuguese expedition to India, had landed there himself, more or less accidentally. At almost exactly the same time, his old colleague Marchionni was realizing through his contacts at the Castilian court that Vespucci held a vital clue to the identity and position of Brazil.

The hope of gold had been so elusive for Columbus, and he had so many faint moments of excitement, only to have them dashed. Back in December 1499, there had been the first sign of what might actually be major gold deposits on the north slopes of the Cordillera Central, fifty miles south of Isabella, in Hispaniola. Columbus had enough self-knowledge to realize that another report along these lines would not be helpful, at least without a ship full of gold to back it up. Now six months later, it was clear that this really was a major gold seam, and in fact it would soon be producing nearly a ton of gold every year. But for Columbus, it was too late.

Ojeda's interview with Ferdinand and Isabella had disturbed them. He handed over a sheaf of complaints against Columbus, described an anarchic chaos on Hispaniola, with Castilian and Aragonite colonists subject to the tyrannical decisions of the foreign Columbus brothers. He hinted at duplicity over the pearl fields and dropped strong hints that the reason so little gold had been forthcoming was that Columbus was siphoning it off for himself. To make matters worse, the court was now being followed by sailors from Columbus's first and second voyages, demanding to be paid. Whenever the sovereigns appeared in public, they would chant "Pay! Pay!" And when either of Columbus's sons—still pages to Queen Isabella—made the mistake of being seen in public without her, there was an uproar. The demonstrators would point to them, shouting that they were the sons of the Admiral of the Mosquitos. It was all very embarrassing.

The sovereigns had appointed Bobadilla to investigate and take over responsibility for Hispaniola if necessary, and then had held back because of the crisis around Granada and unease about their original promises to Columbus. It was clearly now time to send him, and he could take back with him the Taino and Carib slaves who had been freed in Castile.

Back in Hispaniola there was another outbreak of disaffection, when Roldán's old lieutenant Adrian de Múgica rose in rebellion. It was a complicated issue, which involved the defection of Roldán's former mistress and the arrest of her Castilian lover (Múgica's cousin) by Columbus. Since their humiliating compromises with Roldán, the Columbus brothers had veered in the opposite direction, keeping control with the utmost brutality. Those colonists caught stealing had noses and ears cut off and were sold in the town square of Santo Domingo as white slaves. One woman who mentioned that Columbus was a low-class son of a weaver was paraded naked on a donkey by Bartholomew and then had her tongue cut out. Christopher congratulated his brother for defending the family honor. Both also prevented the baptism of local Indians in case it kept them from being sold as slaves back home.

This time, Columbus decided, there would be none of the compromise that he believed had made him ridiculous over Roldán. When the rebel leaders were captured, Columbus insisted that Múgica and his comrades should be hanged. The sentence was delayed because they could not find a confessor, but when the priest finally arrived, Múgica refused to confess, claiming that he had forgotten all his sins. In a rage, Columbus had him thrown into the sea from the top of a tower. As luck would have it, as soon as the sentence had been carried out, and Múgica's battered corpse hung by the neck down by the dock, there were once more sails on the horizon visible from Santo Domingo. Some hours later, who should walk down onto the same dock but Francisco de Bobadilla, bearing letters from the sovereigns addressing Columbus simply as "our admiral of the ocean sea" and omitting his other titles.

For Bobadilla, the gruesome sight that met him at the dockside seemed to confirm every rumor in court about the tyrannical Genoese who had taken power over this island. He eyed the seven copses hanging there with shock and distaste. When he was greeted by Columbus's brother Diego, now a priest, he asked what this meant. Tactlessly Diego told him with some enthusiasm that five more were due to be hanged the following day. Bobadilla showed him his warrant from the sovereigns, asked for the evidence against the men—reminding Diego that they were supposed to be sent home for punishment—and announced that the executions would not go ahead as planned. Diego replied that he took orders only from his brother, and something about the combination of his tone and the extreme situation, and no doubt Bobadilla's exhaustion from a month at sea, catapulted the normally restrained and careful administrator into decisive action.

With fury and determination, he sent his soldiers to seize the fort. Then he ordered the whole population of Santo Domingo to gather in the church—the cathedral was not yet built—and in front of all of them, he asked Diego in the sovereign's name to obey his orders. Having forced the city to witness this, he then moved straight to Christopher Columbus's own house, impounded all his papers and possessions, jailed Diego, and awaited his brothers' return.

Columbus was appalled and infuriated by this latest interruption but convinced that he could fight or talk his way out of the impasse if he had support. Briefly, he planned to enter Santo Domingo with a thousand Indians at his side, prepared to treat Bobadilla as a traitor. But time was running out. He counted on support from the friars because of his known commitment to the Franciscan cause, but even they deserted him. Bartholomew returned from his latest punitive expedition some days later, urging Christopher to fight, but it was too late and the brothers handed themselves over to the sovereigns' representative. None of his former officials were prepared to put their admiral in chains as ordered. In the end, it was the cook who put the iron fetters on Columbus, but then made sure secretly that he was fed some scraps to keep him alive. In the meantime, Bobadilla's officials defined the charges against him: his poor treatment of the Castilian colonists, his refusal to let the Indians be baptized, and his original intention to resist Bobadilla's authority.

For weeks, he suffered hungrily in the stifling heat, cooped up in his own jail. When Columbus was taken out of prison in Santo Domingo at the beginning of October and heard the mob yelling for his blood, he believed he was going to be executed. Instead he was taken, still in chains, aboard the caravel *La Gorda*. Once out at sea, the captain offered to remove the manacles and chains, but Columbus refused. Like the Franciscan habit he had worn on his last return, they were a powerful message that communicated something about how wronged he had been. And so weighed down, he shuffled onto the dockside in Cadiz at the end of the month to begin the battle to clear his name.

# 8

# THE FINISH LINE

*"The crew was so worn down, shaken, ill and overcome by such bitterness that they wanted to die rather than live, seeing how the four elements working against them were cruelly torturing them. They feared fire for its flames . . . so furious and with such wrath—the water and the sea swallowing them up and that of the heavens drowning them."*

BARTHOLOMÉ DE LAS CASAS, after his stormy
crossing to Hispaniola, 1502

*"All great men make mistakes."*

WINSTON CHURCHILL

WHERE WAS CABOT? Nobody knew. His pension had not been paid since March 25, 1499. Mattea was being treated like a widow, even if she had not quite accepted that she was one. The Portuguese diplomatic mission to London that same year, inspired by fears that Cabot was trespassing on Portuguese ocean, was an awkward reminder that he had last been seen disappearing over the horizon from Ireland eighteen months before, and there was still no news. Sadly, London and Bristol had to conclude that he and his fleet were lost, together perhaps with the English dream of making London the new Alexandria. If there *was* going to be a new Alexandria, it looked as if it was going to be Lisbon.

Henry VII's historian Polydore Vergil—the man who took over from Carbonariis as deputy papal collector—writing twelve years later, summed up the situation: "He is believed to have found the new lands nowhere but on the very bottom of the ocean, to which he is thought to have descended together with his boat, the victim himself of that self-same ocean, since after that voyage he was never seen again anywhere." The full tragedy of Cabot is even clearer because, only those few short years later, Vergil had forgotten his name, left it blank in the manuscript, and had to fill it in later.

History has assumed until recently that Cabot disappeared and, in the absence of firm evidence to the contrary, that he did so without making any more significant discoveries in America. Research in recent decades has questioned both those assumptions, sometimes as part of long-running campaigns against the reputation of Columbus but, more recently, by painstakingly putting together the handful of clues that might reconstruct his final voyage.

Browsing in a Parisian curio shop by the Seine in 1832, the Dutch ambassador Baron Charles Walckenaer came across an ancient map. It was damaged and crumbling, painted on ox hide in a strange irregular shape. It was also enormous: six feet long when it was unrolled. Examining it more closely, and with mounting excitement, he discovered an inscription on the bottom. It said it had been made by Juan de la Cosa at Puerto de Santa Maria in 1500.

It transpired that the map had been in the Vatican archives when they were raided by Napoleon in 1810 for a new library in Paris. Most of the booty was returned to Rome later, but this map was mislaid. Walckenaer took it home, and it was bought by the Spanish government when he died in 1853 and is now in the Maritime Museum in Madrid. The map is generally accepted as genuine and the very map that was drawn by Juan de la Cosa, using sketches he had put together on his voyage from 1499 to 1500 with Alonso de Ojeda. It remains controversial not because many academics seriously doubt its authenticity—though some wonder whether it was finished at a later time—but because of whether it sheds any light on the mysterious disappearance of John Cabot and his sons. Because although Cabot's fate remains a mystery half a millennium later, there are some obscure clues: a map, a letter, a lost inscription, and a broken sword—and now possibly also a whole new series of undiscovered archives.

Juan de la Cosa's 1500 map

The reason the map is usually accepted as genuine is because, although it is the first of its kind to show the entire American coastline—minus Central America, which is obscured by a picture of St. Christopher—it does not yet incorporate information brought back from Vasco da Gama's voyage to India. But it is the details that are interesting. The most accurate part of the coastline is undoubtedly that of Venezuela. This is hardly surprising because it incorporated information from two voyages—de la Cosa's and Vespucci's. But it remains accurate *beyond* Cape de la Vela where both Ojeda and Vespucci turned north. So where did de la Cosa get this information?

Some way up the North American coast—it is hard to figure out quite how far, because Florida isn't depicted—there are two sets of English flags with the legend "*mar descubierto por inglese*" (sea discovered by the English). The place names along the North American coast also include names like

Cape de Inynglaterra and St. Nicholas—the patron saint of Bristol's mariner's church. These all imply some connection with Cabot, though they are hard to decipher.*

By itself the map is no proof, but it shows signs that de la Cosa seems at some point to have exchanged information with Cabot or his companions. This may have been information on the maps sent out by the spy John Day to Columbus, or by Castilian diplomats at the English court, but some of the coastline of North America could probably only have been described at that stage by members of Cabot's 1498 voyage. If that is so, there must have been direct contact with him.

The second clue is the letter, in this case a patent given by Ferdinand and Isabella in their gratitude to Ojeda for his achievements, setting out his privileges and duties for his next voyage, and granted in June 1501. These included the following:

> "That you go and follow that coast which you have discovered, which runs east and west, as it appears, because it goes towards the region where it has been learned that the English were making discoveries; and that you go setting up marks with the arms of their Majesties . . . in order that it be known that you have discovered that land, so that you may stop the English in that direction . . . Likewise their majesties make you a gift in the island of Hispaniola of six leagues of land . . . for what you shall discover on the coast of the mainland for the stopping of the English . . ."

The question arises: How did they know the English had been making discoveries along the coast? Was it perhaps that Ojeda met them somewhere before turning north to Hispaniola? If so, it could only have been Cabot's expedition. The Spanish historian Martin Fernández de Navarette confirms this with a tantalizing passage: "It is certain," he wrote in 1829, "that Ojeda on his first voyage (1499) encountered certain Englishmen in the vicinity of Coquibaçoa." But Navarette never revealed where he found the information.

---

*There is a place that used to be called Carbonear on the east coast of Newfoundland. We know Cabot was in the habit of naming places after his friends on board, and this one may refer to Giovanni de Carbonariis.

The third clue is the sword. When Gaspar Corte Real and his Portuguese expedition went ashore on Newfoundland in 1501, they took fifty Beothuk Indians captive. On examination, one had with them a broken sword of Italian design. One of them was also wearing earrings of a type normally worn by boys, and which seemed to have come from Venice. At the time, when the scale of America was still unknown, it was assumed that these artifacts had traveled all the way from the East. But that simply isn't possible, and the only previous expedition, or certainly one carrying anything Venetian, was Cabot's.

The fourth clue is the inscription on a rock in Grates Cove, Newfoundland, now disappeared, but readable by a traveler in 1822. The inscription said IO CABOTO SANCIUS SAINMALIA, which seems to imply a connection with John Cabot and his youngest son, Sancius. The rock itself is variously said to have been taken to Newfoundland Museum or to have fallen into the sea. Either way, it no longer exists for verification.

None of these clues are definitive pieces of evidence. Each one is open to other interpretations. The sword could potentially have been put there on a previous voyage by John Fernandez. The letter could be referring to coasts much farther toward the north, and the map is open to any kind of interpretation, and does not include Florida, which it should have if someone had sailed all the way along the coast. The rock no longer exists. Taken together they may even be contradictory: They imply both a fate at the hands of Ojeda and a wreck off Newfoundland. But, with those important provisos, they do allow us to present a very tentative picture of what might have happened to Cabot and his fleet after his remaining four ships left Ireland heading west in the summer of 1498.

Having linked up after the Atlantic storms somewhere off Newfoundland, the fleet began the long journey toward Asia, but were actually traveling down the eastern coast of what is now the United States of America, putting in to the major rivers, seeking out the telltale signs that China would be looming into sight ahead. As on the other expeditions, as they came farther south, all the ships must have found themselves suffering from increasing effects of shipworm, manning the pumps day and night to keep the vessels seaworthy. As they made their way into the Caribbean sometime early in 1499, some of the ships had to be abandoned and the surviving crews concentrated in just two of them or fewer. It must have been at this point that Cabot or his deputies encountered Ojeda and Juan de la Cosa at Coquibaçoa.

The existence of the map, with all its details, implies that, for a time at least, the encounter was friendly enough. They compared charts and discussed routes and argued about the direction of Asia. These were, after all, the only Europeans—perhaps the only people in the world at that time—who half understood the new geography and could begin to comprehend the size of the continent on the other side of the Atlantic.

Inevitably relations soured and Ojeda pointed out that they were trespassing on Castilian territory and sent them on their way, struggling north in a remaining unseaworthy ship. It was an enormous achievement to have made it so far north as Newfoundland. It may be that the flagship and commander of the expedition had already disappeared on the way south. But either way, Cabot himself and his son Sancio were wrecked along with their crew off Grates Cove, Newfoundland, and carved that mysterious memorial. At least one academic suggests that they hit an iceberg.

Still unaware perhaps of the breadth of the continent they had stumbled so unwillingly upon, they made contact with Beothuk Indians on Newfoundland and used what pieces they had salvaged from the wreck, including the sword and the earrings, to trade for basic food. They knew how unlikely it was that they would be rescued, and perhaps—Cabot being who he was—they then set off on foot westward, believing that Asia lay just beyond the horizon. We do not know how long they survived or where they died.

That would be the best knowledge of Cabot's fate until the end of the twentieth century. But in 2007 evidence emerged, though still unproven, that Cabot might have survived and returned to Bristol after all. The historian of exploration Alwyn Ruddock, who died in 2006 at the age of eighty-nine, found evidence that Cabot did indeed encounter Ojeda but also that he returned to Bristol alive. Fifteen years earlier, Ruddock had been commissioned to write a book to celebrate the five-hundred-year anniversary of Cabot's landing and rumors had been filtering through the exclusive world of Cabot research that she had made some staggering discoveries in some newly discovered archives. But she was dissatisfied with the book, tore it up, started again but never finished—and then stipulated in her will that all her notes and research should be destroyed after her death. More than thirty bags of papers were burned.

The following year, the Bristol historian Evan Jones published an article based on her original book proposal, which set out some of what she found—but without the references to be absolutely certain because, under the terms of her will, they are all gone. There is, though, circumstantial evidence that her findings were based on real documents. But the real bombshell was that Ruddock believed she had evidence that Cabot reached Newfoundland in 1498 and left Carbonariis and his fellow friars there, where they established a church and religious colony, while Cabot and the fleet sailed south along the coast toward the Caribbean and his encounter with Ojeda. Carbonariis sent his own expedition to Labrador, and Cabot himself struggled back north again in the autumn of 1499, reaching England early in 1500.

If that is true, and Cabot did indeed manage to navigate all the way from Newfoundland and down the coast of the new continent to the Caribbean, then it was an extraordinary achievement—though it must have been a bitter disappointment to him to have run up against the same apparent cul-de-sac as his great rival and not to have reached China. The real tragedy for Cabot was that the climate at Henry VII's court was very different in 1500 than it had been eighteen months before when he had set sail. Negotiations for the marriage between Henry's son Arthur, Prince of Wales, and Isabella and Ferdinand's youngest daughter, Catherine of Aragon, were now back on again. Nothing would be allowed to upset the delicate new relationship between England and Spain.

It was clear that Cabot had not just breached the Castilian zone, but he had gone absolutely nowhere near China. A furious Henry canceled his pension and sent him away, together with his backers Thirkill and Bradley, while the diplomats suppressed all information about his voyage. Four months later, and in despair, Cabot was dead. The Castilian court was equally nervous about news leaking out that Cabot had encountered a violent Ojeda in the Caribbean, and that information was also suppressed.

This version of the story looks like a conspiracy theory, and has yet to be confirmed. But if it is true, then Carbonariis was the great hero of the 1498 voyage, setting up the first European church in North America that autumn after they sailed from Bristol, probably in the Newfoundland town of Carbonear, and dedicated to San Giovanni. (St. John's, Newfoundland, continues to bear this name.) Carbonariis and his friars were left behind with the ship *Dominus Nobiscum*, while Cabot sailed south with one ship and the rest of the fleet went home. One of the Italian friars became a hermit on an island for some years afterward, while Carbonariis himself took his Bristol supporter William Weston on the *Dominus Nobiscum* and sailed north to Labrador—before the Portuguese expeditions there. In fact, it was probably his sword hilt and earrings that Corte Real found shortly afterward on Newfoundland. Both returned there to meet Cabot on his way home, but Carbonariis himself remained behind with his church and died in the New World.

The royal wedding was Henry's reward for joining the Holy League against France. It was a key part of Ferdinand's strategy to isolate the French in Europe. It simply had to go ahead, and yet—despite the question of Ojeda's encounter with the English navigators—there were already difficulties. Cabot's voyages were an irritation because the Castilians believed they were taking place in an ocean that was theirs to explore under the Treaty of Tordesillas. The mere existence of Perkin Warbeck, a man claiming to be the rightful king of England, was worrisome enough for Ferdinand. Warbeck was also an excuse for him to withhold some of Catherine's agreed-upon dowry. Castile was undergoing a financial and economic crisis, and the promised dowry was no longer available anyway. By the time Cabot returned, if he did, he had to be sacrificed on the altar of the Castilian alliance.

The execution of Warbeck at Tyburn, on the western edge of London, in the final weeks of the previous century had reassured Ferdinand and Isabella that the marriage between Arthur and Catherine could go ahead. There then followed no less than three weddings by proxy. Finally on November 15, 1501, Catherine herself was shepherded through London by Rodrigo Gonzales de Puebla for a magnificent pageant and a real wedding. The bells rang and the Anglo-Castilian alliance seemed to be a glittering success for Henry's foreign policy, symbolizing the unity between two countries and their joint determination to keep the mighty French in check.

There was not a whisper that an expedition from Bristol had been sent home by an expedition from Cadiz. It may be that the truth about Cabot's mammoth two-year voyage, all the way along the North American coast to the Caribbean, is just now beginning to emerge—along with the evidence about Carbonariis and his church—to take its proper place in history.

Columbus struggled down onto the dockside at Cadiz at the end of October 1500, exhausted by the voyage and weighted down by the shackles around his wrists and ankles. He had become attached to them. The ship's captain had urged him to remove them the moment they were out of sight of Hispaniola. Now his friends and colleagues who greeted him at the dockside urged him to do the same, but he refused. They seemed like a potent symbol of his betrayal. It seemed appropriate to him that he should continue to wear them, just as he had carried on wearing his Franciscan habit after his second voyage.

On board, he had written a desperate letter to Juana de Torres, Queen Isabella's closest friend, hoping that she would drop some of what he saw as the true facts into the queen's ear. "The Comendator Bobadilla wants to gloss over his own wicked deeds and methods by this means," he wrote, describing his deportation. "But I shall make him see with my own right arm tied, that this ignorance and cowardice and intemperate greed have tumbled him into a mistake this time."

Six weeks after his arrival, he was finally summoned to see the sovereigns. It was the moment Columbus had imagined ever since his arrest in the summer, shuffling into their presence in chains. They had ordered him to be released before he arrived, and sent him money—his letter had complained of poverty—to get him to Granada, where the court was staying. But he arrived at the Alhambra Palace on December 17, 1500, still determinedly chained, and came face-to-face with Ferdinand and Isabella for the last time, in the great Moorish palace of gardens and fountains. They had already been furnished with evidence from Bobadilla's officials of Columbus's guilt on all three charges, but they had decided not to punish him any further.

Watching this shuffling symbol of their own misjudgment, the sovereigns were absolutely exasperated, but they were also sympathetic about his plight, explaining that Bobadilla had exceeded his orders and would be sacked. "Your imprisonment was very displeasing to us," they told him, promising to restore his property and position as admiral, but not as viceroy. This would be impossible, they explained, because there was so much land already discovered in the Indies—and who knows how much more to come. One man could not possibly rule it all. Quite apart from that, from what they had heard about the disaffection on Hispaniola, it would clearly be dangerous for Columbus to return.

Columbus was pleased with this justification, though later increasingly angry that he had lost the viceroy's position promised him in 1492. His final years were spent obsessed with very little else. He was still in bad health, but was already beginning to turn his mind to persuading Isabella to send him back to the Indies. There were other more esoteric projects as well.

He already believed he had been singled out by God to "carry Christ" across the Atlantic to the Indies. Now he began an unfinished collaboration with Gaspar Gorrico, a Carthusian monk, to put these achievements in some kind of context. He devoured the esoteric literature of the day, the prophecies, the secret knowledge of the Kabbalah, and he began not just to collect them into a book, but to add references to them to some of his voluminous correspondence with the court. The end of the world was imminent; the world's peoples would be converted to Christianity; Jerusalem would fall back into Christian hands. And—because of a prophecy that those who would restore the Ark of Zion would come from the Iberian peninsula—he decided that Ferdinand and Isabella were destined to lead the conquest of Palestine.

Columbus somehow managed to live half in the esoteric world and half in the very practical world of exploration. Isabella had implied no reason why he should not go back to the Indies, as long as he went nowhere near Hispaniola. It was obvious to her that, while Columbus was a disastrous administrator, he was still a great explorer and it made sense to employ him as such. If the Portuguese now had a spice route around Africa, Castile's advantage—the advantage that Columbus had given them—was that they still had the western routes to explore. If Columbus could find the straits he believed were there from his islands to the Indies, then there was still everything to play for. In the months that followed, he read feverishly through his books of prophecies and piled on the pressure with his letters to the court, urging them to put him in charge of a new expedition.

But he never quite lost his affection for the chains. They had become a symbol for him, of his own failures, or perhaps of the sins he regarded as being committed against him. For the rest of his life he kept them on his mantelpiece and, in his will, he asked to be buried with them.


Vespucci was in Seville suffering from debilitating malaria caught on his voyage, and also from a serious dilemma. If he accepted Ferdinand's proposal and sailed with a Castilian expedition back to Brazil, he knew he would be illegally trespassing into Portuguese territory. If he swapped allegiances and sailed with the Portuguese, he might never be allowed to return home to Seville.

The letters kept arriving from Marchionni in Lisbon, urging him to join a Portuguese expedition that was being prepared, and to advise on precisely where the division in the oceans began and ended. Vespucci replied that he was too ill to make the journey. He gave the same story to the agents of the crown in Seville. But there was a great danger in doing so. Ferdinand and Isabella were now parents-in-law to the Portuguese king, Manuel, married to their daughter Maria. (Manuel had been married to her elder sister, Isabella, who died in childbirth in 1498.) Relations between the rival nautical giants were as good as they had ever been. It would have been terrible if he personally managed to drive them apart again. Vespucci had an enhanced sense of the politics of any situation and he knew, in any event, that he would never be forgiven. To complicate matters further, the paranoia against foreigners had led to a ban on their inclusion on any further Indies expedition. Vespucci knew that the voyage Ferdinand had promised was probably now closed to him.

One spring day in 1501, there was another visitor to Vespucci's lodgings in Seville. It was a Florentine named Giovanni de Giocondo, a silk merchant based in Lisbon.* He had been sent as a special emissary from Marchionni and he was not prepared to accept a simple refusal. Sailing with a Castilian expedition into Portuguese waters was simply unthinkable, said the visitor. Also the Castilians would insist that the voyage made some kind of pointless profit. On the other hand, the Portuguese expedition, financed partly by Marchionni, was intended purely for scientific knowledge. It would not be expected to make a return or to finance itself with those brutal slaving expeditions on the way home. Ambiguity was the cause of wars and only Vespucci was equipped to provide a clear picture of where Portugal's rights began and ended in the Indies. He had to take this opportunity.

Vespucci was also keenly aware of the risks. He may not have actually been under surveillance, as far as he knew, but if any breath of his intention leaked out in Seville, he would be arrested before he could leave the coun-

---

*These are all rather confusing stories. It could also have been Giuliano di Bartolomeo de Giocondo, whose relative Francesco—another silk merchant—was married to the lady who would be immortalized by Leonardo da Vinci as the Mona Lisa. Or was this the Mona Lisa's husband himself who visited?

try. He represented Castilian national interests and he held secrets that were believed to be critical to their future expansion: He would not be allowed to defect to Portugal, even temporarily. Those thoughts ran through his head as he made his decision. His visitor agreed: They would have to leave together, and immediately. Vespucci could not take more than a handful of vital items or say good-bye to his friends and associates, nor could he explain himself to his fiancée, beyond a scribbled note.

So it was that Vespucci, a man given to the science of inoffensiveness—at least to those more powerful than himself—took the greatest political risk of his life, and without explaining why. As he later wrote: "My going was taken amiss by all who knew me."

By far the safest route was by sea. The mysterious visitor had a ship available in Seville, and within a couple of hours since he had received Giocondo, Vespucci was watching the familiar cathedral tower of Seville pass out of sight along the Gualalquivir River. By nightfall, he was past Cadiz and out to sea, heading for Lisbon and service to the king of Portugal.

The Portuguse diplomatic mission to England back in 1499 had not improved relations between the two. Thanks to the Anglo-Castilian marriage, England was leaning toward the Castilian view of the world. The Portuguese diplomats had left London, aware that the English were now hazy about the missing leader of their expedition but convinced that this New Founde Land was probably Portuguese under the treaty. The solution, if the English would not listen to polite diplomatic threats, was to accelerate Portuguese expeditions northward and stake a claim. Portuguese King Manuel's main thrust was still to India, but in 1500 he licensed two rival expeditions, both setting out from the Azores, to go northwest.

The first was led by John Fernandez, from the Azores, the so-called labrador, as we have seen, who rediscovered an icy coast later that year that was probably Greenland. The second was led by a nobleman, Gaspar Corte Real, also from Terceira. Gaspar's father, John Vaz Corte Real, had made a famous voyage westward in 1472 and may even have seen Newfoundland before. Gaspar was also well connected with other explorers. He was a cousin of Columbus's wife, Felipa, and was related by marriage to Columbus's old rival Martin Behaim. Sometime in the summer of 1500, just as

Vespucci was arriving back in Cadiz with his slaves from the Bahamas, Corte Real's expedition to the northwest encountered a mountainous cape, which he described as a "point of Asia," but that was actually Cape Farewell, the southern tip of Greenland.*

The aristocracy of the Azores was a small community, and it became obvious to Fernandez and his partners that the terms given the aristocratic Corte Real family in their patent from the king of Portugal went much further than those in their own patent. Corte Real had been given a widespread trading monopoly covering any land that he found. It looked as though any discovery Fernandez might make in the northern seas would simply be handed straight over to his well-connected rivals. John Fernandez and his colleagues therefore decided to shift their allegiance. They arrived in Bristol early in 1501, in search of new business partners, just as Vespucci was agonizing about which expedition to lead and when Columbus was first back in Castile. Fernandez had been trading with Bristol for nearly a decade. He knew the waters of the Avon well and had many contacts there. He probably knew Cabot. He certainly knew of his achievements and his disappearance.

The arrival of Fernandez in the city brought the battered merchants of Bristol, who had invested and lost money in Cabot's 1498 voyage, around once more to thinking about the far west, and the New Founde Land. They did not yet have access to Juan de la Cosa's map; nor did they yet understand that Cabot's coastline actually led down the coast of a new continent, directly to the islands that Columbus had happened upon, though some may have suspected it.

But even those who guessed the truth had no idea if this long coastline was a narrow strip of land or something more substantial. Asia and the spice trade were still the objectives and if there was land in the way, then the issue was how to get around it. Fernandez and his Azorean colleagues provided a glimmer of hope that had seemed dead when Cabot failed. Perhaps Mattea and Sebastian Cabot, still in Bristol, also hoped they might find or justify their husband and father. Either way, on March 18, 1501, Fernandez achieved his first objective. A royal patent was issued by Henry VII in West-

---

*Although there had been European settlements on Greenland within living memory, the knowledge of Greenland was beginning to die out, even among navigators. A century later, it had been forgotten completely. When Martin Frobisher "discovered" it in 1578, he tried to call it West England.

minster, giving him and his colleagues a ten-year monopoly on any trade from lands they discovered that were "unknown to all Christians."

The patent went further, in an unusual passage missing from all the others: Fernandez and his partners were ordered to punish those "who rape or violate against their will or otherwise any women of the islands or countries aforesaid." Rumors of what really happened when navigators went ashore had obviously reached as far as London.

There were six people named in the patent apart from Fernandez himself. The others were his partners from the Azores, Francisco Fernandez and John Gonsalves, and three Bristol merchants, Richard Warde, Thomas Asshehurst, and John Thomas. The document gave them the right to import goods tax-free for the first four years, and to take one twentieth of the goods that anyone else imported from there for the first ten years. They would also be given the office of admiral—there was no way that the English would be outdone by Columbus.

Fernandez knew what Corte Real was planning because the information was arriving every day down at the Bristol docks. They knew that their rival expedition had returned claiming to have seen land strangely similar to their own discoveries, and would return there. Once again, the race between navigators has been characterized as little more than that. But this was not so much a race to get somewhere first, it was a race to get there with the critical documentation that could secure a lucrative business monopoly—and that required sailing on behalf of a prince capable of enforcing it. That was the essence of the new struggle between Fernandez and Corte Real.

As they battled against time at the Bristol docks to prepare a new expedition, the news arrived that Gaspar Corte Real had set sail again. They did not yet know it, but this voyage was to provide evidence of Cabot's voyage as well as a brutal harbinger of the future.

Corte Real's small squadron sailed north to Greenland again, but then sheered off to the northwest, finding land and following the coast about six hundred miles southward, maybe as far as Maine, staggered at the size of the trees. Landing in Newfoundland on the way home, the expedition surrounded the first village of Beothuk Indians they came to and took the whole village captive, taking the inhabitants down to the boats and onto the ships. It was when they were on board the three ships that Corte Real's men made their discovery of the Italian sword hilt and the Venetian earrings. Cabot was already slipping from people's consciousness. The existence of these trinkets could only mean one thing for Corte Real. The strip of land dividing them from Asia must be very thin, and these objects had been brought all around the world. Never mind the trees, the icebergs, and the bears. They must be near Asia after all.

Two of his ships took the villagers immediately back across the Atlantic to Lisbon, where they were an object of fascination for the diplomatic community. "Their manners and gestures are most gentle," wrote Alberto Cantino, a secret agent for the Duke of Ferrara. "They laugh considerably and manifest the greatest pleasure."

Cantino was posing as a horse dealer and was in the process of bribing Portuguese officials to allow him to copy the secret master map that hung on the wall of Manuel's court. The copy was successfully smuggled out the following year.* It showed Cabral's discoveries in Brazil, brought back by the *Anunciada*, and da Gama's discoveries in India, but it showed no North American coastline, the information which Corte Real's ships were bringing.

Between Cabot, Corte Real, and Juan de la Cosa, the truth about the American coastline was at last becoming clear, less than a decade since Columbus's first landfall, though the breadth of the continent was still a mystery. But neither Cabot nor Corte Real were there to reap the glory. Corte Real's own ship continued the journey south along the coast and was never seen again. Hundreds of mariners searching the ice for the Northwest Passage would share his fate in the centuries to come.

In Lisbon, Vespucci found that the Portuguese caravels were bigger than their Spanish equivalents. He stood on the deck, greeting the commander of his expedition, Gonzalo Coelho, who would lead a series of expeditions to Brazil. It had only been weeks since his fateful decision to escape from Seville, and he was already formulating in his mind a way to be so scrupulously fair to both nations that he could remain on good terms with both. In Lisbon he had also met and spent some time with Gaspar Corte Real, who set out two days after

*It is still in Modena in Italy, though it was thrown out of the window during a riot in the nineteenth century, after which it was used for some time as a screen in a butcher's shop.

Vespucci sailed, heading north via the Azores. On May 13, 1501, Vespucci was rowed out to the ships anchored off the tower of Belen outside Lisbon harbor. Slipping their moorings, they made their way down the Tagus and out to sea. It was broader than the river at Cadiz, which had become so familiar to him.

Vespucci would become contemptuous of Coelho's navigation, but for now, at least, he had no status to complain about it. Coelho set a course directly south along the African coast, heading for Cape Verde—not the islands, but the Portuguese garrison and harbor at Bezebeghe, near Dakar, in mainland Africa—to stock up on the remaining stores they needed and to make some small repairs. Once within the small harbor, they realized that they were not alone. Two battered caravels shared the wharf, and as soon as Vespucci was ashore, he knew where they had come from. These were stragglers from Cabral's expedition to India, which had headed via the coast of Brazil on the way out in case there was anything there. They had lost contact with the main fleet on the way back from India and were now on their way home. Vespucci stayed eleven days talking to them and quickly gained the trust of two of the most extraordinary men he had ever met.

One was the commander of one of the ships, Bartholomew Dias's brother Diogo, who had been carried far out into the Indian Ocean by the storm that had drowned his brother around the Cape of Good Hope, and had made his way back around Africa by himself to Cape Verde. The other was Gaspar da Gama, no relation of the great navigator, but baptized by Cabral as a Christian. He was Jewish, from a Polish family, born in Alexandria, who had fled in his youth to Palestine and thence in various excursions down the Red Sea to India. On one of these, he had encountered Cabral's expedition, offered to act as a navigator and interpreter, and been baptized a Christian, taking this name.

One of their discussions had been about the route that Cabral had used to get to "Terra Santa Cruz" and whether the land he had found was continuous with the coast. Gaspar da Gama had discussed this very point with Cabral because he had advised him widely about geography. But Vespucci had already been to the land that would be named Brazil, back in 1499. There was a great deal to talk about. Vespucci and his new friend spent hours comparing maps and place names, finding that those used by Gaspar da Gama did not correspond with the ancient names used by Ptolemy and the medieval mapmakers. Nonetheless, Vespucci was given access to geographical information for places Gaspar da Gama had only heard about—the spice islands in the furthest reaches of the East, beyond India. He also realized the full significance of the new spice route that could bypass the Mediterranean altogether. The future of Alexandria and Venice as the great markets of the known world were under threat.

If Cabral's discovery of Brazil had made him a hero, his expedition to India was less of a success. It had ended with the bombardment of Calicut and the sworn enmity of the Muslim traders there. Vasco da Gama would be asked to replace him as commander of the next expedition. These were all vital nuggets of information for Mediterranean traders, and Vespucci's first thought was for his home city of Florence. In the remaining days before his expedition set sail from Africa, he wrote to his correspondent Lorenzo di Pierfrancesco, tipping him off about Cabral's progress in India and warning him of what lay ahead.

Vespucci also warned Lorenzo about the journey he was about to begin: "This voyage which I am now making is perilous, to the limit of human courage. Nevertheless I am doing it with bold resolution to serve God and the world." Vespucci knew that if, like Cabot, he never returned, this letter would be taken as his final words.

John Fernandez's expedition of three ships set sail from Bristol later in the summer of 1501. The hopes of the local merchants went with him, though a handful of them stayed aloof from the general celebration: those who had invested in Cabot's last voyage and who shared in Cabot's patent. The phrase "unknown to all Christians" in Fernandez's patent was carefully chosen. It meant that he could claim no rights over the New Founde Land that Cabot had discovered. That remained theirs, with the eighteen-year-old Sebastian Cabot—now training as a cartographer—as the leader of the hopes of the patent holders.

Fernandez himself does not seem to have survived the journey. Nor did Richard Warde, the Bristol merchant on the same ship. But the other four partners returned to Bristol in triumph later in the year, having discovered another island—possibly Baffin Island—and were rewarded in the new year by a grant of twenty pounds from the king. There is a proviso here that is

John Cabot and sons from a later painting

that the main evidence for Fernandez's 1501 voyage was the reward paid to "men of Bristoll that found the isle" in January 1502. But if Alwyn Ruddock was right, and Cabot had returned safely in 1500, this may actually have been a reward to Elyot and Thorne, who were in London that same week, in which case it was a belated honoring of the achievements of Cabot and Carbonariis.

Elyot and Thorne, and Thorne's son William, were also given a grant to buy a large ship from Normandy: the 120-ton *Gabriel*, which brought back a cargo of salt-cured fish from Terra Nova later in the summer. At the same time, in the summer of 1502, their rivals in the Fernandez syndicate were also sailing westward. One of the expeditions—it is not clear which—was recorded as bringing back bows and arrows, "popinjays," and hawks, and later a number of animals described as "cats of the mountain," probably bobcats.*

More important than that was the Fernandez syndicate's mapping of a clear passage through to the East. Fernandez, or those leaders of the expedition that remained alive, charted one end of the Davis Strait, before being pushed back by ice. They also brought back with them some hawks and three Inuit people, who were "clothid in Beestes skynne, and ete Raw flessh, and Rude in their demeanure as Beestes," and displayed them in Westminster, where they excited a great deal of interest. The idea that they ate raw meat and spoke an incomprehensible language particularly appealed to the world-weary diplomats in Henry's court. Two years later, the chronicler Robert Fabyan saw them again at Westminster Palace, dressed as courtiers, and said they were almost indistinguishable from Englishmen.

When the remains of the Fernandez syndicate's second expedition was back in England, the royal court was able to show some interest in exotic "eastern" discoveries. The Bristol consortium needed high-level support if they were going to secure England's claim to the New Founde Land, especially as it was soon clear that the Corte Real family had put to sea again. On January 15, 1502, Gaspar Corte Real's older brother Miguel set sail with two ships to search for his missing brother. This would have seemed a threat to the English court when they heard the news, except that their attention was now consumed by other events. The royal wedding between Arthur and Catherine of Aragon had taken place the previous November, and after only five months, the royal marriage was suddenly and tragically over. In April 1502, Arthur died unexpectedly in Ludlow Castle. He and Catherine had been there to preside over the Council of Wales but, after some weeks, both became ill with the sweating sickness, the mysterious and fatal disease (now extinct) that appeared first in 1485 within days of Henry VII's triumphal entry into London, and spread briefly across Europe. Catherine nearly died herself, and when she did manage to recover, she found she was a widow.

There then followed an agonizing period of uncertainty, which would be

---

*The "popinjays" are thought to have been Carolina parakeets, the last of which was killed in Florida in 1904. As for the bobcats, they were seen regularly by early settlers in New York State and even as far north as Maine. Even so, these trophies are evidence that the explorers were venturing farther down the American coast.

raked over by lawyers in England and Spain in a generation's time. Catherine gave evidence that, because they were so young, the marriage had never been consummated—something only she could know—and on the strength of that, the pope gave a dispensation that she could be engaged to marry Arthur's younger brother, Prince Henry. While these delicate negotiations were going on, the king refused to let Catherine go home and kept what had been paid of her dowry. Ferdinand and Isabella refused to pay the rest of it. The standoff was enough to sour the relationship between England and Castile.

It was a frustrating time for the Bristol consortium. Fearful that the Corte Real family would get there first, they wanted royal support for a proper voyage to find the Northwest Passage to Asia, but could attract no interest. What they did not know was that by then the Corte Real family had been consumed by a second tragedy. The two ships of their new expedition decided to search in different directions along the American coast to maximize their chance of finding Gaspar and agreed to rendezvous on August 20, 1502. One ship found nothing and waited at the point as arranged, but Miguel Corte Real's own ship never appeared. The only clue about his fate was in an ambiguous carving in rock in Narragansatt Bay on the coast of Massachusetts, which appears to be dated 1511—almost a decade after his disappearance—signed Miguel Corte Real, and claiming to have been written by the leader of an Indian tribe.

Gaspar's other elder brother asked Manuel for permission to continue the search, but he refused. The king decided it would be too much for the family to lose all three brothers.

I

*"Sometimes I was so wonder-struck by the fragrant smells of the herbs and flowers and the savor of the fruits and roots that I fancied myself near the Terrestrial Paradise."*

•   AMERIGO VESPUCCI, letter to Lorenzo di Pierfrancesco
de' Medici, 1502

Vespucci's crossing with three large Portuguese caravels was very different than his first westward voyage. Coelho followed what Vespucci understood from Diogo Dias and Gaspar da Gama to have been Cabral's route to the

Indies, a circuitous circle out into the Atlantic. The fleet was battered by storms and lost for periods in the mid-Atlantic. The winds were against them and the sky was overcast, both day and night, which meant observations from the stars were impossible. But on August 15, 1501, three months after they left Lisbon, they made landfall somewhere near the modern city of Recife, and close to the point where Vespucci had been forced to turn back in 1499. Coelho sent one ship on a more southerly course, to see if they could identify the secure harbor that Cabral had found, and told them to turn north again later to meet up. Vespucci himself made for Cape St. Augustine to take some astronomical measurements to calculate the longitude, and set off southward at a more leisurely pace.

Vespucci had long since realized that this landmass he was sailing along was enormous: "a new land," he called it, "which we observed to be a continent." Cabral had been wrong about finding an island. Columbus had also believed that this was a continent, but thought it was just south of China. Vespucci's determination to find a southwest passage implies that, while he may have basically agreed with Columbus, he was beginning to realize that this coastline—which blocked the way to China—ran from the far north to the far south.

This time there was no difficulty getting ashore, and Vespucci and Coelho were determined that they would take the time to understand the continent. The first thing they noticed were the myriad colors. "What shall we say of the number of birds, and their plumage, colors and songs, the manifold species, and their beauty?" Vespucci wrote later. There were also large snakes and wild cats, in fact so many species that he doubted they could all have fit into Noah's Ark. It was fated to be Latin America— Darwin's voyage more than three centuries later—that would finally overturn the literal understanding of Genesis.

Vespucci noted also the aromas and fruits, "many of which are good to taste and conducive to bodily health." There was also dyewood and the brazilwood that would give this whole region its name. But it was the people that fascinated him most. They were entirely naked and lived a simple life that, in many ways, he admired:

Having no laws and no religious faith, they live according to nature. They understand nothing of the immortality of the soul. There is no possession of private property among them, for everything is in common. They have no boundaries of kingdom or province. They have no king, nor do they obey anyone. Each one is his own master . . . Their marriages are not with one woman only, but they mate with whom they desire and without much ceremony. I know a man who had ten women . . . When their children, that is the females, are of age to procreate, the first who seduces one has to act as her father in place of the nearest relative. After they are thus violated, they marry.

He was confused, given this, and with no private property, why the natives still managed to fight such bitter wars with one another. It was a fascinating passage in the literature of the "noble savage," influenced by Columbus's own writings. All early writing about America described it in much the same way, discovering a people who were part innocent, part corrupt. But it also had a pompous air, which was temptingly easy to lampoon. Vespucci was trying to create an aura of navigatory wisdom around himself, even though this was only his second voyage. It was also not a wholly accurate description: we now know the people he saw did have private gardens. Vespucci could not help borrowing from idealistic and fictional reports of travels that were in circulation at the time. He was to run into trouble for this later. But what seems to be the first European description of cocaine has the ring of accuracy:

They were very ugly of demeanor and countenance, and all had their cheeks stuffed out inside with a green grass which they continually chewed like cattle, so that they could scarcely speak; and each had around his neck two dried gourds, one of which was filled with that grass which they had in their mouths, and the other with a white flour which seemed like powdered chalk, and from time to time would dip into the flour gourd a splinter which they would keep moistening in the mouth; then they would insert it into their mouths, powdering the grass therein. Astonished at such a thing, we could not guess this secret, nor for what purpose they did so.

These natives had not yet been exposed to Ojeda and those like him, and were generally welcoming to Vespucci and his small landing parties.

The cannibalism he described was gruesome, but most of his descriptions of life in Latin America tended toward the idyllic, especially his meeting with a man who had great-great-grandchildren and claimed to be 132 years old. All these passages fed the emerging myth of a utopian continent, and yet there was also something monstrous even in Vespucci's descriptions. Their diabolical frenzies in battle, their habit of eating the mothers and children of their enemies. He lived among them at one stage for twenty-seven consecutive days, sleeping at night in a hammock and marveling at their innocence, and then found himself—if we believe him—occasionally buying their prisoners to save them from the cauldron.

The fleet reunited near Porto Seguro on November 3, 1501, and continued southward, exploring the mouths of rivers as they went, hoping that they might turn out to be the strait to Asia, thrilled by the beauty of everything they saw and the aromatic smell that wafted up from the shore. "I fancied myself near a terrestrial paradise," said Vespucci, rather as Columbus had done on his third voyage. But unlike Columbus, he remained skeptical that this was what it was. "I am like one of those followers of St. Thomas," he wrote later, "who are slow to believe."

At the start of 1502, Vespucci passed another great river and harbor, naming it after the month: Rio de Janeiro. Peering at the night sky and doing his calculations, he drew the point on the map marked by the line drawn by the Treaty of Tordesillas, which delineated the boundary of the Castilian ocean. Coelho formally handed over command to Vespucci, as the nearest they had to a Castilian representative, and they named the nearest river Cananor and erected a traditional Portuguese marble column, like the ones that marked the limit of their original voyages down the coast of Africa. Vespucci had been told by Gaspar da Gama that Cananor was the farthest place in India that the Portuguese expedition under Cabral had reached. It was intended to mark the farthest place that Portugal could claim in Latin America under the treaty. It was February 15, 1502, and Vespucci's calculations of the longitude were correct to within two miles. He had been getting better at the technique.

From then on, he kept the charts and the names on them confidential from his Portuguese colleagues, attempting to be fair to Castile, and the fleet sped up. Even so, the names he chose were not always Spanish. A month later, on March 24, it was Guido Antonio Vespucci's birthday, and Amerigo honored his great mentor by naming the San Antonio River.*

The expedition managed a brief exploration of what is now the Plate River before heading farther south, naming it the Rio Giordan. But on April 7, 1502, five days after Prince Arthur's death in Ludlow, the three ships were hit by a massive storm. They hauled down the sails and tried to ride it out far off the coast. It had been dark for fifteen hours when they caught sight of an unfamiliar rocky coast, and sheered away to avoid being caught on the rocks. Coelho and Vespucci agreed that they seemed to be entering a part of the ocean that was particularly dangerous, and it made sense to turn around.

The ships could only just see each other through the gloom, but they managed to signal and set course back north. In fact, they had hit the Roaring Forties—the violent prevailing winds between the latitudes of forty and fifty degrees south—though Vespucci later exaggerated how far they had gone, and claimed to have reached fifty-three degrees. Either way, no European had been this far south before.


Even before Columbus's irritating reappearance in chains, Isabella and Ferdinand had decided to appoint a professional governor of the Indies. Bobadilla had not been intended to establish any kind of permanent rule. The choice of permanent official took longer, but they eventually appointed the aristocratic and trustworthy Nicholas de Ovando, then fifty-two. The arrangement with Columbus, as far as his promised vice-regal appointment, was at an end. Ovando's salary was to be twice Bobadilla's.

The same day that Ovando was appointed, September 3, 1501, the sovereigns issued a series of pronouncements about the future of Hispaniola. From now on, licenses would always be needed to sail for the Indies. All ships would have a notary on board to assess what tax was due to the crown. The Indians would no longer be enslaved, except in certain exceptional cases, but would be converted to Christianity "with much love, and without using force." Of course, the certain exceptional cases expanded considerably on the other side

---

*Guido Antonio had died the previous year, after a stormy session of Florence's council, where his speech had been drowned out by stamping and whistling. To the new generation, he represented the old guard of supplicants to the Medici.

of the Atlantic, but the sovereigns seem now to have been seriously concerned about their new subjects and determined to make sure they were better treated.

Ovando sailed from Sanlúcar de Barrameda at the head of a large fleet of twenty-seven ships, the largest so far sent to the Indies, on February 13, 1502, two days before Vespucci's calculations at Cananor. On board were as many as 2,500 settlers, a number swelled by the deepening economic problems and rising poverty in Castile and Aragon. Among them were Francisco Pizarro, the future conqueror of Peru; and Bartholomé de las Casas, the future campaigner for humanity toward the Indians. The future conqueror of Mexico, Hernán Cortés, would have gone too, but he had hurt his leg jumping out of the bedroom window of a married lady a few days before sailing and had been left behind.

This would be a serious attempt at settlement. No longer would the sovereigns rely on amateurs. Nor would they rely on Columbus to push forward the boundaries of exploration. For the first time, they would attempt to settle the mainland, and armed with his patent that urged him to stop the expansion of the English, the adventurer Alonso de Ojeda was licensed to lead an expedition of three ships to the coast of what is Colombia today. Thanks to the intervention with Ferdinand of his friend Juan de la Cosa, Ojeda was also armed with the title Governor of New Andalusia.

Columbus had forgiven neither of these former friends and associates—Ojeda for his theft of the Pearl Coast map and de la Cosa for portraying Cuba as an island, when he had been one of those on Columbus's second voyage who had made an oath that it was mainland China. Nor had he forgiven the officials who were licensing these voyages of discovery across the ocean he regarded as his own. Peralonso Niño and Vicente Yáñez Pinzón were mapping the Caribbean bit by bit and bringing back a fortune in pearls. But between his vituperations against these former friends, and his book of prophecies, Columbus was making some progress persuading the sovereigns to agree to a fourth voyage. Through the winter of 1501 into 1502 he bombarded the court with letters and proposals, begging for the chance to sail again, and with different plans for the voyage. When he pressed them for a response, they had lost the proposals, and he had to start again. But finally, in March 1502, the voyage was agreed to and the struggle began again to raise the money.

Columbus's original estimate of the cost had been beaten down to a mere

fraction by his usual enemies in the treasury, which is why he was now raising the necessary money from his reliable old contacts in Genoa, the cosmopolitan business families who had first offered him work. At the same
time, the resources to man and supply his four ships were being siphoned off
to the almost limitless needs of Hispaniola's new governor, on whose behalf
the docks of Seville and Cadiz had exhausted themselves preparing a fleet.

The result was that Columbus had serious doubts about the adequacy of
his four ships and supplies. But he was still sick and could not get up enough
energy even to command his flagship, *La Capitana*. Aware that he needed
support on board, he took with him his thirteen-year-old son Ferdinand and
persuaded his brother Bartholomew to come too, on the *Santiago de Palos*,
much against Bartholomew's better judgment. Along with them sailed the
creaking *Gallega* and the tiny *Vizcaína*, which struggled out of Cadiz harbor
on May 9, 1502, after delays waiting for wind.

It is hardly surprising, therefore, that Columbus turned his mind to writing his will before leaving. He wrote to his son Diego asking him to look after his poor abandoned mistress Beatriz, and he wrote to the Bank of St.
George in Genoa, explaining that wherever his body might be, his heart
would always be in the city of his birth. Then he went on board for a voyage
he intended as the crowning achievement of his life and as the final answer
to his critics. Columbus referred to his fourth voyage as the "High Voyage."
It was intended to finally get through to the Indies and to bring back
enough gold to restore his lost titles and privileges. He had employed a
trumpeter on board *La Capitana* in order to impress the Chinese. This journey was to be his most dangerous and disastrous yet.

By June 1502, Columbus's rickety squadron was anchored outside Santo
Domingo harbor in defiance of his strict instructions not to go there. He
had begun by sailing south—directly toward Vespucci's returning ships—to
help a Portuguese fortress on the Moroccan coast, which was under attack.
This was in line with the new friendly relations between Castile and Portugal, which Vespucci was now struggling to preserve. After that, Columbus
made his fastest crossing yet across the Atlantic, just twenty-one days. Even
so, he already had reason to be increasingly concerned about the ships—
especially the *Santiago de Palos*—and the extreme youth of his crews.

Ovando had arrived in Hispaniola as governor, after a difficult crossing three months before, and was installed in Columbus's old home. Columbus's nemesis Bobadilla as well as Roldán and various high-ranking Taino captives were on or near the dockside, watching the gathering winds nervously and preparing to leave for Castile. There was consternation in the town when it was discovered who was in the ships they could see waiting offshore, afraid that the hated Columbus brothers were about to stage a return to power.

There were reasons why Columbus had broken his promise not to land. The first was that he was determined to swap the *Santiago de Palos* for one of the other ships in Ovando's fleet, which he knew would still be in Santo Domingo harbor. But there was a more urgent reason. He had seen the unusual swell from the southwest, watched the racing clouds, and sensed the oppressive feeling in the air, which for Columbus meant only one thing: they were in for a dreadful storm. He could see the preparations on the dockside, and realized that the fleet was about to sail, and it was vital that they were delayed. He was also determined to shelter his own ships in the harbor. He sent the captain of the *Gallega* ashore with a letter, warning Ovando that he must keep the fleet in port until after the storm.

Ovando was by the docks himself when this letter arrived, supervising the dispatch of Hispaniola's latest consignment of produce, by far the most valuable cargo which had yet crossed the Atlantic. There were thirty ships now heaving in the lively swell, their flags and pennants flapping wildly in the wind, and in their holds was nearly three years worth of full-time gold mining. Surrounded by some leading colonists, Ovando dealt with their fears by reading out the letter in a sarcastic voice, and he sent the captain back with a stark refusal. Astonished and horrified, Columbus took his own ships farther around the coast to take shelter in the bay of Azúa de Compostela. "Was there a man born who would not die of despair—excepting Job himself," he wrote, "at being denied refuge at the hazard of his life and soul . . . in the very land which, by God's will, and sweating blood, I won for Spain?"

As he predicted, the hurricane struck some hours later, and it did so with unprecedented force. The new city of Santo Domingo was nearly flattened. Roofs were torn off and wooden walls were demolished. The storm surge swept through the devastated streets, drowning those near the shore and their animals, smashing the boats and remaining ships in the harbor, transforming the new city into piles of debris. The church which had been so laboriously built there since Bartholomew Columbus had laid the foundation stones five years before was left in ruins. Three of Columbus's small squadron broke free of their moorings and managed to survive only by extraordinary seamanship. Only *La Capitana* held firm.

The returning fleet, under Columbus's friend Antonio de Torres, was not so lucky. The ships had just reached the particularly dangerous straits between Hispaniola and Puerto Rico when the wind rose to hurricane force, tearing off masts and sails before the crews had the chance to take them down. The ships were scattered and succumbed one by one to the rage of the sea. As many as five hundred lives were lost, together with nearly all the gold, including the so-called Great Nugget, a lump of gold said to have weighed over three hundred pounds. All the papers about Bobadilla's governorship went down with the ships, along with Bobadilla himself and all his staff. Also drowned were Roldán and his former ally Guarionex, as well as the fleet commander de Torres himself and the navigator Peralonso Niño. Three surviving ships staggered back to Santo Domingo in the following days, dismasted and battered. Only one ship, the unseaworthy caravel *Aguja*, in which the authorities had entrusted Columbus's own gold, made it all the way back to Castile.


Vespucci's expedition had arrived off Sierra Leone on the African coast on May 10, 1502, a month before these events, and the day after Columbus had sailed from Cadiz. One of his ships had become unseaworthy and it was beached and set on fire. He then sailed north again to the Azores at the end of July and stayed there for two weeks to rest. There seems to have been a reluctance to actually get home and begin the diplomatic wrangling that Vespucci was going to have to do in both royal courts if he was going to survive with his reputation unscathed.

It had been an achievement. Not one crewman had been killed—or possibly only one, based on a later story that one had been eaten by native women. No native villagers had been seized and sold into slavery. Two rival maritime nations, he hoped, would see clearly where their rights lay and be able to avoid stumbling into war by mistake. Before his voyage the assumption among navigators was still that this landmass, so inconveniently in the middle of the Atlantic, was just a final hurdle before the Indies. After Vespucci's voyage, it was clearer that this was a whole continent, running from the Arctic to the Antarctic. There was at least a possibility that it was no more part of Asia than Europe was.

This was an insight that derived not solely from Vespucci, but also from the series of explorations now so feverishly continuing in Central America, and on those of Cabot, Corte Real, and Fernandez in the north. But this New World—a term coined back in 1493 by Peter Martyr and used increasingly by Vespucci—was not yet of great interest to many of the explorers in its own right. For the next decade, the challenge was to find a passage, south, north, or central, that would take them through to Asia and the spices. Vespucci had studied the continent for its own sake, using his astrolabe and quadrant, and was trying to shift the debate to a more technocratic level. He may have had no formal training at sea, but he knew his science, or so he argued, and had a great deal to teach the seagoing community.

His problem was that he and Coelho had taken Marchionni at his word. They had brought back no gold or slaves, but holds full of rather ordinary dyestuffs like brazilwood. They had discovered no new hope of profit, and as a result, they were disturbed to find that their investors were no longer very interested. For the Portuguese, the problem was that all those passages, if they existed, probably lay on the Spanish side of the treaty line. For the Spanish, the danger was that the Portuguese had already found their own route to India. Diplomats began debating whether the Tordesillas line extended around the other side of the world as well.

Nervous about his reception, Vespucci finally landed in Lisbon on September 7, 1502, bringing parrots, monkeys, and logwood, and immediately began writing his regular report to Lorenzo di Pierfrancesco, explaining that "I reached the region of the Antipodes, which according to my navigation, is the fourth part of the world." In fact, he was bitterly disappointed by his reception in Lisbon, where he had hoped to be hailed as a great discoverer. A month later, he was sailing up the Guadalquivir back home to Seville.


Columbus was still in the Caribbean. He had escaped the hurricane in June only to be lashed by the most extraordinary weather. His four caravels crossed the Windward Passage along the southern coast of Jamaica and made the journey to Honduras in only three days. There Bartholomew took a party ashore and discovered a sophisticated galley, eight-feet wide, rowed by a crew of twenty-five local Indians. He seized the elderly skipper of this canoe as an interpreter for the expedition.

The objective was the straits that would take them through to India, but it was unclear which way to search. Columbus believed they had arrived somewhere near the Malay Peninsula, and therefore ought to sail southeast. But the winds and the current were against them and, for the next twenty-eight days, they sailed through thunder, lightning, and almost continuous torrential rain. The crew was permanently soaked. He wrote how guilty he was to have brought Bartholomew, against his will.

> The ships were lying open to the skies, the sails broken, the anchors and shrouds lost, as were the cables . . . and so many supplies went overboard, the crew were all sick and all were repenting their sins and turning to God . . . The distress of my son, who was then with me, wracked my soul, for he was only thirteen years old . . . but the Lord gave him such courage that he cheered the others.

Finally on September 14—a week after Vespucci arrived back in Lisbon—they rounded Cape Gracias a Dios and found favorable winds and currents. Two days later they anchored in the mouth of the Rio Grande where disaster struck. Two of the sailors were drowned when their boat capsized in the surf. It was an omen for the voyage. For the next 130 miles, all the way to what is now Costa Rica, Columbus explored every channel, questioned every group of natives, and heard just what he wanted to hear— that they were in between two seas, just ten days from the Ganges. Certainly he was unable to grasp the truth, which was that the River Ganges lay far beyond the next sea, which was itself more vast than any other ocean on earth, almost halfway around the world again. Columbus was also now suffering from his old condition, confined to his cabin in *La Capitana*, bleeding from the eyes and in great pain in his joints and bladder, and he rarely went ashore. He was never good at looking at evidence objectively, but it was all the harder when that evidence was conveyed to him secondhand.

There was no strait. So on December 5 he gave up and turned the ships around. Now the winds that had helped them down the coast were against them again and once more there was torrential rain. The dreaded shipworms that bored little holes into the hulls of ships in this region, which had become such a nuisance to mariners in the Indies, were making the vessels leak and weevils had been at the ships biscuits. "God help me," wrote Columbus's son Ferdinand later. "I saw many wait until nightfall to eat the porridge made from it so as not to see the worms."

On December 13 Columbus roused himself to rescue the fleet from a waterspout, reciting the gospel of St. John on the deck and drawing a protective circle with his sword around the fleet. Having escaped that hazard, the ships were then becalmed, running short of food and reduced to eating shark. It was a damp and miserable Christmas at the site of what is today the mouth of the Panama Canal.

On January 6, 1503, they finally anchored off a river they named Belén in western Panama, an area they knew as Veragua, where Columbus decided he would set up his trading settlement, squeezing over the sandbar at the river's mouth. It was clear from what they saw and the locals they met that there was considerable gold in the area. But even here, the problems multiplied. It rained for a month, and the locals became increasingly threatening once they knew these visitors were intending to stay. As soon as the rain stopped, the river dropped so much that the sandbar prevented their escape. Worse, according to their interpreters, the locals were planning to attack. Diego Tristan, captain of *La Capitana*, was captured along with most of his crew and killed.

It was here that Ferdinand repeated the mysterious discovery made by Vespucci in the south: "The colonial chief and his dignitaries never neglect to put in their mouths a dry herb and to chew it, and sometimes they would use a certain powder, which they carried with the herb mentioned, which seems a very ugly thing."

On Easter night they managed to get three of the ships over the sandbar and into deep water, but the *Gallega* was too ridden with shipworm and had to be abandoned. The other three were barely in better shape and the pumps had to be manned all day and all night just to keep the ships afloat. Near Puerto Bello, where Sir Francis Drake would eventually be buried at sea a century later, the *Vizcaína* had to be abandoned as well. They took off all the stores and she slowly sank.*

---

*The *Vizcaína* may be the remains of the ship rediscovered in the area in 2001, now the subject of a series of legal actions in Panama. If so, it is the only one of Columbus's ships to come to light.

It was at this point, in the driving wind and rain, desperately trying to coax his remaining worm-eaten ships away from the coast, that Columbus had his most mystical experience yet. At the height of the storm, he painfully climbed the mast of *La Capitana* and begged God to stop tormenting him—and this time he believed he heard a response. "Be not afraid, but of good courage," the voice said. "All our afflictions are engraved in letters of marble and there is a purpose behind them all."

Yet the afflictions continued. It seemed highly unlikely that the other two ships could make it to Santo Domingo, let alone back across the Atlantic, especially when having reached Cuba on May 13, they collided with each other in a gale. This was the moment when it became clear that even Hispaniola was beyond them, and on June 23, the struggle became too much. The crews were exhausted from pumping and from lack of food. Columbus himself was in serious pain and nearly blind. He decided to run the ships aground on St. Ann's Bay in Jamaica. They dragged the ships onto the beach and used the wood to build shelters with thatched roofs fore and aft.

If Cabot or the Corte Real brothers had survived whatever had befallen their ships, they would have found themselves marooned on an unfamiliar coast with no hope of rescue. This was the nightmare of the transatlantic explorers. Without their ships, there was no way back, and the last of Columbus's ships had been destroyed in the collision. But Columbus was in a different situation. There would be no passing ships, but it might just be possible that there would be a search that could bring him home.

That was the humiliating position in which he and his men found themselves. The only chance of rescue was to make the hazardous four-day journey by canoe over the sea-lane to Hispaniola, to walk to Santo Domingo, and to raise the alarm. Diego Méndez, chief clerk of the fleet, had managed to lead a small party into the bush, negotiate with the local villages, and agree to buy regular supplies of food. He now heroically volunteered to attempt the crossing—five hundred miles across the Windward Passage. Setting up a mast and sail, recruiting six Indian paddlers, and building high sides to the canoe, Méndez set out.

"I am wholly ruined," wrote Columbus in one of the letters requesting help to the sovereigns that he pressed on Méndez as he left. "Hitherto I have wept for others. Now, may heaven have pity on me, may earth weep for me."

. . .

In Italy the summer of 1503 was unusually hot. In early August of that year, Pope Alexander VI was dining in the garden belonging to Cardinal Adriano Castellesi, his former secretary and also Bishop of Hereford, and Carbonariis's employer as papal collector back in England. Toward the end of the meal, Alexander was taken ill with a sudden fever. He was taken home and bled. He died on August 18, five days later. Poison was suspected, possibly even the pope's own poison, intended for someone else. His notorious son, Cesare Borgia, who was also taken ill, was too sick to come to his father's bedside, but he was able to send his trusted agent to the Vatican to seize the keys to the papal treasure house. He then used the money to pay troops loyal to him to occupy Rome and intimidate the cardinals as they gathered to choose the next pope.

As the cardinals struggled to agree, Alexander's body lay unburied in the heat, his face blackened and swollen, his tongue lolling out. According to the Venetian ambassador at the funeral, it was "far more horrifying than anything he had ever seen or reported before." One witness said that when the time finally came to deposit his remains in a coffin, they had to jump up and down on the corpse to force it in.

The cardinals chose as the new pope the Sienese church reformer Francesco Piccolomini. He took the name Pius III and refused to have mass said over his predecessor's body. Less than a month later he was dead too, officially from a gangrenous ulcer on his leg but possibly also from poison. The exhausted cardinals were faced with another funeral and another conclave. This time they took no chances, within a few hours and almost unanimously, they elected the bitter enemy of the Borgias, Giuliano della Rovere. He became one of the most powerful popes of any age, Julius II, as at home in armor leading his troops into battle as he was behind the altar. Julius may have been the right man to sort out the diplomatic confusion of Italy, but he was the wrong man to unite a church that was already bitterly unpopular among laypeople all over Europe.* Between Alexander's corruption and Julius's ambition they have been blamed for provoking the Reformation in the generation to come.

---

*It was said in London that no jury would acquit a priest brought before them, no matter how innocent he was.

Cesare had negotiated an alliance with Julius, but it did not last. Giu-liano della Rovere had devoted every waking moment to unseating the Bor-gias for more than a decade. He had Cesare arrested and shipped him to Spain, where he died in battle in Navarre in 1507.

Julius forged a military as well as a spiritual power. He founded the Swiss Guard to protect him, and they still protect the pope to this day. He forced the tyrants out of cities like Bologna, and he confronted Venetian rule over cities in the heart of Italy, which was now divided three ways: between French-dominated Milan in the north, Spanish-dominated Naples in the south, and the center of Italy, where the pope and the Venetians eyed each other with distrust. Over the next five years, Julius negotiated a new net-work of European alliances, which would allow him to take on Venice for this central belt of Italy. The League of Cambrai was eventually signed in 1508 by Margaret of Austria, the brilliant regent of the Netherlands, who had been the rejected child fiancée of Charles VIII of France, then the widow of young Juan, heir to Ferdinand and Isabella.

England's Henry VII did not join this holy league of Cambrai. He offered to mediate between Venice and the pope, but it was too late. In 1509 the French marched into Venetian territory, accompanied by two archbishops, three cardinals, five bishops, and an abbot, and divided it between other members of the league, culminating in the decisive battle of Agnadello. Venetian power, which had dominated the eastern Mediterranean for cen-turies, battered by the loss of Constantinople and the new spice routes to Lisbon, never really recovered.

When Vespucci arrived back in Seville, he was reunited with his nephew Giovanni and his fiancée, Maria, and he finally took the opportunity to marry. Maria Cerezo is a mysterious figure who may have been the illegiti-mate daughter of El Gran Capitan, Gonzalo Fernández de Cordoba, Ferdi-nand's brilliant general in the Naples campaign, but this has never been proven. If so, Vespucci was marrying into influential but dangerous com-pany: Ferdinand was jealous of El Gran Capitan's success.

Yet Vespucci had learned the art of diplomacy at the feet of his mentor, Guido Antonio, one of the foremost diplomats of the age, and he had learned well. Few other navigators could have returned to Castile, having effectively disappeared and shipped out with their great rivals in Portugal, and found his way back into royal favor. Unfortunately the process took time, and his business life had long since disappeared in Seville. He had made careful arrangements so that the voyage would be scrupulously fair, keeping from the Portuguese the details of coastline on the Castilian side of the Tordesillas line and vice versa, and that was a foundation on which renewed trust could be built. He explained that although he had made the voyage partly in the name of science and partly, of course, for glory, it was primarily to protect the peace between Castile and Portugal.

Even so, with the Medici family dead and gone, and with no obvious future in Seville, this was not going to be an easy period. "Amerigo Vespucci will be arriving here in a few days," wrote one Florentine from Seville. "He has undergone great hardships and has derived small profit." Exactly what these hardships were, apart from his recurring malaria, has never been clear, but it seems likely that he had little or no money and was bitter about his treatment by the Portuguese. Even so, he began to regain the good opinion of the sovereigns because they trusted his judgment and were impressed with his prestidigitation with instruments. Vespucci was consulted by them in their attempts to regulate the business of the Indies. So in January 1503, while Columbus was still at sea, they decided to set up an institution that could manage these issues, based in Seville, which, although it was a hundred miles from the sea, was becoming the source of most decision-making about the Indies. Isabella was now ill, and the order was signed instead by her daughter and heir, Juana.

It was called the Casa de Contratación, and it would act partly as a registry of ships, licensing the voyages and captains, partly as a mint for coins for the New World, partly as a center for information about routes and navigation, and partly as a training organization. It would be both customhouse and courthouse. It had wide powers, including the power to arrest and imprison those who disobeyed. It was, in effect, the institution that would extend the role that Bishop Fonseca had done hitherto. To confirm this, Fonseca's associate Jimeno de Bribiesca, the royal treasurer who Columbus had assaulted shortly before sailing on his third voyage, was appointed as the first notary. For the next two centuries, the Casa de Contratación would rule over business with the Spanish empire, based in the old arsenal in Seville, firing a cannon whenever a ship bound for the Indies was ready to sail. It enforced

Seville's domination over the Atlantic trade and made the city what it was to become: the proud, overcrowded melting pot of different cultures, home to both the indescribably wealthy and the most hellish and degrading vices.

The Casa's first task was to set up its own postal service, so that news and instructions could be exchanged with the royal court within forty-eight hours, wherever it happened to be. Its second task was to forbid the importation of African slaves to the Indies. The few that had already been sent to Hispaniola had been involved in a small revolt.

The Casa also had to deal with complaints, and there was no shortage of those from Hispaniola. One of the most common was now about the quality of the goods that were being sent there for them to buy. Why, for example, in such a hot climate, were they being sent thick woolen cloth from England? The Casa, backed by the sovereigns, decided it was time to open up trade to the Indies to all Spaniards. From the summer of 1503 they would be allowed to export anything they wanted, and bring back anything except brazilwood. Columbus was now marooned on the coast of Jamaica, but this might have been designed to infuriate him. It flew in the face of the privileges he had been promised in 1492.

The first attempt by Columbus's crews to escape Jamaica by canoe ended in a skirmish with natives at the other end of the island. But Méndez set out on a second attempt, using another canoe, together with the Genoese captain of the *Vizcaína*, Bartholomew Fieschi. On the first day, their Indian paddlers drank their whole water supply, and by the third day some of them were beginning to die of thirst. But on the fourth day, the exhausted occupants reached an island off the tip of Hispaniola and made the short crossing to finish the journey. The indefatigable Méndez then set off on foot, first to Santo Domingo, and then—because Ovando was absent—to the western peninsula of Jaragua, the former stronghold of Roldán and his supporters.

Ovando was organizing a new kind of administration for Hispaniola. He was struggling under an epidemic of syphilis among the new settlers, nearly a thousand of whom had died in the first year of their arrival. He had ordered cattle for the pastures, which were taking the place of the island's plummeting Taino population. He had ordered mulberry trees to start a silk industry and sent back samples of rubber and a new kind of root that he thought would yield madder, the ingredient used in making red dye. When Méndez finally caught up with him, Ovando was in no hurry to see the return of his predecessor to Hispaniola. For seven long months, he kept Méndez by his side in Jaragua, as he continued to press his case for rescue.

Ovando was also launching a policy of ferocious pacification across the island, starting with Jaragua, where Méndez was forced to witness one of the most notorious massacres in the history of the New World. Ovando had brought a powerful force with him to see Queen Anacoana, the widow of Caonabo, the last independent chief on the island. She held a three-day fiesta in his honor, with dancing and music. As always, this enjoyment accompanied rumors among Ovando's men of a conspiracy to take them by surprise. So he offered a display of arms, to Anacoana's delight, but when he put his hand on the gold cross around his neck, it was a prearranged signal for the soldiers to open fire on the villagers. Anacoana was captured and hanged and the other local chiefs gathered there were surrounded in a house and burned alive.

So it was a thoughtful Méndez who accompanied Ovando back to Santo Domingo, to pursue his punitive policies in the east of Hispaniola. Ovando had promised to deal with the marooned Columbus on his return but, when he got back, he changed his mind and refused to let Méndez use the small ship in the harbor there to mount a rescue. There was no alternative but to use Columbus's own money on the island to hire the next ship that arrived.

By then Columbus and his brother had faced down their first revolt by those crewmen who were already deeply suspicious of him. On January 2, 1504, Francisco de Porras, the captain of the *Santiago de Palos*, burst into his cabin and accused Columbus of not trying to get home. He led about half the remaining crew on what was left of the masts of the beached ships, shouting "For Castile!" They then seized some canoes that Columbus had bought from the locals, burned the nearest villages, and took some of the locals by force to paddle them to Hispaniola.

But the seas rose and the waves began washing over the sides, and Porras and his men panicked, throwing their captive native paddlers into the sea to lighten the canoes. Eighteen of them drowned. Then the mutineers struggled back to the bay, and set up an alternative camp near the beach, continuing to harry the local villagers, who had been supplying the crews with food. Unsurprisingly, both sides found that the food supply dried up very rapidly.

The situation was becoming desperate. Without some kind of food, there was no doubt that the crews would die, but getting food depended on good relations with the locals. At this point, Columbus had one of his most brilliant ideas. He had brought an astronomical almanac with him, presumably to measure longitude using the method that Vespucci had set out. In this, he discovered that there was an eclipse of the moon due on February 29. Bartholomew therefore summoned all the chiefs nearby to meet them that night and, when they had arrived, Columbus told them that if no more food was forthcoming, God would punish them by making the moon disappear. Right on cue, the shadow began to cover the moon and the villagers begged him for forgiveness. Timing his response carefully, he said it would only reappear if they promised to bring regular supplies of food. The supplies began again the following day.

Some weeks later, a small caravel did arrive on the horizon, but, when it anchored off shore, it was clear that Méndez was not on board. It had been sent by Ovando and captained by one of Roldán's old lieutenants, who handed over a cask of wine and a haunch of pork and then set sail again. This fleeting and peculiar glimpse of freedom was enough to break the uneasy truce with Porras and his followers, and here Bartholomew's battlefield skills saved his brother and those that remained loyal to him.

When Porras and his supporters struck on May 19, they surrounded Bartholomew on the beach. But in a series of deft moves, Bartholomew killed five of those in front of him, before Porras struck him so hard in the shield that he could not pull his sword out again. Bartholmew knocked him down, disarmed him, and took him prisoner. The rest of the mutineers begged for forgiveness, while the villagers watched fascinated from the edge of the forest.

Columbus was afraid that Ovando's delay was motivated by the fear that he was trying to supplant his successor as governor. He needed a scheme to reassure him, and over the next six weeks, he puzzled over how to solve the problem. But then, finally, on June 28 there was another sail on the horizon, and it was clear that Méndez had succeeded after all. He had chartered a ship and here it was.* Barely able to believe it, Columbus and his crews boarded and set sail. On September 12 he embarked from Santo Domingo

---

*Scholars have doubted the Méndez story, on the grounds that he told most of it himself. But when he died he asked that a canoe be carved on his tombstone.

to Castile for the last time, in the same leaky caravel that had rescued him from the beach.

II

*"An old man, broken with the storms of state*
*Is come to lay his weary bones among ye;*
*Give him a little earth for charity."*

WILLIAM SHAKESPEARE, *Henry VIII*

When Columbus landed at Sanlúcar de Barrameda on November 7, 1504, he was exhausted and barely able to move. His first thought was of the queen. He had learned through bitter experience how vital it was to get his story in first, especially as Porras had been freed by Ovando and might tell his. She was also the only person likely to restore the lost privileges, which he had hoped to leave to his son Diego. Columbus was taken by boat upriver to Seville and then carried to a rented house in the parish of Santa Maria, where he remained bedridden, a chest of gold coins beside his bed, complaining to everyone about his abject poverty and obsessing about his scandalous treatment.

There was the question of all the other expeditions to the Indies, unlicensed by him as admiral. But there was also the question of the various shares he was expecting—the third, eighth, and tenth—from his 1492 agreement. Not to mention his removal as governor of the places he had discovered. But the news on the dockside had been bleak: Isabella was ill and had been ailing for some months.

In fact, Isabella had been sick almost since Columbus left. She had been weighed down by the economic problems of her combined kingdom, the continual crop failures and resulting hunger, and the worrying question of why gold seemed to be flooding out of the country. Most rulers had not yet grasped the idea of balance of payments: gold was leaving Spain because they were importing more than they were exporting. By May 1504 she was too ill to carry on working, and she retired to her bed in Medina del Campo in great pain and with a constant fever. She suffered from insatiable thirst, but the sight of food made her vomit. Columbus had hoped that, if he could only make the journey to visit her on her deathbed, he could get her to promise that Diego could inherit his privileges, but his own condition just did not allow it.

Isabella died on November 26, less than three weeks after Columbus landed. They never met again. Her body, dressed as a Franciscan, was drawn on a litter draped in black through the appalling storms and swollen rivers, all the way to her burial in Granada. Her will urged her successors to conquer Africa. If Columbus had not already discovered the Indies, that is no doubt what Isabella would have tried. A last-minute codicil urged her navigators to instruct the Indians in the Catholic faith. But for all this detail, the will left out information that it really should have included. Who was going to succeed her as ruler of the kingdom of Castile, given that her husband was only king of Aragon? The strong implication was that it should be her eldest surviving daughter, Juana, supported by her husband, Philip Hapsburg. He was the son of the Holy Roman emperor Maximilian, the heir through his mother to the extraordinary wealth of Burgundy and the Netherlands. But would Ferdinand really relinquish his hold?

Philip had been the most eligible bachelor in Europe. He was known as "Philip the handsome." He was a man with everything, and on top of that was articulate and highly intelligent. His sister had married Ferdinand and Isabella's tragic eldest son, Juan, so he was bound into the family already. He was also an obsessive womanizer, and this was having a devastating effect on his wife's mental state, the beginning of her reputation as Juana the Mad. The complication was that because Ferdinand could theoretically still father a son, the court in Aragon refused to recognize Philip and Juana as his heirs there. Even the senior officials in Castile were worried about news of Juana's fits of uncontrollable rage and violence. Claiming to be Juana's protector, Ferdinand made an abortive attempt to be named regent of Castile, and then waited nervously for the heirs to make their arrangements to leave on their long journey by sea from the Netherlands.

All the decisions required from the courts of Castile and Aragon had to wait as officials delayed to see which way they should jump. There was little chance that Ferdinand would focus on an irritant like Columbus's forgotten privileges.

Meanwhile, Vespucci was beginning to reestablish himself in Seville. It seemed as though he had been at least partially forgiven by the court for his disappearance and defection to Portuguese service, but for a while he remained rather a pathetic figure, ill and impoverished, staying briefly in Columbus's own lodgings. He borrowed Columbus's books and witnessed at least one draft of his will. People trusted Vespucci as they always had, at least those people whom he needed—he castigated mariners who knew nothing of navigation instruments both in print and conversation. Columbus was no exception.

Vespucci may have taken part in a journey that broke Columbus's monopoly on voyages to the Indies, but it was quite clear that Vespucci's objective was fame as much as it was enrichment, and it was money that really bothered Columbus. Columbus was terrified that time was running out for him to make sure that what he believed he was owed would be passed on to his sons. Columbus was not, in fact, impoverished—it was the ship he owned, filled with gold from Hispaniola, that had been the only one to survive the hurricane of 1502 unscathed. But he *felt* poor.

Neither he nor Vespucci was well. Columbus was all but bedridden and in great pain in the limbs and bladder. He obsessively railed against those who had betrayed him and criticized his son Diego for squandering money. Vespucci was suffering from recurrent bouts of malaria. Apart from their ailments, they shared unprecedented knowledge about the geography of the Indies, and though their understanding of it diverged considerably, they had a great deal to talk about.

It was also clear that their positions were beginning to reverse themselves. Vespucci had begun as a manager for the company that was investing in Columbus's first two voyages of discovery. He was a very junior partner in the relationship, a mere accountant and fixer, a supplicant to the Admiral of the Ocean Sea. But now he was a navigator with claims for the attention of history, an experienced explorer who was not—as Columbus was—locked in a dispute with the crown. Their conversations must have been awkward to begin with. Vespucci's successes were a measure of Columbus's failures, and it was his failures that obsessed him, and the failure of those around him to recognize his achievements.

Vespucci was at least able to travel. Columbus could not sit on a horse. He had tried to borrow the same litter that brought the body of the archbishop to Seville, but his doctor told him he was too ill to travel. Vespucci therefore agreed, on his visit to the court early in 1505, that he would press Columbus's claims while he was there. Columbus in turn wrote to his son Diego, asking him to help Vespucci:

He has always been desirous of serving me and is an honorable man, though fortune has been unpropitious to him, as to many others, and his labors have not been as profitable as he deserves. He goes on my account, and with a great desire to do something which may redound to my advantage, if it is in his power.

Vespucci was already more famous than Columbus around the world, and both may have known it. But it is a touchingly trusting letter, and one that proves to some extent the falsity of later claims that Vespucci was deliberately trying to steal Columbus's reputation. Right to the end the two men were friends, even if they were not necessarily in agreement. Also right to the end, Columbus maintained his position that his Indies were only a few days' journey from Asia.

Even so, Vespucci was not wholly trustworthy. His own claims came first when he reached the court. He made little headway with Columbus's, but he was successful on his own account. He was wholly forgiven for his Portuguese escapade and was made an honorary citizen of Castile.

In the spring of 1505, after Vespucci's failure on his behalf at court and the winter weather began to break, Columbus finally felt well enough—or at least desperate enough—to make the journey to see the king. He rode a donkey, which was strictly illegal in Castile because they were reserved for military transport, and was accompanied by Bartholomew and a great deal of luggage. His son Ferdinand had been acting as his secretary and he came too, but it was a five-hundred-mile journey, and it was exhausting even for someone in good health.

The party left Seville in May 1505, picking their way carefully along the rutted roads and tracks, and managed to reach Segovia, where he met his son Diego. Columbus and the king finally came face-to-face a few days later. Columbus had never trusted Ferdinand and he expected little from this encounter. He was also planning to write to Philip and Juana, and seems to have been thinking about an appeal to the pope as well. But Ferdinand was friendly and proposed a new contract between them, and offered to find a mediator who could help them agree about exactly what Columbus was owed. Columbus agreed.

As soon as the admiral was gone, painfully carried back to his lodgings, Ferdinand wrote to Ovando and told him to make sure the Columbus family received what was due to them. But the rest did not work out quite as planned. The frenetic activity preparing for the arrival of his daughter and son-in-law pushed the business of the new contract out of the forefront of Ferdinand's mind. Even so, the agreed-upon mediator set to work and in due course handed down his decision. The so-called tenth applied solely to the sovereign's share of the money from the Indies, and was therefore a tenth of a fifth—a fiftieth—rather than a tenth of the whole amount. The eighth referred to the share of Columbus's profits from his own direct investments and therefore had nothing to do with the crown. The third was pure imagination, said the mediator. It was based on the tradition that the other admirals in Castile were allowed to collect a third of the tax on the waters under their jurisdiction. This had never been extended to Columbus. He was left, therefore, with one fiftieth.

Columbus gave up. "Since it seems that his highness has no intention of keeping the promises he made on his honor and signed in his hand together with the queen, may God keep her soul, I believe that to fight it any longer would be, for me, who is an insect, like flogging a dead horse." He spent most of the rest of the year exiled in Segovia, with its medieval Alcazar high on a rock and its tremendous Roman aqueduct. There was little, away from Seville, to distract his bedridden thoughts from his mission and the bitterness of betrayal. The winter was also bitter that year. His sons felt it was too cold to be in Segovia and began to persuade him to move again.

The months passed by. He was unable to read anything. In April 1506 he dictated a last hopeful letter to Philip and Juana, expected in Castile at any time, asking for their support. He urged his sons to meet them, swear an oath of allegiance to them, and to beg them for help.

Columbus was by then very weak, and they moved him to Valladolid, where he owned a two-story brick house. He was taken upstairs and put to bed on the top floor, where his mind wandered and his nights were filled with the most violent and grandiose dreams. There he dictated his final will, leaving his titles and privileges to his son Diego. In his final days, he was looked after by the Franciscans. On the night of May 20, with his sons and his friends Fieschi and Méndez in the room, he died. He was only fifty-four.

His reputation had suffered so much in the intervening years that there was hardly any contemporary mention of his death.

Columbus was buried in the Franciscan monastery at Valladolid, after a funeral at the parish church of Santa Maria la Antigue nearby. Diego then commissioned a family mausoleum in the Carthusian monastery of Las Cuevas in Seville, and in 1509 his father's remains were moved there, along with his mother, Felipa's body, which was brought from Madeira. It was to be the first of many moves that their bones were to make.

Only a few years after this burial, Diego changed his mind about the mausoleum. It would be more fitting if his father was buried in Hispaniola instead, the heart of Columbus's discoveries. So Diego ordered the building of a convent of the Poor Clares at Concepción on Hispaniola, but this was unfinished by the time he died in 1526, and he was also buried in Seville, along with his parents and his uncle Bartholomew, who had died in 1514 leaving behind one six-year-old illegitimate daughter.

Diego's son Luis Colón, the third admiral, moved all their remains to Santo Domingo in 1541. He agreed that Hispaniola was the place they belonged, initially at least in a space next to the high altar in the new cathedral. The plaque on the vault, marking the spot, was removed just over a century later in 1655, when the authorities were afraid that the city would be sacked by Admiral William Penn, and the remains of the Columbus family would be an obvious target.

It was a sign of things to come. The Spanish empire had been drained of its wealth during the seventeenth century, and the island of Hispaniola—with no Tainos left alive—was partitioned. The Spanish gave away the western half, named Haiti—the original Taino name for the whole island—to the French in 1697. The other half, which eventually became the Dominican Republic, was also handed over to France a century later. It was unthinkable that Columbus's bones should lie in a French cathedral. The headquarters of the Spanish empire was moved to Havana, Cuba, and so with great ceremony, the commander of the Spanish imperial fleet opened the tomb and found a small stone vault with some bones and ashes inside. These were put into a lead casket with iron locks and taken to Havana, where they were put in a niche in the side of the altar of the cathedral there.

But only two generations later, there was confusion about exactly what was where. In 1877 repairs were being made on the cathedral of Santo Domingo and a previously unopened vault was found. In it were a casket with some bones, some dust, and one unexplained bullet. There was a notice with them that said that these were the remains of "the illustrious and famous gentleman Sir Christopher Columbus." When they were put back a year later, another label, engraved on silver, was found among the bones, which said they were the last of the remains of Columbus. Both notices were crude and clearly not made in the sixteenth century, but on the strength of this information, the archbishop of Santo Domingo announced that the remains were still there, and that the bones sent to Havana must have been those of Columbus's son Diego. The archbishop happened to be an Italian, which made the Spanish authorities even angrier, and they insisted that Columbus's bones were in Havana and would remain there.

Yet not even that was permanent. Only two decades later, the Spanish-American War led to Cuban independence. The Spanish empire had shrunk to just a few Caribbean islands, and it was once more unthinkable that Columbus's remains should slip outside Spanish territory. So at the end of the year they were taken out of their niche and sailed to Cadiz. There they were taken by the royal yacht, flying the Spanish flag at half mast, up the Guadalquivir, and back to Seville. They arrived there in January 1899 and were put behind a little door in the side of the impressive monument in the cathedral that is seen to this day, with a giant coffin held aloft by four medieval kings, representing the nations of Spain: Leon, Navarre, Aragon, and Castile.

But the dispute rumbles on. The Dominican Republic still argues that they have the genuine bones, and they built a new monument shaped like a lighthouse to house them in preparation for the five-hundred-year anniversary of Columbus's discovery held in 1992. There is still quite a lot left unexplained, with experts supporting either side of the argument, and many unanswered questions. What, for example, was the bullet doing there? What happened to Columbus's beloved chains? There are those who say that, in fact, the Franciscans would never have allowed Columbus's body to leave their friary in Valladolid and that he remains there. That is how the Italian historian Giovanni Granzotto came to believe that he was buried under what was by then the pool table in a small beer cellar called the Café del Norte.

An examination by surgeons in 1960 concluded that there were actually bones from at least two bodies in the Seville tomb, and that is where matters have stood for the past generation. But there is a new clue. Columbus's younger brother Diego had a peculiar, but definite tomb. He ended his life as a priest and died in 1515 and was buried in a monastery in Seville. The building eventually closed, and by the nineteenth century it had become part of a ceramics factory, under English management. Diego's remains were exhumed from behind the wall where they had been for three centuries and kept in a box, and so, by our own time, they were available for scientific examination.

In 2006 a team led by the forensic geneticist José Antonio Lorente took DNA from Diego's bones and from those in his brother Christopher's supposed tomb in Seville—the bones taken from the niche in Havana in 1899. They were also given permission to open the tomb of Ferdinand Colón, also in the Seville cathedral. Their results coincided with the five-hundred-year anniversary of Christopher's death and confirmed that the few bones in Seville were indeed those of a close relative of Diego's.

The authorities in Santo Domingo were predictably furious, but, as the experts pointed out, there were so few bones involved, and the tomb had been moved so often, that there was no reason why both cathedrals should not actually house some of the remains of the great explorer.

# 9

# THE NEW WORLD

*"There are three stages in the popular attitude towards a great discovery: first, men doubt its existence; next they deny its importance; and finally they give the credit to somebody else."*

ALEXANDER VON HUMBOLDT

*"Had our father Adam made them his sole heirs?"*

FRANCIS I, King of France, complaining
about the Treaty of Tordesillas,
dividing the world between
the Portuguese and Spanish

IN THE SMALL town of Saint-Dié in April 1507, in the disputed territory between France and Burgundy, and in the home of a local intellectual, Gaultier Lud, one of the most important maps ever printed was taking shape. Columbus had been dead for less than a year. Pope Julius had just announced his notorious indulgence to pay for the new St. Peter's Basilica in Rome, and Leonardo da Vinci was back in Milan, finishing the *Virgin of the Rocks*. Here in the Vosges mountains, a thirty-three-year-old German printer called Martin Waldseemüller was just pulling from the press the first proof of a section of his new world map. There was the potent smell of ink.*

These were the great days of printing. It was only half a century since Johannes Gutenberg had first set type in a way that could be rapidly and widely reproduced, and already there were 10 million printed books in circulation in Europe, in 27,000 different editions. Aldus Manutius had founded his famous press in Venice only fifteen years before, and now there were novels and compendiums of knowledge, from ancient to downright dangerous, throughout the continent, spreading the ideas of the Renaissance outside Italy, and the methods of business far beyond the great banking and trading cities. In every university town, and many other places, the presses were at work, with their ink warming on the stove and the clicking sound of assistants setting up the type, before the great presses began to turn out more pages—each one precisely the same as the last.

A thousand copies of the Saint-Dié map were to be printed in twelve large sheets, designed to be attached on a wood support to make up a plan of the world just under ninety-five-inches wide. It was a thrilling moment for Waldseemüller and his colleagues, and the printing assistants they had brought in from Strasbourg and Basel to help, all of them clustered around the press. They believed this was the most accurate representation of the world ever produced, it showed a clear gap between the New World and the Far East—though the Pacific had not yet been seen by any European—and incorporated the discoveries of Columbus, da Gama, Cabral, Cabot, Vespucci, and their colleagues and competitors.

Waldseemüller was a graduate of Freiburg University in Germany and the son of a butcher, with a fascination for geography and a playful excitement about words and wordplay. He was one of the young scholars attracted to Saint-Dié by Duke René II of Lorraine, who was himself thrilled by the new geography. Lud was another of these. Later to be director-general of the duke's mining operations, he had invested in a printing press back in 1494 and set it up in his home.

---

*There is not much of Saint-Dié left. It was burned down in a great fire in 1757, bombarded in World War I, and destroyed by retreating German forces in November 1944.

Lud had a dream. He was going to lead a project to publish a new printed edition of Ptolemy's *Geography* and had recruited a number of young scholars to help him. They met regularly at his home and called themselves the Gymnase Vosgien, a literary circle of the kind that was now flourishing in German cities. It included a young mathematician and poet from Heidelberg named Matthias Ringmann, who was recruited to do the new translation of Ptolemy, just as Waldseemüller was asked to organize the printing.

Waldseemüller was particularly excited because of the possibilities of naming things. His own Latin tag, coined by himself and used for this map, was "Hylacomylus." With the enthusiastic encouragement of his colleagues, he believed he had finally given credit where it was due on this new map. On the top are two figures presiding over the world: Ptolemy and Amerigo Vespucci. And on the left, marking the southern part of the new continent, is the name America. It is the first time, as far as anyone knows, that the word had been coined.

How was it, then, that it was a version of Vespucci's name—albeit his first name—that came to be on the map? The arguments have resounded ever since, and will probably never be resolved, but it was a series of accidents—made possible by the phenomenal growth of printing—that seems to have given America its name.

What had happened was that Vespucci's former Popolano employer had died in June 1503. He had been immensely proud of the letters that Vespucci had sent him, and showed them to visitors, or indeed anyone that asked. Many of the paragraphs were copied and passed around. When Lorenzo died the letters suddenly became the property of his executors. It was clear to them that these letters were of value, not just the ones that have survived but the fragments of others that circulated along with them. Somebody in their circle—calling themselves Jocundus—believed these should have a wider audience, and gathered as many fragments as he could with a new text that held the various genuine clips together in some kind of order. These were published later that same year, immediately after Lorenzo's death and only shortly after Vespucci's return from Latin America, and given the compelling title *Mundus Novus*, or New World.

"We may rightly call them a New World," writes Vespucci of the places he had visited, "because our ancestors had no knowledge of them and it will be a matter wholly new to those who hear about them."

*Mundus Novus* was an immediate success way beyond Florence. In its first two years, it ran to twenty-three editions and was immediately translated into a range of different languages. It was short and concise, and even if it was a little disjointed, it gave the impression of the intelligence behind it. Although Vespucci had not written it himself, it had clearly been constructed by someone with access to at least some of his letters—though probably not the major ones, which didn't come to light until the eighteenth century. The book did more than anything else to spread the news throughout Europe that there was a New World, and its very existence became linked irrevocably with the author's name.

The success of *Mundus Novus* did not go unnoticed in Florence, and it occurred to one of Florence's new printers that a longer book might sell profitably. There were no more letters forthcoming, so they employed a hack writer to construct one for them. This was the genesis of the book that would gild and then undermine Vespucci's reputation around Europe. *The Four Voyages of Amerigo Vespucci* was published partly as a simple matter of making a profit and partly about lampooning Vespucci himself among the skeptical reading public of Florence, for whom he had become a distant figure of some pomposity, suspiciously supplicatory to the old Medici regime.

Not only was Vespucci a devoted servant of both branches of the Medici family, by then derided in most corners of Florence, but he was already engaged in an angry correspondence with critics back home who doubted aspects of his claims. He was furiously, and rather pompously, sending ammunition to his uncle Giorgio to use on his behalf ("And if any invidious and malign person refuses to believe it, let him come to me and I will declare it to him, with authority and with testimonies"). *The Four Voyages* was written as if it was another letter, but to someone it was absolutely inconceivable that he would ever have written to: the city's new gonfalconier, the representative of the republic, Piero Soderini, who Vespucci had known and disliked at school.

Soderini's main accomplishment to date, apart from hanging on to his position, was to lure Michelangelo back to Florence in 1500 and point him in the direction of a large lump of marble in the cathedral workshop, which had been abandoned forty years before. The result was the extraordinary seventeen-foot-tall statue of David, which has become a symbol of the city's

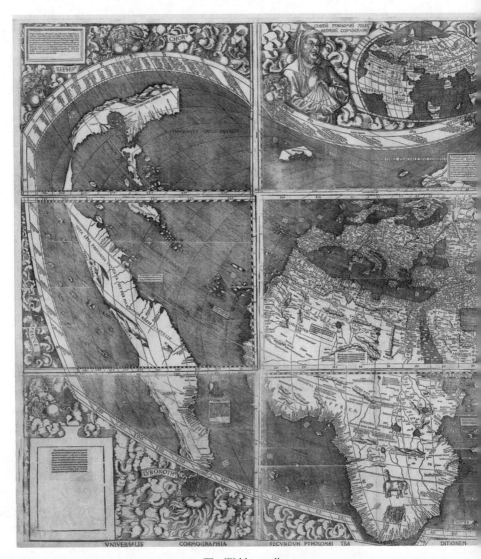

The Waldseemüller map

pride. An entire wall of the cathedral compound needed to be demolished to get it out. The idea that the pawn of the Medicis, remembered as a servant to aristocratic absolutism, might write to the leading figure of the new republic—who he was known to dislike—made the Florentines laugh.

The author used information from *Mundus Novus* for the two voyages, but he added two more voyages of his own, one in 1497 to Florida, which would have given Vespucci a claim to being the first navigator to find the mainland of America the same year as Cabot, and another to Brazil in 1503. The so-called Soderini letter was published in Florence in September 1504, just as Columbus was setting sail for home having been rescued from Jamaica. It was an immediate success in its home city and was soon carried to other places, where the jokes at Vespucci's expense were less obvious. It may not have sold as well as *Mundus Novus*, but *The Four Voyages* had cannibalism, sex, and the thrilling hope of a cure for impotence, contained in the news that the women of the New World used herbs to stimulate their menfolk to prodigious sexual feats.

The letter also caricatured Vespucci's coy and slightly lascivious habit of drawing a polite veil over anything he considered improper. In the Soderini letter, this is taken to ludicrous lengths.

> They do not employ the custom of marriage. Each one takes the women he wants and when he repudiates them he does so without constituting an offence or shame for the women, for in this the women are as free as the men. They are not very jealous, but they are lascivious . . . and the women much more so than the men . . . they showed a great desire to have carnal knowledge with us Christians.

Then, having titillated the readers, Vespucci is made to say that "out of decency, I refrain from telling of the expedients they employ to satisfy their inordinate lust."

Offered their wives and daughters as a sign of friendship, the author had Vespucci drawing the veil once more: "It would be out of the question for me to tell you all the honor they did us." The readers in Florence must have laughed at so cruel a lampoon, almost as much as they enjoyed the mental pictures. The sexual gratification of explorers is little studied. Even now, we have to read between the lines, but it was clear that for the contemporary audiences, almost as much as the crews themselves, sex was one of the enjoyable aspects of discovery that was not generally written into the reports of the captains.

The letter had a particularly damaging influence on European attitudes toward the people of the New World. On one occasion it described how a posse of native women killed a young crewman, cutting him up, roasting, and eating him before the horrified eyes of the crew. This horrific cannibal scene was depicted over and over again in drawings on the maps in generations to come. Something about it deeply impressed those who read it. The passage did almost as much as Vespucci's noble savage descriptions to fix in the minds of Europe this sense of the "other" across the Atlantic, although Vespucci made it clear enough in other letters that he was staying with people who ate their enemies. Cannibalism, or tales of cannibalism, were used for centuries to justify the most brutal treatment of those who lived in Latin America before Columbus. Soon European pictures of demons were being modeled on Vespucci's cannibals, and the noble savage had come full circle.

*The Four Voyages* was full of inaccuracies, grammatical errors, and pretend Spanish words, to imply that Vespucci had been so long abroad he was almost foreign. It made him out to be boastful and dishonest about and reveling in his expatriate status. The whole production implied a comment on his perceived snobbery. Even so, the humor that had been aimed at Florence was lost on the rest of Europe, and the letter was not recognized as a forgery until 1879.

While *The Four Voyages* was circulating around Europe, a copy of *Mundus Novus* had made its way to Saint-Dié. Ringmann had been thrilled by the book, translated it again into Latin, and given it to his colleagues. When a copy of *The Four Voyages* fell into his hands soon afterward, he shared it with excitement as well. Waldseemüller had decided on the strength of this that they would write a short introduction to the map, to which Ringmann contributed a poem. In this introduction, also published in 1507, Waldseemüller set out clearly why he had named the new continent in the way he had.

Now, really these parts [Europe, Africa and Asia] were more widely traveled, and another fourth part was discovered by Americus Vespuccius (as will be seen in the following pages), for which reason I do not see why anyone would rightly forbid calling it (after the discoverer

Americus, a man of wisdom and ingenuity) "Amerige," that is, the land of Americus or "America," since both Europe and Asia are names derived from women. Its location and the customs of its people will be easily discerned from the four voyages of Americus which follow.

This is not the only explanation of the name. It has been suggested that Waldseemüller was not coining a term, but trying to explain one he had already heard—either because the name was derived from Amerrique, a district of what is now Nicaragua, a local name, or because Cabot called it after his patron Richard Amerike. But none of these explains the process of how the name reached Saint-Dié. Waldseemüller also removed the name in later editions, which implies that he did invent it. So this remains the best explanation so far.

Having finished the first edition of the map, the Gymnase went back to preparing the edition of Ptolemy's *Geography*. But it was a long struggle. Ringmann died of tuberculosis in 1511, and Lud ran into financial difficulties, and the project was taken on by two Strasbourg lawyers. But the *Geography* appeared in 1513 and was a great success. Waldseemüller himself realized by then that he had been mistaken about Vespucci and had failed to give enough credit to Columbus. His second edition of the famous map removed the name America and replaced it with *Terra Incognita*, but the name had a popular a ring to it, which seems to have been the main reason why he had coined it in the first place.*

Meanwhile, other forgeries were circulating around Europe describing increasingly bizarre voyages by Vespucci, including one he was supposed to have undertaken to India in 1505, the year he was making Columbus's case at Ferdinand's court. There is no evidence that Vespucci ever claimed the name America. When his nephew Giovanni drew up an innovative world map in 1526, he didn't call the continent anything at all.

Nor is there any record the other way: of Vespucci complaining that a continent had been named after him. Equally there is no record that the map reached Seville in his lifetime. Nor, in fact, did *Mundus Novus* circulate much there either. As for *The Four Voyages*, he must have known about its

---

*Only one copy of the original map has ever been found. It came to light in Wolfegg Castle in Germany in 1901, where it had been used centuries earlier to reinforce the binding of a book.

publication, and cringed when he read its caricature of his pomposity, but it was never widely known in Spain. As a good Florentine, he knew it was a joke directed primarily at himself and he assumed that the rest of Europe knew it was intended as such. Unfortunately for his later reputation, the letters were taken at face value. The first generation was thrilled by them but after that the grotesque voice in which the Soderini letter was written—and the obvious inaccuracies—were attributed to Vespucci himself.

The main reason it was assumed around Europe that Vespucci was somehow responsible for discovering America was the book title *Mundus Novus*. Actually, the term "New World" had been coined as early as 1493. The words "the New World" were first attributed to Vespucci, though in *Mundus Novus*, which, while not actually written by him, was largely culled from his letters to Lorenzo di Pierfrancesco.

But it is not clear that Vespucci was the first to recognize what they had all discovered on the other side of the Atlantic. By the time his books were published, most educated opinion in Castile agreed that Columbus had probably not discovered the Indies, even though the pope was still talking about it as part of Asia. But even Columbus recognized, as early as his third voyage, that he was sailing alongside a new continent. He was just mistaken about where it was. He clung to the idea that it was just south of China rather than a long way east of it. What Vespucci did was to add considerably to people's understanding. After his own second voyage from 1501 to 1502, down the eastern coast of Latin America, the problem was clear for the policy makers of Europe: how to get through this landmass to the Indies, either north of the new continent, or south of it—or possibly, as Columbus hoped to the end, through an undiscovered passage in the middle.

But the critical factor in the naming of America after Vespucci rather than Columbus was simply the enormous growth in printing and literacy over the previous generation. Columbus's letters about his discoveries had been published and printed, but they just referred to the Indies. It was a new route he was claiming, not a new continent. Nor did they carry the whiff of erotic adventure that Vespucci's forgeries claimed. Columbus's writings were vivid but included a tone of self-justification that undermined their potential for bestseller status. When a book called *The Ship of Fools* was published in

1494, describing new countries filled with gold discovered by Castilians, it included no mention of Columbus at all.

If Columbus had remained obsessed with a passage through Central America to China, and the Bristol rivals were obsessed with a Northwest Passage, Vespucci was now driven by the hope of going farther than his last voyage and finding a *southwest* passage to Asia. He spent Columbus's last months in Seville, preparing the case for a new voyage. Together with Vicente Yáñez Pinzón and Juan de la Cosa, Vespucci had persuaded Ferdinand to invest in their planned expedition and, just as Columbus was failing, they were busy fitting out three ships for the journey. But the preparations were taking place while the uncertainty about who should succeed Isabella to the throne of Castile was rumbling away in the background, during Ferdinand's long wait for the arrival of his daughter Juana and her husband, Philip of Burgundy.

By the new year 1506, when Columbus was still sick and bedridden in Segovia, the Castilian government had almost ground to a halt, constipated by the uncertainty about the succession. Juana and Philip were finally making their long-delayed journey, leaving their young son, Charles, under the care of Margaret of Austria back in Brussels, when there was an enormous storm in southern England. It was one of those storms that is remembered for centuries. The weathervane of St. Paul's Cathedral in London was blown down, and the royal couple limped into the tiny harbor of Melcome near Weymouth to take shelter. They were immediately whisked to London, where Juana's younger sister, Catherine of Aragon, performed Spanish dances for them. It was a rare public appearance by Catherine, who was increasingly sidelined at court after the death of her husband.*

When Philip and Juana finally arrived in Castile, landing at Corunna in April 1506—just as Columbus was making his last journey to Valladolid— they found that Ferdinand was remarried, to the eighteen-year-old Germaine de Foix, in a desperate attempt to produce another son. A peculiar game began as Ferdinand dashed to see his daughter and son-in-law, but the royal couple dodged him and he finally caught up with them near the Por-

---

*It was this unplanned and unexpected visit that is supposed to have given rise to the nursery rhyme "I had a little nut tree," which explains that "The king of Spain's daughter came to visit me/And all for the sake of my little nut tree."

tuguese border. It became evident when he did that Philip would accept no limitations on his rule over Castile. There was to be no power sharing, and Ferdinand had no choice but to retire to his own kingdom of Aragon. Philip was proclaimed Philip I of Castile and the tragic Juana was kept under lock and key, where she remained for most of her life.

The sudden disappearance of Ferdinand was a disaster for Vespucci's new voyage. Desperately he set out to see Philip instead, and spent some time explaining the intricacies of the New World to him, and the importance of a southwest passage to bypass the Portuguese voyages to India. Vespucci now had better access to the court than Columbus had ever had, and Philip grasped the idea immediately, promised financial support, and urged Vespucci to speed up the preparations. But four months had been lost since Ferdinand's retreat.

On September 25, Philip was at a monastery at Miraflores, playing a game of pelota—an Iberian version of tennis—and shortly afterward was overtaken by a fit of shivering, which they said at the time had been caused by drinking icy water when he was sweating. Before nightfall, he was dead. Juana was sent over the edge of insanity by her grief, refusing to eat, dress, or speak, and she refused to allow her husband's body to be buried. She kept it next to her, decomposing, in her room.

Once more, Vespucci's voyage was in doubt, along with the succession to the throne of Castile. Ferdinand himself was in Naples and showed no haste about returning until his supporters had smoothed the way for him to be regent for his six-year-old grandson, Charles, back in Burgundy. The new court was more nervous than the old one, and they felt that if a voyage of exploration for a southwest passage was to go ahead they ought really to consult the Portuguese, because it would mean sailing along the Brazilian coast, and that was clearly theirs.

Unsurprisingly, the Portuguese objected. In fact the Portuguese court was going through their own periodic frenzy of paranoia. King Manuel had even gone so far as to make the possession of globes illegal, in a desperate attempt to prevent the secret routes to the Indies leaking out. Juan de la Cosa, sent as an emissary to Lisbon to discuss the voyages, was arrested as a spy and was only released after high-level intervention.

In this form at least, Vespucci's voyage could not go ahead. A year passed, while Ferdinand made sure his support was in place for a return to the throne of Castile, and then summoned his leading navigators—Vespucci, de la Cosa, Pinzón, and Juan de Solís—to meet him in Burgos. They arrived more than a year after Philip's death and found that Ferdinand wanted to discuss whether they could learn anything from the Portuguese about how to make sure the latest developments of navigation could be better used.

This was an excellent idea. Almost everything about the Portuguese arrangements for discovery were better organized, and Vespucci had been urging something similar for some time. He was busy conducting a war against those critics who did not accept his methods of navigation and who claimed he had barely any knowledge of the sea. Many navigators angrily rejected anything of the kind and regarded any claims to be able to measure longitude using means other than dead reckoning as vain and conceited.

As a result of the meeting in Burgos on November 26, 1507, Ferdinand sent Solís and Pinzón to find the southwest passage, and Juan de la Cosa to the Pearl Coast where he was lobbying to return with Ojeda. But Vespucci was appointed to a new post at the Casa de Contratación, called pilot major. It was a consolation prize for not being allowed to join the expeditions, and a way to formalize and spread his undoubted knowledge of the theoretical aspects of navigation. Under the agreement, he would open a school for navigators in his own home, which was a large house in the Postigo del Car-bón, rented from Bishop Fonseca, next to the Torre del Oro, between the city walls and the new shipyards, and near the enormous crane that domi-nated the wharves. From his home with Maria and Giovanni, he could hear the clattering of metal and wood as the ships bound for the New World took shape, just as he was instilling the principles of good navigation on the skeptical men who had been at sea twice as long as he had. "No-one shall presume to pilot ships or receive pay as a pilot," Ferdinand wrote to him in confirmation. "Nor may any master receive them on board, until they have first been examined by you, Amerigo Vespucci, our chief pilot, and have been given a certificate of examination and approval by you."

It is hard to imagine Columbus being appointed to such a post, and that Vespucci was given the job was a measure of the respect that he had achieved, and of his successful reinvention of himself from failed func-tionary to scientist-navigator. It would now be his allotted task to draw up and develop a master chart, incorporating all the new information that any of the expeditions brought back, just as the Portuguese did. This task he del-egated to Giovanni, who rapidly became one of the foremost cartographers

in Castile. Before any navigators set sail for the New World from Seville—
and Seville was now the official point of departure for all voyages there,
even if they actually left from Cadiz—they would need a certificate of com-
petence from the Vespucci household. Then, and only then, would they be
allowed to take a copy of the master map.

It was a difficult time to be in Seville. There were terrible floods in 1507,
and the influx of adventurers, prostitutes, criminals, and beggars was bringing with it the most devastating waves of plague and famine. In the midst of
all this, Vespucci's first task was to tackle the perennial problem of shipworm. It was already four years since Columbus had returned from an expedition where his entire fleet had been destroyed by precisely this problem.
From then on, Vespucci declared, all ships built to go to the New World
would have to be fitted with lead-plated keels.

As the Castilians were bracing themselves for another search for the southwest passage, the search for the Northwest Passage was beginning to run out
of energy.

After the initial successes of John Fernandez and his Bristol allies, there
had been a flurry of activity from Bristol, fueled by rivalry between those
who held rights under the patent given to him and those who still held
rights under Cabot's patent. By 1504 there were records of priests leaving
Bristol for the New World, an unmistakable sign that somewhere on Newfoundland the Bristol merchants had set up a permanent settlement to dry
cod, collect timber for masts, and harvest the wild cats for their furs.

Resources were not inexhaustible, given that the promised Northwest
Passage had not actually been found, and it began to make sense for the two
sides in Bristol to pool their resources. Between them, the heirs of Fernandez and his colleagues, and the heirs of Cabot and his partners, organized a
joint charter and formed themselves into one company: the Bristol Company Adventurers to the New Founde Land.

It was not a success. The problem was that half the fishing communities
in northern Europe were now using the waters around Newfoundland. Led
by the Basques and the Portuguese, the cod that Cabot had discounted had
launched a whole new industry. Newfoundland was even being described by
its Portuguese name, *Terra de Baccallos* (a Basque word) in reference to the

cod. It was too late to regulate or control the business there. The new company had no means of enforcing their monopoly. All they could do was to haul back a few consignments of dried fish and some mountain cats. The promised Northwest Passage to Asia remained elusive.

The company disintegrated in acrimony when Hugh Elyot sued Francisco Fernandez for £100 he said was owed him and had him arrested for debt, while Fernandez countersued for £160. The company ended up in the courts, and the king lost interest. Elyot went back to his old occupation, trading with Spain from his office on Broad Street in Bristol.

The Portuguese explorers were no more successful. They were nervous about northern exploration after the disappearance of the Corte Reals. They sent one more expedition to search for them in 1506, but there was no sign. They were also beginning to capitalize on their new route to India and the spice trade, and in itself this was already shifting the balance of economic power around the Mediterranean. The first cargo of Indian goods to England, which came via Lisbon, arrived in Falmouth in 1504.

This was an unprecedented disaster for the economy of the eastern Mediterranean, from which it has never quite recovered. In response to the catastrophic loss of trade, the sultan of Egypt threatened to destroy the Christian holy places in Jerusalem unless these voyages around Africa were stopped. The monastery on Mount Sinai was so concerned that they sent a messenger to plead with the pope to put pressure on the Portuguese. When the news reached Lisbon, Manuel decided he must press on faster. He appointed Francisco de Almeida as governor and viceroy of Portuguese India. Almeida destroyed an enormous combined fleet of Turks, Levants, and Arabs in 1509, which guaranteed the Portuguese presence in the region, and was killed in Africa on the way home. But the commercial empire of the Portuguese was now firmly established in the East.

I

*"You can only predict things after they have happened."*

EUGENE IONESCO

The aftermath of Columbus's death was unsurprisingly complicated for his family. There were the inevitable discrepancies in his accounts, kept by his cousin, and an equally inevitable investigation by his enemies at the royal treasury. His agent in Santo Domingo was working tirelessly on his behalf, and even if he had trouble extracting the money owed to the family in Seville, it was still flowing in.

Ironically, now that it was too late to influence Columbus's ruined reputation at the Castilian court, Hispaniola was beginning to turn a serious profit. By 1505 the famous *quinto*—the fifth of the profits due to the crown—was bringing in 22 million maravedis a year. The sheer productivity of the island was also accelerating thanks to the policies of Ovando, who had begun to bypass the exhausted and enslaved local population when looking for labor. It was clear now that the Tainos were not suitable for heavy work in the mines or the fields. They were not used to it. Ovando reversed his policy on slaves from Africa and began to bring them into Hispaniola in twos and threes. That same year Ferdinand intercepted a request for more and ordered a hundred black slaves for the New World. It was a fatal turning point, and the beginning of a trade which would involve up to 30 million Africans and eventually engulf the northern part of the new continent in civil war.

But even Ovando could not retain his popularity with everyone, and once more complaints about the governor began to mount. In August 1508 Ferdinand decided to replace him, and in an ironic gesture, given that Columbus believed he had set his face against the whole family, he decided to replace him with the admiral's eldest son, Diego Colón.

Diego was twenty-eight-years old, and a sophisticated product of the Castilian court, where he had spent most of his life. He had attracted Ferdinand's notice as an effective administrator and had made a highly fashionable and advantageous marriage to the niece of the Duke of Alba, another favorite of the king. In 1509 he sailed to take up his appointment as governor, together with his uncles and his brother Ferdinand. He made an easy crossing with his wife on the *Que Dios Salve* and set up home in the governor's palace from which Bobadilla had ejected his father. Against all odds, Christopher Columbus's governorship had been inherited by his eldest son.

The Bristol Company Adventurers may have wound up in disputes about debts, and the whole business of exploration may now have been seriously out of favor as the health of Henry VII began to decline, but there was one youthful advocate in Bristol who would not be silenced. John Cabot's son Sebastian was alive and well and desperate to capitalize on the patent that had been made out in 1496 in favor of his father and his brothers. For Sebastian the central problem remained how to get past this continent, the so-called New World, to reach the spices, gold, and wealth of the East. It also seemed to him that he had inherited some clues. The series of expeditions from Bristol, starting in 1497, had revealed a whole range of still-unexplored inlets, one of which must go through. For Sebastian, the Northwest Passage was still there to be discovered.

The year Columbus died, Sebastian was twenty-two. The young Cabot moved to London and married a Londoner named Joanna, who soon gave birth to a daughter named Elizabeth. Sebastian had inherited not just his father's convictions, but also his ability to charm an audience. His cartographic skills quickly impressed the king, and he was given a ten-pound annuity by Henry VII for his "diligent service and attendaunce." He also managed to find a new source of investment for westward exploration.

Where Cabot differed from his father was that his lifelong quest to match those achievements led him sometimes, perhaps, to believe his own rhetoric a little too much. He claimed he had raised the money from Henry VII; in fact, it seems to have come from the Netherlands. Even so, it was enough to hire and equip two ships, and it was the opportunity of a lifetime. At the back of his mind, as well, he may have hoped to vindicate or rediscover his father, and assumed—knowing John Cabot's personality—that he had discovered the elusive passage himself before leaving the stage.

The new Cabot expedition set sail early in the summer of 1508 and headed for the Hudson Strait, and to Sebastian's excitement, he found that it opened out into what seemed like a sea, but which we now know was Hudson Bay. It was a perilous expedition. The ice floes were everywhere. The unknown seemed even more unknown than it should have, a misty, insubstantial white emptiness, so far north that the sun never set. It is hardly surprising that he faced the same problem his father did. The crew would not go on, and insisted that he turn around. He held them off throughout the winter of 1508 into 1509 in a small camp on the north coast of Labrador, and when spring came he made another attempt, managing to get as far north as Baffin Island, searching for ways through before the crew finally had enough.*

It was an enormous disappointment to Sebastian, and a fatal moment in his life. He never stopped believing that had he been permitted to go on, the Northwest Passage would have been before him. From then on, he kept the route a closely guarded secret, aware that it was sometimes senseless—sometimes actually dangerous—to reveal it, and battled to return there until he died. But a bigger problem loomed as they arrived at the mouth of the Avon in the early summer of 1509—the king was dead.

Henry VII had not been well for some years. He had suffered from cataracts since 1505 and ever since his wife had died had developed an obsession with the poor incarcerated widow Juana the Mad, since meeting her during her brief stay in England after she was nearly shipwrecked in the English Channel in 1506. He already loathed Ferdinand, who was still refusing to send the rest of Catherine of Aragon's dowry, and he became convinced that Juana was being deliberately shut away with her husband's coffin and wasn't mad at all.

Ferdinand deftly avoided all Henry's diplomatic requests that he should marry Juana himself. Henry developed "consuming sickness" (probably tuberculosis) and died on April 21, 1509. He was only fifty-two. His heir since Arthur's death was his seventeen-year-old son, also called Henry, who had, according to John Cabot's Venetian friend Pasqualigo, an "extremely fine calf to his leg."

The young Henry VIII was tall, handsome, and magnetic. His first act on succeeding to the throne was to sort out the ridiculous scandal of the treatment of Catherine of Aragon. He wanted a sumptuous coronation and he wanted a queen beside him, now that the pope had given him permission to marry his brother's widow. Henry buried his father in Westminster Abbey on May 10 and went straight from there to Greenwich for a quiet wedding to Catherine, who was ten years older than he. The following month, Henry wore crimson and gold ornamented with flashing diamonds, rubies, and emeralds to parade through London for his coronation. Catherine followed,

---

*These waters were fatal for the early navigators. Sebastian Cabot faced mutiny in 1509, but Henry Hudson himself was murdered by his crew, set adrift in Hudson Bay in 1611.

with her long red hair flowing behind her, wearing white satin and sitting on a golden cloth.

Ojeda's expedition to found a colony of New Andalusia on the mainland, the project which was supposed to stop the English, was a disastrous failure. He had struggled back to Hispaniola, to find his great ally Queen Isabella had died. But after the famous meeting between Vespucci, de la Cosa, and Ferdinand in Burgos, and a period raising the money and lobbying in Castile, Ojeda set out again in the *Magdalena* and three other ships to the site of the new colony. Among those on board, apart from de la Cosa, was Ojeda's friend and ally Diego de Nicuesa, the future conquistador Pizarro, and three hundred men.

They landed near what is now Cartegena. The brutal capture of slaves had become an obsession with Ojeda. De la Cosa, now sixty years old, strongly advised him against going on to Calamar in search of slaves, but he was overruled and the two of them led a slaving party of seventy men deep inland. They made one of Ojeda's trademark surprise attacks on a nearby village, capturing sixty locals, and pursued the rest into the jungle, where Ojeda and his men soon found themselves isolated and surrounded and attacked by waves of enraged local Indians, finally taking revenge for the cruelties meted out by Ojeda. On February 28, 1510, the rescue expedition found Ojeda unconscious, hiding in a mangrove swamp. Juan de la Cosa's body, horribly swollen and covered with poisoned arrows, was found in a hut. The former captain of the *Santa Maria* was dead.

Undeterred, Ojeda moved on to found his colony at San Sebastian. He sailed back to Hispaniola in search of new supplies, leaving Pizarro in charge, and was shipwrecked on the way. Only after a terrible struggle did he finally make his way back to Hispaniola, to find that a new generation under the leadership of Columbus's eldest son was now in charge there and had no time for him. He died in poverty, taking the vows of a Franciscan shortly before his death in 1515.

The settlers on Hispaniola were excited about the arrival of the first Dominican friars, who had a reputation as brilliant speakers. Entertainment was in short supply for them, and the prospect of some thrilling sermons was enough to provide a frisson of excitement. The Franciscans were less keen on the arrival of their rivals, who were known for their reforming zeal, but the Dominicans kept to themselves when they arrived in 1510, and it was not until December 4, 1511, that the first of their preachers opened his mouth.

Antonio de Montesinos was asked if he would deliver a sermon in the large thatched church at the center of Santo Domingo, which was being used as a temporary cathedral. It was packed for the occasion, but what the settlers heard froze them in their seats. "This voice says that you are in mortal sin, that you are living and may die in it, because of the cruelty and tyranny which you use in dealing with these innocent people," thundered Montesinos from the pulpit. He had watched the treatment of the Tainos with mounting horror for over twelve months. "Are these not men? Have they not rational souls? Are you not bound to love them as you love yourselves?"

At the end of his sermon, he walked straight out of the church. A group of prominent settlers went to see Diego Colón, who complained to the senior Dominican and asked him to tell Montesinos to withdraw his remarks. He was told that Montesinos would preach again the following Sunday, and the crowds packed the church again to hear his apology. But the second sermon was more condemnatory than the first. At the end of it, he said he would hear no more confessions of settlers until this injustice was brought to an end.

The settlers pulled what political strings they could to demand Montesinos's recall, and his colleagues sent him home to argue on his own behalf. Ferdinand was appalled at what he heard and convened a group of theologians to meet in the Casa del Cordón in Burgos, where he had received Columbus in 1496. It was a high-level committee, including the fearsome Fonseca, and it met twenty times to debate and hammer out a solution. One professor of law dismissed the Indians as "animals who talk." The Franciscans accepted that the Tainos were free people, but said it was their duty to help them overcome their tendency to laziness. The debate rumbled on and resulted in the so-called Laws of Burgos, not quite what the Dominicans had intended and in many ways disastrous for what remained of Taino culture. There should be new villages built for them, the committee decided. The old ones would be burned. They must not dance or sing, paint their bodies, or get drunk. And in return they would be taught. Talavera, now bishop of Granada, and once the chair of the commission that dismissed the idea of the Indies enterprise, was invited to write a small book of instruction for Indian children. The Dominicans argued for some relaxation and that the labor they must give to landowners was limited to nine months a year. They must be allowed three months a year to work on their own farms.

But all these laws were subject to a major qualification: Indians must accept the Church of Rome and their new Castilian rulers or they would be made slaves. This outline of what was required of them, the so-called *Requerimiento*, was read in the villages, usually in a language the residents could not understand. It was often used in a symbolic way, read in Spanish to empty fields by the newly arrived conquerors. It was read to a deserted village on Darien by the conquistador Pedrarias, to the laughter of his military guard in June 1514. If the natives took no action, it would mean they could reasonably be enslaved or attacked.

After only four years as pilot major, Vespucci's health was also deteriorating. His attacks of malaria were more pronounced and more frequent, though he had no conception of what the disease was. His reputation had also been damaged by the revelation that he had been selling versions of secret maps and was forced to swear an oath never to do it again. Through the early months of 1512, while Michelangelo's *Creation of Man* was taking shape in the Sistine Chapel, Vespucci was growing increasingly sick. One of his last recorded acts was to verify the signature of Columbus on a map. He did so knowing it would deeply displease his masters.

He lay in his sickbed at home, listening to the hammering from the shipyards across the street, a constant reminder of oceans and coastlines still to be explored, and the smell of the tropical forest reaching far out to sea. He died at home on February 22 with Maria and his nephew Giovanni at his bedside.

Vespucci was only fifty-eight and was not a wealthy man. His will set out the extent of his failed investments in Columbus: Berardi's estate still owed him 144,000 maravedis, but Maria was to get a pension of 10,000 maravedis, which was inherited twelve years later by her sister Catalina, who had lived with them in the same house. The pilot major left his books and maps to his nephew Giovanni, later a Florentine spy in the service of the Medici pope Leo X. Vespucci also asked that a ruby and a pearl, left in his brother's custody when he departed from Florence in 1491, be sold to pay for a requiem mass and thirty-three masses for his soul in the church of Ognissanti in Florence, where his portrait as a youth remains on the walls.

He was buried, like so many of his other navigator contemporaries, in the robes of a Franciscan, probably in the church of San Miguel in Seville, which burned down in the early twentieth century. He was succeeded as pilot major by Juan de Solís, just back from the Plate River.*

If western exploration had faltered in England and Portugal, the Castilian voyages and settlements were now in full swing. Columbus, Vespucci, and Juan de la Cosa were dead; Ojeda was ruined. But there were plenty more in Castile willing to take their places, and the generation who would bravely and brutally found the Spanish empire in Latin America was now on its way to the place officials still referred to as the Indies.

Jamaica had been invaded in 1509. Cuba had been conquered by Ovando's protégé Cortés two years later: the Cuban leader was offered a Christian death, including eternal life, and is supposed to have said that if that meant eternity in the company of Spaniards he would prefer not and was burned as a pagan. Juan Ponce de Leon had scourged Puerto Rico with the utmost bloodshed, nearly wiping out the native population. His large red dog played such a vital role in the routing of the local Indians that it was given the salary of a crossbowman, before master and dog sailed in 1513 for Florida in search of a rumored fountain of everlasting youth. And so on toward the great and terrible exploits of the conquistadors in Peru from 1530 and Mexico from 1535.

It was Vasco Nuñez de Balboa, a stowaway fleeing from creditors, who finally solved the central problem set by Columbus. Balboa emerged as the effective leader of a new attempt to settle in the region of Darien, who sent an unwisely enthusiastic letter home to Ferdinand, accompanied by a consignment of pineapples, where he used the overblown phrase "rivers of gold." Faced with this temptation, the royal court roused themselves to finance their first expedition since 1493, under a seventy-year-old soldier named

---

*Solís lasted less than four years. Landing in what is now Uruguay in February 1516 with seven men, he was killed by locals and cut into tiny pieces. Survivors of his expedition were still being rescued by Sebastian Cabot's expedition a decade later.

Pedro Arias Ávila, known as Pedrarias. As soon as Balboa heard the news that there was an expedition planned, he realized it would make sense to go inland immediately and find these rivers of gold himself.

Collecting as many armed men on the colony as he could, Balboa marched inland in September 1513. It was an exhausting journey through swamps and jungles. He managed to make peace with some of the tribes he encountered. Where this was impossible, he had their representatives torn apart by dogs on the peculiar grounds that they were transvestites. Heading up the first mountain peak, he reached the summit on September 25, 1513, and saw finally the sight that had eluded Columbus, Vespucci, and Cabot before him, and for which in their different ways they had given their lives. Far off, stretching into an impossible distance, was the blue of another ocean to match the Atlantic.

Balboa raised his hands and saluted the ocean that would one day be known as the Pacific, then he made his way down the other side of the mountain, fought a short engagement with the local chief, and marched to the edge of the ocean. There he waded into the water wearing his armor until he was breast deep, raised his sword, and arrogantly took possession of it in the names of Ferdinand and Juana.

The problem that had obsessed Columbus was now solved. The new continent was two vast landmasses, connected by a narrow strip, with an ocean on either side. The question of whether this was a large ocean or a small strip of sea before China, was as yet unanswered, but the sea that had eluded Columbus for so long had now been seen by Europeans.

The admiral's heir Diego Colón was as effective an administrator as his father had been a useless one. He was tall, good-looking, charming, and dignified. He spent his first years as governor building a base of personal support in the Indies and did so by quietly failing to report when the landholdings, the *encomiendas*, fell vacant—as he was required by the crown in Castile to do—then appointing his own supporters to fill them.

Just after midnight on January 23, 1516, King Ferdinand died in an unfurnished house in the tiny village of Madrigalejo, having recalled Diego for consultation. Diego remained in Castile as the young Charles V inherited the joint throne, and Castile and Aragon finally merged as the nation of Spain, under an imperial ruler who, through his mother, also ruled Burgundy and the Netherlands, the most powerful monarch in Europe, and the beginning of the mighty Hapsburg dynasty. Diego charmed the young emperor, and he was reappointed as governor in 1518. He was there for another five years before failing revenues and conflict with campaigners like Bartholomé de las Casas led to his final return home in 1523. But he never abandoned his father's claims. It was just that from his intricate knowledge of the Castilian court, he had a more subtle way of going about pursuing them. While accepting the position of governor, he also quietly pursued a series of long-running lawsuits to enforce what he believed had been promised his family.

The first legal decision, in 1511, had confirmed Diego's rights over the land discovered by his father, though this was limited to the places actually found by him, and these rights were circumscribed in various ways. Both sides took exception to the decision, and Diego appealed. The next phase concentrated on whether the family had the right to vice-regal power over the areas that were the focus of settlement activity, Veragua, Urabá, and Darien, all on the coasts of mainland Latin America. It meant that a string of witnesses were called to question whether Columbus had actually set foot on any of them. Under questioning, his brother Bartholomew claimed that because Christopher was ill, he had gone ashore and claimed them for Castile.

By 1515 Diego was sure he was winning the case, when the government solicitor managed to complicate it further with a legal masterstroke. He collected thirteen friends of the Pinzón family, who claimed that it was actually Martin Alonso Pinzón who had made the journey possible in 1492 and had discovered the Indies. By now the money the Colón family was claiming amounted to a massive 55 percent of all royal revenues from the Indies and the government simply could not afford to let him win.

Throughout this period Diego's brother, Ferdinand, acted as his legal agent. It was a task that took his whole life, but he had time for the occasional journey between hearings to visit Genoa and to accompany the emperor Charles V on long journeys across Europe, especially the two-year trip he made beginning in 1520, from Brussels to Worms, taking in London and Switzerland. Everywhere he went he bought paintings and books. Ferdinand's share of the Columbus fortune was invested in a library that ran to as many as fifteen thousand volumes.* It was he who was largely responsible for the next favorable decision, but Diego was still not satisfied and appealed again. The strain of the lawsuit, and his period in Hispaniola, had exhausted Diego, and he died in 1526 at the age of only forty-six. The case was carried on by his wife. Even then, the so-called Judgment of Deuñas in 1534 left some questions unanswered.

Diego's son, Luis, the third admiral, continued the case. But he was perpetually in debt and settled out of court in 1537, giving up his rights to administrative office in the Americas in return for an annuity and the hereditary title Duke of Veragua. Not long after that, he was convicted of bigamy and sentenced to a heavy fine and ten year's military service in North Africa, where he married for a third time, much to the rage of his previous wives. He died at fifty and was buried alongside his forebears in Santo Domingo Cathedral.

But even that was not the end. The legal actions, known collectively as the *Pleitos*, continued in some form or another well into the eighteenth century. Luis had no legitimate sons, and his nephew Diego inherited his pension, laying the foundations for a long-running dynastic dispute. Luis's grandson Cristóbal died without an heir in 1601, having lived on handouts from other members of the family, and the titles were passed on through cousins to other families. The legal battle over which family line should inherit the titles began in 1650 and lasted until a final court decision in 1790, nearly three centuries after Columbus made his first discovery. The pension that Luis had accepted in his out-of-court settlement was still paid into the 1830s, and the dukes of Veragua continue to this day.

While Diego was fighting in the courts, there was a parallel argument about the Americas that would also continue through the generations, which began with Antonio de Montesinos's brave sermon in 1511. The primary figure in the campaign to defend the Indians was Bartholomé de las Casas. He had been born in Seville, and when he was nine had witnessed Columbus's

---

*This became one of the biggest libraries in Europe at the time, now the Biblioteca Colombina, still based in Seville, where Ferdinand died in 1539.

triumphal return in 1493 and his procession with the first Taino captives. He went to the Indies himself with Ovando in 1502, when he was eighteen, to manage some land given to his father. He also witnessed the brutal subjugation of the west of Hispaniola by Ovando, and was there while Méndez desperately tried to get Columbus rescued from the Jamaica beach.

Las Casas had been at the church of Santo Domingo and heard and sympathized with Montesinos's sermon. But it was not until he was appointed military chaplain to the 1513 expedition to conquer Cuba that he really experienced a revelation about the evil that was happening as the conquest extended. He renounced his own *encomienda*, contacted Montesinos, and sailed home with him to confront Ferdinand a second time, urging him to break up the *encomienda* system, which was destroying the Indians. He had noticed the decline in Tainos in Hispaniola and calculated that there were now only twelve thousand Tainos left on the island.

Together he and Montesinos worked out a series of ambitious plans, some of them utopian, of special new orders of chivalry, or a line of Spanish forts to protect the Indians in their old ways, as well as practical plans to compensate the *encomienda* owners and to organize new villages for the Indians. But time after time, these plans were undermined by the bitter opposition of the colonists and the inability of the court in Spain to enforce their will across the Atlantic.

Las Casas was an inspired campaigner, and Ferdinand and then Charles, for reasons of their own, were both sympathetic. But campaigning is always subject to the laws of unintended consequences, and the most powerful objective fact at their disposal was that the Tainos and other Indians were not used to heavy work in the mines or on the new cotton plantations. They tired easily, and if they were worked too hard they simply died. Administrators and settlers alike heard the message of Las Casas and Montesinos. They chose to look elsewhere for people to do their heavy work and found the source largely in Africa. It was one of those ironies of history that it was a powerful humanitarian campaign that drove the development of the slave trade.

African slavery was, at the start of this story, largely the preserve of Genoese businessmen, many of them, like Berardi and Marchionni, operating in Lisbon and Seville. But over a generation, slavery was becoming big business, disposing of all the Moorish captives after the fall of Granada or populating the plantations on the Canary Islands. A century before, most right-thinking, God-fearing people condemned slavery as an ancient God-less evil; now they had embraced it as a business necessity. And at the very epicenter of this new trade was Berardi and Vespucci's old colleague Jerónimo Grimaldi from Genoa, who built a large warehouse in Santo Domingo to house the slaves he had brought across the Atlantic. Those that survived the grueling journey were branded with letters on their faces and put to work.

This and other matters occupied the studies of Las Casas, locked away from the world in a convent on Hispaniola for ten long years, and when he finally emerged, he was completely radicalized. From now on, he could accept no compromise between Spanish and Indian interests. The material and spiritual interests of the locals came before Spanish interests every time, and any wars and conquests that claimed temporal power over the Indians were illegal, because he said these powers had not been given by the pope. In those circumstances, only one method could be used to persuade the Indians to convert to Christianity, and that was "love, gentleness and kindness."

His history, A Brief Account of the Destruction of the Indies, was used as propaganda by Spain's enemies for generations to come, as it detailed the cruelties suffered by the Indians in horrific detail. "I believe that because of these impious, criminal and ignominious acts, perpetrated unjustly, tyrannously, and barbarously upon them, God will visit in his wrath and his ire upon Spain for her share, great and small," he wrote. The book was published shortly after his famous debate with the humanist Juan Ginés de Sepúlveda about whether wars against the Indians could be justified. Sepúlveda won, in the sense that Charles V agreed with his position that Indians were "natural slaves" as defined by Aristotle, because of their wild and sinful sexuality—the influence of Vespucci was already felt here. But there was to be a peculiar twist. Horrified by the black slave trade he had done so much to begin, he worked away at Charles's conscience, only to find he had overdone it. Instead of insisting on emancipation, Charles decided his own soul was in peril. He abdicated and went to live in a monastery in Extremadura.

After Sebastian Cabot's return from his failed Arctic search, exploration took a backseat in the new court of Henry VIII. The marriage with Catherine of Aragon had renewed the friendship between the English court and her father, Ferdinand. This and the pugnacious enthusiasm of the new young English king toward his French neighbors meant that some kind of attack on France was inevitable. Henry organized an ambitious expedition in June 1512 under Thomas Grey, Marquis of Dorset. The English troops were sent by sea to Gascony, with an agreement that Ferdinand would strike simultaneously, annexing the old kingdom of Navarre on the French border. But having done so, Ferdinand allowed the English to carry the rest of the burden of fighting. As it turned out, there was precious little of that either, but over two thousand English soldiers died of fever and dysentery.

Also on the expedition, feverishly working on maps of the French coast, was Sebastian Cabot. One of the only lasting effects of the abortive English invasion was that Sebastian continued the journey to Castile and stayed there, in the employment of the Castilian court, making maps in the Casa de Contratación. He was assiduous in his mapmaking, as he had been in London, and rose quickly, boasting rather inaccurately about his long experience in exploration. When Juan de Solís died in 1518, Sebastian was appointed to succeed him in Vespucci's old position of pilot major. It was a job he held for nearly thirty years.

Seville was then the European capital of western navigation, so he had to be there. He spent most of his working life in the city, becoming friendly with some of the great writers of the age. He talked to Peter Martyr at length and became friends with him, and Peter Martyr was close friends with Vespucci's nephew Giovanni. The problem was that Sebastian nursed a secret: the Hudson Strait, which he had seen in 1508 and which he still believed held the secret of the Northwest Passage that came to dominate his life. It made him careful with people, and so secretive that he was heartily disliked by his subordinates in Seville, and on his later expedition up the River Plate.

Sebastian had access to all the records of the Casa de Contratación, and must have had suspicions, which he also dared not name, about his father's confrontation with Ojeda. He anyway preferred not to speak too much about his father's exploits for fear that they would take away from his own. Perhaps he was afraid to remind his Castilian employers that the name of Cabot had once raised diplomatic fears that the English would beat the Spanish to Asia.

There was also a major problem for his ambitions. The Northwest Passage was his objective, but the Spanish would never organize an expedition there, for fear that it would bypass their own empire in the Caribbean. So throughout his period as pilot major, Sebastian was feeling his way toward some scheme to go back to the open sea he believed he had glimpsed beyond the New World. In 1521 he engineered a visit to England, where he contacted Henry VIII's principal adviser Cardinal Thomas Wolsey, and convinced him secretly that the English should mount a new expedition for the Northwest Passage. The Merchant Venturers of London agreed to supply one ship and pay the crew, but they needed other investors in London, and here the scheme began to unravel. The drapers' and mercers' guilds held out, and we get a glimpse of the skepticism with which Sebastian was regarded in some London circles, complaining that he "was never in that land hym self." Their definite refusal culminated in an apt proverb: "He sayls not surely that sayls by an other mannys compass."

While he was in London, ostensibly on business for the Spanish court, he also put out feelers toward his native city of Venice, making a quiet contact through their representatives in England. But he returned to Seville without any reply from them, a deeply disappointed man.


Despite the knowledge of the Breton and Norman fishing fleets, now joining with the Basques, Portuguese, and English in the seasonal hunt for cod on the Grand Banks off Newfoundland, France had been slow to join in the business of western exploration. They had been too concerned with the great game in Italy to look in the other direction. But the Renaissance was moving north to France, partly because of their invasions of Italy, and with it came a belated interest in the New World. Something about the Renaissance went hand in hand with a fascination for America, because the continent on the other side of the Atlantic became symbolic of human possibility.

The new French king, Francis I, was a Renaissance man in all senses. He founded the art collection that eventually became the Louvre, while his mother—also a collector of Renaissance painting—nagged him about getting involved in overseas exploration. It was he who commissioned Leonardo da Vinci to construct a mechanical lion to enliven the latest peace talks in Italy, following his recapture of Milan in 1515 and then lured him to France and became his close friend. The great artist lived in a manor house called Clos Lucé near the royal palace at Amboise, and when he died in May 1519, it was said that he died in the arms of the French king.

This new awareness of the Atlantic brought the French into conflict with the Treaty of Tordesillas, which divided the world between Spain and Portugal. "Had our father Adam made them his sole heirs?" asked Francis, rhetorically, adding their monopoly on navigation to his quarrel with Charles V. He was determined to find his own shortcut to the spice islands, preferably outside the Spanish zone, and the obvious place to look was northwest. A powerful alliance of businesspeople and financiers in Dieppe, and silk importers in Florence, put together the funds for a French voyage of discovery. In 1524 the expedition sailed from Rouen led by the Florentine mariner Giovanni da Verrazzano.

Verrazzano was followed a decade later by Jacques Cartier, who had been one year old when Columbus first landed in the Americas, and who made three voyages, during which he founded the first French colonies in the Americas and coined the name "Canada" for the coast along the St. Lawrence River. The English claims to Newfoundland and its environs were allowed to lapse.

In August 1519, five ships under the Portuguese captain Ferdinand Magellan sailed from Sanlúcar de Barrameda on the mouth of the Guadalquivir, in search of the elusive southwest passage. Magellan had been to India with Almeida but had been accused of trading illegally with the Moors, and other misdemeanors, and was sent home. Most of the charges were dropped, but he was told he would not be employed again, and had therefore offered his services to the Spanish. He evaded a Portuguese squadron sent to intercept him, battled down the coast of South America, and finally located a passage through what are now known as the Magellan Strait, at the tip of what is today Argentina. He found out for himself the vastness of the Pacific Ocean and was killed in a tussle with locals on the beaches of the Philippines in April 1521, but his ship *Victoria* did finally circumnavigate the world. The questions that had been set by Columbus and Cabot were finally answered.

But at the beginning of the voyage, at the height of a storm off the coast of what is now Uruguay, Magellan is said to have shouted at his crew: "We cannot go back here, because this is as far as Vespucci arrived. We have to go beyond."

When the *Victoria* arrived back in Spain in 1522, under the command of his Spanish deputy Juan Sebastián Elcano, Sebastian Cabot was extremely worried. Revealing the existence of a Northwest Passage to foreign powers, as he had done, was one thing. But doing so secretly when Spain now had proven access to a rival southwest passage might look treasonable. He lived in terror that his mission to London was going to be revealed. If only he had not been so foolhardy as to mention the matter to the Venetians.

Some months later he was horrified to be approached in Valladolid by the Venetian ambassador, who brought a letter from the council in Venice asking for more details of his plan. As Sebastian read the letter, he went pale, begging the ambassador: "I earnestly entreat you to keep the thing secret, as it would cost me my life."

The news did not leak. Sebastian's secret was safe, for the time being. In fact, the emperor Charles V thought highly of him, and in 1526 asked him to lead a Spanish expedition to search for a more convenient southwest passage, convinced that Vespucci's original exploration of the River Plate had not gone far enough. The expedition was not a success. Sebastian irritated his subordinates by his secrecy and could not summon up the considerable willpower required to prosecute the expedition as determinedly as he needed to, perhaps because his heart lay farther north. He lost his flagship and was forced to send another of his ships, the *Trinidad*, under the command of his deputy, the Englishman Roger Barlow, home across the Atlantic to get reinforcements.

The reinforcements were never sent, Barlow was sent home by the English ambassador Sir Thomas Boleyn, and still Sebastian delayed.* Once more he faced dissension among the crew, furious at his indecision, and he returned without having discovered a new route to the Pacific. When he finally got there, he faced a judicial inquiry into the failure of the voyage and was sentenced to banishment in Morocco. As so often happened, the sentence was never carried out.

---

*Boleyn's younger daughter, Anne, was just then beginning a flirtation with Henry VIII that would end in their disastrous marriage.

Sebastian was becoming increasingly aware of the instability of his position. If he led an expedition and found any of these elusive passages, he
would have been showered with wealth. But if he failed to find one, he
would have been barred from further work in either Spain or England.
He had married again, Catalina de Medranao from Seville, but it was clear
there was little future in Spain for him, and even that future was likely to be
unpredictable. He clung to Seville for fear of what would happen to his
property there if he left, never wholly honest with anyone about his plans or
his past. The first volume of history by the Venetian historian Giovanni
Battista Ramusio described meeting a Mantuan man who had seen Sebastian some years before. Sebastian was said to have boasted that he knew a
shorter way to the Indies and had also sailed all the way down to Florida in
1496. It seems to have been a half-remembered conversation, and confused
Sebastian's voyage of 1508 with his father's earlier expeditions. This is the
basis of the story, which has endured, that Cabot claimed his father's discoveries. Ramusio may just have been remembering a distant conversation
rather inaccurately.

In any case, Sebastian was now very careful. His father's story was sensitive in Spain: if John Cabot had been attacked by Alonso de Ojeda, his son
would have uncovered the evidence in Seville. And since he spent most of
his life desperately talking up his own qualifications for further expeditions,
it seems to have been convenient, if not to actually claim he made the 1497
voyage himself, then to simply omit his father's name. Perhaps he retained
some animus toward his father after the 1498 voyage, or perhaps he never
really forgave him for failing to return. Sebastian spread confusion by being
the first to accuse Vespucci of falsely claiming to have discovered the New
World. Sebastian Cabot and Vespucci shared a common propensity for self-
promotion and exaggeration, and this may have irritated Sebastian particularly. In any case, Vespucci was dead and that made it difficult for him to
reply.

His reputation was then growing in England and, in 1547, the English
privy council sent the money for him to come home. Without telling his
Spanish employers, Cabot quietly left Seville, never to return, but pursued
by furious demands that he should be extradited back there. So Sebastian
found himself back in Bristol. It was a very different place than the city he
had left four decades before. Protestantism had swept through. The old

abbey was now Bristol Cathedral. There were no monks for the mayor to battle with, and the merchants were unexpectedly reticent about their style of religion. The Cabots soon moved again, to London, where Sebastian was given the title of grand pilot and a salary to go with it. He spent a good part of the next few years engaged in a wild scheme to send an Anglo-French expedition up the Amazon to take Peru from the rear, endless lawsuits in Seville and Venice to secure his family's property, and investing in voyages to Barbary and Guinea.

Being in England relieved his main fear. Nobody might listen, but at last he could speak freely about what he believed the shape of the world to be. There was no fear of arrest, no looming fear of a Moroccan exile. But it was hard to quite shake off his lifetime habit of affecting the deliberate air of one who keeps secrets, and he did not trust people to know the full truth about his own past. Only this time, the aura of mystery seemed to work in a way that it never did when he was a younger man. "The people of London set a great value on the captain's services, and believe him to be possessed of the secrets of English navigation," wrote the German ambassador to London about him.

Sebastian grew an impressive forked beard and became a respected figure in navigatory circles. He became a governor of the Muscovy Company, dedicated to searching for northeastern passages along the northern coast of Siberia, as well as northwestern ones. As late as 1550 he was applying for a reissue of his original 1496 patent from the boy king Edward VI, Henry VIII's sickly son. Our last glimpse of Sebastian is as an old man in 1555, coming on board a small ship on the Thames called the *Serchthrift* before it sailed in search of an Arctic passage to the East via Siberia.

> The 27 being Munday, the right Worshipfull Sebastian Cabota came aboord our Pinnasse at Gravesende, accompanied with divers Gentlemen, and Gentlewomen, who after that have viewed our Pinnasse, and tasted of such cheere as we could make them aboord, they went on shore, giving to our mariners right liberall rewards: and the good olde Gentleman Master Cabota gave to the poore most liberall almes, wishing them pray for the good fortune, and prosperous successe of the *Serchthrift*, our Pinasse. And then at the sign of the Christopher, hee and his friends banketted, and made me, and them that were in

the company great cheere; and for very joy he entered into the dance himself, amongst the rest of the young and lusty company.

It was no simple journey—Sir Hugh Willoughby's expedition had frozen to death on the coast of Lapland the previous year—and Sebastian was then about seventy-one. Around this time also, he was painted, holding a globe and a pair of dividers, the very model of an ancient mariner. But it was again a difficult time to be prominent in English society. Two years later Philip II, Charles V's son and Isabella and Ferdinand's great grandson, was in England, effectively including England in his vast empire by marrying Queen Mary, and was setting about the business of rolling back Protestantism. He was King of England for fourteen months and during that time he briefly canceled Sebastian's pension.

Sebastian died sometime toward the end of 1557. Characteristically, one of the last statements he made on his deathbed was that the ability to measure longitude—Vespucci's great claim—had been revealed to him by God.

Of all the main players in this story, Sebastian Cabot lived the longest, except for one: Bartholomé de las Casas. When Las Casas died in July 1566, there truly was a New World, with Mary Queen of Scots and Elizabeth I on their respective thrones. Francis Drake was already sailing the Spanish Main. Walter Raleigh—who would found the abortive Virginia colony at Roanoke—was then twelve years old, and William Shakespeare was two. A different world, but within living memory of Columbus's first landfall.

## II

*"All hail, and welcome, nation's of the earth*
*Columbia; a greeting comes from every state.*
*Proclaim to all mankind the world's new birth."*

PROFESSOR JOHN KNOWLES PAINE,
"Columbia March," 1892

Columbus died a wealthy man, despite his protests, but in some obscurity. The expansion of the empire in the Indies was going ahead with extraordinary energy without him. He was not from any of the Spanish nations, so his privileges—and the long-running legal actions by his family—were resented for different reasons by the Spanish establishment and the colonists. When the historian Francisco López de Gómara said in 1552 that the discovery of America was the greatest event since the birth of Christ, he did not give Columbus the credit.

The court cases had also confused the history. The Pinzón story and the sale of many of the key documents by Columbus's grandson Luis confused the picture still further. What revived interest in Columbus was the need for a founding hero by the revolutionary leaders of what was about to become the United States, and this was satisfied to some extent by a new concept: "Columbia." This referred to an idealized state of liberty and the pursuit of happiness, and it was used first in the *Boston Gazette* in 1775 by Mercy Warren, the wife of a revolutionary general. It was taken up by the first known African American poet, Phyllis Wheatley, in a poem that included the lines: "Fixed are the eyes of natives on the sails / For in their hope Columbia's arm prevails."

General Washington liked it, and Tom Paine reprinted it in his *Pennsylvania Gazette*. Columbia was emerging as an idea, associated increasingly with Columbus himself, of rebellion in the name of intellectual and political liberty. When a friend of Jefferson and Madison, Joel Barlow, wrote his *Columbiad* in 1787, it included Columbus dying in prison and vouchsafed a vision of the grandeur of America to come. Columbus was, in fact, beginning to be regarded as a figure like Galileo, a kind of proto-Protestant, who had defied both church and accepted wisdom by sailing into the unknown. He was therefore a fitting hero of the new revolutionary nation. Jeremy Belknap explained in his "Ode to Columbus and Columbia," for the third centenary in 1792, that Columbus had rebelled against a world where "Black superstition's dismal night / Extinguished Reason's golden ray."

Columbus was emerging from history again as a semireligious symbol in his own right, a savior who brought his own kind of Advent moment for the world by his discovery. Columbia was adopted as the name of the administrative district around the new capital city of the United States, and in 1819 revolutions in Latin America led to a new republic of Great Columbia, incorporating modern Ecuador, Venezuela, and Panama.

By then, there were historians on both sides of the Atlantic delving into the details of the real story of Columbus and his discoveries. In Spain a former naval officer named Martin Fernandez de Navarette was asked by King

Carlos VII to track down some of the documents that had been sold by Luis Colón, and to piece together the full story. The writer Washington Irving, author of *The Legend of Sleepy Hollow*, met him in Spain, was asked to translate some of his work, and used it as the raw material for the four-volume *Life and Voyages of Christopher Columbus*, which was published in 1828 and made his name.

It was hard work. When the naturalist Alexander von Humbolt traveled widely in North and South America two generations earlier, he said he could find not a single stone to commemorate Columbus. When the young Roman Catholic priest Giovanni Mastai-Ferretti did the same shortly afterward, he agreed: no statues, no memorials, nothing. Two decades later the doors to the U.S. capitol in Washington, D.C., depicted scenes from Columbus's life, and the young priest had become Pope Pius IX and was starting the process to make Columbus a saint. This bid limped on for three decades before it finally collapsed—not because of the slaughter that had happened as a result of his discovery, or any of the other ugly rumors of brutality, but because he was not married to Beatriz de Harana when Ferdinand Columbus had been conceived, and because he had diverted the reward money to her when it should have gone to the man who first sighted the New World in 1492.

Spain had also failed to erect any statue to Columbus for the first 350 years after his landfall, but marked its four-hundred-year anniversary by unveiling enormous monuments in Seville, Barcelona, Huelva, Salamanca, and Madrid. The Spanish government also designed and built replicas of the *Santa Maria*, the *Niña*, and the *Pinta* as a present for the American people.* Chicago won the chance to host a massive exhibition and it opened on May 1, 1893, in the presence of President Grover Cleveland and Columbus's heir, the Duke of Veragua, on 664 acres next to Lake Michigan, with forty buildings and 24 million visitors. It was the largest crowd—or so they claimed at the time—in the history of the world.

The rediscovery of Columbus in the United States meant a corresponding drop in Vespucci's reputation. Although there was no friction between Columbus and Vespucci in their lifetimes, those who were brought up on

---

*They were repaired for the 1912 silent film *The Coming of Columbus*, which also used the log of Columbus as a prop.

Washington Irving were irritated that Vespucci's name appeared to have been given to their continent. "Strange . . . that broad America must wear the name of a thief: Amerigo Vespucci, the pickle dealer at Seville," wrote Ralph Waldo Emerson, "whose highest naval rank was boatswain's mate on an expedition that never sailed, managed in this lying world to supplant Columbus and baptize half the earth with his own dishonest name."

Vespucci's reputation remained high in Italy, and particularly in Florence. In 1719 a tablet was erected on the Vespucci mansion there that referred to Vespucci as the "Amplifier of the World." It was also Italian historians who began to rescue his reputation. The idea that *The Four Voyages* was a forgery waited until 1879 even to be suggested. The case was not considered proven until the Florentine historian Alberto Magnaghi tackled the subject in 1926, though even as late as 1955 some biographers were still assuming Vespucci actually wrote it himself. If Vespucci had not claimed to have discovered America, it was time to look more closely at his life, and historians have been doing so ever since.

John Cabot's reputation was more difficult to recover because he had been almost entirely forgotten, partly because his son Sebastian seems to have edited him out of the narrative. A copy of the original patent to Cabot, the basis of the English claim to North America, hung on the wall in Whitehall Palace in Queen Elizabeth's day, but the careers of father and son became confused and soon the only known portrait of Sebastian was confused with his father too. It hung in Whitehall Palace in the reign of James I, and survived the fire which burned down the palace in 1698, but not the one that destroyed the Pennsylvania home of the congressman, lawyer, and author Richard Biddle in 1845. The confusion continues to this day. The Canadian post office used the portrait of Sebastian Cabot on stamps in 1997 to commemorate his father's achievement. Even in 2006 a major exhibition in Seville attributed the 1497 voyage to Sebastian.

By 1897, the fourth centenary of Cabot's landfall, scholars had begun to reconstruct his story, and a steady stream of documents began to come to light that added details to the story, culminating in the peculiar discovery of the John Day letter to Columbus in 1956, filed wrongly under "Brazil" in the Spanish archives. Just as Florence became the center for preserving the memory of Vespucci, so Bristol and Newfoundland became centers for remembering Cabot.

In Canada the leaders of the English community looked at the Columbus exposition in Chicago in 1893, jealous about the apotheosis of Columbus as a fearless, modern, and freedom-loving hero. They had been searching for some similar hero of their own to counter this growing nationalism from the United States. Moses Harvey, the pastor of the Presbyterian church in St. John's, Newfoundland, urged the Royal Society of Canada to claim Cabot as its founder and to celebrate him in the same way. "As surely as Columbus pioneered the way in the South," he wrote, "did the Cabots open a pathway to a far nobler civilization in the North."

The man he wrote to, the society's secretary, Samuel Edward Dawson, was skeptical about whether Cabot had even landed in Canada— Newfoundland was at that time not part of Canada—but he soon became the most enthusiastic advocate. "The English tongue was heard, of all the languages of Europe, the first upon this great continent," he wrote. But this was inflammatory in a nation with sizeable French and Italian populations, who firmly believed that it was Verrazzano and Cartier who were the founding navigators of their nation.

Three decades later, when the first Fascist party cell was formed in Montreal, they decided to hold a competition to encourage Italian Canadians to have pride in their Italian heritage.* The result of this, a decade later, was a statue of Cabot, forged in Florence and unveiled in Montreal in 1935. The Italian Canadian newspaper *L'Italia* celebrated with the headline HALF OF THE WORLD WOULD BELONG TO ITALY IF WE WERE TO CLAIM ALL THE LAND DISCOVERED BY ITALIANS.

But while Cabot was becoming a symbol of Italian achievement for Italian Canadians, he remained a symbol for the Canadian establishment of their different origins to the superpower south of the border. The United States had their founding heroes already, and had no need of symbols of staunch English values in Canada. But Cabot has more recently, and more oddly, become a symbol of Protestantism. Cabot was not English and he may have died before the word "Protestant" was even coined. Yet because he was not Columbus, and sailed from a country that would in one short generation be officially Protestant, he has been hailed more recently in

---

*A similar project was launched in the United States concerning Antonio Meucci, the Italian candidate for inventor of the telephone.

North America as the hero of those who see themselves as struggling against Roman Catholic conspiracies to defend American life. To this day, the main source of information on the Internet about Cabot's life is on a maverick Protestant Web site.

For the English, on the other hand, Cabot became in the twentieth century a comforting reminder of their own status as underdogs. Cabot had been marginalized by Columbus, just as Britain had been sidelined by the United States. His memory dovetailed neatly with the postwar mood of lost empires and economic recession. It also reinforced a link with Canada that had been strengthened by two world wars, and a memory that Cabot had probably sacrificed his life to build that link. In 1947, 450 years after Cabot's landing, a new model of Cabot's ship the *Matthew*, built to replace the one destroyed in the heavy wartime bombing of the city and docks, was unveiled in Bristol, and Bristol Cathedral was filled for the occasion with leading members of the Canadian armed forces. "Let us leave this cathedral, with all its historical association long before and long after John Cabot set sail," said the dean, Harry Blackburne, "with the thought in our hearts and minds that, God willing, we too will serve."

The most recent centenary was celebrated with new replicas of the *Santa Maria*, the *Niña*, and the *Pinta*—still moored near Palos—and of the *Matthew*, now moored in Bristol, but regularly traveling around the United Kingdom and Ireland and sometimes beyond. Expo 92 in Seville was the equivalent of the Chicago exhibition a century before, next to the river in Seville and including the site of the monastery that contained Columbus's second tomb.

Newfoundland, only part of the Canadian union since 1949, seized the initiative for the 1997 anniversary, announcing that the celebrations of Cabot's 1497 landing would be held there in June. The *Matthew* replica repeated the journey in forty-six days, arriving at Bonavista, Newfoundland, which was the official landing site chosen for the celebrations. On June 24, the *Matthew* was joined by a flotilla of nearly a hundred other boats, with Queen Elizabeth II and Prince Philip aboard one of them.

The difference between the end of the nineteenth century and the end of the twentieth is that Columbus has become a far more controversial figure in the Americas, just as the whole concept of "discovering" a continent that was already peopled has become more dubious. Columbus has been emerging as the very opposite of the enlightened "Columbia" and instead as a symbol of imperial presumption and oppression. Venezuela has renamed Columbus Day (October 12) as the Day of Indigenous Resistance. Columbus's statue was pulled down in Caracas in 2004. When Brazil celebrated the five-hundred-year anniversary of the arrival of Cabral in 1500, thousands of landless farmworkers and members of Brazil's indigenous tribes arrived at the same time, marching to Porto Seguro. They found the road blocked and were attacked by police with batons, tear gas, and rubber bullets, injuring 30 and arresting over 140. The discovery of the evidence of the cruelty of the Columbus brothers on Hispaniola given to Bobadilla, published for the first time in 2006, is likely to further undermine his reputation.

The truth is that all three figures, Columbus, Cabot, and Vespucci, remain symbols of different kinds of nationalism, depending on taste, all now deeply complex, so much so that it is still hard to get through all the layers to the truth. With some notable exceptions historians stick to their national icons without straying too far into the lives of their rivals, while the historical figures become political symbols that shift into different shapes for each generation.

Brazil was settled by the Portuguese, so it was Cabral's arrival they celebrated, partly because he was Portuguese and partly because the evidence that Vespucci sailed along the coast a year earlier is not absolutely clear-cut. One of the few places left in the world that celebrates the arrival of Vespucci is the island of Bonaire, in the Netherlands' Antilles, but even here Bonaire Day (September 6) every year is as much a political festival and an assertion of national unity for a tiny island as it is historic. Perhaps the depth of confusion and symbol is inevitable, if Francisco López de Gómara was right, and the accidental arrival of Europeans in America was indeed the most important event since the birth of Christ. And maybe it was.

# 10

# THE MEANING OF THE
# NEW WORLD

*"New islands, new lands, new seas, new peoples; and,
what is more, a new sky and new stars."*

PEDRO NUNES, *Treatise of the Sphere*, 1537

*"In discovering America, Europe had discovered itself."*

J. H. ELLIOTT

IN HIS SPARE moments between negotiating with Charles V in the Burgundian city of Bruges in 1515, the future chancellor of England, Thomas More, was writing what would probably be his most influential book. In just over two decades, he would be lying in prison awaiting execution for defending the rights of Ferdinand's daughter Catherine of Aragon against her husband, but for now he could afford to be a little satirical. He told his friend Erasmus that he had dreamed he was king of an island called Utopia. As he wrote up the result of this dream, he spent some time in the nearby city of Antwerp—the city that was replacing Florence as the European financial center—a new city spectacularly taking shape before his very eyes.

His Utopia is an island off the New World, shaped like an enormous crescent exactly the same size and on the same latitude as England, with a principle city remarkably like London, but with at least one massive difference:

In it there is no greed or pride. The streets are laid out in a sensible grid. The men and women dress alike and eat communally. Like Vespucci's Indians, they have no private property. They have never heard of Christianity and there are also no lawyers. More also imagines that there is no need for money, and safes are never locked. It is a place where there is so much gold that it is made into chamberpots and chains for slaves, and, when foreign ambassadors arrive in gold chains themselves, the Utopians mistake them for servants.

The story begins outside the brand new Antwerp Cathedral, where he sees a friend talking to a sunburned stranger with a long beard and cloak, who is introduced as a Portuguese traveler named Raphael Hythlodaeus. He describes him as a former shipmate of Vespucci's, who had gone with him on his last three voyages "of those four that be now in print and abroad in every man's hands." Like everyone else, More had devoured the forged letter of Vespucci to Piero Soderini.

*Utopia* was and still remains an ambiguous book. More was a humorist and was using this imaginary place to make fun of the people, institutions, and mores of those around him. He was making serious points about the way society ought to be managed. *Utopia* was originally called *The Best Condition of Society*. But he also set out to confuse and lampoon his readers. More occasionally hints that Hythlodaeus has made Utopia up, just as it was beginning to be agreed that Vespucci had made up some of his famous *Four Voyages*, and that *Mundus Novus* was not quite the whole truth about the discovery of America. The first of Vespucci's four voyages in that letter definitely never happened, and the fact that not even Hythlodaeus had been on that voyage may have been More's way of saying that he knew at least some of the real facts.

Just twenty-three years after Columbus's discovery, and eighteen years after Cabot's, the New World was entering into the imagination of European thinkers and reformers. It is the habit of idealists to grasp the next frontier, in geography as in technology, and proclaim that this time it will all be different. Europe may have sunk their own continent in a confusion of corruption and hypocrisy beyond unraveling, but there was a New World where humanity might have a fresh start.

The history of the Americas from the moment of discovery contains this same strand of idealism, from Columbus's excitement at the innocence of the Tainos to Vespucci's wonder at their simplicity, and the literature about the noble savage ever since. America, and especially revolutionary America, was born with this sense of hope for new beginnings and rational, tolerant social arrangements.

There were two problems with this. One was that the idealization of America by the European humanists meant that they blinded themselves to the complexity and diversity of what America actually was. The other problem was that the European settlement of America, the great project of the 1490s that led to the link between old and new worlds, was born out of a business venture. It was intended as profit-making, and it was monstrously profitable, though without benefiting those who took the original risk. It was a business proposition that gave Columbus and Cabot their edge. Other pioneers might have stumbled on the coastline across the Atlantic before they did, but Columbus and his colleagues had worked out a way to profit from it personally.

Then, tragically perhaps, what began as a business proposition for an equal trading relationship with the Asian powers—hence Columbus's letters of supplication to the Great Khan—ended with an unequal relationship with a continent that looked unowned, and seemed very much more like plunder. "License my roving hands, and let them go / Before, behind, between, above, below," wrote the English poet John Donne a century after Columbus's death, in his great seducer's elegy. But he then characterizes the victim of his seduction like this:

> "O my America! my new-found-land,
> My kingdom, safeliest when with one man manned,
> My mine of precious stones, my empery,
> How blest am I in this discovering thee!"

Historians will always debate how much the events described in this book were inevitable, but given the shape of the planet, there was bound to be a time when the mariners of Europe became so advanced in their technology and their conceptual thinking that they stumbled across America. The ferment of the end of the fifteenth century, and the burgeoning trade, with ships fifty times the size of the little *Matthew* plying their wares along Europe's politically complicated coasts, probably determined that it had to happen around the time it did. That was when Europe began to look westward and away from the advancing Turks and the closed markets of the East. If it had not been Columbus, Cabot, and Vespucci who set out the shape of the world to the west, it would have been one of their contemporaries, and history would now celebrate the names of Dulmo, Corte Real, or Fernandez the labrador instead. It could have been Martin Behaim, an equally complex character, both as well and as badly connected as Columbus.

"It is even a mortal question whether the two worlds would not have been far happier had they remained forever unknown to each other," said the great French Columbus scholar Henry Harrisse. But the possibility really doesn't arise. No alternative future was possible.

But the way that the Americas were colonized by Europe, while it was highly likely, may not have been absolutely inevitable. The fact that this colonization came about as an unexpected side-effect of a failed business plan, one which had to produce a profit—and its failure to do so—may at least have sped up the plunder. But these are marginal, almost theological, questions. The relationship between the old world and the new developed in the way it did partly because of the need for profit, but largely because Europe was driven by a similar motive. The innocent, hopeful, idealistic America was inevitably pushed aside by the seducer's because that was the way Europe was. Only in Vespucci's encounter with the "giants" of Curaçao do we get a glimpse of a more equal relationship that might have been.

The so-called Columbian exchange, the flora and fauna that passed from East to West and vice versa, had to come. The diseases that spread so rapidly—the smallpox that destroyed the Incas and the syphilis that ravaged Europe in return—had to happen in the same way. It may be possible to imagine a different combination of the awe, joy, and greed with which Europe pounced upon the Americas, but given Europe—given humanity perhaps—it is hard to imagine any other result.

Those in Europe today who rather smugly criticize America and American mores might consider that what made that continent—and what drove this story—is not the nature of America, but the nature of Europe. It was European values that built the continent which came to dominate the twentieth century. Now that it gives back some of that mixture of values—the idealistic New World as well as the drive for profit—it remains a mirror of the European world that created it.


It was the best of times; it was the worst of times. It was the golden hope of a brave new start for humanity, of new cultures of sophistication and tolerance; it was the cruel destruction of whole races, forests, and knowledge. It was the source of unparalleled wealth; it was the cause of impoverishment. It was the crucible of empires; it was the destroyer of nations. The collision between the Old World and the New was all those things.

Most immediately, it was the source of an extraordinary exchange between East and West of produce, flora, fauna, and know-how that took place over the following decades. Not all of this happened immediately. It was not until 1586 that the English adventurer Francis Drake is supposed to have seized a cargo of potatoes from what he believed to be a Spanish treasure ship from America, and caused their introduction into the European diet, especially among the poor.* There are rival stories that the first potatoes in Ireland, which was the first nation to embrace them as a food, washed ashore there from the Spanish Armada two years later.

Along with potatoes also came pumpkins, squash, peanuts, tomatoes, avocados, tobacco, papayas, mahogany, rubber, cocoa, and maize—from the Arawak word *mais* meaning "stuff of life." Like potatoes, maize took a roundabout route to Europe, seized by Barbary pirates preying on Spanish shipping and taken to Turkey, which meant it was known originally as turkey wheat (turkeys also came from the New World). Tobacco came to dominate the world's economies, despite the best efforts of England's King James I, whose pamphlet *A Counterblaste to Tobacco* was published in 1604. Cocoa plus sugar became chocolate. Chocolate was believed to have health-giving effects while tobacco was always known to be harmful. We know about their successors all too well: Cocaine arrived in the very late stages of the Columbian Exchange.

Going the other way were wheat, barley, almonds, mulberries, cherries, walnuts, apples, indigo, oranges, lemons, grapefruit, and rice—sent for the

---

*That same year, Queen Elizabeth I's chef is supposed to have cooked the potato leaves for her and thrown away the actual potato.

first time in 1512, the year Vespucci died. Most of these were undoubtedly enriching for both sides.

Perhaps it was the New World that gained most from the exchange of animals, when the descendants and successors to the few horses and cattle in the holds of Columbus's second voyage spread out across the continent. Horses had been extinct in the Americas for ten thousand years, but by the 1580s massive wild packs of them were storming north, and for the Indians who adopted them, they enormously broadened their conception of manageable areas and distances. Cattle ranching also expanded enormously during the same period, although not to the benefit of the indigenous population in the same way. Cattle became a product, like sugar and cotton, which was exported to the Americas to export back to the Old World. A century after Columbus, massive fleets carrying hundreds of thousands of cattle hides were making their way back across the Atlantic.

The enterprise of the Indies was born out of two men steeped in the European cloth trade, sailing from the cloth trade centers of Seville and Bristol, so it is hardly surprising that one of the exchanges from which Europe benefited was an expanded sense of color. The colors of the parrots and the plants staggered Columbus and Vespucci; all three pioneers sought out brazilwood and other dyestuffs. But they were particularly driven by the demand among Europe's merchant classes for ever more brilliant versions of red, and here the New World delivered after the conquistadores came across Aztecs selling cochineal in the marketplaces of Mexico in 1519. This was a dye so powerful and brilliant that it overshadowed all previous methods of making scarlet dye. Its source was kept obsessively secret by the Spanish, and it was still banned by the Venetians two generations later. The portraits of European rulers that followed gloried in the new reds. When the peasants of Germany rose in revolt in 1526, one of their demands was the right to wear red.

But of all the colors of discovery, it was the gold that had obsessed Columbus and the others above all. The staggering increase in precious metals flowing into Europe through Seville made Spain, for a while, the richest place in the world. Once vast silver deposits had been found in Bolivia in the 1540s, this process began to accelerate. But Spain was simply a staging post. The Spanish used this vast influx of money to buy the spices, silks, and Eastern luxuries they craved, and the silver and gold began to filter through those intricate networks of merchants that Cabot had failed to un-ravel in Mecca in 1485, and out to India and China. Often it found its way into the hands of merchants from Portugal and then England who had fol-lowed Vasco da Gama to the East in search of wealth. These were the days when a small sack of cloves brought back from there could set up a trader with a mansion outside London or Lisbon.

The silver and gold also filtered north, partly because of the activities of pirates who preyed on the Spanish convoys, and partly because of the con-sumption of dried cod on the Iberian peninsula. The English had also hoped for spices, silks, and gold from Cabot's voyages, and when all they got was a profusion of cod off the Newfoundland coast, they temporarily gave up the whole idea of serious exploration. In fact the European discovery of cod in the frozen north was to have even wider political implications, and, by the end of the sixteenth century, they were being hauled out of the North At-lantic at the rate of 200 million a year.

Two centuries after Cabot, when war broke out between England and France in 1689, it was a dispute about cod off Newfoundland that was at the heart of the dispute. By 1784 one English politician could say that the New-foundland fishery "was a more inexhaustible and infinitely more valuable source of wealth than all the mines in the world." The supreme irony was that the dried cod caught off Newfoundland in the centuries to come was beginning to earn the gold and silver from Spain that they were mining and transporting so laboriously from the New World.


If these were the long-term positive effects of Columbus, Cabot, and Vespucci, and their contemporaries, on that same side of the scales must be thrown the later history of the Americas—the struggle for democracy, the tolerance of the United States Constitution and its example to the world, the great culture of music, painting, and literature from the American Arctic to the Antarctic that has emerged in the centuries since, the grandeur of the landscape and its effect on the world, the experiments in living, and the lessons of liberty. Also the weight of American civilization in our own times, flung to the defense of Europe in two world wars, and the haven for the dispossessed of Europe in the centuries before. Whatever crimes may have been committed by North and South Americans since independence, none can quite outweigh those contributions to the world.

But the other side of the scales weighs heavily too, and perhaps heaviest has been the miserable cruelty with which the native Americans were treated in the north and the south; the destruction of their landscapes and cultures, their torture and enslavement, the murder of their families that goes on deep in the Amazon even today, as indigenous tribes come up against loggers or rubber-plantation bosses. The natives of both North and South America faced what amounted to a last stand as independent people in the 1870s, after which their mere existence has depended largely on the whims of the descendents of the European settlers and their economic interests. Though recent events in Bolivia and Ecuador suggest they may be making a political comeback.

Even by the time Las Casas was writing his books, he believed the discovery of America had led to the deaths of up to 40 million Indians. His figures have remained controversial ever since, but it was quite clear that a terrifying number had died, either from disease and poverty, or being forced to sell their children and their land to pay taxes—or from outright murder. There was a similar story in the north, where there was no record of royal concern, as there had been in Castile. The Fernandez brothers and their Bristol colleagues had brought back three Inuit men, presumably against their will. By the 1520s Giovanni da Verrazzano was taking an Inuit baby with him to Europe just to be able to demonstrate what it was like back home. By the middle of the century on Newfoundland, the Beothuk Indians were being hunted down and shot by official policy, on the grounds that they carried disease. Like the Tainos, they were extinct by the twentieth century.

The Spanish inherited the blame for what has been a continuing crime, a horrific blot on human history, and the Protestants of northern Europe justified their piracy against the Spanish empire partly by this "Black Legend" of Hispanic cruelty. But in some ways the northern settlers were worse. There was no enslavement and no conversion to Christianity that followed the early settlements in what is now Canada, because to the English-empire builders the Indians were less than human.

Here Vespucci was a key influence, from the precision with which he set out the nature of the indigenous people of the New World, as the intellectuals back home struggled to define their legal position. They were human. Vespucci lived among them and described them as fellow human beings. They were innocent and therefore not pagan, and having never heard of Christ, deserved tolerance. Vespucci the slave trader would not have encouraged profits from slavery, based on these descriptions. But he also described them particularly as owning nothing. the implication of this was that their status was like that of a European serf: they were bound to the land and therefore to the landowner. Vespucci may not actually have been an apologist for slavery, though he profited from the sale of American Indians, but he was, thanks to his definitions, an apologist for the notorious *encomienda* system, which dominated the development of Latin America.

It is true that had Columbus not arrived, the poor Tainos of Hispaniola would undoubtedly have been wiped out with equal cruelty by the advancing Caribs, who were themselves well practiced in the art of taking slaves, and also possibly eating their enemies. But the European colonization was done in the name of God, and with a cruelty and recklessness that implied that the New World was so far away, that neither God nor the colonial authorities could see the truth of what was happening. It was a cruelty meted out by colonists drawn from a class of adventurers who often were seriously in debt or former convicts, uncontrolled by anything approaching the rule of law.

It also paved the way for a new kind of industrial-scale slavery, bringing Africans to the New World to fuel the new industries and investments. In the quest for sugar, rubber, cotton, and tobacco on the new plantations, 10 million Africans were enslaved and shipped to the New World, to the great profit of Columbus's adopted home of Seville and Cabot's adopted home of Bristol, where the street names Whiteladies Road, Blackboy Hill still reveal the truth about how the proud mansions and broad avenues were paid for.

But the most ferocious result of the fusing of the two worlds was probably that great peril of any kind of globalization: disease. Europe encountered syphilis and polio in the New World, and it spread rapidly eastward. In return they brought smallpox, measles, diphtheria, plague, typhoid, cholera, and influenza, against which the native Americans had no resistance. The arrival of smallpox among the Aztecs was a major factor in the extraordinary conquest of Mexico by Cortés, just as it was a factor in the Christian conversion of the Indians, who watched this terrifying epidemic sweep through their communities while it left the Christian newcomers unharmed.

Also in this Columbian balance are the unintended consequences of the benefits to Europe of the encounter. The arrival of wheat turned the great grasslands of South America into wheat fields, and the great forests were felled and turned over to cattle ranching: By 1900 there were 20 million head of cattle in Argentina alone, displacing those who had lived there and threatening the ecosystems of the world. By the end of the twentieth century, cod was almost extinct from the Grand Banks off Newfoundland. The fate of the Amazonian rain forest—the guarantee of a temperate climate for mankind—now also hangs in the balance.

Having tamed the Atlantic, the European pioneers, with their shared terror of the wild, began the slow but inexorable process of taming the wildness they found in the Americas, making way for their ranches and plantations. And the final results of this still-unresolved process seem a frightening prospect for humanity itself.

The other peculiar side-effect emerged from the very wealth the Spanish dragged home across the ocean. Once the gold from the New World began pouring into Europe, it was used less as an investment in production and more for the purchase of Eastern luxuries from the Portuguese empire. This caused galloping inflation, which eventually came to ruin the Spanish empire itself. The silver and gold, which were the justification for empire at the beginning, were the seeds that guaranteed its eventual destruction.

By 1660 the amount of silver in Europe had tripled, Spanish money was worth a third of its value in 1505, and most of the fifths of this massive injection of wealth siphoned off by the Spanish kings had been frittered away to service debts incurred for their incessant European wars. Bankers profited but the Spanish crown did not. Worse, Spain soon forgot how to make things, believing that the import of money itself was sufficient for their economy. As much as 80 percent of the goods shipped from Spain to their new colonies had been imported from elsewhere in Europe. The business of money for its own sake, the sophistication of financial services, tends to price other productive businesses out of existence, and that was the corrosive effect it had on the Spanish economy.

The idea of gold had achieved a powerful grip on the European imagination. It wasn't just that it represented stability in a period of economic and political uncertainty in the days of Columbus, Cabot, and Vespucci, but it represented the secret heart of a body of esoteric knowledge that was suddenly popular in intellectual circles. The Renaissance fascination for forgotten classical wisdom and alchemical texts gave gold a mystery and luster that it had never quite attained before. Columbus used to insist that his men go to confession before collecting it. He even told Pope Alexander that he had found King Solomon's mines on Hispaniola. Pope Julius was treated in his final illness with molten gold. This religious fixation on gold, as well as the economic fixation, redoubled the inflationary confusion of the generations that followed. Gold—and therefore money—became more important than the wealth it represented, and so drove out productive wealth.

The inflation soon took hold across Europe, under the impact of Spanish spending. The more precious metal there was, the more bankers could extend their credit. The more interest-bearing debt was in circulation, the more power went to bankers and the more prices rose. Even in England, prices of manufactured goods had risen by 300 percent by the end of the sixteenth century, and food prices had soared by 700 percent.

Precious metals came to be the meaning of the New World for southern Europeans. (Northern Europeans were stuck with cod.) The silver settlement of Potosí came to be the largest city in the New World, and the silver convoys made their way first to Lima, then along the coast to Panama, across the land to Cartagena, then to Havana, and then home by convoy. These transport systems proved an overwhelming temptation to the adventurers of those European countries locked out by the Treaty of Tordesillas.

Ironically it was the gold and silver Sir Francis Drake stole from Spain on his circumnavigation of the globe, and which provided Queen Elizabeth of England with a profit of nearly 5,000 percent, that formed the basis of all British overseas investment. The great economist John Maynard Keynes described how the money was used to set up the Levant Company, and the profits from that to set up the East India Company, and that Elizabeth's forty-thousand-pound windfall at average rates of interest came out to the total of British investment in 1930, when he was writing. If the Spanish empire mined the money, its effects were widespread, far-reaching, and unpredictable.

I

*"The idiocy of the man who killed his goose that he might*
*get the golden eggs, was wisdom compared to the folly of*
*the European nations, in outraging and destroying the In-*
*dian races, instead of civilizing them . . . and the wonder-*
*ful variety of their natural productions which they would*
*have sent us in exchange."*

WILLIAM HOWITT, English quaker, 1838

The fall of Constantinople was one event that spurred the explosion of exploration in the 1490s. So was the development of navigation techniques
and technology, the emergence of the astrolabe and the caravel. But then so
was the Renaissance, and its fascination with classical knowledge. The first
texts of Ptolemy's *Geography* came to Europe via the Crusades, but it was the
Renaissance scholars who translated it in the generation before Vespucci,
and who made it available and so launched the fascination for cosmography
of which Toscanelli was such a pioneer. It is no coincidence that people like
Botticelli, Ghirlandaio, Michelangelo, and Leonardo da Vinci appear in
this story: the New World was a Renaissance project.

But the story described here is primarily about business. Columbus,
Cabot, and Vespucci were all in their own ways ambitious but rather unsuccessful merchants, determined to find a mixture of fame and wealth, but
primarily wealth, and armed with a method—at least Cabot and
Columbus—to profit by their discoveries that their rivals lacked. It was this
insight that made Columbus a true pioneer. Other people had gone to
America before, blown off course, glimpsing it through the mist, maybe
even settling there like the Vikings, but it was a business idea that made it
possible for Columbus to go there and to profit by it, and that made the risk
worthwhile.

That the model was flawed—Asia was not on the other side of the
Atlantic—does not take away from the fact that it was a business plan that
took him there in the first place. Of all the many ways in which Columbus
and Vasco da Gama shifted the course of history, even if such a shift was inevitable, the changes in the geography of business were probably the longest
lasting.

The discoveries of the 1490s meant that Europe was able to bypass the great markets of the Middle East, the vast selling spaces of Alexandria, Beirut, and Mecca where the people of East and West met through intermediaries to exchange their produce. By 1504 there were no spices available in Alexandria. Just as Amsterdam replaced Venice as the center of the sugar and spice trades, so the Middle East lost its defining economic role. The new Ottoman empire was expanding over a beach from where the economic tide had receded. And apart from the discovery of oil there in the twentieth century, the Middle East has never recovered from this devastating blow. The political consequences of their impoverishment, and the consequent economic marginalization of the heart of the Islamic world, are still being worked out today.

After business, the most immediate effect of Columbus and his contemporaries was the growth of empire. By accidents of birth, death, and dynasty, Spain had become a powerful European empire. The addition to this of the New World made it temporarily vastly wealthy and powerful, though that wealth began to seep eastward and northward. While Spain was seizing the new American continent, Portugal was tightening its grip on the East, capturing Malacca in 1511 and Goa in 1512, and placating the Medici pope Leo X by the timely donation of a performing elephant from India. For the first time, the economic interests of the Christian and Muslim world were wholly opposed, and it was important to the Portuguese that the pope not intervene in defense of the threatened Christian outposts in the Middle East.

But the Portuguese empire was to be even more short-lived than the Spanish, and was in decline by 1550. Portugal was too small a country to maintain an empire in Brazil as well as the East, and to provide the inspirational leaders they needed when only one in ten of those who went to administer and trade there ever returned home. The English did not immediately grasp the possibilities of empire until Sebastian Cabot was an old man, though the benefits of gold-earning cod were becoming clearer.

The third shift caused by the encounter with the New World was intellectual. The first interpretations of what was there came from an inevitably imperial mindset, which limited the understanding of Columbus and Cabot about what it was they were finding in the New World. Everything from the animals and plants to the people there had to be filed according to the existing European categories, though so much of it demanded new ones. But the possibility of a New World, a place where humanity could start afresh, began to filter through the intelligentsia, to emerge again through the centuries, especially in North America, with new ways of thinking and organizing. The New World implied that other ways were possible.

There is no doubt that the sudden discovery that a large part of the earth's landmass had lain beyond their knowledge all that time did shift the way people thought. Before Columbus and his contemporaries, arguments about the shape of the world were theological. After Columbus, they were based on experience. When four centuries later, after the 1893 World's Columbian Exposition in Chicago, the adventurer Joshua Slocum sailed solo around the world, he was approached by three Boers in Durban who asked for his help to prove the world was flat. "They seemed annoyed when I told them they could not prove it by my experience," he wrote later. That was the shift that happened: from henceforward, with some hiccups along the way, humanity would progress their knowledge according to what their senses told them, and would make the traditions of the ancients subservient to that.

These major effects on the lives of the generations that followed Columbus, Cabot, and Vespucci continue to reverberate today. But telling this story has been a historical experiment in its own right, weaving these disparate tales together as they were originally lived. Doing so has cast light on different aspects that perhaps have not been emphasized enough before—the international nature of the journeys of exploration, the business idea at the heart of them, and of course the continuing uncertainties about the details of what happened. But there are other conclusions we might draw as well.

The destruction of the Tainos, and other Indian peoples later, derives from a misunderstanding about wealth and value—a common misunderstanding that remains the besetting sin of the business world. Columbus's fixation on gold, and the fixation of those who followed him about financial profit, blinded them to the value of what they found in the New World. They saw a land that could be exploited only in terms of plantations or extraction, and did not see what they could have learned. It was immediately an unequal encounter, where the charm of the natives gave way quickly to irritation that they were not faster in their extraction of gold. Columbus believed they were ignorant about the real value of things, and wrote about the "trifles" he exchanged with them; he was actually deluding himself about real worth.

We do not know Cabot's attitude, but Vespucci's betrayed some of the same naiveté. "As soon as he got the hawk's bell," he wrote about one innocent native who handed over a thousand ducats worth of pearls in return, "he put it in his mouth and was off into the wood, and I did not see him again." It was almost as if the failure of the natives to grasp what was, in fact, a mistake about value, was a justification for enslaving them.

This is not just pious rhetoric about learning from the ways of the noble savage. The failure of the early settlements in the New World, and the struggles of those that survived, demonstrated just how much the settlers needed to understand about local agriculture. Indian plant breeding also seems to have been more sophisticated than that of Europeans at this time. They had a better understanding of practical obstetrics and pharmacology. Only in the late twentieth century have we come to understand the cornucopia of medical knowledge and pharmacological possibility hidden in the rain forest species that are fast disappearing as we study them day after day. Ironically, pharmaceuticals were emerging in Europe at exactly the same time, but as an underground movement in opposition to the medical profession, calling for a "chemical revolution" that would give medical knowledge to ordinary people.

It is true that as well as the new plants, Columbus brought back the idea of the hammock, which simply emphasizes how little he and his contemporaries learned, compared to what they could have.

One other business lesson, perhaps, is the power of international regulation. The eight negotiators of the Treaty of Tordesillas, who decided the ownership of the planet in a small Castilian village in the summer of 1494, drew a line down the middle of the Atlantic, which drove the competing powers to develop their knowledge about their own designated slice of ocean. They succeeded in keeping the peace by doing this, but it also drove forward the pace of discovery. A major motivation for Columbus's later voyages and for Vespucci's was to ascertain exactly what the line meant in practice.

Yet because it took no account of any nation except Castile and Portugal, it also inadvertently encouraged the growth of piracy, first by the

French and then the English in the West, and by the Dutch in the East, as they challenged the Spanish and Portuguese empires respectively. The regulations protected the original innovators but drove a kind of terrorism two generations later, which saw Drake burning the settler city of Cartagena. It is no coincidence that Drake's bloodiest outrages coincided with the temporary merger between Spain and Portugal. There were virtually no alternative options open to other nations when all the rights to the world had been vested by the pope in one rival.

There is another, more disturbing, lesson about regulation. What the authorities were not able to do was to prevent the cruelty and the bloodshed, and there is no doubt the Spanish authorities tried, and that for all their complaints about Spanish barbarism, the English barely did. (Though it was the British who took the lead to end the slave trade three centuries later.) Las Casas persuaded the Spanish rulers to act against slavery in the New World, but again and again, they were too far away to do so and were defeated by the intransigence of the colonists. As early as 1514, the Medici pope Leo X argued that both nature and the Christian religion cried out against slavery. Yet the slavery continued, along with the most brutal cruelties.

European rulers in the next generation were about to develop the concept of "religious freedom," which meant the right to impose *their* religion on their subjects. In the same way, the first concept of freedom in America— the one that led in the end to the overthrow of the Spanish empire—derived from the right to treat "our" Indians as we see fit.

Maybe if the Spanish had wanted to enforce humanitarianism enough, or if the English had wanted to enforce it at all, they could have done so. But it was probably beyond their power. We have become accustomed in our own century to believe we can prevent any abuse across the world. But this story is evidence of just how difficult that can be.


Despite this, there is still a hopeful message here. It is the extraordinary achievements of which human ingenuity is capable. In 1492, when Columbus set sail from Palos, Europe worked with a geography of the world that assumed Jerusalem was the center of an amorphous landmass surrounded by ocean—where the spherical nature of the earth was a generally accepted truism that nobody had actually tested. Just two decades later, with the return of Magellan's ship *Victoria* from his circumnavigation, the basic shape of the globe was finally clear. There were landmasses that remained shadowy on the atlas, but America, the Pacific, Africa, and India now all took their correct shape, and all because of the temerity of a handful of pioneers who had traveled those sea routes themselves.

It was done with few resources and originally by a handful of adventurers on the margins of mainstream business and navigation. What is more, the foreign and trade policies of the nations involved adapted over and over again in that short space of time to meet the new challenges of new discoveries and new questions. New institutions were created and tested to drive forward more knowledge. Europe and its governments and institutions—and of course its mariners—were able to make gigantic intellectual and scientific leaps in the space of a generation. Those doubters today, who wonder whether humanity can adapt fast enough to meet the challenges it faces, might look back on Columbus, Cabot, Vespucci, and the others, and those that made their voyages possible, and realize that if the will is there, and if our leaders agree at least to let it happen, then massive and peaceful intellectual and practical revolutions are possible.

So when we tell the story of these three merchant venturers, we see not just blindness and cruelty, but also courage and determination. That is what the story says about human beings and particularly about Europe—because this is a story primarily about Europe: that all these qualities exist and we need to work with them. We have to make sure that our courage includes the presence of mind and self-knowledge to look into the unknown future and to see things as clearly as we can. In many ways, Columbus, Cabot, and Vespucci, for all their flaws and vanities, created the modern world, and we need to learn from their mistakes and borrow from their courage, so that we can push forward into the unknown ourselves.

# POSTSCRIPT
## STARS AND STRIPES

*"If that Americo Vespusio who discovered those western
Indies which the geographers deem to be a fourth part of
the world became so famous in the doing, that all that land
is called America after him . . . how much more reason
could this part of Asia which this valiant captain of ours
discovered be called Gama."*

DIOGO DO COUTO, speech to Goa municipal council,
around 1600

*"Then came a great shout from the flag . . . I am whatever
you make me, nothing more."*

SPEECH BY FRANKLIN LANE, U.S. secretary of the
interior, Flag Day 1914

BY THE YEAR 1908, four centuries after these discoveries, the Spanish empire was a half-forgotten memory. The British empire, which succeeded it, was at its most-pompous zenith, its characteristic pink on its atlases marking a quarter of the world, including India, Canada, and parts of the Caribbean. On May 21 that year, in the polite Bristol suburb of Clifton, a genteel outpost above the great gorge through which Cabot sailed to America, a local architect and church restorer named Alfred Hudd rose to address the local antiquarian society with a discovery he believed would turn the history of Columbus and Cabot upside down.

Hudd was an enthusiast for the emerging history of medieval Bristol, and it was his detailed research into the marks medieval merchants used to distinguish their shipments that had led him to the theory on which he was about to expound. The merchant mark belonging to the Bristol trader and former customs officer Richard Amerike, or ap-Meric, had made him wonder whether the prevailing theory about the origins of the word "America" was correct.

If Amerike had backed Cabot's voyage, was it not reasonable to suppose Cabot had returned the favor by naming the new continent after him? Maybe hidden on that furtive map of Cabot's 1497 voyage, copied by John Day and sent to Columbus in Seville, was that very word, which filtered eventually through to Waldseemüller and his famous map. Maybe Waldseemüller's explanation about taking the name from Amerigo Vespucci was an ambiguous translation, and that what he meant was that he believed that "Amerigo" was the origin of a word he had already seen on other maps. This is the heart of what might be described as the English conspiracy theory.

Nearly every European nation has its own conspiracy theory about the discovery of America. The Portuguese theory talks about evidence that John of Portugal knew of Brazil before 1492 and that Columbus was a double agent in his pay. The Danish conspiracy theory invokes the voyages of John Scolvus, and the secrets of the Vikings that Columbus heard in Iceland. There are Spanish conspiracy theories (Alonso Sanchez, the mysterious pilot who gave Columbus a map before dying). There are Basque conspiracy theories and even Jewish conspiracy theories. Many of them have added considerably to the knowledge about the period and contain more than an element of truth. When Hudd was at work the English conspiracy theory was already emerging around the Bristol voyages from 1480. There was considerable evidence, set out most recently by the historian David Quinn, that Bristol merchants and fishermen had indeed secretly been to the American coast before Columbus. But the Amerike connection added an extra frisson: the possibility that the continent itself might have been named after a Welshman.

Amerike himself died in 1505 and his estate above the gorge was inherited by his daughters, one of whom—Johanna Broke—is buried in St. Mary Redcliffe church in Bristol, just near the tomb of the owner of the *Trinity*, John Jay, and the shipping magnate William Canynges. The difficulty about

The Amerike coat of arms

the Amerike theory is that it is reasonably clear how Waldseemüller developed the name America, because he explains how he did so. This does not rule out a slightly different translation of Waldseemüller's explanation but, even so, the idea that it was called after Amerike is a more complicated theory than the one we have. For the time being, at least, without further evidence, we have to assume that the continent was indeed named after Amerigo Vespucci, and probably without his knowledge.

But then there was a peculiar twist to the whole story. The Amerike coat of arms is available in descriptions of his daughter's tomb and is also in the Lord Mayor's Chapel, just across from what is now Bristol Cathedral, but which in Cabot's day was the abbey. His coat of arms was, bizarrely, the stars and stripes. The stripes were yellow and blue and the stars were white on a red background, but even so it is a peculiar coincidence.

That is almost certainly all it is, though it is a coincidence that has fed the English conspiracy theory over the years. Every citizen of the United States of America knows the story of how Betsy Ross was commissioned to design their new revolutionary flag in 1777. But in fact, although Amerike's stars and stripes must be a synchronistic twist of history, there is in fact a link between the famous Stars and Stripes of today and the days of Columbus and Cabot, and it reveals a central truth about the whole story.

On the morning of December 3, 1775, moored on the Delaware River in Philadelphia harbor, Lieutenant John Paul Jones raised for the first time the naval flag of the revolutionary states on the quarterdeck of his ship the *Alfred*. It was known as the Grand Union Flag, and contained thirteen horizontal red and white stripes, with a Union Jack in the top corner. *Alfred* had been the merchant ship *Black Prince*, which had already plied a brief career between America, Bristol, and London, and was one of the five ships in the new United States Navy. The first ship was called *Columbus* and the second *Cabot* "after Sebastian Cabot," said a contemporary newspaper, rather inaccurately, "who completed the discoveries of America made by Columbus." The flag had been commissioned by Jones from a local milliner named Margaret Manny, with cloth charged to the account of the *Alfred*. The question is: where did Jones and Manny get the design?

The answer is, almost certainly, that the horizontal red stripes came from the flag of the British East India Company, known as "John Company's Gridiron," which was identical. Exactly how Jones came to choose this flag has never been verified, but he was an experienced sailor himself, who had trained as a midshipman and mate on voyages to the West Indies. The *Alfred* must also have had a full complement of flags of convenience, for visiting foreign ports, and he may have had something similar on board already. The East India Company had been banned from using their red and white striped ensign outside Indian waters, but they continued to use it when they were attacking or resisting pirates. Many English merchant ships had used red and white striped flags in the reign of Queen Elizabeth, and a century or so later were only allowed to do so in those specific circumstances. My suggestion is that Jones knew the implications of the flag—it implied an aggressive challenge—and he chose it for that very reason.

In fact, striped ensigns were carried by ships of many nations and ports by the eighteenth century. The flags of Tunis, Wismar, and Bremen included red and white horizontal stripes. French merchant vessels flew blue and white horizontal stripes, and Portuguese ships flew green and white stripes. The East India Company originally flew their red and white stripes with a red cross in the corner, the St. George's Cross for England—the same emblem flown by ships from Genoa. They eventually dropped the cross because it upset the Japanese. They seem to have chosen the red and white stripes to distinguish their ships from those of the Portuguese, who licensed local ships in India in the sixteenth and seventeenth centuries using their green and white striped ensigns. It is possible that Vespucci's second great voyage, along the coast of South America, flew under just such a striped Portuguese flag.

There is some knowledge, too, about the flags used by Columbus and Cabot. Columbus carried the royal flag of Castile and flags of his own design, which had a green cross with the initials F (Ferdinand) and Y (Is-

The flag of the British East India Company

abella) on either side of it, and a crown above each letter. Cabot used the royal standard of England, and the flags of Venice and the pope, when he landed in 1497. But wander through the Alcazar in Seville today, and look at the sixteenth-century paintings of ships heading to the New World, and it is immediately clear that horizontal red and white stripes were a feature of Spanish shipping all the way back to Columbus's generation. The famous painting *Virgin of the Navigators* shows at least one ship flying this flag from the stern. But here the trail back into history to find the origin of these elusive red stripes goes cold.

Was it adopted, as in India, to distinguish Spanish ships from Portuguese? Did it borrow the red and white stripes of the Austrian flag part of the legacy that the Hapsburgs brought to the Spanish coat of arms—a faint memory of the bloody surcoat of Duke Leopold of Austria fighting on the walls of Acre in 1191? Was it actually related to the red and yellow stripes of Aragon? Was it just because stripes had become a tradition for mariners at the time? Many paintings of contemporary galleys in the Mediterranean at the time have striped awnings over their quarter decks. But since the flag in *Virgin of the Navigators* is so definite, it is much more likely to be by deliberate design, even if it was an informal one.

There were no set rules for flags in those days. There is even evidence

The flag of Ferdinand and Isabella

that Portuguese merchant vessels were wearing red and white horizontal stripes by the eighteenth century, in which case the flag seems to have come rather informally to refer to ventures to the Indies, both Western and Eastern. But beyond mere tradition, there are some possible explanations.

It may have come from Ferdinand's coat of arms, part of which included red and white horizontal stripes, borrowed from the house of Anjou, the previous rulers of Naples, when Aragon began its rule over that city in 1442. The Anjevins, in turn, added red and white stripes from the Hungarian royal coat of arms when they married into that family. It may be that, in searching for distinctive flags that demonstrated Aragonese power in the Mediterranean, red and white stripes were seen as an appropriate weapon.

But there is another possibility. The powerful figure of Bishop Fonseca, Columbus's implacable enemy, and the man who dominated and controlled the early shipping to the New World, was related to the Hungarian royal family. Perhaps the red and white stripes were originally his innovation—a cheeky reference to his own origins, which were defensible because of their other connotations. In which case, it was Fonseca who sent those ships so symbolically to the New World with the stripes fluttering from their masts.

How those red and white stripes came to be adopted then by the British in India and from there by the new revolutionary states of America is unclear now, and probably always will be. But it does say something about the international nature of the story of Europe's arrival in the New World. The end of the fifteenth century was a time when national identity was still fluid and had more to do with loyalty to rulers than to frontiers. The perilous risks of the enterprise of the Indies were taken largely by stateless mercenaries, from the city-states of Italy, acting for monarchs who were only just developing the idea of nationhood around them.

We have lived through centuries of nationalism where this kind of confusion of national identity seemed incoherent—where every European nation needed their own conspiracy theory about how they got to America first. Now we are in an age where national boundaries are once again more fluid, and where national identity is harder to pin down. The idea that the flag of the United States has a hidden history that stretches back, via the original pioneering navigators, to medieval Naples or Hungary, might allow us to understand the polyglot history of discovery a little more clearly.

# Acknowledgments

I went to school in Bristol, and spent more weekends than I care to remember on the Clifton Downs, staring into the gorge, two hundred feet below, through which Cabot set out across the Atlantic. On my very first day in the city, the steamship *Great Britain* returned on the last leg of its journey from the Falklands Isles. Because of that, I should have been aware of the maritime heritage around me, and of Cabot in particular, but I don't think I was.

It was decades later that his story caught my imagination. I have always been fascinated by powerful characters who have somehow slipped through the sieve of history, the details about them and those around them lost, leaving us to discern the truth—and imagine the color—as much from the shadows on the wall as from the facts.

But there are still traces of Cabot in Bristol: St. Nicholas Street, where he lived, is rather disheveled, but it is there. So is the medieval St. Nicholas Market nearby, and the church where he worshipped. The dock the *Matthew* probably sailed from was filled in during the twentieth century to make way for a tram interchange, but you can imagine it and walk along its edges.

In the same way, you can still see the house where Vespucci grew up in Florence, and at least the street where he died in Seville, still next to the medieval tower by the river he knew so well. Cadiz, Lisbon, Huelva, and Southampton still remain, though scarred by twentieth-century-traffic horrors like the motorway that soars above the waterfront in Genoa, where Cabot and Columbus were born. Even the tram interchange in Bristol is now a traffic island.

But of all these sites, probably the most peculiar and atmospheric, though in an unexpected way, is Palos de la Frontera, from where Columbus sailed in 1492. The harbor has long since become silted up and is home to a series of small ramshackle market gardens. The dockside, "improved" for the 1992 celebrations, is now cracking and overgrown. Exploring Palos with my father, and discovering the Pinzón family home just up the road, and wandering around Seville where all three central characters fleetingly came together, was one of the most enjoyable periods of researching this book.

In fact, my father's support, translation, and widespread reading has been so enthusiastic that I suspected, by the end, he knew more about many aspects of the subject than I did, and I am enormously grateful to him—for this and for the trip—and dedicate the book to him. I couldn't have written it without him.

One of the peculiarities of the research for this book was that every nation involved has its own traditions, convictions, and even spellings. At the time, those involved used generic or Latin versions of their own names, or—like Columbus—changed them completely. Instead of deciding to use one language rather than another, I have tried to call all those involved by the usual styling of their name in the English-speaking world: thus it is Columbus, Cabot, and John of Portugal, but Amerigo and Bartholomé de las Casas. It may not work for the purists, to whom I apologize, but it does at least have the virtue of being simpler.

I would also like to thank Evan Jones from Bristol University, who read most of the manuscript, and whose criticisms were incisive and invaluable, and without whose guidance this book would have been very much poorer. I didn't always take his advice, I fear, so any mistakes that remain are mine. Also Glyn Redworth, for his excellent historical advice, Silvia Evans for all her research in Genoa and help with Italian sources, Tatiana Villegas for her fascinating conversation and book loans, John Ormond for reading some of the chapters and helping with the background material on the Renaissance, Felipe Fernandez-Armesto for answering my out-of-the-blue peculiar queries, Alex Macgillivray for his advice and his inspirational book *A Brief History of Globalization*, Sandra Stokes for reading the whole manuscript as it was written, Andrew Simms for his excellent ideas, and Gill Paul for her editorial reassurance. Thanks also to Rob and Roger and the crew of the *Matthew* for everything I learned sailing with them up the Bristol Channel. Also, as always, my mother and stepfather for reading the early chapters and encouraging me, and for everything else.

I could not have written the book either without the help of the staff at the London Library, the British Library, the Matthew Society, and the Naval Museum in Madrid. Or without the support and encouragement of my agent, Julian Alexander, my publisher, George Gibson, and my tireless and brilliant editor, Michele Lee Amundsen, all of whom I especially want to thank for their belief in this project from the beginning and all their efforts to make it better.

But the biggest thanks must go to Sarah, Robin, and William (born during the final chapter), for their love, patience, ideas, tolerance, and fun during the writing of the book.

# Notes

Books that are fully cited in the bibliography are cited here by author's name and in the case of an author having more than one book listed in the bibliography, by title, sometimes in shortened form. All other works are fully cited here.

## Prologue: Setting Sail

**ix** "One glass is gone": The Royal Navy, famously conservative, kept time with half-hour glasses until 1839.

**1** On August 6, 1497: A replica of the *Matthew* was built in Bristol in 1997 and remains a seagoing vessel and open to the public. See www.matthew.co.uk/home/home.html.

**3** The last few years have: see D. Quinn, *European Approaches to North America*, pp. 32–33.

## 1: Paradise Lost

**5** "There will come a time": Tiphys was the pilot of the Argonauts. Thule is generally agreed to have been the ancient name for Iceland. See also: D. Clay, "Columbus' Senecan Prophecy," *American Journal of Philology*, Vol. 113, No. 4, Winter 1992: 617–20.

**5** "The world is fair": Walther von der Vogelweide as quoted in G. G. Coulton, p. 253.

**6** Behind them waited the great city: the classic account of the fall of Constantinople is in S. Runciman.

**7** He flung off his imperial insignia: Constantine's death is described in S. Runciman, p. 144.

**8** One of them, Cardinal Isidore: Cardinal Isidore was one of those who played a leading role in the efforts to reunite the Catholic and Orthodox churches. His escape is described in S. Runciman, p. 141.

**9** As early as 1347: For more on John VI's diadems see S. Runciman, p. 5.

**10** The Ottoman advance: The growth in trade is described in P. Spufford, especially pp. 385–89.

**10** This susceptibility to borrowing: Fugger used to employ a personal fortune teller to advise on investments. His silver monopoly is described L. Jardine, p. 111.

**12** "When you perceive the miserable corruption": quoted in K. Sale, pp. 29–30.

**12** "I think I have given myself more honor": For new attitudes to wealth see H. Baron, pp. 158–257.

**12** The inspirational preacher Thomas Couette: described in D. Hay, p. 321.

**12** The Quentin Matsys portrait: The description of the portrait of Erasmus is from L. Jardine, p. 33.

**13** "Men sooner forget the death of their father": quoted in Machiavelli's *The Prince*, Chapter 17.

**15** The way through to the Silk Road: For descriptions of Genoa in the 1450s see, particularly, S. A. Epstein.

**16** When the news: John Cabot is traditionally believed to have been born in 1449, supported by the fact that he joined the Scuole Grandi in Venice in 1470, when he was twenty-one and had children while in his early thirties, which is not unreasonable to assume. But the simple fact is that we really don't know his date of birth. See J. A. Williamson, pp. 33f.

**17** There are even some rumors: In 1837 the English historian Rawdon Brown established that Cabot was indeed Venetian. But many years later, in his own copy of the book he wrote on the subject, he scribbled two marginal notes, which said that in 1855–56 he had found documents in the Venetian archives that proved Cabot came to Venice in 1461 and married a Venetian, but was by birth an Englishman. These documents have never come to light. See J. A. Williamson, *The Cabot Voyages*, p. 139.

**17** "Genoese like Columbus": See J. A. Williamson, *The Cabot Voyages*, p. 228.

**17** "son of a Genoese": See J. A. Williamson, *The Cabot Voyages*, p. 140.

**18** There are hints that the family: If Guilo Cabot was involved in the salt trade, it would explain why he went to Venice. The Venetians rival in salt production and export and would have welcomed his insider knowledge. See P. Macdonald.

**20** Life in Genoa was dominated: Genoa's political divisions are from G. Granzotto, pp. 22–23.

**21** Sometime between: Nobody has proven beyond doubt that Cabot and Columbus ever met, but the circumstances suggest they did. They were almost the same age, born in the same city, and went into the same profession. That they were both members of families affiliated with the Fregoso clan is my assumption based on the fact that the Cabots left Venice when the Fregoso cause collapsed, but if that is correct that would be more evidence. A family called Caboto had strong links to Savona when the Columbus family was there. They both also frequented the dockside at Lisbon at the same time, and—as has become clear only recently—they were both plunged into debt at the same time. It is the argument in this book that this debt was incurred in part as a consequence of an early phase of a joint enterprise involving the Indies. The respected expert on northern Atlantic exploration, Professor David Quinn, argued for a definite connection between the two men. See D. Quinn, pp. 32–33.

**22** "In the city of Genoa, I have my roots": See, for example, S. E. Morison, *Admiral of the Ocean*, p. 8. But since the recent discovery of Bobadilla's evidence shows that contemporaries were complaining that he was a weaver's son from Genoa, the accepted story of his birth seems more secure.

**22** The tiny house has consistently disappointed visitors: H. Harrisse, *Cristoforo Colombo*, p. 176.

**24** The family made the difficult and risky decision: The evidence that Cabot and his family moved to Venice in 1461 comes primarily from documents that confirm John Cabot was granted full Venetian citizenship in 1476, since newcomers to the city had to wait fifteen years before they could become citizens. See J. A. Williamson, *The Cabot Voyages*, pp.190–91.

**25** Amerigo Vespucci was born: This date comes from Vespucci's baptism record in F. J. Pohl, p. 14. There is a slightly different account of Vespucci's birth in F. Fernandez-Armesto, *Amerigo: The Man Who Gave His Name to America*, p. 18. The details of a previous deceased brother called Amerigo are in this same book, pp. 17–18.

**25** Amerigo was named after the young Leonardo da Vinci: A. V. G. Arciniegas, p. 26.

**30** "Bright shining star": E. L. S. Horsburgh, quoted in A. V. G. Arciniegas, p. 35.

## 2: MAPS

**32** "Our land is the home": Letter from Prester John in S. Baring-Gould, pp. 38–46.

**32** "Map me no maps": Quote from Henry Fielding's 1730 play *Rape upon Rape*, Act 1, Scene 5.

**33** The legend of Prester John: See N. Jubber.

**34** One of the new printed editions: The quotations from Marco Polo are in J. S. Collis, pp. 16–21.

**35** Or the legend of St. Brendan: See G. R. Crone, pp. 15f.

**36** One by one, each voyage pressed farther south: The navigators had a rhyme about the perils of passing Cape Non, or Cape Nun, as it is now called. "When Cape Nun hoves into sight, turn me back, lad—or else goodnight!" B. Keen, p. 56.

**37** Toscanelli was the grand old man: See F. J. Pohl, pp. 20f. It is not absolutely certain that Giorgio Vespucci introduced Toscanelli to his nephew, but it seems highly likely that he did. Vespucci's employer, Lorenzo di Pierfrancesco de' Medici, also had Giorgio as a tutor, and as a result understood some cosmography (F. Fernandez-Armesto, *Amerigo*, p. 20), and it seems likely that this is what began Vespucci's fascination as well.

**38** In the 1460s: See A. Vallentin, p. 22.

**38** With Toscanelli he saw: Toscanelli, who had spent time in Rome in his youth, must have known that successive medieval popes had appointed bishops to oversee the spiritual needs of Markland and Vinland. See F. J. Pohl, p. 21.

**39** "If you knew": Quoted in J. J. Norwich, p. 103. Galeazzo Maria Sforza was assassinated in church in 1476 in Milan, and then dismembered and eaten by the hungry crowd.

**39** At first it was the salt trade: See P. Spufford. There is little evidence about Guilo Cabot's activities, but some authorities list the salt and spice trades (see, for example, P. Macdonald). If the Cabots were involved in salt—the source of great rivalry between Genoa and Venice—it might partly explain why they were welcomed to Venice so enthusiastically.

**40** This was a city so bound: It is hard to be absolutely definitive about the Cabot family home, but tradition points to one mansion on the corner of the via Garibaldi—though the via Garibaldi was then a canal.

**40** He signed his name: See E. Giuffrida, in R. M. Zorzi, p. 61.

**40** He must also have frequented: See P. F. Brown in H. A. Abrams, p. 136.

**41** Not just any club either: See E. Giuffrida in R. M. Zorzi, p. 62. It can only be speculation as to what catapulted Cabot to membership of such a prestigious club. If he was older than twenty-one, he may, of course, have simply had his name down on the waiting list for years. But the circumstantial evidence not only indicates that he was relatively youthful but that he also paid less than the other members.

**41** The great Venetian navigator: See Ibid., pp. 64–65.

**42** Soon Christopher was carrying out: The evidence of Columbus's piratical activities is set out at length in A. Ensenat de Villalonga. See also C. Varela, *La Caida de Cristobal Colon*, p. 238.

**43** René was theoretically: It is usually believed that since Columbus was revealing this story in a letter to Queen Isabella of Castile—who was married to the Aragonese king he was supposed to have been fighting—that it was too uncomfortable a story to have been made up.

**44** But Doge Mocenigo: See J. J. Norwich, p. 100.

**45** Cabot was also putting: See E. Giuffrida in R. M. Zorzi, pp. 65–66.

**45** Even the traditional sources of furs: See P. Spufford, pp. 334–38.

**45** But so much more would: See J. A. Williamson, *The Cabot Voyages*, p. 190.

**46** As they weighed anchor: There remains doubt about almost everything that Columbus did before 1492, and that includes his 1476 convoy departure and subsequent shipwreck. But the battle is well documented and there is no major reason to doubt his word that he was there.

**47** Help was also on the way: See P. E. Taviani, pp. 59–62.

**48** The relationship between Bristol and Iceland: D. Quinn, *European Approaches to North America*, pp. 20–21. In fact, Hull was the main English port trading with Iceland at this time and Bristol had been reducing its involvement with Iceland for two decades.

**48** Southampton, on the other hand: See A. Temple Patterson.

**48** Once in Bristol: See R. Broome, p. 18.

**48** The voyage was a twenty-day: The description of Columbus's circumnavigation is based on what history suggests he did, and on what was possible at the time. See D. Quinn, *European Approaches to North America*, pp. 20–21.

**49** But in the heaving seas: There remains some controversy about whether Columbus actually went to Iceland, on the grounds that he claimed the fifty-foot tides were there and not in Bristol. But since he was writing many years later, this is definitely not conclusive. Many, but not all, English historians now believe that he made it up. See A. A. Ruddock, "Columbus and Iceland: New light on an old problem," *Geographical Journal*, 1970, pp. 177–89. On the other hand, the facts are muddled and not completely outrageous, and this implies that Columbus was definitely in Bristol, so it is unreasonable to conclude, without specific evidence to the contrary, that his boasts to have visited Thule (Iceland) were no more than that.

**49** The previous summer: See I. Wilson, p. 41. There is a series of denunciations of other pre-Columbian discoverers in S. Morison, *The European Discovery of America: The Northern Voyages*.

**49** "Most unusual appearance": These words are written in the margin in Columbus's own copy of *Historia Rerum*.

**51** It soon became clear: See A. V. G. Arciniegas, pp. 53–56.

**52** To lead the Florentine delegation: See A. V. G. Arciniegas, pp. 58f.

**53** As he glimpsed: See, for example, F. J. Pohl, p. 20.

**53** He consigned all this to memory: G. R. Crone, p. 40.

**55** He began the habit: Felipa's family also were originally Italian immigrants, but the surname is intriguing and may have intrigued Columbus too. It means "by the stars," or "navigators."

**56** "behaved honorably": B. Keen, p. 39.

**56** Columbus was a master: The idea that Columbus left so suddenly after his wedding to such a hopeless destination because he had been found out is my interpretation, but it does explain a peculiarity.

**56** Nearby Madeira: I. Wilson, p. 60.

**57** A one-eyed sailor told him: B. Keen, pp. 51–52.

**60** Would it, by any chance: This letter has remained controversial ever since it was written. There was an attempt a century ago to argue that it was a forgery (see H. Vignaud). But it is now generally accepted that the letter was real.

**60** In the meantime: See E. Giuffrida in R. M. Zorzi, p. 64.

**62** The penalty for anyone: R. A. Skelton, p. 33.

**62** Lorenzo Berardi had been: The earlier sources describe him as Lorenzo Giraldi and suggest that he was simply an intermediary, receiving a copy of the original letter for Columbus direct from Toscanelli. But I have followed Consuelo Varela's suggestion that this was Berardi, and that it was also Berardi who showed the original letter to Columbus: (see C. Varela *Colon y los Florentinos*). That would explain why Columbus had to copy it down, and the fact that he did copy it down in his own handwriting is some evidence that the letter itself was not forged (see P. E. Taviani, p. 31n).

**63** Toscanelli received the letter: For some time this letter was also believed to have been a forgery, until the French historian Henry Vignaud found that Columbus had inscribed it in his own handwriting inside one of his books. See H. Vignaud.

## 3: The Enterprise

**64** "Between the edge of Spain": Quoted in I. Wilson, p. 77.

**64** In Bristol, in July 1480: T. F. Reddaway and A. A. Ruddock (eds.). "The accounts of John Balsall, purser of the Trinity of Bristol, 1480–81," *Camden Miscellany*, Vol. XXIII, London, 1969. See the use made of this in I. Wilson, pp. 60–68, 89.

**65** The charge was illegal trading: The documents from Croft's trial only came to light as recently as 1935, and provided welcome evidence for historians of the period that the exploratory voyages from Bristol actually did take place. See J. A. Williamson, *The Cabot Voyages*, pp. 188–89.

**66** But the evidence: For the circumstantial evidence that the 1481 expedition discovered something, which they subsequently lost again, see D. Quinn, *European Approaches to North America*, pp. 29–31.

**67** His own tentative maps of the world: See Ibid., p. 30.

**68** But what we know: See Ibid., pp. 32–33.

**68** But in northern cities like Paris: There is a wonderful description of Paris at this time in L. Febvre, pp. 4–6.

**69** "These things carved from marble": See Ibid., p. 8.

**70** Columbus was living: The evidence that Columbus had detailed knowledge of sailing in the English Channel is in A. Ensenat de Villalonga, pp. 429–30.

**70** The new Portuguese king: See E. Sanceau.

**71** Cabot was now: The assertion that Cabot was already fascinated by the idea of the Indies and finding it on the other side of the Atlantic is not absolutely certain. But a look through a list of his closest associates in Venice is considerable evidence that he was. See E. Giuffrida in R. M. Zorzi, p. 66.

**72** "he gives the impression": See F. Fernandez-Armesto, *Columbus on Himself*, p. 14.

**73** "If you knew how universally hated": See J. J. Norwich, p. 103.

**76** One story says that when he arrived: See M. Kurlansky, p. 58–60.

**77** There are records: See R. Gallo, "Intorno a Giovanni caboto," *Rendiconti dell'Accademia Nazionale dei Lincei*, S VIII, Vol. 3, 1948: 220.

**77** Fame was very nice: This plan is the heart of the story, and, of course, it no longer exists. But it is strongly implied by the circumstantial evidence of coincidental links between Cabot and Columbus, not least the fact that they both plunged almost simultaneously into ruinous debt. For academic discussion of the likelihood that Columbus and Cabot were partners at one point, see D. Quinn. *European Approaches to North America*, pp. 32–33.

**79** Edward IV had begun: See C. L. Scofield, pp. 404–11 and E. Power, "The English wool trade in the reign of Edward IV," *Cambridge Historical Journal*, vol. 2, 1926: 21–22. One of the London merchants most involved in Edward's business was Richard Whittington—not the original Dick Whittington, who died in 1422, but possibly a descendant. He was involved in one contract to import four lions from Africa into England for the king. The historian David Quinn suggests that this might have been how the legend of Dick Whittington came to be associated with cats: see, D. Quinn, "Edward IV and Exploration," *Mariner's Mirror*, July 1935: 278n.

**80** Both the partners: Most of Columbus's projects until 1483 seem to have been linked to the Centurione, di Negro, or Spinola families. I have used the Centurione family here because of the instruction in his will to repay money to them. It has always been assumed by historians that this relates to the incident of the sugar in Madeira in 1479, but it could also relate to the reason he was in debt. We know who Cabot's creditors were because they were named on the letters sent to the cities where he was living after 1488. They all had strong commercial links with London, one of them buying woolen cloth and the other exporting wine from Crete to Sandwich in Kent. (See E. Giuffrida in R. M. Zorzi, p. 67.)

**80** To make the situation doubly tragic: It is, once again, impossible to know exactly how or when Felipa died. There is particular ambiguity about when: Most sources suggest that she had died before Columbus approached the king of Portugal in 1484, but Columbus himself later wrote to Isabella of Castile claiming that he had abandoned his wife and family to enter her service, which would mean she may have died sometime later. But this was probably the hype of a desperate man. The argument that plague killed her, and maybe other children of hers, is in M. Barreto, pp. 489–90.

**82** Reuchlin had been sent: See A. V. G. Arciniegas, pp. 83–85.

**83** "Find out what he wants": Quoted in F. Fernandez-Armesto, *Amerigo*, p. 37.

**83** "My word is as good": See A. V. G. Arciniegas, p. 91.

**83** He was also responsible for: See F. J. Pohl, p. 29.

**84** Under Vespucci's discreet guidance: It has been suggested that Vespucci was acting as a pimp himself (see F. Fernandez-Armesto, *Amerigo*, pp. 38–39), and although this goes beyond the direct evidence, he was clearly a man who would fix things for those wealthier and more powerful than he.

**85** "If someone were to bring together": Quoted in L. Jardine, p. 365.

**86** Poliziano, the poet and translator: See A. V. G. Arciniegas, pp. 121–22.

**86** "In the end, I hold the things of heaven": Quoted in F. Fernandez-Armesto, *Amerigo*, p. 24.

**86** With reverence, they repeated: Plato's dialogues *Timaeus* and *Critias* are the only known references to Atlantis.

**87** He made sure he ate in public: See E. Sanceau, p. 281.

**89** Armed with the sketchy maps: Admiral Morison describes Bartholomew with Columbus at the meeting. See S. E. Morison, *Admiral of the Ocean Sea*, p. 69.

**90** "get your head examined!": See *El Nuevo Mundo* by Lope de Vega in *Three Major Plays*, ed. G. Edwards (Oxford: Oxford University Press, 1999).

**91** "The king found this Columbus": This is from *Decades of Asia* written on 1552 by João Barros in C. E. Nowell, "The Rejection of Christopher Columbus by John of Portugal," *University of Michigan Historical Essays*, 1937: 25–44.

**91** "vain, simply founded on imagination": Quoted in S. E. Morison, *Admiral of the Ocean Sea*, p. 97.

**92** The ghetto in Venice: See B. Ravid, "Curfew Time in the Ghetto of Venice" in E. Kittell and T. Madden, p. 237.

**92** There were powerful laws: More about the Venetian dowry law can be found in E. Kittell and T. Madden, pp. 149f.

**92** While it was being refitted: There is a great deal of confusion about when and where Sebastian was born, mainly because he told a number of conflicting stories, which are now considered wholly untrustworthy. Most of his statements on the subject claim that he was born in England, but also that he was a Venetian citizen. This appears to be contradictory—which has confirmed the view of most historians—but it may actually be true. "Sebastian Caboto, borne at Bristow, but a Genoway's sonne," according to Thomas Lanquet's *Epitome of Chronicles* in 1559, quoted in C. R. Beazley, p. 38.

**93** Columbus needed to leave Lisbon: There have been other reasons, including the possibility that Felipa's family was connected in some way to the executed Duke of Braganza. See G. Granzotto, pp. 64–65.

## 4: In Debt

**94** "It is difficult for us to realize": C. S. Lewis, *The Discarded Image* (London: Cambridge University Press, 1964).

**94** It was about an adventurer: See S. Baring-Gould, p. 543. The legend of Fernando de Alma was also retold by Washington Irving in *Chronicles of Wolfert's Roost and Other Papers* (Edinburgh: Constable, 1855).

**96** Instead, once he had landed: Some biographers believe that, either then or later, Columbus took the vows of a tertiary Franciscan, the lay division of the order. He certainly shared the order's spiritual conviction, but perhaps not the commitment to poverty.

**96** There he knocked on the door: This famous scene remains controversial among historians, some of whom believe it actually happened on Columbus's way through Palos in 1491. The introduction from Berardi is argued in C. Varela, *Colon y los Florentinos*, p. 47.

**97** Having done that he boarded: My evidence for this is simply that it was the best way to slip unnoticed out of the country. He was in the habit of accompanying cargos from Lisbon and would not have attracted attention. See B. Keen, p. 60.

**97** There are no details: Like Christopher's journey to Spain, we have no information about how his brother made the journey to England, which was so rudely interrupted. Nor do we know when the pirates struck. I have used the coast of Gascony because it was the scene of ruinous long-running wars, and those mercenaries left behind in the fifteenth century often turned to activities like piracy. See Ibid.

**99** They were on the front line: See H. Thomas, p. 41.

**100** As the visit progressed: This is not proof, but it is evidence that Columbus did not ask the Portuguese for titles and honors, because he seems prepared at this stage to accept nothing more than investment and continuing rights.

**100** We also know that he was searching: We know this because of the evidence of Cabot's London friend Raimondo de Soncino, see J. A. Williamson, *The Cabot Voyages*, p. 210.

**101** Like the European adventurers: For a description of other Europeans who made the same journey, see Z. Freeth and H. V. F. Winstone.

**101** The first part of the journey: See R. Burton, *A Personal Narrative of a Pilgrimage to al-Madinah and Meccah* (London: Bell, 1906), p. 31.

**102** Mecca was a sweltering city: It is tempting to imagine that Cabot followed the rest of the caravan to drink the waters from the Zemzem well, said to have been revealed to Abraham's wife, Hagar. If so, he might perhaps have agreed with a Victorian traveler who followed in his footsteps that it tasted like a "weak solution of Epsom salts." See T. F. Keane.

**104** "Then take a little Allom": See www.elizabethancostume.net/dyes.

**105** "Tell me how your daughter": Quoted in F. J. Pohl, p. 30.

**108** "My proposition was a thing of mockery": There is some evidence, but slight, that Columbus also approached his own city of Genoa and asked for two ships at this time. They rejected the idea. See P. E. Taviani, pp. 491–92.

**109** It may be that Columbus's intensity: The description of Columbus is from B. Keen, p.34.

**113** But the reason he went there: F. Fernandez-Armesto, *Amerigo*, pp. 48–50.

**113** "Welcome and good luck!": see E. N. Symons, p. 86.

**115** In fact, there was a studious silence: See R. Broome, p. 65.

**116** Columbus realized that this was: C. Varela, *Colon y los Florentinos*, pp. 37f.

**116** He wrote to the Portuguese king: J. Martins da Silva Marques, *Descobrimentos Portugueses*, III, Lisbon, 1971: 341–2.

**117** The Genoese colony on the Thames: The Spinola family may have been his brother's creditors, and they did have an office in London at the time.

**125** "Know then that this opinion": A. V. G. Arciniegas, p. 231.

**125** "Find out what sort of person he is": Ibid., p. 98. The fact that Vespucci did not actually go is pointed out by C. Varela, *Colon y los Florentinos*, pp. 38f.

**126** The definitive manual for bookkeeping: This was the period when Leonardo was perfecting his flying machine. He advised that it should be tested over a lake, and told pilots they should "carry a large bladder bound to you so that if you fall you will not be drowned."

129 "You have come to tell me": A. V. G. Arciniegas, p. 119n.

130 Anne of Beaujeu was twenty-eight: see P. Matarasso and M. de Lauwe.

131 "colossal errors": G. Granzotto, p. 83.

## 5: TRIUMPH AND DISASTER

133 "This night of October 11–12": S. E. Morison, p. 233.

134 "You do well to grieve": A. V. G. Archiniegas, p. 129.

135 This time he presented the monarchs: This map came to light in Paris in 1924 and has been controversial ever since, but it includes notes from *Imago Mundi*, which are remarkably similar to the ones Columbus has underlined in his own copy. David Quinn believes that it is actually the map Bartholomew Columbus showed to the English; see D. Quinn, *European Approaches to North America*, pp. 29f.

137 Isabella protested: B. Keen, p. 65. It has also been suggested that this sudden change of heart came because a chart stolen from Lisbon revealed that there was indeed land on the other side of the Atlantic.

138 The cost of fitting out: the Castilian currency converted to pounds of gold at the rate of about 49,000 to the pound. See L. Vigneras, *The Discovery of South America and the Andalusian Voyages*, pp. 41–43.

140 Vespucci was being included: See T. Goldstein, "Geography in Fifteenth-Century Florence" in *Merchants and Scholars: Essays in the History of Exploration and Trade*. (Minneapolis: University of Minnesota Press, 1965), p. 30. For the argument that this was the moment that they met, see also C. Varela, *Colon y los Florentinos*, pp. 44f.

141 Pope Innocent lay in a coma: D. Seward, pp. 63–64.

142 "We're in the wolf's jaws": D. Seward, p. 64.

142 His experience as a construction engineer: These first came to light only in 1943, when a series of letters was found referring to John Cabot Montecalunya. No explanation of the Montecalunya has ever been found, but the discovery of letters from Cabot's debtors to the authorities in Valencia confirms that he was there at the time. See Ballesteros-Gaibros, M. "Juan Caboto en Espana" in *Revista de Indias*, 1943, Vol. IV, pp. 607–27. The description of the existing jetty is in J. Gil, pp. 77–81.

143 All mention of the Indies: This omission has led some conspiracy theorists to suggest that Columbus was not actually making for the Indies at all.

144 Their special expedition banners: See S. E. Morison, *Admiral of the Ocean Sea*, pp. 158–59.

144 The ships carried provisions: See F. Fernandez-Armesto, *Columbus and the Conquest of the Impossible*, p. 83.

146 "so that if the voyage were long": See S. E. Morison, *Portuguese Voyages to the Americas in the Fifteenth Century*, p. 199.

146 "The savor of the mornings": See S. E. Morison, *Admiral of the Ocean Sea*, p. 201.

146 On a visit to Rome: See Ibid., pp. 137–38. For more than forty years after his death,

Pinzón's family continued a long-running court case in Spain claiming that Columbus had wanted to turn back for home but Pinzón had persuaded him to go on.

**147** "Like a little wax candle": See Ibid., p. 223.

**147** "Señor Martin Alonso": See S. E. Morison, *The European Discovery of America: The Southern Voyages*, p. 62

**147** Columbus took the royal standard ashore: S. E. Morison believed there was really no doubt that this island was the one now known as Watling Island, and that has been the official view. But there are other candidates, both to the north and the south: See essay on landfall controversy by W. E. Washburn, pp. 401f.

**147** "and many things of slight value": S. E. Morison, *Admiral of the Ocean Sea*, p. 229.

**148** "No-one would have believed it": From Columbus's published letter to the sovereigns, quoted in Ibid., p. 231.

**148** There were some iguanas: See C. Jane (ed.), *The Four Voyages of Columbus*, Vol. 1 (New York: Dover, 1988), pp. 120–23, quoted in M. de Asua and R. French, p. 3.

**150** "I am still determined": See H. Thomas, p. 107.

**150** It was time for Cabot's second meeting: See J. A. Williamson, *The Cabot Voyages*, pp. 39–40.

**150** It is hard to imagine: There is no absolute proof that Cabot was still in Valencia when Columbus passed through, or that he was in the crowd, but J. A. Williamson, the leading Cabot scholar, believed so. See Ibid., p. 41.

**152** "O man of little comprehension": See S. E. Morison, *Admiral of the Ocean Sea*, p. 346.

**152** As he sailed out of Lisbon harbor: Day was in Lisbon at this time, and this seems like the moment they may have met—if they hadn't met before—but this is speculation on my part. See D. Quinn, *England and the Discovery of America* p. 56.

**153** "We have seen your letters": See S. E. Morison, *Admiral of the Ocean Sea*, p. 355.

**155** "By this post I am sending you": See A. V. G. Arciniegas, p. 145.

**155** Across the city: There is a full discussion of this in L. Formisiano.

**156** Cabot was also in town: See E. Giuffrida in R. M. Zorzi, p. 69. See also J. A. Williamson, *The Cabot Voyages*, p. 42f. We do not know whether he was lobbying to lead a voyage himself, but it seems highly likely that he was. Recent evidence about his stay in Seville and his plans for the pontoon bridge are in J. Gil, pp. 77–81.

**156** Columbus's letter to Santangel: The letter to Santangel seems to be identical to another letter written to Gabriel Sanchez, which seems to create confusion in the early editions about who actually held the post of royal treasurer.

**157** The Duke of Ferrara understood: See G. Weare, p. 84.

**157** "I do not deny it entirely": See H. Thomas, p. 121.

**157** "the famous Columbus": See S. E. Morison, *Admiral of the Ocean Sea*, p. 383.

**158** Almeida's argument prevailed: See H. Thomas, p. 132. There is a legend that Almeida did in fact sail and discover Brazil, but that can almost certainly be dismissed.

**158** "our dear son Columbus": See Ibid., p. 133.

**158** *Inter caetara Divinae*: G. Weare, p. 65.

**158** "living peaceably and going naked": G. Weare, p. 65.

**159** there was a contingent of *hidalgos*: See J. Edwards, "Cordoba in the time of Ferdi-nand and Isabella" in H. J. Hames.

**160** *Dudum siquidem*: See S. E. Morison, *Admiral of the Ocean Sea*, pp. 372–73.

**160** "Martin does nothing": E. G. Ravenstein, p. 42.

**161** Almeida's fleet was stood down: In a note to the sovereigns after his return from the second voyage, Columbus clearly believed that Almeida's fleet had actually been dis-patched but had failed to find the West Indies. There is, however, no other evidence for this. The main evidence is in G. Zurita. *Historia del Ray Don Fernando el Catolico* (Saragossa, Spain: 1610), pp. 30–32.

**162** "had the genital organ cut to the belly": See S. E. Morison (ed.), *Journals and other Documents*, p. 211.

**162** Columbus did not stay: See S. E. Morison, *Admiral of the Ocean Sea*, p. 405.

**164** "The fish here": Quoted in F. Fernandez-Armesto, *Columbus on Himself*, p. 61.

**166** "Gentlemen, I wish to bring": Quoted in S. E. Morison, *Journals and Other Docu-ments*, p. 227.

**166** There was no gold: H. Thomas, p. 108.

**166** He became convinced: M. de Asua and R. French, pp. 4–5.

**175** The answer, they believed: The evidence for this voyage is in Michele de Cuneo's letter, written later in 1495 (see S. E. Morison, *Journals and Other Documents*, p. 227). He himself did not know the outcome of the voyage, but it seems likely that it never took place. The interruption of Guaniguana's army and the hurricane seem to have been fatal.

## 6: HEADING NORTH

**176** "I see that the world": Quoted in P. M. Watts (1985), p. 83.

**177** A passerby immediately recognized him: See I. Arthurson, p. 1. See also A. Wroe, pp. 47–48.

**178** a small clique of Bristol merchants: The evidence of a discovery in 1494 is a map with annotations, apparently by Cabot's son Sebastian, that give 1494 as the date, though it is widely but not unanimously agreed that this was a misreading of the Roman numerals for 1497. The evidence that John Day knew about the voyage is in his letter to Columbus, explaining that "men from Bristol" had found land before 1497; see J. A. Williamson, *The Cabot Voyages*, p. 213.

**179** Whatever the merchants: The fact that Cabot was allowed to pursue his enterprise in one tiny ship, which would have to bring back a cargo of fish to pay for the expedition, suggests that only a handful of local merchants backed the voyage. The secretive nature of the previous voyages of discovery suggest that a reason why this might have been, and a reason why it may have been the customs officer Richard Amerike—who had replaced Thomas Croft, who had backed the *Trinity* voyages—who backed Cabot. But although this is the role set out for Amerike in many recent books, there is actually no evidence that he was formally involved, only the hint in Alwyn Ruddock's work that she had finally found some link; see E. Jones.

**180** Cabot had probably always known: See E. Giufrida in R. M. Zorzi, p. 70.

**180** If it was an island: Evidence of this is that the map which was discovered in Paris in 1924, perhaps the one which Columbus presented to Ferdinand and Isabella outside Granada in 1491. The map shows three small islands, similar in shape, grouped together like present-day Newfoundland. They are placed directly to the west of the British Isles, and labeled Antillia. This is clear evidence that Columbus—and therefore probably Cabot—knew about the Bristol voyages and had access to some information about what they had found. See D. Quinn, *European Approaches to North America*, pp. 28–30.

**181** Genoa had been deeply unpopular: This was a bigger disaster than it seems since 128 sailors might have been about 3 percent of the adult male population of Bristol.

**181** His successor, Richard Amerike: The exact role that Amerike played in Cabot's voyage has never been quite pinned down, though it is a central tenet of what I call the English conspiracy theory (see p. 469) that Amerike was a major backer. And constructing a narrative like this one does imply good reasons why it was Amerike who listened to Cabot when others failed to. Alwyn Ruddock's mysterious book, destroyed after her death, seems to have uncovered evidence of the role he did play (see p. 345), but that awaits a new generation of researchers to follow her lead.

**181** Bristol Broadmead cloth: P. Fleming and K. Costello.

**185** "The bishop will use your ships": F. de Navarette, *Colección de los Viajes y Descubrimientos*, Vol. II (Madrid: La Imprenta Nacional, 1825–37), p. 199, quoted in A. V. G. Arciniegas, p. 151.

**187** "made bets": B. de las Casas, *A Short Account of the Destruction of the Indies.* p. 15.

**189** "His guilt is written": C. Varela, *La Caida de Cristobal Colon*, p. 123.

**190** "my agent and special friend" See F. J. Pohl, p. 44.

**190** By now Berardi was too weak: See F. Fernandez-Armesto, *Amerigo*, p. 59.

**191** Cabot was in London: There are no records about when he opened negotiations in London, except that the patent was signed early in March 1496. But these things were not arranged quickly.

**191** to put their case to the Danish ambassador: H. Harrisse, p. 40.

**191** Giovanni Antonio de Carbonariis may have been: See J. A. Williamson, *The Cabot Voyages*, p. 93, about Carbonariis's time in Milan. Most of the information about his time in London seems to have been uncovered by Alwyn Ruddock before her death, and the destruction of her findings shortly afterward, so it can't be absolutely certain. See page 345, but also E. Jones, "Alwyn Ruddock: John Cabot and the Discovery of America," for more detail. We don't, of course, know whether Cabot first met Carbonariis in Milan, but it seems likely.

**191** Austin Friars, with its dominating spire: W. A. Cater, "The Priory of the Austin Friars 1253–1538," *Journal of the British Archaeological Association*, March/June 1912.

**192** Playing cards: P. Ackroyd, p. 382.

**193** Warbeck was now in Scotland: C. Varela, *Ingleses en España y Portugal, 1450–1515*, p. 61.

**194** "one like Columbus": See J. A. Williamson. *The Cabot Voyages*, p. 48. When de Puebla talked about "another Genoese" like Columbus, he knew what he was talking about: He regularly accepted bribes from London's Genoese community: See G. E. Weare (1897), 112.

**195** "To eat.": See F. Tarducci, p. 10n.

**195** When de Puebla was writing: See J. A. Williamson, *The Cabot Voyages*, pp. 50–51.

**196** almost on its side: The modern *Matthew* was tilted like this in storms in this same region.

**196** Robert Thorne and Hugh Elyot: Robert Thorne and Hugh Elyot were the names listed by John Dee as having discovered America in 1494; the date is generally thought to have been a misreading of the Latin numeral LXXXXVII for LXXXXIV. And since we know that Cabot had two Bristol merchants on board, presumably investors, it would explain the statement by Robert Thorne in 1527: "my father, which with another merchant of Bristow named Hugh Elliott discovered the Newfound Landes." See J. A. Williamson, *The Cabot Voyages*, pp. 28–29.

**197** The crew, even in medieval times: See D. Burwash, *English Merchant Shipping, 1460–1540*: University of Toronto Press, 1947, pp.60–65; quoted in E. Jones.

**198** His other backers: E. Jones, "The *Matthew* of Bristol and the Financiers of John Cabot's 1497 Voyage to North America," *English Historical Review*, Vol. 121, No. 492, 2006.

**198** Henry VII had sent Catherine: See J. A. Williamson, *The Cabot Voyages*, p. 54.

**199** "The more I said": See F. Fernandez-Armesto, *Columbus on Himself*, p. 116.

**200** "Why, the coasts": Quoted in Ibid.

**200** Columbus began signing his name: F. Streicher.

**200** Those disillusioned Franciscans: See R. O. Jones, p. 7.

**201** Despite these obstacles: C. Varela, *Colon y los Florentinos*, p. 57.

**202** "Here lies Margot": See S. E. Morison, *Admiral of the Ocean Sea*, p. 555.

**204** "Be prepared, I tell you, Rome": See D. Seward, p. 149.

**205** wrote to Bartholomew: See S. E. Morison, *Admiral of the Ocean Sea*, p. 511.

**206** island of the Amazons: See J. de Tuleda Buesco, quoted in F. Fernandez-Armesto, *Columbus on Himself*, p. 11.

**207** In the early months: History suggests this delay, but there is no documentary evidence for it. It is also suggested that the pilot who guided the *Matthew* down the Avon was named James George Ray: See S. E. Morison, *The European Discovery of America, The northern voyages 500–1600*, p. 167.

**209** Cabot named it St. John: There is ambiguous evidence that Cabot's crew also came across polar bears and large stags and moose, because this was included in the so-called eighth legend on the Paris map, published 1544, which claims to be a copy of one made by Sebastian Cabot, and was discovered by a Bavarian count in 1843. I have followed those historians who have argued for a landing in Nova Scotia, because of Cabot's overwhelming need to ascertain whether he had encountered a mainland coast running southwest. He seems to have satisfied himself on this enough to sail back northeast, and it seems unlikely that the confusion of Newfoundland and the St. Lawrence River would have made it nearly so clear to him. Day's descriptions of the tall trees imply Nova Scotia. The Paris map also suggests Cape Breton was the spot: See P. E. Pope.

**211** Over the next two weeks: There are only two major sources of information about where the *Matthew* went next, and they contradict each other. On the one hand, there is Raimondi de Soncino's letter, which discusses how Cabot will make his way to Cipangu along the coast he found, which implies that he felt sure the coast would lead there—and that meant exploring southwest. On the other hand there is the English merchant John Day, who says that Cabot sailed northeast until he reached the same latitude as Dursey Head in Ireland, when he turned for home. It was possible that Cabot was starting the search that would so obsess the English for the next few centuries—a northwest passage to the East. But it is far more likely, if he was seeking a way to the Indies, that he actually needed to turn south initially, to satisfy himself that this was a continental coastline that went south. I am therefore assuming that Day left out the first part of this journey. Cabot first turned south along the coast, and only then turned around and sailed north the same distance, back to where he had begun and beyond to Newfoundland, and then turned for home. He was erring on the side of safety on this voyage, and that was the safe solution to his basic question. See J. A. Williamson, *The Cabot Voyages*, pp. 70–71.

**211** The *Trinity* and those other adventures: The interpretation was suggested by the English spy John Day who implied that the previous Bristol explorers had discovered what is today Newfoundland and believed it to be an island, when actually it was a promontory of the mainland. It was an island, in fact, but it was easy to see why they were confused.

**212** It was a small whale: See G. E. Weare, p. 110.

**213** Cabot's return journey: The precise dates of Cabot's voyage were recorded in a Bristol chronicle known as the Fust MS: See J. A. Williamson, *The Cabot Voyages*, p. 206.

**214** Caxton had actually died: B. Weinreb and C. Hibbert, *The London Encyclopaedia*, revised ed. (London: Macmillan, 1993), p. 970.

**214** On August 10: This is the sequence of events that seems to have been set out by Alwyn Ruddock before her death: See E. Jones.

**215** The jaw bone of the whale: This entry was republished in the *Bristol Observer* in 1868, though the original has never been found.

**215–16** having been granted his pension: See H. Biggar (ed.), p. 16.

**216** a Venetian merchant named Lorenzo Pasqualigo: See J. A. Williamson, *The Cabot Voyages*, p. 84.

**217** Raimondi de Soncino: Ibid., p. 210.

**217** "As I have made friends": Williamson Ibid., p. 211.

**218** Diplomats had various methods: See G. Mattingly, p. 99.

**218** We know the great lengths: See for example, A. Cortesao.

**218** The merchant king Edward IV: See D. Quinn, "Edward IV and Exploration," *Mariner's Mirror*, July 1935.

**219** A generation later: Catherine of Aragon's marriage papers are from G. Mattingly, p. 147.

**219** the English merchant John Day: See Ruddock, A. "John Day of Bristol and the English Voyages across the Atlantic before 1497," *Geographical Journal*, June 1966, Vol. 132, Part 2. For Day's career with Berardi, see C. Varela, *Colon y los Florentinos*, p. 44. Day eventually inherited a house in London, under his real name of Hugh Say, but lost all his wealth in a legal dispute in 1505.

**219** "In payment for some services": See J. A. Williamson, *The Cabot Voyages*, p. 214.

**219** *Inventio Fortunata*: It is a pity Day mislaid his, because no copy of this important book has ever come to light since, though the Elizabethan magician John Dee spent years trying to find it. See D. Quinn, *England and the Discovery of America*, p. 109.

**221** "It seemed as if God": A. R. Scoble (ed.), p. 280.

**222** "the verdict in their bosoms": See D. Seward, p. 229.

**222** "a place where every man pissed": The phrase comes from Philippe de Commines, quoted in J. Norwich, p. 124.

## 7: Strange Meetings

**223** "The land which God has newly given": Quoted in F. Fernandez-Armesto, *Columbus and the Conquest of the Impossible*, pp. 175–76.

**223** "God made me the messenger": Quoted in P. M. Watts, "Prophecy and Discovery: On the spiritual origins of Christopher Columbus' enterprise of the Indies," *American Historical Review*, Vol. 90, No. 1, Feb. 1985.

**223** On the one hand: See P. Ackroyd, *The Life of Sir Thomas More*, pp. 79–83.

**224** The accounts we have: See Raymond Soncino's letter in J. A. Williamson, *The Cabot Voyages*, p. 210.

**224** "The English run after him": See Pasqualigo letter in Ibid., p. 84.

**224** "the land and isles of late found": Ibid., p. 91.

**225** In early May 1498: We have no descriptions of this, and don't even know the exact date, so the idea that the departure of his fleet would be marked in this way is an assumption of mine. But I believe it is a reasonable one: Expeditions of that size did not set sail without attracting excited interest.

**225** "slight and gross merchandises": See J. A. Williamson, *The Cabot Voyages*, p. 320.

226 another Friar Boyle: Ibid., p. 228.

226 "Your father loves you": Quoted in H. Thomas, p. 102. This was how he always closed his letters to Diego.

227 The *Niña* had experienced: See S. E. Morison, *Admiral of the Ocean Sea*, pp. 511–12.

227 "God willing, you will try": Quoted in F. Fernandez-Armesto, *Columbus and the Conquest of the Impossible*, p. 144.

228 "May our Lord guide me": Quoted in Ibid., p. 166.

231 But then a chastened Thirkill: Bradley also returned safely: He was an interpreter to an English mission to Castile in 1503: See D. Quinn, *England and the Discovery of America*, p. 102n. But Alwyn Ruddock's new evidence may provide a different interpretation of this—that they returned not in 1498, but with the other crews in 1500 (see p. 345).

231 "The king of England sent": See G. E. Weare, pp. 159–60.

231 "I have seen the map": Ibid., pp. 161–62.

233 "large mainland": Quoted in H. Thomas, p. 199.

234 "Now I observed the very great variation": Quoted in F. Fernandez-Armesto, *Columbus on Himself*, p. 158.

235 he was the "Christ-bearer": Quoted in P. M. Watts, "Prophecy and Discovery: On the spiritual origins of Christopher Columbus' enterprise of the Indies," *American Historical Review*, Vol. 90, No. 1, Feb. 1985: 74.

235 Ojeda and the stolen map: That there is no direct evidence that Ojeda stole the map in this way, but nor is there any that he took a copy home with him, and it is unlikely that Columbus let the map out of his cabin.

236 Maiobanex held firm: See J. S. Collis, pp. 154–55.

237 "Even if they die now": Quoted in F. Fernandez-Armesto, *Columbus and the Conquest of the Impossible*, p. 147.

237 "What power of mine": Quoted in H. Thomas, p. 203.

238 The Great Chronicle of London: See J. A. Williamson, *The Cabot Voyages*, p. 220.

239 "where all women were communal": See, for example, J. Perez de Tuleda Bueso.

240 "It was my intention": Quoted in F. J. Pohl, p. 50.

241 The mild-mannered Vespucci and Ojeda: I am basing this on what we know of both their characters, and on Vespucci's behavior since. Vespucci seems to have been very careful, once he had separated from Ojeda's ships, to stay studiously apart from him afterward. In fact, Ojeda described Vespucci later as a "pilot" and it is not clear what his status was on the voyage, and whether he exaggerated it. See F. Fernandez-Armesto, *Amerigo*, pp. 66–71.

242 "We launched the boats": From the letter to Lorenzo di Pierfrancesco, quoted in G. Masini, p. 12.

244 "Rationally, let it be said": Quoted in F. J. Pohl, p. 81.

244 and lines from Dante's *Purgatory*: Quoted in Ibid., p. 79. See also F. Fernandez-Armesto, *Amerigo*, p. 78.

**246** "We encountered an ocean current": Quoted in F. J. Pohl, p. 78.

**247** "They all go naked": Quoted in Ibid., p. 83.

**248** Vespucci turned north somewhere: Again this is controversial territory. Not all historians accept that Vespucci was telling the whole truth, since the reports are not confirmed by any other document, but the maps imply some support for his description. See F. Fernandez-Armesto, *Amerigo*, pp. 70–71.

**250** "Our people here": Quoted in F. Fernandez-Armesto, *Columbus and the Conquest of the Impossible*, p. 136.

**252** On September 23, 1499: We know very little about Vespucci's time there and why he seems to have stayed aloof from both sides—or indeed if he really did. But this explanation makes the most sense, given that, unlike Ojeda, he managed to keep his friendship with Columbus. He did clearly link up with Juan de la Cosa to discuss the famous map.

**252** But longitude was a tougher proposition: There is still controversy about exactly how much of Vespucci's claims are true. For a convincing explanation, including the idea that he borrowed Columbus's earlier readings, see F. Fernandez-Armesto, *Amerigo*, pp. 77–85.

**253** "In the endeavor": F. J. Pohl, p. 94. The fact that Lorenzo di Pierfrancesco understood geography is from F. Fernandez-Armesto, p. 21.

**256** He set sail in spring: See F. J. Pohl, p. 87.

**257** but called the new land Labrador: See S. E. Morison, *Portuguese Voyages to America in the Fifteenth Century*, pp. 55–56.

**261** When the rebel leaders: These revelations have been uncovered in the archives in Simancas by archivist Isabel Aquirre. See C. Varela, *La Caida de Cristobal Colon*.

**262** As luck would have it: The evidence that the Columbus brothers planned to fight was collected by Bobadilla's officials, revealed in documents only published in 2006. See ibid., pp. 69f.

## 8: The Finish Line

**265** Browsing in a Parisian: See J. A. Williamson, *The Cabot Voyages*, pp. 108–9.

**265** Examining it more closely: See A. Davies, "The Last Voyage of John Cabot and the Rock at Grates Cave," *Nature*, Vol. 176, November 25, 1955, p. 77. The original reference to the wording was in Cormack, W. *Narrative of a Journey across the Island of Newfoundland* (St. John: Morning Post, 1856), p. 77.

**267** The second clue: See J. A. Williamson, *The Cabot Voyages*, pp. 109–10.

**267** "It is certain": F. de Navarette, *Colección de los Viages y Descubrimientos*, Vol. III (Madrid: *Imprenta Real*, 1829); quoted in I. Wilson, pp. 136–37.

**269** At least one academic: See A. Davies.

**270** the Newfoundland town of Carbonear: See J. A. Williamson, *The Cabot Voyages*, p. 93n.

**272** "The Comendator Bobadilla": Quoted in F. Fernandez-Armesto, *Columbus on Himself*, p. 194.

**272** "Your imprisonment was very displeasing": Quoted in B. Keen, p. 221.

**274** These are all rather confusing stories: We know little about this strange meeting. There have been suggestions that the visitor was Giocondo, partly because he was also identified as Jocundus, the translator of Vespucci's supposed book *Mundus Novus* (see F. A. Ober, *Amerigo Vespucci*, New York: Harper & Brother, 1907, pp. 198–99). Whether Marchionni really offered the chance to go on a voyage without any expectation of profit is still debatable. It may be that this is what Vespucci said, after the event, to justify his failure to produce any. The idea that they left by sea from Seville, by far the safest way if they wanted to escape detection, is mine.

**275** "My going was taken amiss": Quoted in G. R. Crone, p. 149.

**275** He was a cousin: See M. Barreto, p. 150.

**276** When Martin Frobisher: See S. E. Morison, *The European Discovery of America: The Northern Voyages*, p. 212.

**277** "who rape or violate": Quoted in J. A. Williamson, *The Cabot Voyages*, p. 252.

**278** "Their manners and gestures": Quoted in S. E. Morison, *The European Discovery America: The Northern Voyages*, pp. 215–56.

**278** Cantino was posing: See S. E. Morison, *The European Discovery of America: The Southern Voyages*, pp. 272-73.

**280** "This voyage which I am now making" Quoted in F. J. Pohl, p. 130.

**280** The hopes of the local merchants: I am arguing that Bristol's merchant community was divided, and had been since the secrecy of the voyages of 1480–81. Some were in on the secret of the *Trinity*'s discovery; those that were not backed Cabot. I am assuming here that this division continued, between the old guard who saw Fernandez as a way to claw back the ground lost to Cabot and his sons, and those who still had rights under Cabot's patent of 1496.

**280** another island—possibly Baffin: See J. A. Williamson, *The Cabot Voyages*, p. 216.

**281** Elyot and Thorne, and Thorne's son: I am extremely grateful to Dr. Evan Jones for pointing out this implication of Alwyn Ruddock's research.

**281** the 120-ton *Gabriel*: See A. A. Ruddock, "The reputation of Sebastian Cabot," *Bulletin of the Institute of Historical Research*, No. 47, 1974.

**282** "Clothid in Beestes skynne": Quoted in J. A. Williamson, *The Cabot Voyages*, pp. 220-23.

**282** Robert Fabyan saw them again: See J. A. Williamson, *The Cabot Voyages*, p. 128.

**283** The only clue: See M. Barreto, pp. 150–52.

**283** Coelho followed: There is some evidence about who commanded this expedition. Most academics agree that Vespucci was not in command, though he again clearly enjoyed some influence as a representative of the investors. See S. E. Morison, *The European Discovery of America: The Southern Voyages*, pp. 280–81.

**284** "a new land": Quoted in F. J. Pohl, p. 130.

**284** "What shall we say": Quoted in Ibid., p. 132.

**284** "many of which are good to taste": Quoted in ibid.

**284** "Having no laws": Quoted in Ibid., pp. 132–33. See the discussion about the accuracy of this description in F. Fernandez-Armesto, *Amerigo*, p. 154.

**285** "They were very ugly": Quoted in G. R. Crone, pp. 146–47.

**286** "I fancied myself ": Quoted in F. J. Pohl, p. 132.

**286** "I am like one of those followers": Quoted in ibid., p. 135.

**286** Coelho formally handed over: A fuller explanation of the name Cananor is in F. J. Pohl (p. 225), who suggests that Vespucci and Coelho exchanged formal command of the expedition at this point.

**287** In fact, they had hit: If we believe Vespucci, he must have reached the Roaring Forties some time before getting as far south as he claimed, but some academics dispute that he got that far. See F. Fernandez-Armesto, *Amerigo*, p. 96.

**287** "With much love": Quoted in H. Thomas, p. 232.

**290** "Was there a man born": Quoted in F. Fernandez-Armesto, *Columbus on Himself*, p. 220.

**291** the so-called Great Nugget: See B. de Las Casas, p. 20.

**292** "I reached the region": See also the translation in F. J. Pohl, p. 131.

**293** "The ships were lying open": See H. Thomas, p. 250, or for another translation, F. Fernandez-Armesto, *Columbus on Himself*, p. 221.

**294** and weevils had been: See B. Keen, pp. 240–41.

**294** "The colonial chief " Quoted in ibid., p. 244.

**295** "Be not afraid": Quoted in F. Fernandez-Armesto, *Columbus on Himself*, pp. 226-27.

**295** "I am wholly ruined": Quoted in K. Sale, p. 211.

**296** "far more horrifying": Quoted in J. Burchard, translated by Geoffrey Parker, *At the Court of the Borgia*, Folio Society, London, p. 225.

**297** Maria Cerezo is a mysterious figure: See F. Fernandez-Armesto, *Amerigo*, pp. 55-56.

**298** "Amerigo Vespucci will be arriving": Quoted in F. Fernandez-Armesto, *Amerigo*, pp. 249-50.

**305** "He has always been desirous": Quoted in Ibid. There are clearly two views about Vespucci. The cynics might suggest that he was taking advantage of Columbus here, and that his visit to court was entirely about his own enrichment. We shall never know for certain, but Columbus believed in him, and there is no evidence that Vespucci was unworthy of his trust.

**305** thinking about an appeal to the Pope: See Ibid., p. 209.

**306** "Since it seems that his highness" Quoted in G. Granzotto, p. 271.

**308** a small beer cellar: See Ibid., pp. 283–85.

## 9: NEW WORLD

**310** "There are three stages": A. Humboldt, *Examen critique de l'histoire de la geographie du Nouveau Continent et des progress de l'astronomie nautique aux quinzieme et seizieme siecles.* (Paris: *Librairie de Gide*, 1836–39).

**310** "Had our father Adam": Quoted in G. E. Weare, p. 111.

**312** "We may rightly call them": Quoted in F. Fernandez-Armesto, *Amerigo*, p. 147.

**313** *The Four Voyages of Amerigo Vespucci:* Although the realization that the Soderini letter is a forgery, and Vespucci was not therefore claiming all four voyages, is a twentieth-century revelation, there does remain some doubt. The best argument lies in the first lines of the clearly genuine letter to Lorenzo the Popolano in 1500: "It is a long time since I have written to your excellency, and for no other reason that nothing has occurred to me worthy of being commemorated." (See F. J. Pohl, p. 76.) If he had in fact been discovering Florida since 1497, he might have mentioned it.

**313** "And if any invidious or malign person" Quoted in F. Fernandez-Armesto, *Amerigo*, p. 118.

**316** had cannibalism, sex, and the thrilling hope: See J. F. Moffitt and S. Sebastian, pp. 145–58, and in F. Fernandez-Armesto, *Amerigo*, p. 169.

**316** "They do not employ": F. J. Pohl, p. 155.

**318** Only one copy: This was found by Professor Josef Fischer when he was searching for information about Norse settlements in America. See J. Fischer and F. von Weiser.

**319** the Soderini letter was written: The final nail in the coffin of the letter as a genuine composition by Vespucci was hammered in by A. Magngahi.

**320** "I had a little nut tree": Opie, Iona & Peter, *The Oxford Dictionary of Nursery Rhymes* (London: *Oxford University Press*, 1975).

**322** "No-one shall presume" Quoted in H. Thomas, pp. 312–33.

**323** harvest the wild cats: See J. A. Williamson, *The Cabot Voyages*, p. 216.

**326** "Diligent service": Quoted in Ibid., p. 265.

**329** Antonio de Montesinos: See H. Thomas, pp. 334–36.

**330** His will set out: The will revealed that one of his household slaves was from the Canary Islands, and it has been suggested that her two children might have been Vespucci's, but there is no evidence one way or the other: See C. Varela, *Ingles en España y Portugal*, p. 75.

**331** Solís lasted less than: See S. E. Morison, *The European Discovery of America: The Southern voyages*, pp. 301–3.

**331** Cuba had been conquered: See H. Thomas, pp. 357f. The story of the style of death chosen by their leader is in B. de las Casas, *A Short Account of Destruction*, p. 28.

**336** "I believe that because of these impious": Quoted in K. Sale, p. 158.

**338** "He sayls not surely": Quoted in S. E. Morison, *The European Discovery of America: the northern voyages,* p. 221.

**340** "We cannot go back here": Quoted in G. Masini, p. 36.

**340** "I earnestly entreat you": Quoted in J. A. Williamson, *The Cabot Voyages*, p. 151.

**342** "The people of London": Quinn (1974), 156.

**342** a small ship on the Thames: See S. E. Morison, *The European Discovery of America: the northern voyages*, p. 222.

**346** "Strange . . . that broad America": R. W. Emerson, *English Traits* (London: Routledge & Co., 1856).

**347** "As surely as Columbus pioneered": E. Giuffrida, p. 88, from M. Harvey. "The Voyages and Discoveries of the Cabots," *Collections of the Nova Scotia Historical Society 1893–95:* p. 17.

**347** "Half of the world would belong": Ibid., p. 125.

**348** "Let us leave this cathedral": E. W. Lennard, "John Cabot of Bristol," *United Empire*, May–June, 1947.

## 10: The Meaning of the New World

**350** an island called Utopia: See Logan, G. M., R. M. Adams, and C. H. Miller (eds), *Utopia*. Cambridge: *Chatto & Windus*, 1995. See also P. Ackroyd, *The Life of Sir Thomas More*, pp. 161–75.

**352** One was that the idealization: See J. H. Elliott, pp. 26–27.

**352** "License my roving hands": This is John Donne's Elegy XIX "To his mistress going to bed."

**353** "It is even a mortal question": Quoted in K. Sale, p. 367.

**354** a cargo of potatoes: See H. Hobhouse, pp. 191f. The French initially believed potatoes caused leprosy.

**355** Aztecs selling cochineal: See A. B. Greenfield, p. 39–42

**356** It was the gold and silver stolen: J. M. Keynes, "Economic Possibilities for Our Grandchildren," *Essays in Persuasion* (London: Macmillan, 1931), p. 361–62.

**361** "The idiocy of the man": See Howitt, W. *Colonization and Christianity* (London, 1838), p. 504; quoted in T. J. Ellingson, pp. 225–26.

**363** The adventurer Joshua Slocum: A. Macgillivray, p. 49.

**364** "As soon as he got the hawk's bell": Quoted in A. Fernandez-Armesto, *Amerigo*, p. 165.

**364** calling for a "chemical revolution": H. Trevor-Roper, *Renaissance Essays* (London: Secker & Warburg, 1985), p. 149–99.

## Postscript: Stars and Stripes

**367** "If that Americo Vespusio": Quoted in S. Subrahmanyam, p. 17.

**367** "Then came a great shout: Quoted in S. Guenter, p. 15.

**367** church restorer named Alfred Hudd: A. Hudd, "Richard Ameryk and the Name America," *Proceedings of the Clifton Antiquarian Club*, Vol. VII, Part I, 1909–10: 1–9.

**370** "after Sebastian Cabot": L. Balderston, p. 26.

**370** a local milliner named Margaret Manny: B. Tuchman, p. 45.

**370** known as "John Company's Gridiron: C. Fawcett, "The Striped Flag of the East India Company and its Connection with the American Stars and Stripes," *Mariner's Mirror*, Vol. XXIII, No. 4, October 1937.

**370** attacking or resisting pirates: W. G. Perrin, p. 129.

**370** In fact, striped ensigns: *Bowles' Universal Display of the Naval Flags of the World*, London: *Bowles and Carver*, 1790.

# Selected Bibliography

Ackroyd, Peter. *The Life of Sir Thomas More*. London: Chatto & Windus, 1998.

———. *London: The Biography*. London: Chatto & Windus, 2000.

Arciniegas, A. V. German. *Amerigo and the New World: The Life and Times of Amerigo Vespucci*. Trans Harriet de Onis. New York: Alfred A. Knopf, 1955.

Arthurson, Ian. *The Perkin Warbeck Conspiracy 1491–1499*. Stroud, UK: Alan Sutton, 1994.

Asua, Miguel de and Roger French. *A New World of Animals: Early Modern Europeans on the Creatures of Iberian America*. Aldershot, UK: Ashgate, 2005.

Balderston, Lloyd. *The Evolution of the American Flag*. Philadelphia: Ferris & Leach, 1909.

Baring-Goald, S. *Curious Myths of the Middle Ages*. London: Rivingtons, 1872.

Baron, Hans. *In Search of Florentine Humanism*. Princeton, NJ: Princeton University Press, 1988.

Barreto, Mascarenhas. *The Portuguese Columbus: Secret Agent of King John II*. Trans. R. A. Brown. Basingstoke UK: Macmillan, 1992.

Beazley, Charles R. *John and Sebastian Cabot*. London: Unwin, 1898.

Biggar, Henry (ed.). *The Precursors of Jacques Cartier, 1497–1534*. Ottawa: Canadian Archives, 1911.

Brinkbaumer, Klaus and Clemens Hoges. *The Voyage of the Vizcaina: The Mystery of Columbus' Last Ship*. Trans. Annette Streck. Orlando: Harcourt, 2006.

Broome, R. *Terra Incognita: The True Story of How America Got Its Name*. Seattle: Educare Press, 2001.

Brown, Patricia F. *Art and Life in Renaissance Venice*. New York: Harry Abrams, 1997.

Burchard, John. *Diaries 1483–1492*. Trans. Arnold H. Mathew. London: Francis Griffins, 1910.

Childs, Wendy R. "England's Icelandic Trade in the Fifteenth Century: The Role of the Port of Hull." London: in Holm P. Janzen, O. and Thór, J (eds) *Northern Seas Yearbook*, Egsberg, Fiskeri-og Sø fartsmuseet, 1995.

Collis, J. S. *Christopher Columbus*. London: Macdonald & Jame's, 1976.

Cortesao, Armando. *Cartografia e cartografas portugueses dos seculos XV e XVI*. Lisbon: Seara Nova, 1935.

Coulton, G. G. *Medieval Panorama: The English Scene from Conquest to Reformation*. New York: Meridian Press, 1955.

Crone, Gerald R. *The Discovery of America*. London: Hamilton, 1969.

D'Arienzo, L. "Un documento sul primo arrivo di Amerigo Vespucci a Siviglia" in *Columbeis* Genoa: University of Genoa, 1988.

Ellingson, Terry J. *The Myth of the Noble Savage*. Berkeley: University of California Press, 2001.

Elliott, J. H. *The Old World and the New*. Cambridge: Cambridge University Press, 1970.

Ensenat de Villalonga, A., *El Cristóbal Colón Histórico*, Ayuntamiento del Valladolid, 2006.

Epstein, Steven A. *Genoa and the Genoese 958–1528*. Chapel Hill, NC: University of North Carolina Press, 1996.

Febvre, Lucien. *Life in Renaissance France*. Trans. M. Rothstein Cambridge: Harvard University Press, 1977.

Fernandez-Armesto, Felipe. *Amerigo: The Man Who Gave His Name to America*. London: Weidenfeld & Nicolson, 2006.

Fernandez-Armesto, Felipe. *Columbus and the Conquest of the Impossible*. London: Weidenfeld & Nicolson, 1974.

Fernandez-Armesto, Felipe. *Columbus on Himself*. London: Folio Society, 1992.

Fischer, J. and F. von Weiser. *The Oldest Map with the Name America of the Year 1507 and the Carta Marina of the Year 1516 by M. Waldseemuller*. Innsbruck and London: Henry Stevens, Sons & Stiles, 1903.

Fleming, Peter and Kieran Costello. *Discovering Cabot's Bristol: Life in the Medieval and Tudor Town*, Bristol, UK: Redcliffe, 1998.

Formisano, L. (ed.). *Letters from a New World: Amerigo Vespucci's Discovery of America*. Trans. David Jacobson. New York: Marsilio, 1992.

Freeth, Zahra and H. V. F. Winstone. *Explorers of Arabia: From the Renaissance to the End of the Victorian Era*. London: Allen & Unwin, 1978.

Gil, Joan. *Mitos y Utopias del Descubrimiento 1: Colon y su Tiempo*. Madrid: Alianza Universidad, 1989.

Granzotto, Gianni. *Christopher Columbus: The dream and the obsession*. Trans. Stephen Sartarelli. London: Collins, 1986.

Greenfield, Amy B. *A Perfect Red: Empire Espionage and the Quest for the Colour of Desire*. London: Doubleday, 2005.

Guenter, Scot. *The American Flag 1777–1924: Cultural Shifts from Creation to Codification*. Cranbury, Vancouver: Farleigh Dickinson University Press, 1990.

Hames, Henry J. *Jews, Muslims and Christians In and Around the Crown of Aragon*. Leiden: Brill., 2004.

Harrisse, Henry. *Americus Vespuccius: A critical and documentary review of two recent English books*. London: B. F. Stevens, 1895.

Harrisse, Henry. *Cristofo Colombo e il bancodi St Gorgio*. Genoa: Sordomuti, 1890.

————. *Discovery of North America*. London: H. Stevens & Sons, 1892.

————. *John Cabot the Discoverer of North America and Sebastian his Son*. London: Stevens, 1896.

Hay, Denys. *Europe in the Fourteenth and Fifteenth Centuries*. Basingstoke, UK.: Macmillan, 1966.

Hobhouse, Henry. *Seeds of Change: Five Plants That Transformed Mankind*. London: Papermac, 1992.

Horsborgh, E. L. S. *Lorenzo the Magnificent and Florence in her Golden Age*. London: Methuen, 1908.

Horwood, Harold. *The Colonial Dream 1497–1760*. Toronto: Natural Science of Canada, 1978.

Hudd, Alfred. "Richard Ameryk and the Name America," *Proceedings of the Clifton Antiquarian Club*, Vol. VII, Part I, 1909–10.

Jardine, Lisa. *Worldly Goods*. London: Macmillan, 1996.

Jones, Evan. "The *Matthew* of Bristol and the Financiers of John Cabot's 1497 Voyage to North America," *English Historical Review*, Vol. 121, No. 492, 2006

Jones, Evan. "Alwyn Ruddock: John Cabot and the Discovery of America," *Historical Research*, April 7, 2007.

Jones, Royston O. *The Golden Age: Prose and Poetry in the 16th and 17th centuries*. London: Emesv Benn, 1971.

Jubber, N. *The Prester Quest*. New York: Doubleday, 2005.

Keane, T. F. *Six Months in Meccah: An account of the Mohammedan pilgrimage to Meccah*, London: Tinsley, 1881.

Keen, Benjamin (ed. and trans.). *The Life of Admiral Christopher Columbus by his Son Ferdinand*, London: Folio Society, 1960.

Kittell, Ellen, and Thomas Madden (ed). *Medieval and Renaissance Venice*. University of Illinois Press, 1999.

Kurlansky, M. *A Basque History of the World*. New York: Walker & Co., 1999.

Las Casas, Bartholomé. de. *History of the Indies*. Trans. Andree Collard. New York: Harper & Row, 1971.

Las Casas, Bartholomé de. *A Short Account of the Destruction of the Indies*. Ed. Nigel Griffin. London: Penguin, 1992.

De Lauwe, Chombart. *Anne de Beaujeu: La passion du pouvoir*. Paris: Tallandier, 1980.

Lester, C. Edward, and Andrew Foster. *The Life and Voyages of Americus Vespucius*. New York: Baker & Scribner, 1846.

Macdonald, Peter. *Cabot and the Naming of America*. Bristol, UK: Petmac, 1997.

Macgillivray, Alex. *A Short History of Globalization*. London: Constable & Robinson, 2006.

Magnaghi, Alberto. *Amerigo Vespucci: Studio critico*, Rome: Fratell: Treves, 1926.

Masini, G. *How Florence Invented America*. New York: Treves, 1926.

Matarasso, Pauline. *Queen's Mate: Three Women of Power in France on the Eve of the Renaissance*. Aldershot, UK: Ashgate, 2001.

Mattingly, Garret. *Renaissance Diplomacy*. New York: Dover, 1988.

Moffitt, J. F. and Santiago Sebastian. *O Brave New People: The European Invention of the American Indian*. Albuquerque: University of New Mexico Press, 1996.

Morison, Samuel. E. *Admiral of the Ocean Sea*. Oxford: Oxford University Press, 1942.

———. *The European Discovery of America: The Northern Voyages 500–1600*. New York: Oxford University Press, 1971.

———. *The European Discovery of America: The Southern Voyages*. New York: Oxford University Press, 1974.

——— *Portuguese Voyages to America in the Fifteenth Century*. Cambridge: Harvard University Press, 1940.

———. (ed.) *Journals and other Documents on the Life and Voyages of Christopher Columbus*. New York: Heritage Press, 1963.

Northup, George T. *Vespucci Reprints: Texts and Studies*. Princeton: Princeton University Press, 1916.

Norwich, John Julius. *Venice: The Greatness and the Fall*. London: Allen Lane, 1981.

Pagden, A. *European Encounters with the New World: From Renaissance to Romanticism*. New Haven: Yale University Press, 1993.

Perez de Tuleda, Juan. *Mirabilis in Altis: Studio critico sobre el origin y significado del proyeto descubridor de Cristobal*. Madrid: CSIC, 1983.

Perrin, William G. *British Flags*. Cambridge: Cambridge University Press, 1922.

Phillips, J. R. S. *The Medieval Expansion of Europe*. Oxford: Clarendon Press, 1998.

Pohl, Frederick J. *Amerigo Vespucci: Pilot Major*. New York: Columbia University Press, 1944.

Pope, Peter E. *The Many Landfalls of John Cabot*. Toronto: University of Toronto Press, 1997.

Quinn, David. *England and the Discovery of America 1481–1620*. London: University of Allen & Unwin, 1974.

Quinn, David. *European Approaches to North America, 1450–1640*, Aldershot UK: Ashgate, 1998.

Ravenstein, Ernst G. *Martin Behaim: His Life and His Globe,* London: George Philip & Son, 1908.

Runciman, S. *The Fall of Constantinople 1453*. Cambridge: Cambridge University Press, 1965.

Sale, K. *The Conquest of Paradise: Christopher Columbus and the Columbian Legacy*. London: Hodder & Stoughton, 1991.

Sanceau, Elaine. *The Perfect Prince: A biography of the King Dom João II*. Porto: Livraria Civilizacão, 1954.

Scoble, Andrew R. (ed.). *The Memoirs of Philippe de Commines*, Vol. II. London: Bell, 1900.

Scofield, Cora L. *The Life and Reign of Edward IV*. London: Longmans & co, 1923.

Seward, Desmond. *The Burning of the Vanities: Savonarola and the Borgia Pope*. Stroud, UK: Alan Sutton, 2006.

Simons, Eric N. *Henry VII: The First Tudor King*. New York: Barnes & Noble, 1968.

Skelton, R. A. *Explorers' Maps: Chapters in the Cartographic Record of Geographical Discovery*. London: Routledge & Kegan Paul, 1958.

Spufford, Peter. *Power and Profit: The Merchant in Medieval Europe*. London: Thomas & Hudson, 2002.

Streicher, Fritz. *Die Kolumbus-Originale: eine palaographische Studie in Spanische Forshungen der Gorresgesellschaft*. Munster, Ger.: Görresgesellschaft, 1928.

Subrahmanyam, S. *The Career and Legend of Vasco da Gama*. Cambridge: Cambridge University Press, 1997.

Tarducci, Francesco. *John and Sebastian Cabot*. Trans. Hery F. Brownson. Detroit: Brownson, 1893.

Taviani, Paolo E. *Christopher Columbus: The Grand Design*. Ed. John Gilbert. London: Orbis, 1985.

Temple Patterson, Alfred. *Southampton: A Biography*. London: Macmillan, 1970.

Thomas, Hugh. *Rivers of Gold: The Rise of the Spanish Empire*. London: Weidenfeld & Nicolson, 2003.

Tuchman, Barbara. *The First Salute*. London: Phoenix, 2000.

Vallentin, Antonina. *Leonardo da Vinci*. London: Victor Gollanz, 1939.

Varela, Cansuelo. *Amerigo Vespucci: Un nome per il Nuovo Mondo*. Milan: Fenice, 1994.

———. *Colon y los Florentinos*. Madrid: Alianza America, 1988.

———. *Ingleses en España y Portugal 1450–1515*. Lisbon: Mercaderes Edjções Colibri, 1998.

———. *La Caida de Cristobal Colon: El juicio de Bobadilla*. Madrid: Marcial Pons, 2006.

Vignaud, Henri. *Toscanelli and Columbus*. London: Sands, 1902.

Vigneras, Louis (ed.). *The Journal of Christopher Columbus*. Trans. Cecil Jane. London: Hakluyt Society, 1960.

Vigneras, Louis. *The Discovery of South America and the Andalusian Voyages*. Chicago: University of Chicago Press, 1976.

Washburn, W. E., in S. A. Bedini. *The Christopher Columbus Encyclopaedia*. Basingstoke, UK: Macmillan, 1992.

Watts, P. M. "Prophecy and Discovery: on the spiritual origin of Christopher Columbus' enterprise of the Indies," *American Historical Review*, 90, 1, 1985.

Weare, George E. *Cabot's Discovery of North America*, London: J. Macgreen, 1897.

Williamson, James A. *The Cabot Voyages and Bristol Discovery under Henry VII*. Cambridge: Cambridge University Press, 1962.

Williamson, James A. *The Voyages of the Cabots and the English Discovery of North America under Henry VII and Henry VIII*. London: Argonaut Press, 1929.

Wilson, Ian. *The Columbus Myth*. London: Simon & Schuster, 1991.

Wroe, Ann. *Perkin*. London: Jonathan Cape, 2003.

Zorzi, Rosella M. (ed.). *Attraversare gli Oceani: Da Giovanni Caboto al Canada multiculturale*. Venice: Marsilio, 1997.

Zweig, S. *Amerigo: A comedy of errors in history*. New York: Viking Press, 1992.

# Index

Note: Page numbers in *italics* refer to illustrations.

# A Note on the Author

David Boyle is also the author of *Troubador's Song*, *The Sum of Our Discontent*, and *The Money Changers*. He lives with his family in Crystal Palace, London.